DR. SNOW

HOW THE FBI NAILED AN IVY LEAGUE COKE KING

BY CAROL SALINE

NAL BOOKS

NEW AMERICAN LIBRARY

NEW YORK AND SCARBOROUGH, ONTARIO

Published simultaneously in Canada by The New American Library of Canada Limited.

 NAL BOOKS TRADEMARK REG. U.S. PAT. OFF. AND FOREIGN COUNTRIES
REGISTERED TRADEMARK—MARCA REGISTRADA
HECHO EN CHICAGO, U.S.A.

SIGNET, SIGNET CLASSIC, MENTOR, ONYX, PLUME, MERIDIAN
and NAL BOOKS are published *in the United States*
by NAL PENGUIN INC., 1633 Broadway, New York, New York 10019,
in Canada by The New American Library of Canada Limited,
81 Mack Avenue, Scarborough, Ontario M1L 1M8

Library of Congress Cataloging-in-Publication Data

Saline, Carol.
  Dr. Snow : how the FBI nailed an Ivy League coke
king.

  1. Lavin, Lawrence W.   2. Narcotics dealers—United
States—Biography.   3. Dentists—United States—
Biography.   4. Cocaine habit—United States—Case
studies.   5. Narcotics, Control of—United States—
Case studies.   I. Title.
HV5805.L375S36   1988   364.1′77′0974811   88-1413
ISBN 0-453-00593-4

First Printing, June, 1988

1   2   3   4   5   6   7   8   9

To Jack, Sharon, and Matthew with my love
and thanks for their patience, confidence, and support.

Acknowledgments

In the early fall of 1985, Ron Javers, my editor at *Philadelphia* magazine, called me into his office. "I think I've got an angle on that cocaine piece we've been wanting to write," he said and handed me a slip of paper with the name Ron Noble and a phone number. "He's the U.S. attorney working on that yuppie conspiracy drug ring. See if he'll give you the inside story." The yuppie conspiracy was the FBI's description of a twelve-state cocaine organization masterminded by Larry Lavin, a personable, preppy young dentist recently graduated from the University of Pennsylvania. Javers and I had been searching for a fresh approach to an article on cocaine, something that wouldn't cover the same tired ground and would appeal to a city magazine's readers. This seemed like a natural.

Noble was too busy to meet with me right away and suggested his trial partner in the case, Tina Gabrielli. We had lunch and discussed what the U.S. attorney's office could and could not reveal about this ongoing investigation. Clearly there was plenty to work with. Next I met with Sid Perry, one of two FBI agents who'd broken the ring. My research had begun.

The article, *Dr. Snow*, appeared in the March 1986 issue of *Philadephia* magazine. Readers were both shocked and fascinated by the tale of a massive cocaine operation buried under the respectable cover of the Ivy League. I mentioned to my agent, Jay Acton, that I thought it would make a good telemovie and asked him to see if he could sell it. With that I forgot about *Dr. Snow* and returned to my normal life: hosting a daily talk radio program in the morning and writing for *Philadelphia* magazine in the afternoon.

A month or so later I received a phone call from a woman who introduced herself as a literary agent from Los Angeles. It seemed she'd been visiting someone in the Philadelphia suburbs, had read *Dr. Snow,* and taken the liberty of sending it to Kevin Mulroy at New American Library. He was interested in developing the magazine piece into a book. "Do you have an agent?" she asked. I answered, "Yes," thanked her and immediately called Jay Acton.

"Do you knew Kevin Mulroy at NAL?"

"I sure do," Acton said. "We had lunch last week."

"Please call him right away. I think he wants me to do a book."

I relate the origin of *Dr. Snow* because people are so often curious about how a book is born. In this instance, the gestation period equalled the length of my two childbirths and was, in retrospect, a lot more difficult. The manuscript was researched and completed in nine months of ten-hour days and required the help of many people in many ways. My warmest thanks go to all of them.

To Ron Javers for encouraging me to expand my horizons as a journalist and granting me a leave of absence from *Philadelphia* magazine while allowing me to retain my office as a workplace.

To Frank Ford, John Harmelin, and Bill Davol at Talk 900 AM for generously giving me time off the air to research and write whenever I needed it.

To Alan Halpern, who taught me most of what I know about writing, for his excellent editing and enthusiastic support.

To Ron Noble, Tina Gabbrielli, Chuck Reed, and especially Sid Perry for always returning my calls, providing the material I requested and cooperating in every way possible. Also to the FBI for allowing the agents to work with me.

To Kevin Mulroy for seeing the potential of a book in a magazine article and shepherding it to fruition.

To the following attorneys for facilitating access to their clients: David Gendelman, Peter Scuderi, Jack Meyerson, Michael Mustakoff, Greg Magarity, Steven Morley, David Shapiro, Charles Peruto, Jr.

To the following state and federal prison officials who permitted me to conduct interviews with inmates in their facilities: Jim Youngman, Charles Bender, Tom Frame, Warren Diesslin.

To the many people who shared their time and information with the promise they be granted anonymity. You know who you are.

My appreciation also goes to David Ackerman. At his behest, and in return for his cooperation on this project, a percentage of the proceeds from the sale of *Dr. Snow* will be donated in his name to a treatment center for cocaine addiction.

Finally, to my family and good friends go my gratitude for their patience and loving encouragement during the year I took a sabbatical from life to write this book.

1

PHILADELPHIA
WINTER, 1983

"Okay, Kim. I want you to keep your eye on the quarter. Watch it carefully."

Slowly Larry Lavin passed the coin in front of the frightened child's face while her pale blue eyes followed his hand up and down. Then, in a flash, the quarter vanished.

"Well, imagine that," the young dentist said. "Maybe it's hiding in your ear." Lavin waved his hand over the five-year-old's blond curls and the quarter reappeared. Kim giggled, all traces of her fear gone.

"Now, let's open up and have a look at that tooth."

Six months earlier Kim McKinley had fallen off her bike and broken half a front tooth. Her mother had taken her to dentist after dentist, but the little girl wouldn't sit still for any of them. When a brochure came in the mail announcing that Dr. Larry Lavin and Dr. Kenneth Weidler, recent graduates of the University of Pennsylvania Dental School, were opening an office in her Philadelphia neighborhood, Mrs. McKinley decided to try still another time.

Kim took to Dr. Lavin immediately. He joked with her, did magic tricks, and never seemed to be in a hurry to get on to his next patient. Tall and lanky, with slightly drooped shoulders and a narrow frame, he was not as frightening as the other dentists. He dressed more casually, sporting Docksider boat shoes and often not wearing socks. His pale skin seemed almost chalky against his coarse dark hair, an unruly mop that perpetually seemed in need of combing and swept his forehead. Had Kim been older and more susceptible to his other charms, she might have singled out Lavin's smile as his best feature. That was something women he met usually remembered. Although his lively green eyes were small and overshadowed by a straight prominent nose, he was often described as handsome because of his warm, open smile.

Dr. Lavin handled Kim so successfully that her mother soon booked appointments for her other two children and recommended the appealing new dentist to several of her friends. They all agreed that the twenty-seven-year-old Ivy Leaguer not only had a winning personality but also was an extremely capable practitioner. Eventually Kate McKinley found herself in Dr. Lavin's chair. She'd been anxious for permanent bridgework to replace teeth knocked out in an auto accident, but because her health coverage did not include cosmetic dentistry, she was concerned about being able to pay for the work. A day after mentioning her financial dilemma to Dr. Lavin, he called and said he'd found a way to handle the payments and that he could make the bridge for just $250. When Kate McKinley commented to the hygienist how considerate Dr. Lavin had been to fix her teeth so cheaply, she was told, "Larry's like that. He can afford to help some people out. He's a self-made millionaire."

"You can rinse now, Kim," Dr. Lavin said. "Want to see your tooth all fixed up?" He scooped the child up in his arms and carried her to a mirror, noting that the clock on the wall next to it read 11:30. That was good. He had just one more patient and he'd be finished for the day. He booked only until noon on Saturdays and today he was particularly eager to leave on time. He was hosting a bachelor party at the Playboy Casino in Atlantic City for his college roommate, Paul Mikuta, and he wanted to get there ahead of the other guests. Lavin's bashes—lavish extravaganzas of drugs, liquor, and beautiful women paid to do whatever his guests desired— were the kind of bachelor parties that indulged every fantasy, no matter how expensive.

Out in the waiting room, Dr. Lavin chatted briefly with Mrs. McKinley, thoughtfully inquired about her other children, and then walked his next patient to the inner office. Fortunately, it was only a routine cleaning and by 12:30 he was behind the wheel of his BMW, speeding back to the elegant white brick colonial home he'd recently purchased in Devon, an exclusive Philadelphia suburb. He had lunch with his wife, Marcia, and complained bitterly about how he wished he didn't have to give these parties, explaining that they were business obligations. She kissed him good-bye with just a trace of annoyance when the limousine arrived in midafternoon to transport him to the shore. Larry told her the limo was simply part of the glamour of a first-class bachelor party, but it served another purpose. The sleek black car made a second stop to pick up Paul Mikuta, the guest of honor, and a third to get the call girl. The party began.

As the limousine sped down the Schuylkill Expressway toward the bridge that connected Pennsylvania to New Jersey, Dr. Lavin took a plastic sandwich bag filled with the purest, whitest cocaine from his jacket pocket, scooped out a tiny spoonful to snort, then passed the bag to the others. Within minutes a warm rush coursed through his body and he went from feeling good to feeling extraordinary. Images of factories, warehouses, trees, and speeding cars leapt through the darkened limousine windows like rapidly moving slides, each one sharp and memorable. The three of them all took a second toot, then a third, and started talking and laughing at once. Larry reminded the girl that she hadn't been brought along to tell bedtime stories. She licked her lips, smiled, slid down to the carpeted floor of the car, and unzipped Mikuta's fly.

By the time the limousine pulled up at the glittering entrance to the Playboy Casino one hour later, the cocaine bag was empty. Lavin and Mikuta checked into one of several suites overlooking the ocean that had been reserved for the party, left the call girl to take care of any early arrivals, and went downstairs to the tables. Lavin enjoyed gambling and often made day trips to the casinos. Although he rarely bet more than $100 on a football game, he thought nothing of wagering $1,000 a card at baccarat and won as often as he lost. The Playboy Casino considered him one of its high rollers and as a courtesy, often provided complimentary rooms for his parties.

By dinnertime a dozen or so of the forty invited guests had arrived and Larry Lavin ushered everybody into the casino's most elegant dining room. The dinner bill came to $2,500, most of it spent on wine. Larry liked Bordeaux and ordered several bottles of the best Lafite Rothschild on the wine list. Anybody observing the group in their blazers, striped ties, and penny loafers would have thought they were young executives in town for a convention. Only someone who knew the real meaning of their buzzwords would have realized the get-together centered around drugs. For Lavin, these bachelor parties were a perfect way to combine business and pleasure and to touch base with people he usually dealt with only by telephone. Since the majority of his drug customers were school friends from Phillips Exeter Academy or the University of Pennsylvania, he used his bachelor bashes as much for entertaining clients as to celebrate the toll of wedding bells.

After dinner, a few of his guests drifted off to the craps tables. The rest returned to the suites, which by now had been stocked with food and liquor. Lavin made sure that everybody's favorite brand was on hand. Imported vodka for his dental partner, Ken Weidler; Wild Turkey for the airline pilot from up-state Pennsylvania whom Lavin kept in coke; and Courvoisier for the dental-school dropout who ran the drug business for Lavin. There were trays of cold cuts, fresh fruit, platters of shrimp and clams on beds of ice. But the food was barely touched. The refreshment of preference was clearly cocaine. There were mounds of it for casual snorting lying around on tables, on top of the television set, on the bureaus in the bedrooms. Lavin was a generous host and saw to it that his guests had an endless supply of not only uncut cocaine but also top-grade Hawaiian marijuana and Quaaludes.

It took a while for things to get going, even after the six call girls arrived. They, too, were top-quality and charged $1,000 apiece for a party like this. Each one was young, attractive, and skilled.

On the surface, things looked like the old fraternity days. Guys milling around noisily with drinks in their hands and sex on their minds. None of them had much experience with calls girls. Occasionally a couple wandered off to a bedroom. It was all rather discreet until Billy Motto arrived.

Motto, in his mid-twenties like the rest, was obviously from another league. There wasn't a thing about him that suggested Ivy. In height and build he resembled his idol, actor Al Pacino. Motto's fine sandy hair was carefully shaped in a layered cut and his nails were freshly manicured. He wore alligator shoes, an Italian designer suit, and a silk shirt open at the neck exposing a thick gold chain. A diamond sparkled on his pinky and around his wrist was a bracelet with MOTTO spelled in half-inch diamond letters. Billy Motto, a kid who'd grown up shooting heroin in the shadow of Philadelphia's Italian produce market, had cleaned up his act and gotten rich selling drugs supplied to him by Dr. Lavin. Although he wasn't socially friendly with the crowd, Larry liked him immensely and invited him to the party because he was a major customer. For Motto, the party was more of a business meeting. The only thing about it he didn't understand was why these rich college boys needed to pay for sex. And as long as prostitutes were here, he intended to have fun. Hell, he'd been running with hookers all his life and he never missed a chance to have a good time.

"Hey, what's the matter with you? You got hookers here. These ain't the girls you date in college. You don't hold hands with hookers. You gotta abuse 'em." Billy grabbed two of the girls, unbuttoned his pants, and jumped on the sofa. "Let's go."

By now everyone had had enough coke and booze to follow his

lead. "Who wants to get tied up?" Lavin hollered, and a short fellow with a big belly who'd dropped out of college to deal drugs volunteered. One of the girls removed his clothes while a couple of guys pulled off their silk ties and fastened his wrists to the head-board of the bed and his ankles to the foot. Two girls stripped and climbed on top of him. Soon the room was crawling with naked bodies. Two girls on a guy; two guys forming a sandwich with a girl as the filling, or two girls languidly licking each other's breasts while the boys watched. Anybody interested in group sex jumped in. Those, like Lavin, who preferred their sex in private, stood on the sidelines offering kinky suggestions and waiting for the orgy to peter out so they could form their own threesomes behind closed doors. It was a scene straight out of the stag movies they'd all drooled over as boys. Only this was the real thing. Thanks to the fortune he made selling drugs, Dr. Larry Lavin didn't have to watch movies anymore; he could produce his own.

Lavin kept the action moving by replenishing the mounds of coke. For Larry, cocaine was the ultimate party drug. A high lasted about thirty minutes, obliterating inhibitions and leaving none of the foggy aftereffects of booze. Coke cut the appetite, but it fueled the sex drive and ignited incredible bursts of energy. With enough snorting, hookers worked nonstop for hours and men had erections that lasted as long as the Sunday Night Movie.

Well after midnight, the party began to wind down. Lavin took several wrapped stacks of hundred-dollar bills from his gym bag, paid the girls their $6,000 and sent them back to Philadelphia in a limousine. Some of the guys stayed in the suite doing lines, while a few, Lavin included, were too wired to sit still and headed for the casino.

Toward dawn, the long night of sex and drugs began to take its toll, and as the coke wore off, Lavin's body cried out for sleep. He crawled into one of the twelve rooms he'd reserved, but every time he closed his eyes somebody banged on the door begging for more coke. Lavin, who'd done just about everything imaginable in col-lege, from pot to acid to coke, was no longer a heavy user. Drugs interfered too much with business, so except for parties like this, where he did line after line to keep awake, he'd reduced his snorting to a minimum since leaving dental school.

Not all of his drug customers were that controlled. Once they started partying, their craving was insatiable. They'd never let him alone if they thought he had any coke left, and his chances of getting any sleep if he remained at the hotel ranged from little to none. As the sun rose over the waves, casting its pale light on the white sandy beach, Dr. Lavin borrowed a car and drove home to his pregnant wife. He told her, as he always did, how dull the weekend had been. "Just another one of those boring bachelor parties, Marcia. I'd much rather have stayed at home."

2

FBI HEADQUARTERS, PHILADELPHIA
SUMMER, 1982

Lavin . . . Lavin . . . Lavin. The name kept jumping out at FBI agent Chuck Reed as he sat at his desk poring over the records of a bankruptcy case that had recently fallen into his hands. A BMW purchased for Dr. Larry Lavin. A $25,000 salary from the Martin Luther King Arena paid to Larry Lavin. The Celebrity Limousine Company with its exclusive contract to ferry gamblers to and from the Playboy Casino, partly owned by Larry Lavin. Impact Productions, a company that owned and promoted prizefighters, showing checks to Dr. Larry Lavin. On the books of WMOT Records, a rhythm-and-blues recording company, thousands of dollars in the name of Larry Lavin. "Who the hell," Reed wondered, "is this guy Larry Lavin?"

In July 1982, the White Collar Crime Squad in the Philadelphia office of the FBI was brought into the bankruptcy investigation of WMOT Records when the scent of fraud wafted over the case. One of its artists, Frankie Smith, a black rap singer, had cut a song called "Double Dutch Bus" that climbed to the top of the soul charts, sold a million copies, and earned a gold record. Smith filed a complaint with the court, alleging that Mark Stewart, owner of WMOT, was siphoning off money paid to him from the record's distributor that should have gone to Smith as part of his royalties.

The agent initially assigned the case was too busy to handle it and dropped it on Chuck Reed's desk. "You might find this interesting. Fraud. Big bucks. A record company."

Good FBI agents are always on the lookout for cases that will hold their attention. This one appealed to Reed. He enjoyed plowing through financial data and had, in fact, come into the Bureau in 1979 through one of its most popular entry routes:

accounting. In his eyes, investigations were quite similar to audits; the paper trail pointed the way to the crime.

Tall and square with broad shoulders and a somber expression, Reed exuded dogged determination. His straight brown hair fell in bangs over his forehead and his round face was accented by the thin line of a closely clipped beard. Built like a former football player, the 31-year-old agent was actually anything but an athlete.

He received his degree in accounting from Bentley College in Boston and went on to become a CPA with the idea that he would someday go in business for himself. Soon after joining an accounting firm, Reed quickly realized that he didn't have the personality to engage in the social games necessary to win clients. When a former FBI agent he met on an audit suggested the Bureau could use his skills, Reed was ready. He took the entrance test, scored well, and within three months he became Special Agent Charles Reed. He brought to the job the tendency of a man trained in numbers to view the world as a balance sheet. Issues were black and white. People were good guys or bad. Woe to the man who didn't add up.

Chuck Reed believes accountants make the best FBI agents because of the way they're trained to analyze information. He did not wear blinders, though. For him business records were only a tool. His real fascination was with human behavior. Through his steel-rimmed photo-gray aviator glasses, he peered into a suspect's mind. "What makes this guy tick? How does he think? If I were in his shoes, what would I do?" Those were the questions he asked himself as he studied the bankruptcy schedule of WMOT Records and began to piece together a picture of the company's officers, their assets, and their liabilities.

The first name to emerge from Reed's examination wasn't Larry Lavin's. It was Mark Stewart's, the man with whom Lavin chose to invest his enormous drug profits. The thirty-eight-year-old Stewart was a real-estate entrepreneur who specialized in putting together tax shelters—the kind in which his lawyer and physician clients would invest $10,000 and wind up with a $100,000 tax credit. A short, well-built man with muscular arms, Mark Stewart was a born hustler. His deep-set brown eyes never missed the slightest detail. His thick, wavy dark hair grew from a widow's peak that emphasized the pointed tip of his nose, which, along with his small perfect teeth, gave him a Mephistophelian air. Stewart was a flashy dresser who wore custom suits and shirts with French cuffs. Although his shoe collection included a pair of $2,000 alligator loafers, he preferred boots—they made him look taller—and owned over fifty pairs.

Stewart grew up in a row house in a predominantly middle-class Jewish section of Northeast Philadelphia. His father owned a gas station; his mother worked for the government. Stewart might have kept his given name, Murray Slingbaum, and developed into a decent commercial artist if he'd stayed with the sign-painting business he started in high school. But the lure of big money attracted him to real estate. He made a good living as a broker, earned enough to buy a Jaguar, trade it for a Porsche 911, and join a country club to indulge his passion for golf. But Stewart wasn't content buying and selling property. He wanted bigger bucks, bigger opportunities, and was always promoting the kinds of deals—from sports management to tax shelters—that could bring him a bonanza. For the most part, they were more imaginative than shady. "Being inventive, aggressive, and creative is not illegal," he was fond of saying.

Eventually Reed would discover that Larry Lavin had become involved with Stewart while still in dental school. Lavin had needed a way to make some of the enormous profits from his cocaine business appear as legitimate income. An Ivy League college graduate confident he could outsmart the law, Lavin searched for a sophisticated way to recycle his cash and earn money on his drug proceeds. He found the ideal investment counselor when he met Mark Stewart. The two were a perfect match. Each had what the other needed. Larry, cash; Mark, a way to launder it.

In time, Reed learned that Lavin had been introduced to Stewart's personalized money-laundering service by one of his cocaine customers whose attorney also represented Stewart. Lavin initially turned over $500,000 that he'd stockpiled from selling cocaine. In return for his investment Stewart gave him equity in several apartment buildings and a record-distribution business that he owned. They also formed a company called Larmark (for Larry and Mark), which made Lavin an equal partner in any future enterprises Stewart created.

Reed's investigation would show that through 1980 and 1981, Larmark prospered. Stewart put the $500,000 into certificates of deposit which he turned over to a bank and used as collateral for a $1.2 million line of credit. That provided operating capital for a host of new businesses. One was Celebrity Limousine Company. Stewart, in addition to everything else, talked himself into a lucrative position as a sports and entertainment consultant, booking events for the Playboy Casino in Atlantic City. He was soon also ferrying high rollers into Playboy in the newly formed Celebrity's thirty Cadillac stretch limousines. (Stewart was later dumped by Playboy when state gaming-commission officials found he'd been providing free prizefight seats to Mafia kingpin Nicky Scarfo.) Another new enterprise was WMOT Records, one of the companies from which Lavin received a paycheck. When "Double Dutch Bus" broke the million sales mark and was awarded a gold record, Larry proudly displayed the plaque in his home and told neighbors he was making a fortune in the recording industry.

The record company was in fact losing a fortune and it was alleged that WMOT Records had cheated its artists, which is how Chuck Reed came to be examining its books. And how he stumbled on the information that Mark Stewart not only was involved in the WMOT bankruptcy fraud but also was a suspect in an arson case. Only later would Reed come to understand the relationship. He'd see that Lavin's money had given Stewart the opportunity to buy a decaying complex that the entrepreneur envisioned revitalizing as the Martin Luther King Arena, a sports and entertainment mecca for the Philadelphia black community. A more prudent businessman would have realized the project was doomed from the start, but Stewart stubbornly poured more and more cash into it. As a result of juggling the books of one company to pay the expenses of another, his cash flow dwindled to a trickle. Pressured by Larry, who wanted a return on his $500,000 investment, Stewart decided his only recourse to cash was the $1.4 million insurance policy he'd taken on the King Arena. But he was in such desperate financial condition that, having made the decision to torch the building, he had to ask Larry to give him the $5,000 down payment to hire the arsonist.

Shortly after midnight on the evening of October 4, 1981, when the King Arena had no scheduled events and stood dark and deserted, James Holt, a tough member of the Pagan motorcycle gang, let himself into the Arena with a key he'd been given. Holt, whose nickname was "Horrible," also carried in his pocket his $2,000 share of the down payment and the card of an attorney supplied by Stewart whom he was to call if he got caught. Holt carried several plastic containers filled with gasoline and armloads of rope made from rags that had been knotted together. After laying the rag rope around the building, he soaked it with gasoline. The match that ignited the blaze illuminated the deep scars that ran down Holt's cheeks. As soon as he saw the first flames, he ran for the back entrance, hopped on his bike, and roared off into the night.

It wasn't Holt's fault that his mission failed. Rather it was Stewart's bad luck that a fire truck answering an alarm in the neighborhood happened to see the flames on its way back to the firehouse, called for extra help, and quickly extinguished the blaze.

That didn't prevent Stewart from filing a claim six weeks later and then suing the insurance company when they refused to pay because they suspected foul play. Not only was the damage insufficient for collecting the insurance but also there was enough evidence in the partly charred remains to charge Stewart with arson.

Horrible Holt never got paid either. He was promised the remainder of his fee when the insurance money came in, but didn't live long enough to learn the check would never arrive. Months after the fire, his body, riddled with bullets, was dumped on the steps of the emergency room of a center-city hospital. It was hard to understand why his assailants had bothered to bring him for help. By the time doctors found him, he was already dead.

The details of the arson would not become clear to Chuck Reed until later in his investigation. It was enough for him to realize that Mark Stewart was a suspect in the burning of the King Arena for his interest in the case to heighten considerably. Reed contacted an agent at the Bureau of Alcohol, Tobacco, and Firearms, which has jurisdiction over arson cases. As soon as they pooled their information, it was decided to bring in the Internal Revenue Service and proceed on a joint front. They subpoenaed the records of Stewart's other businesses—all told, some forty corporations—to ferret out, among other things, a motive for the arson. Was there a company that was in such dire straits that only the insurance money could salvage it?

The boxes of jumbled records arrived one after the other until, stacked floor to ceiling, they practically filled a ten-by-twenty foot room. The contents were so disorganized that it seemed they'd been dumped from a wastebasket. Day after day the agents sat at a long wooden table chewing through the piles of paper like patient termites. Slowly a path emerged leading from WMOT to a bank account that showed over and over again checks bearing the name Larry Lavin. He surfaced as well on the payroll of the King Arena at a $25,000 annual salary and as the recipient of a BMW automobile. Reed, meanwhile, began conducting interviews with people who might help with the arson investigation. Since divorced women are known to be fonts of valuable information about their former husbands' activities, he paid his first call on Stewart's ex-wife. She suggested he look at the four musketeers: Larry Lavin; his college roommate, Paul Mikuta; his dental partner, Ken Weidler; and a kid who'd dropped out of dental school, David Ackerman. All of those names had already shown up on payroll records and checks issued by Stewart's various corporations. They were good leads, but not nearly as important as the most salient word in her interview: "cocaine."

Now the case comprised fraud, arson, and drugs, far more than Reed had expected. From the mess the records were in, it looked like it would be impossible to prove all three quickly, and certainly not bankruptcy fraud. The money from all the corporations was so commingled and the records so confused that it might take years to weed through it all.

In any FBI investigation, decisions are made at every turn which have a crucial effect on the direction of a case and who is ultimately prosecuted. The determining factor in whether to proceed—and if so, how—is the answer to a very practical question: can the case be proven? Solving a case is the easy part; amassing sufficient evidence to win it can be a far bigger problem. There's no point spending the government's money if it looks like the case won't stand up in court. Reed was certain that bankruptcy fraud had been committed, but he doubted he'd ever be able to substantiate the charge. A drug case seemed pretty weak as well, but he went to his supervisor and told him he'd heard rumors that Stewart's associates might be drug dealers. "If we can prove it," Reed said, "I want to work the case. I don't want it switched to the drug squad." The supervisor promised that if a drug case developed, Reed could keep it.

That left arson as the strongest possibility for prosecution, and Larry Lavin as a promising source for background on Mark Stewart. In the early stage of an investigation, the FBI looks for red flags—odd little facts that jump out because they don't make sense. Such as: why were students Lavin, Mikuta, Weidler, and Ackerman earning big salaries at the King Arena for jobs they obviously didn't perform—for instance, running the hot-dog concession? How did Lavin, whose name was on more checks than anybody else's, come to own a lovely home in an exclusive Phildelphia suburb, a town house in a gentrified center-city neighborhood, and a costly BMW? Reed decided to zero in on Dr. Lavin, pay him a visit to tell him the FBI had good reason to believe he was a drug dealer. That ought to scare him enough to become a cooperating witness in the arson case.

Late in February 1983 Chuck Reed parked across the street from Larry Lavin's dental office and watched him through the window working on a patient. The sun had already set, and despite the heat in the car, Reed shivered in the damp cold. Lavin's office was located in a working-class neighborhood of row houses and small single homes not far from the city's Holmesburg prison. In fact, a little sign that hung on a post in front of the unpretentious office, which had been converted from a house, said, "Holmesburg Dental Office." Lavin's silver BMW 733, the motor company's most expensive sedan, was parked in the driveway. Reed waited until the last patient left the office. After the receptionist walked down the front steps, he got out of his car.

Lavin was standing behind the reception desk when Reed entered without knocking. He introduced himself in a flat voice with the metallic edge of a Vermont twang. "Dr. Lavin. My name's Chuck Reed." He extended his wallet to show the identification card with his picture and the familiar gold badge. "I'm with the FBI, investigating the arson of the Martin Luther King Arena. I'd like to talk to you about it. Maybe get your cooperation. I understand you might be able to help us out."

Lavin clearly disliked him. Reed surmised that Lavin already knew from Stewart that his business records had been subpoenaed, and also suspected that Lavin had been warned by a lawyer to expect a visit from the FBI.

Although Lavin's heart had begun pounding when he spotted Reed's car parked in front of the office, he appeared calm and controlled. At that moment Lavin had no idea how much the Bureau knew about his drug activities and dreaded finding out. Just like Reed, he decided to fish for information. He didn't ask the agent to sit down, but he figured he'd be polite and see what Reed would reveal.

"Sure. What would you like to know?"

"First I need some data on you. When were you born?"

"March 14, 1955, in Haverhill, Massachusetts."

"Where do you reside now?"

"Devon."

"Married?"

"Yes."

"Wife's name?"

"Marcia."

"Where did you attend school?"

"I went to high school at Phillips Exeter Academy. I went to college and dental school at the University of Pennsylvania. Graduated two years ago."

"When did you first meet Mark Stewart?"

"About two and a half years ago. We started Larmark Corporation together."

"How much money did you invest?"

"None. I didn't invest anything in Larmark. I was supposed to drop out of school and run the King Arena but I decided not to do that."

"What exactly did you do for Stewart?"

"Mostly I did promotions for the record company. There was a real-estate deal I was advising him on, but it didn't work out." Lavin's answers were short, with little elaboration. He was cool to the point of being arrogant. Everything in his bearing said: You're wasting your time.

"Did you have anything to do with the arson at the King Arena?"

"Nothing at all."

"How about Stewart. What was his part?"

"Mark told me he had nothing to do with it."

"Are you involved with any of Stewart's corporations other than Larmark?"

"No."

Reed paused for a moment. "Have you ever sold illegal drugs?"

"No."

Most of Lavin's answers about Larmark were lies, and Reed knew it. He'd swear that Lavin knew he knew it, too, but his smirk seemed to say: You'll never prove anything against me. Reed had the feeling the young dentist could glibly answer questions for hours without implicating himself or Stewart. It was time to stop pretending this was a harmless little chat and see whether Lavin was going to cooperate. Time to bring up the BMW. Reed knew the car had been paid for by Mark Stewart and provided an undeniable financial link between the two of them.

"About your BMW out in the driveway, Larry. Where'd you get it?" Reed asked with his thin lips curled in a sneer.

"I got it through Larmark. No, wait, I actually bought it by mortgaging my house." Lavin's cool then turned to ice. He now had a sense of how much the FBI had on him and he was finished talking. "I think this has gone on long enough. I won't answer any more questions without my lawyer."

The interview was over.

Something about Lavin rubbed Reed the wrong way. It wasn't so much that he lied. Lots of people lie to the FBI. It was his attitude. He acted like he was above the law. Untouchable.

The cold air that hit Reed's face as he left the office only made him more conscious of the fire inside his belly. Lavin was an offensive smartass. One thing Reed wouldn't tolerate was an arrogant crook.

"Who is this cocky kid anyway?" he asked himself. "He deals drugs, burns buildings, and thinks he can get away it. Thinks he's smarter than we are. Well, he's not gonna stick it to the system." He turned the ignition key and decided then and there to leave the arson investigation to the ATF agents. He was going to pursue the drug case. No matter how tough it might be or how long it took, he was going to put Larry Lavin in jail for dealing cocaine.

3

PHILADELPHIA
SPRING, 1983

Larry Lavin was as much an enigma to his neighbors as he was to the FBI. When the outgoing young dentist and his reserved, pretty wife, Marcia, moved to the Main Line suburb of Devon and into their quarter-million-dollar white-brick colonial home in 1982, they were just twenty-seven years old and by far the youngest couple on Timber Lane, a long winding road of large, custom twenty-year-old homes on beautifully landscaped wooded tracts. Larry had a dental degree but no job, and he didn't seem to be looking for one either. Yet without any visible source of income they seemed to have more money than anybody else on the quietly affluent block where wealth was never paraded and definitely took a back seat to respectability. A retired Navy admiral lived across the street from the Lavins and John Eisenhower, the son of a former United States president lived next door. His wife, Barbara, wondered how this "awfully pleasant young man" could afford to buy a house in an area where most families were enjoying the financial fruits of middle age, then go on to install expensive additions like a pool, a greenhouse, and a solar heating system. While there was the usual gossip, most of the neighbors accepted Lavin's explanation that he'd gotten into the record business in college and had become very successful managing rock bands.

Dr. Lavin made a point of reinforcing his successful image by inviting neighbors like Mrs. Eisenhower into the tastefully decorated house and proudly showing them the framed gold record hanging in the bedroom he'd converted to an office. Usually the gregarious dentist did the house tour, happily chatting about the marvels of solar energy and his plans to remodel the recreation room, while Marcia Lavin kept to herself and puttered about the kitchen. Larry was always the friendlier and more visible of the two. He spent a lot of his time gardening and encouraging neighbors to borrow his tools or offering to help them with chores like putting in a new azalea bush. When he discovered that the retired admiral across the street was also a dentist, he made a point of walking over to discuss some new technique he'd just read about in a dental journal. The admiral thought it odd that someone so interested in dentistry didn't seem interested in working at it, until Larry mentioned he was looking around for the right opportunity. He finally found it that spring about a year after he'd graduated, when he bought a small practice in Philadelphia that catered to patients on public assistance. Based on the elegant life-style he'd established, the neighbors viewed his dental practice as more of a rich man's hobby than an economic necessity.

Indeed when FBI agent Chuck Reed visited Dr. Lavin at his unpretentious office early in 1983, the dental practice was in better shape than Lavin's drug business. He'd probably sold one thousand kilos of cocaine in the last five years, and if he included the money pocketed by all the principals in his ring, the total earnings came to nearly to ten million dollars. His personal share of that had been a million annually since 1981. Money wasn't the problem; it was management. Brian Riley, a kid he'd brought down from New England to buy coke for him in Florida and distribute it out of his Philadelphia headquarters, was threatening to walk out. That left him with only Bruce Taylor—another New Englander, a tough biker type and cocaine addict with tattoos on his forearms. What little brains Taylor had brought with him into the world were well on their way to being fried by all the cocaine he used.

On top of Larry Lavin's business problems, and unquestionably more serious, was the increasing heat of a tax-evasion case. During the investigation of the WMOT bankruptcy the government had found at least seven $50,000 checks along with other receipts of monies paid to him through various Mark Stewart enterprises, on which he'd never paid income tax. He'd hired a lawyer to handle his tax problems and knew there was a chance he might go to jail. And in addition to all this there was Marcia's ongoing pressure to get out of drugs so they could lead a normal life. Maybe the time had finally come to take up an offer from one of his suppliers to buy him out.

Lavin had heard through the grapevine that Franny Burns wanted to purchase his business. He'd been getting cocaine indirectly from Burns for several months, ever since he'd had trouble finding top-quality product from his usual Florida sources. A mutual friend connected them—and acted as broker—so Burns and Lavin never met face-to-face, although, oddly enough, they lived quite close to each other in the vicinity of Valley Forge National Historic Park. Despite the geographical proximity, the dentist and the dealer lived worlds apart. Lavin, the young professional, was the product of an exclusive private school and Ivy League college and resided in luxury at a prestigious Main Line address. Burns, a high-school dropout, was educated in the streets, owned a Dairy Queen ice-cream franchise, and rented a nice but undistinguished house in a middle-class development. Drugs were all they had in common. But that was enough.

What Lavin had to sell Burns was nothing more than a tiny hand-held computer-calculator that contained the names and phone numbers of all his drug customers: his company's total assets. There was no inventory and no property, just this valuable list of some fifty upscale users and dealers that Lavin estimated had a market value of $750,000 because it would give Burns exactly what his business lacked. Burns had connections to purchase first-rate cocaine, but he needed better financing. Lavin's carriage trade would be able to provide him with the front money to make ten-, twenty-, or thirty-kilo deals with the Colombian and Cuban whole-salers in Miami as well as a network to unload the increased volume. Lavin was at the time selling twenty-five to thirty kilos of coke per month; Burns dealt about fifteen. The merger, when completed, would boost Burns to forty-five kilos a month, which at a minimum profit of $10,000 a kilo meant he could make $4.5 million in a single year.

Their initial business meeting wasn't held in a fancy lawyer's office. Lavin and Burns met alone at a McDonald's on Route 202 between the King of Prussia Mall with its magnificent glass-fronted Bloomingdale's and a strip shopping center where Burns's Dairy Queen was located. The stumbling block to completing the sale was not price. Lavin had been forewarned that Burns would pay only $500,000 and he was prepared to accept that offer. It was not as if he had a variety of options or could turn to a business broker to find him a better deal. The problem was Lavin's commitment to his manager, Bruce Taylor. Larry believed that people like Bruce needed him, or at least he used them as a rationalization for staying in the drug business long after common sense told him to stop pushing his luck. More than once he'd said to friends, "I can't get out. Too many people depend on me to support their families." Lavin refused to abandon Taylor, and Burns refused to hire him. Finally Larry found a compromise. Instead of Franny giving Bruce a job, Larry would turn over to him the small, less-than-a-kilo customers he'd been servicing already. All that Franny had to promise was that he'd supply Bruce with cocaine. That settled, they had more coffee and worked on a plan for a gradual buy-out whereby Larry, over the summer and fall of 1983, would personally introduce Franny to his heavy hitters and Franny would pay him off as the profits developed.

The key customer at the top of Lavin's list was Billy Motto, the South Philadelphia produce distributor who sold far more coke than tomatoes. Without Motto's agreement to buy from Burns, there was no deal. Actually, Lavin had offered the business to Motto first by telephoning him one evening at Bookbinder's, a seafood restaurant near Philadelphia's historic district. It was one of the spots where Billy could boast that his car was "always front-parked and I don't need no credit cards. I can run a tab." One of Motto's underlings took the call. "Tell Billy I'm selling the business," Lavin said. "Ask him if he wants to buy it." Motto's answer was: Definitely not. "He's hot as fire. I'm not buying his heat." Lavin was in deep tax trouble and Motto wasn't interested in anything that might tie him to Larry's problems and bring him under FBI scrutiny.

Several weeks later, on a Sunday in late August when the temperature was sweltering, Lavin traced Burns to Atlantic City and told him to drive back to Philadelphia that afternoon because he'd arranged for him to meet Billy Motto. Burns arrived as instructed at Bookbinder's. Lavin was waiting inside the door like a nervous matchmaker to lead Franny to a booth in the back where Motto sat. He'd already given them a complete rundown of each other, telling Burns what a loyal customer Billy was and how quickly he paid his bills, and telling Motto that Franny had access to the best coke at good prices.

"Fran, this is Billy South Philly." They shook hands and Franny eased his flabby six-foot frame next to Billy's slight, trim, immaculately groomed body.

"So you're gonna be taking over," Billy said. "Well, if my pal Larry tells me you're all right, I'll take his word. I can do a lot of weight for you so long as the price is right and the quality is right. I don't buy no shit. Lately, the quality ain't been right, but I hear you'll change that."

"Yeah," Burns said. "Larry told me all about you too. I understand you only buy the best."

Billy smiled, showing off a set of sparkling teeth cleaned by Larry the day before in his office. "I only want pure and uncut. Nothing else. And when I front you bread, I buy cheaper. So you got two prices, one before and one after."

"No problem."

"So how we gonna get together? You wanna give me your beeper number?" Because of their fear of wiretapping, the dealers avoided direct phone calls as much as possible and contacted each other through beepers similar to the kind carried by doctors, and then established voice contact on pay phones.

"Yeah. You can use the same twenty-one code you use now for Larry and then put a sixty-eight at the end of the number so I'll know it's you." They exchanged beeper numbers while Larry jabbered on about how much they'd like each other and how good this was going to be for both of them.

"So I'll beep you when I'm ready and you'll send stuff for me to look at," Billy said. He was very particular about picking and choosing his coke.

"Well, I'll be going to Florida soon to cop a deal, so I'll have plenty of product."

"Now you've got it straight," Larry said, wanting to be certain everything would go smoothly. "Billy, you'll call Franny and you two will work together."

"Yeah. So that's it," Franny said. "My old lady's waiting in the car and I gotta get moving."

They stood up and shook hands. Billy said, "You treat me right, I'll treat you right. You know what I mean."

Three weeks later Motto beeped Burns, who called him back at a pay phone near his produce business and ordered four kilos of cocaine. They arranged that a runner would deliver the coke in a paper bag to a man standing in front of the Melrose Diner with a newspaper under his arm and that Burns would arrive shortly afterward to get the money. Everything went exactly as planned. Franny pulled into the diner lot after his runner left and soon got a message on his beeper where to reach Billy. He walked to a phone booth on the corner, returned the call, and was told that Billy would drive by in a Cadillac and he should get in his car and follow him. Their destination was a small row house on one of the narrow streets in South Philadelphia.

"Everything looks real good," Billy said as soon as they were inside. "If you can get me a better price, I think I can do more. We're gonna do real good together. Hey, maybe you're hungry. Lemme get you something to eat. Whaddya want? Whaddya like?" Billy sent out for asparagus-and-egg sandwiches, Franny's favorite, and along with the food came a man carrying a gym bag full of cash. While they ate, they checked the money—$188,000—for four kilos selling then at $47,000 a kilo with a resale value of $65,000 each.

A few days later Franny paid Larry his first installment on the buy-out. The dentist was delighted that the turnover had been accomplished so smoothly. If things went as well as his other big customers, especially Priscilla in New England, he'd be paid off in no time. With his business problems apparently solved, Lavin could now turn his attention to finding a way to beat the FBI's tax-evasion case.

4

MASSACHUSETTS
1970

The snow-packed streets of downtown Haverhill were usually deserted by ten P.M. The depressed mill town where Larry Lavin grew up was one of many once-prosperous villages on the outskirts of Boston that never recovered from the demise of Massachusetts' shoe industry. By the late 1960's most of Haverhill's footwear factories had closed and the town had the air of an old panhandler who'd enjoyed better days but had no hope of ever seeing them again.

Nobody noticed the oversize van as it pulled up in front of one of Haverhill's snowmobile dealerships. Painted an awful shade of army olive drab, it blended easily into the dark, moonless night. Glenn Fuller was driving and his high-school classmate Larry Lavin was seated next to him. As Glenn braked, Larry hopped out of the passenger seat carrying a wire cutter. He snipped the chain that locked the fence protecting the snowmobile dealership from trespassers and pulled open the gate. As soon as Glenn drove inside, Larry carefully rewound the chain so nothing would look suspicious. The two might have been inexperienced thieves but they weren't stupid. The day before, Glenn had been offered a few hundred dollars by a high-school classmate if he could get his hands on a snowmobile. It was a perfect caper for the street-wise kid who, at thirteen, had been driving his father's Cadillac without a license and swilling inexpensive wine on weekends. Snowmobiling had become a popular local sport but the vehicles were too expensive for the average teenager to buy legitimately. Glenn had little difficulty persuading Larry it would be easy to steal the buggy—and fun besides. For Larry the adventure was as seductive as the money. One of the reasons he hung around with Glenn, even though he knew he was a bad influence, was that they did crazy things like that.

Glenn parked the van near the rear of the building, as far as possible from the street. Whatever nervousness the boys initially felt had been quelled by a couple of beers, followed by a bottle of wine and the prospect of a few hundred dollars and a weekend skiing at Killington. They walked around the lot until they found what looked like a suitable vehicle, pulled the van alongside, slid open its large doors, and stared at each other. The body of the van was more than three feet off the ground and the snowmobile must have weighed at least one thousand pounds.

"How we gonna get this thing in the van?" Larry asked.

"We'll lift it," Glenn replied.

"Are you kidding? I'll rupture myself."

"Shut up and heave."

Both the fifteen-year-old Lavin and his sixteen-year-old buddy were big kids who'd already reached their six-foot adult height. Larry had a swimmer's body, slender with strong arms and shoulders. Fuller was beefier, with muscles to match his rough manners. Between the two of them they somehow jockeyed the front wheels of the snowmobile onto the floor of the van and pushed the rest of it inside. They scrambled into the front seat and drove off the lot after carefully winding the chain around the fence and positioning the lock so it would look as if it hadn't been touched. Their high spirits collapsed when they arrived at the garage where they'd planned to hide the snowmobile and got a good look at their booty in better light.

"Christ Almighty, this thing's a piece of crap," Glenn Fuller said. "Look at these dents. The paint's all scratched. It's not worth fifty bucks." Furious, he kicked the rear fender, adding another dent. "C'mon. We'll get a newer one."

They climbed back in the van and headed for a different dealership on the other side of town, where they repeated the wire-cutter routine and parked far in the back where they were well-hidden from the main road and could shop more leisurely. They cased the lot carefully and chose an almost new snowmobile that gleamed even in the dark. For some reason, no matter how hard they pushed this time, they couldn't lift the vehicle off the ground into the van. Despite the twenty-degree temperature, Lavin was sweating.

"This is fucking ridiculous, Glenn. Tarzan couldn't move this thing."

"Cool it. I got an idea."

Fuller jumped on a forklift parked nearby, thinking he'd use it to raise the snowmobile even with the floor of the van and they'd force it inside. As he turned the ignition key, a deafening noise like the revving of a jet engine ripped apart the silence of the dark night.

Larry sprinted toward the road as if an army were chasing him, an army of cops. "Whaddya, nuts?" he hissed. "They can hear that thing in Boston. It's got no exhaust."

"C'mon back," Fuller hollered. "Nothing's gonna happen."

Lavin, his heartbeat slowly returning to normal, started back to where he'd left Fuller, when he noticed an empty fifty-five-gallon oil drum standing near the service area. It occurred to him they could use the drum to raise the snowmobile to the level of the van. He flipped it over and kicked it in front of the van's big sliding doors.

"We're gonna try something, Glenn," he said. "I think we can lift this thing off the ground by working the front wheels up onto the drum. Use your shoulders and push hard."

"Okay. I'm ready. One. Two. Push."

"Hey, it's working. Take it slow. Don't let it slip back."

Grunting and groaning, they managed to ease the front end of the snowmobile partially up the side of the overturned drum, and by using the revolving motion of the cylinder they could hoist the rear end and roll the vehicle into the van. For good measure, Fuller ran back and grabbed some mechanic's tools lying nearby and added them to the booty. He knew they'd be easy to fence.

"Not bad if I say so myself." Larry Lavin grinned and smacked Glenn Fuller on the back. "A couple pros couldn't have done better."

Apparently the town's newspaper reporters agreed. An article about the theft in the local paper said it must have been carried out by a band of professional thieves. It was considered one of the cleverest heists in Haverhill history. But not clever enough to keep the audacious amateurs from getting caught. When it came time to deliver the snowmobile, Glenn made the mistake of insisting they show the new owner how it worked. They rode off to a vast snowfield behind a school that the locals used as a makeshift racecourse. Ironically, one of the men trying out his brand-new Skiddoo that same afternoon recognized the stolen snowmobile as the very vehicle he'd returned to the dealership because something was wrong with the rubber tracking. Sensing something amiss, he headed straight for a phone booth and called the police. The boys were arrested the next day but never had to serve time. After the snowmobile and tools had been returned, Glenn got two years' probation; Larry slithered away scott-free, partly because his father had connections in the judge's office and partly because he was a good student with no criminal history. Moreover, because they were juveniles, the records were expunged. The theft might have been big local news, but Larry Lavin's name was never attached to the publicity. It would be the first of many times that he would tangle with the law and slip through its net unscathed.

Any other bright middle-class kids caught red-handed by the police would have been, at the least, chastened by their narrow escape from a felony indictment. Not Larry and Glenn. They were neither frightened nor guilt-ridden, just annoyed that they'd done something stupid after their brilliant execution of the heist itself. Both would go on to bigger and better crimes. Lavin, when he later recounted the episode, managed to distort his first criminal adventure into nothing more serious than a prank. What a kick it had been! What a thrill! What an exciting way to make a fast buck. The worst part about it had been facing the hurt and disappointment of his parents, especially his mother, who couldn't understand why this wonderful son of hers would do such an awful thing. Frankly, Larry had been less concerned about their reaction than what might happen to him legally, and since he got off with a mere official scolding, he carried away the message that stealing was easy. His mistake was getting caught. That wouldn't happen again. As time went on, he would feel more and more sure that he had the ability to get away with anything.

Larry Lavin spent his childhood in a pleasant two-story gray frame house within walking distance of a junior college. From the weedless front lawn to the brick patio in the back, the yard was picture perfect, and no landscaper could take the credit. Everybody in the family helped with the planting and trimming. There were flowerbeds in abundance and a tall pine tree that grew just close enough to Larry's bedroom so that he could climb down the trunk at night to cavort with his pals. Larry was the baby of the family, ten years younger than his oldest brother, Paul. Jill, the only daughter, was the second oldest. She and Larry had some friends in common and would ultimately share drug interests as well.

Closest to Larry was Rusty, two years older, who inherited his mother's looks and his grandfather's bright orange hair but none of his brothers' intellectual curiosity. Rusty simply didn't have their scholastic gifts. What he did have was mechanical ability, but when he begged his parents for permission to attend a vocational school, they wouldn't hear of it. As it turned out, Rusty dropped out of high school in his last year to enter the construction business. The summer before, he'd found a job building roads and decided he belonged in the work world, not the academic. He continued working after school and by spring of his senior year was employed full-time. Every morning he'd get on the school bus, get off a few blocks away from home, and thumb a ride to the job. His parents, who often berated him for not being more like his brothers, were very angry when they discovered he'd quit, but couldn't persuade him to return. Eventually Rusty got his equivalency diploma when his baby brother, Larry, took the exam for him.

Although the elite ranks of the town were rather thinly populated, the Irish Catholic Lavins were considered to be among the more privileged in the Bradford suburb of Haverhill. Both Mr. and Mrs. Lavin had come from families who owned summer homes and never worried about not having cash in their pockets. "My father's father was one of the richest men in town until he lost his money in the depression," Larry remembers, "and my father had been educated at Notre Dame and MIT." His mother, a graduate of Simmons College in Boston, had, like most women of her generation, chosen to stay at home and raise her family. Pauline Lavin—called Pauli by her friends—was a tall, dark-haired woman whom Larry describes as "an overly gushy, extremely religious, loving mom." She enjoyed having company and filled the house with people— bridge parties for her friends, dinner for her children's schoolmates, or huge barbecues for the whole neighborhood. Pauli's specialty was flower arranging. She sold her dried centerpieces to local restaurants and gave lessons in her basement to supplement the family's income.

Larry's father, Justin, whom he most closely resembled, was a tall proud man with the body of a track star and a receding hairline. A rigorous disciplinarian and decorated Navy Hellcat pilot, he was too busy struggling with financial setbacks when Larry was born in 1955 to see to it that his youngest son adhered to the rules. "By the time I came along my dad was in his forties and he just didn't give me anywhere near the restrictions he laid on my brother Paul, who wasn't even allowed off the block. I could pretty much do whatever I wanted as long as I brought home good grades. I knew I was expected to do well, and if I did, I'd be left alone." Larry saw his father more as an emotionally detached authority figure than a pal. "He couldn't show his love to me, and he was too tired from working so hard to take me to ballgames or stuff like that. I did those kinds of things with my friends' dads." Larry sometimes complained he'd been cheated because his father was older and almost burnt-out on parenting when his fourth child arrived. Still, the youngest Lavin son felt supported by his parents and considered himself to have had a happy family life.

What Larry remembers most about growing up is the family's increasing difficulties with money and the embarrassment he often suffered as a consequence of being a poor boy in a rich neighborhood. Justin Lavin started married life as the prosperous owner of a factory that manufactured heels for the area's thriving shoe industry. By Larry's infancy, foreign competition had forced his father out of business and into a financial decline from which he never really recovered. Using his college degree in chemical engineering, Justin landed a job recruiting for a specialized employment firm in Boston. Frugal by nature, he'd leave for the city with his lunch in a brown bag and more often than not return home without having made a placement or earned a penny. Sometime months would pass between paychecks.

Meanwhile the bills mounted and young Larry felt the social sting of his father's periodic penury. "I remember in grammar school they'd call the roll in the morning and anybody whose parents hadn't paid the twenty-five-dollar tuition had to stand up in front of the class. At first I didn't even know why I was forced to stand there, and when I found out, I felt awful. In the cafeteria I'd watch my neighbors buy hot lunches, but since they cost fifty cents I brought lunch from home and got milk for a dime. It was hard when I'd go to the dentist knowing my mother owed twelve hundred dollars for her dentures. I'd often be asked by the school or a store owner to bring a note home to my parents. I'd sneak a look in the envelope and it would say: This is your fifth notice; please pay. I can remember going to the corner grocery store where everybody charged things and being told I couldn't charge anymore because we owed too much. At home there'd be fights about money all the time. Once I put a quarter in the jukebox at a luncheonette and a little while later in the car my father pulled over at a bridge and screamed at me, 'Why don't you get out now and throw your money into the water if you're going to waste it like that.' "

Larry couldn't understand why his parents didn't sell their home and reduce their expenses instead of struggling to pay the taxes and maintain their upper-middle-class public image. (In the early seventies, unable to pay the taxes on the big two-story home where they'd raised their children, the Lavins finally were forced to sell it and move to a moderately priced town-house complex, a giant step down.) From their behavior, Larry got the message that financial hardship was something to be ashamed of, and resolved to provide a financially stable future for his own children. "I had some friends whose families had similar problems, but they didn't have any pretense about being poor. I always felt it was this thing that no one should know. I never wanted my kids to go through the same embarrassment. I wanted a nice house and a pool. I wanted to be able to give my kids everything so they wouldn't have to hang around somebody else's house to play with their toys, but friends would come to them."

One thing seemed obvious to young Larry Lavin: money was the cause of life's problems and also the solution. He was always hustling to pick up any odd-job he could find. The struggle to present an appearance of wealth and status while fighting to keep the wolf from the door had a profound effect on shaping his character and aspirations. He vowed he would never fall into his father's predicament. "I was always a very logical thinker and I didn't want the ups and downs of my father's life. When I was in fifth grade one of my jobs was cutting the lawns of two dentists. I looked at the way they lived and decided that was the life-style I wanted when I grew up. It was even better than being a doctor because you made a lot of money and didn't get awakened in the middle of the night for emergencies."

For the first dozen years of his life, Larry was a model child and star student, but in junior high school his halo began to tarnish. The kid who used to snatch cigarettes out of friends' mouths because smoking was bad for their health got turned onto pot by his sister, Jill, and his best friend, Ricky. "When I first found out that Ricky was smoking pot I thought it was horrible. I couldn't believe he was doing something that could really hurt him. But by the end of the year I was getting high with him and I had a whole different attitude." Suddenly it was no longer cool to be straight, and if Larry needed a guide to where the wild side was, he found it in Glenn Fuller.

The two met at Cardinal Cushing Academy, a Catholic prep school, and gradually Larry began to live the dual existence that would characterize the rest of his life. At home and in school he was, in the main, the perfect son and conscientious student. At the same time, he was initiated by Glenn into a subculture where the spoils of petty thievery were considered badges of honor and symbols of success. By his junior year in high school he'd become adept at stealing stereos from the town-house complex where his family now lived and selling them to a fence. He always needed money to buy himself the luxuries his rich friends had or to help pay for things his family couldn't afford. But he concedes that stealing satisfied something deeper than his material needs. "I always got off on pushing myself to the limit. Even as a little kid I can remember climbing trees to a phenomenal height where I could definitely die. There was a thrill for me in figuring out how to get away with the theft, then executing the plan. Stealing wasn't like the false excitement of skiing fast downhill. It was true danger, a way to test my limits. More exhilarating than any drug I ever took."

It would always surprise close friends who knew Larry's lust for lawbreaking that he retained so many of the old-fashioned middle-class values fed to him along with his mother's cooking and his father's puritanical admonitions to work hard and be a good provider. The pleasures of home and hearth and the respect of his neighbors remained very important to Larry Lavin. At the same time, an equally powerful force railed against the dreary middle-class constrictions with which he'd been raised and urged him to resist any authority other than his own. Rather than let one side of himself control the other, he simply gave full expression to both.

By Larry's sophomore year in high school he had decided he deserved a better education than he was getting at Cardinal Cushing Academy, and he applied to Phillips Exeter in nearby New Hampshire. He entered in January 1971 as one of Exeter's many scholarship students, which meant that his parents paid only about $600 of the schools $3,200 tuition, bringing the cost more in line with Cushing. Since he was neither an athlete nor the son of an alumnus, he must have stood out academically to the admissions committee.

An exclusive private boarding school, Phillips Exeter Academy was founded by a Harvard graduate in 1782 to "regulate the tempers, enlarge the minds, and form the morals of youth." It has, in its two-century history, educated some of the finest minds in the country from some of the finest families. The 142-acre campus encompasses manicured playing fields for a dozen different sports, from lacrosse to soccer, and handsome red brick school buildings and dormitories covered with ivy. In winter, Exeter looks like a Currier & Ives print, with icicles dripping from the eaves of the white chapel steeple. In spring, bicycles meander along the grassy banks of the Exeter River, which flows through the campus.

When Larry Lavin arrived at Exeter the serene campus belied the unrest simmering in the student body. While the school was as rigorous academically as it had always been, the political and social dust from the upheavals of the sixties lay scattered everywhere. Girls had just been enrolled in the formerly all-male school, adding another element of disorientation to student life. Pot smoking was as common as pizza parties. A faculty members recalls, "We just didn't know how to deal with the drug culture when it hit us. We didn't even know why we disapproved so strongly, except that we thought we should." Larry Lavin's personality was well-suited to this climate where the strict disciplinary rules that had for so long glued everything tightly in place now seemed to exist purely to be tested.

But he didn't test the rules right away. To the sixteen-year-old Lavin, with his shoulder-length Prince Valiant haircut, a mouth full of braces he paid for himself and a broad, provincial Massachusetts accent, Exeter was an intimidating place.

Among the thousand or so students were a goodly number of monied sophisticated kids who spent most of their ample allowances on drugs. Another segment of the student body was made up of the intellectually gifted who chose Exeter as a guaranteed route to a top Ivy League college. A third element comprised political. activists who tried to reform student government and experimented with the liberating aspects of LSD. Everyone felt the intense pressure to excel and the desire to be accepted by one of these groups. Larry Lavin gravitated toward the wealthy potheads. "I couldn't believe the drug scene at Exeter. Every single night from the day I got there until the day I left, we got high."

Almost immediately Lavin found for a mentor his roommate—a brash, irreverent kid named Jeff Giancola who was short and scrappy with penetrating brown eyes under bushy brows that gave a shifty expression to his otherwise attractive face. Giancola's forte was shocking people. In an era when it was chic to be liberal, Giancola stood apart as a staunch conservative. When presidential candidate George McGovern spoke at Exeter, Giancola tore down his campaign banner in the middle of his presentation.

Larry was not as committed to right-wing politics as Jeff, but he'd been raised in a family of Republicans, and once he was old enough, would cast his vote repeatedly for the GOP because he felt it was the best way to protect his money. The anti-Vietnam-war movement of the early seventies did not attract him, and if he had a hero, it was William Buckley. That put him very much in the minority at Exeter, which fit perfectly with his fondness for non-conformity. He was possibly the only long-haired student who campaigned for Richard Nixon. He also worked on the conservative student paper, the *Plain Dealer*. The paper had been started by two boys from Cleveland as an alternative to the official school paper, the *Exonian*, which they considered a left-wing rag. Staff members of the *Plain Dealer* say Lavin was conscientious and reliable although he never seemed to write much. His title on the masthead was "sports editor," but he was never a serious athlete. He played lacrosse and water polo and stood out more for his competitiveness than his skills. A teammate recalls, "He was very tough on defense, a real animal. Whatever Larry did, he was driven to win."

Giancola was far more flamboyant than Lavin, and clearly the leader. He was considered the intellectual and Lavin the schemer. The roommates quickly became known for their derring-do. They'd get drunk (Larry had a reputation for not holding liquor very well), climb out on the slanted roof of their four-story dorm, and perch precariously on the edge with their legs dangling over the rain gutter. Now and then they'd steal a bicycle just for the hell of it. They bragged about cheating on their College Boards by switching the parts so that each could take only the tests on subjects in which he excelled. Lavin did the math and Giancola did the English. Lavin's score on the exam they took together was over 1,200. On a later SAT he took on his own, his score was lower.

Even without Giancola, Lavin was capable of dreaming up ways to thwart authority. One weekend he created a contest to see how many of Exeter's sacred rules could be broken in a twenty-four-hour period. There were five rules of campus behavior popularly known as "mortal sins"—no drugs, no drinking, no girls in dorm rooms, no leaving campus without a pass, no sneaking into a dorm after check-in curfew. It was something of a rite of passage to break at least one rule before graduating. What most boys did was sneak out to the Crater, a grassy bowl near the railroad tracks about a half-mile from campus, and get high. But only Lavin would have conscientiously set out to challenge the entire list of infractions at one time. And succeeded.

Young Lavin had no trouble attracting female companions. As time went on, he used his girlfriends to enhance his image as a risk-taker. One girlfriend remembers him as "very gentle and tender and not at all shy or awkward." Initially, he flouted the rules by sneaking dates into his dorm room. When that was no longer a challenge, he invited two girls to spend the same weekend with him. One, from Haverhill, whom he had met over the summer at his lifeguard job, he installed in a hotel in town. The other, who also attended Exeter, he smuggled into his room. Then he jockeyed back and forth between the two, delighted by how cleverly he kept them from discovering each other. He might have been lucky keeping the girls apart, but he wasn't as careful when he was with them alone. The Haverhill girlfriend got pregnant, and although Larry wasn't convinced the baby was his, he paid for her abortion by stealing some stereos.

What helped Larry pull off his bold stunts was style. He was a likable kid whose low-key manner belied the audacity of his activities. Some of his most loyal fans were the underclassmen in the dorm, the gangly, awkward boys nobody else had time for. One recalls, "Larry would look you in the eye and make you feel very important, even if you weren't part of his cool group. Once some of us asked him what would happen if he got caught smoking pot and kicked out of school. He shrugged like it was no big deal and said he'd get an equivalency diploma and go to college anyway. I marveled that he didn't seem to care about having to go home and face his parents if he got in trouble. Later I recognized him as having the classic profile of a con man. But back then I thought he was terrific."

Not everybody saw Lavin in such a positive light. Those who didn't know him intimately and never got to see the lively side describe him as being rather quiet, more of a loner than a leader. And his prep-school friends could never quite understand why he held on to his former high-school friends—even punks like Glenn Fuller, who used to come to Exeter to drive him home on weekends. "There was a rough side to Larry," says an Exeter classmate. "Once we were walking in town and two guys taunted us about being preppies. Larry pulled out a penknife and chased them for a block or so. Then he stopped, picked up a rock—the kind you need two hands to hold—and hurled it at them. He aimed it to land just short of where they were standing. He terrorized those kids and enjoyed every minute of it. I never saw him laugh so hard. He loved winning, no matter what the challenge."

Outside his small circle of friends, Lavin's impact on Exeter was negligible. He had few extracurricular activities. Despite a knack for speaking well in class and picking up the gist of a discussion even if he hadn't done the homework, his grades, by Exeter's tough standards, were average and only good enough to get him into the University of Pennsylvania, which was considered the bottom of the Ivy League. The A students at Exeter were admitted to Harvard, Yale, and Princeton. In a public high school Lavin would have been an honor-roll student, but at Exeter he could only muster B's in math and physics, C's in English, French, chemistry, and biology, and a D in music. His faculty adviser, Donald Dunbar, says, "Larry didn't stand out in any way. If I were asked to describe him, I'd say he was a nonentity, a loser. He was one of those nondescript kids that nobody on the faculty remembers."

Often Lavin seemed reticent only because his behavior was judged in comparison with the noisy activism of his constant companion, Jeff Giancola. In the fall of their senior year, during an assembly to air complaints about Exeter's stifling regulations,

Giancola strode up to the microphone as cocky as usual and lectured the student body. "Look. You guys know the rules. I know the rules. And if you get caught, you know the consequences." The implied message was: Do what you want, but be smart and you'll get away with it. A week later Giancola got roaring drunk and passed out in front of the proctor at sign-in. He was expelled the next day. A week later the *Exonian* ran a cartoon showing Giancola in the garb of Julius Caesar surrounded by the faculty brandishing daggers. Giancola's expulsion was the start of a discipline backlash. By the end of the year, twenty-four students had been dismissed from Exeter for drug or alcohol abuse, the highest number in the school's history. Giancola managed to matriculate at Columbia University, where he was elected student-body president, and continue on to law school. He never lost touch with his pal Larry. Years later, while practicing law in Washington, he was one of Lavin's regular cocaine customers.

With Jeff out of the picture at Exeter, Larry had the spotlight to himself and he brazenly filled it with an array of stolen goods. From the library where he worked part-time as a student aide, he slipped out—on permanent loan—an oak table and a tape recorder, which he displayed like trophies in the center of his dorm room. He even rigged the recorder with a timer to wake him in the morning with his favorite music. Next he set about stocking his pantry. Langdell Dormitory, where Larry lived, was one of two dorms connected by a dining hall in the middle. He found a way to sneak into the kitchen at night through the boiler room in the dorm basement. Sometimes he'd fill huge plastic bags with potato chips, which he'd take back to his room and share with his friends. He also pilfered institutional-size cans of Bartlett pears and peaches in syrup, which he'd stack on his bookshelves like a rack in a supermarket.

The food stash impressed the boys in the dorm and came in handy for late-night snacks. When his own cupboard was bare, Lavin would pound on the door of his next-door neighbor, Nick Vanderbilt, the very proper scion of a prominent American family. Long after midnight, he'd rouse Nick from a sound sleep, amiably yelling, "Hey, Vanderbilt, whaddya got to eat?" The groggy freshman, who dared not refuse an upperclassman's bidding, tumbled from bed and handed over the Lorna Doones his mother had sent. Lavin and his pals sat on the floor in Vanderbilt's room eating cookies and chatting as if they'd dropped in for afternoon tea.

By his senior year Lavin was heavily into drug experimentation. One weekend he camped out with friends at Watkins Glen for a huge rock-music event featuring the Allman Brothers and spent most of the three days in limbo, tripping on LSD laced with angel dust. At school he smoked marijuana on a nightly basis as a way to unwind after a hard evening hitting the books. After Giancola was expelled he lived alone in a corner room on the fourth floor of his dormitory. Because the room had been designated as a double it had a fairly large closet, which struck Lavin as an ideal smoking den where he and his friends could indulge their illegal activity. He carpeted the floor, hung a Jimi Hendrix poster on the wall, and hooked up a "black" light for atmosphere. When the smoking regulars gathered for the nightly pot party, they'd huddle in the closet, shut the door, and stuff towels along the bottom to prevent the sweet-scented smoke from escaping. Lavin even devised his own early-warning system to protect the group from faculty invaders. He connected an intercom to another room on the floor, where a lookout was posted. Once a friend pretended to be the dorm supervisor and gave Lavin and his friends a bad fright by shouting into the intercom, "Boys, I know you're in there."

Lavin's year of living dangerously came to an ignominious end a month before his graduation. On a routine check one night, a faculty member came to see if he was in his room. What he found, instead of Larry, was the stash of stolen food, the smoking den, and a water pipe. On May 11, 1973, Larry Lavin was expelled from Phillips Exeter. The reasons listed on his record say: "For illegal removal from the library of a tape recorder, for taking food from the food-storage area, and the use of marijuana in his dorm room." Calling his father to tell him what had happened was much worse than explaining the snowmobile heist. Julian Lavin screamed his outrage and disappointment. Finally Larry shouted back, "Then don't come get me. I'll just go to California and disappear." But of course his father came and the ride back to Haverhill seemed to take days instead of hours. While his father railed on and on, Larry sat next to him, his belongings piled in the trunk and back seat of the car, thinking how stupid he'd been to get caught. It never crossed his mind that he deserved to be punished for breaking the rules. Quite the contrary.

Larry was annoyed at being expelled but felt neither guilt nor embarrassment, and a week later blithely returned to campus to party with what would have been his graduating class. Nor did he harbor resentment toward Exeter. Years later, as a young dentist, he responded to alumni fund-raising appeals with generous checks of fifty and one hundred dollars when his former classmates were giving a mere twenty-five.

Fortunately for Lavin, his expulsion came after he'd received his acceptance to the University of Pennsylvania. All he had to worry about was whether they'd still take him without a diploma. Exeter's policy in cases like Larry's was to send a form letter to the college saying so-and-so is no longer a part of the student body. Period. No explanation. Lavin contacted an admissions officer at Penn and persuaded the man to overlook his problems. Most colleges by then viewed minor drug infractions far more leniently than high schools did. Penn took the unofficial posture that if a student was basically okay and the incident was not part of a pattern of addiction, it would not withdraw its approval. The lack of a diploma wasn't an obstacle either, since there was a precedent of admitting extremely bright students to Penn directly after their junior year in high school.

For Larry Lavin, his expulsion from Exeter mirrored the snowmobile incident. He'd gotten into trouble by being a little sloppy, but had managed to escape the consequences. If anything, he was rather proud of once again having crossed the line and coming away unscathed. When his father learned about the expulsion, he warned his son, "That's two strikes. You only get three, Larry. Three strikes and you're out."

Larry figured differently. He'd gotten two balls and the worst he'd ever get was a walk.

By the early 1970's marijuana had become as integral a part of college life as underage drinking. Not everybody smoked pot. Not everybody waited until age twenty-one to order a beer at a bar. But nobody much cared who did either one. The prevailing attitude in the student body was that the laws ought to be changed, the drinking age lowered and marijuana legalized. Compared with the antidrug zeal at Exeter, Penn was like a party at the Playboy Mansion. The administration didn't condone drug activity; it preferred to ignore it.

Lavin fit into this milieu as if it had been custom-designed for him. He no sooner had met his roommate than the boy whispered, "As soon as we're alone I'll show you this great pot I brought." Within an hour they'd unpacked their pipes, bongs, and roach clips and gotten high. And that was just the beginning. Every weekend, and sometimes during the week as well, Larry was doing some kind of drug. He was introduced to Quaaludes, dropped acid a few times, and developed a reputation as a pothead. "We had a smokathon one weekend where one of the fraternities bought a half-pound of pot and everybody sat around taking hits on the bong. I was one of the three guys who outlasted everybody else."

It seemed to Lavin that "Penn was overwhelmingly influenced by drugs. Everybody was always talking about what kind of acid or speed they had or what great pot. Drugs were the major influence in our lives. The only negative view I can ever remember was one time when my brother Paul [who was attending medical school at the University of Pennsylvania] refused to drive me home for Christmas vacation because I had some pot in my pocket and he was afraid of losing his license if we got caught." Getting caught was never something Larry worried about. If he had had any intention of putting drugs behind him when he enrolled at Penn, it had disappeared by the end of freshman orientation. By his sophomore year he'd escalated from a steady user to a dealer. "I always thought I was smarter than the cops. There were times when I'd break out in a cold sweat because I was doing something wrong and close to getting caught, but I always believed I could get away with anything."

Lavin's outgoing personality quickly established him at Penn as a party looking for a place to happen. He became known as the crazy kid with the BB gun, aiming at squirrels, pigeons, and pets, not to mention people. He and his roommate would race across the campus like gangsters on a shooting spree. It didn't occur to Larry until he got disciplined that he might hurt somebody. He was just having harmless fun.

Shortly after unpacking his gear at Penn's Jacobean-style freshman dorms, he found the perfect outlet for his high jinks in a Phi Delta Theta pledge bid. The college fraternity system provided the ideal environment for Lavin to display his bravado. Traditionally, pledges show their mettle by breaking into rival frat houses and stealing their flags or filching the sign from the campus tavern. Lavin, already an old hand at thievery, excelled at this kind of game. He stole the moose head hanging over the mantel of the Zeta Beta Tau house, shot at pigeons with his BB gun, and just to be outrageous, invited people off the street and into his room for beer and conversation. But his most imaginative deed was the Great Stereo Robbery, which he pulled off with Paul Mikuta, a Penn classmate who became Lavin's best friend.

If there was something that couldn't or shouldn't be done, Paul and Larry had to do it. Paul was just as reckless as Larry, but not as smart. His specialty was streaking—that short-lived fad that sent college kids running naked through the streets. His picture made the local paper and prompted an angry call from his mother, who recognized the bottom she'd diapered eighteen years earlier. Both boys were tall and slender, but there the resemblance ended. Mikuta was a handsome young man with a fair complexion and light brown hair, whose only disturbing feature was his darting brown eyes, which sometimes gave him the look of a cornered animal. Unlike Lavin, who could successfully compartmentalize his life into drugs, pranks, and studying, Mikuta was a lousy juggler. He flunked out at the end of his sophomore year. By then he was rooming with Larry at the Phi Delt house in quarters that Lavin had painted black and furnished with a waterbed. When he was bored he'd practice swan dives off the bureau onto the bed.

The stereo heist was part of Lavin's fraternity-pledge challenge—to steal something sensational. The inspiration for the caper came to him while he was selling fraternity raffles in the dorm. Every freshman had a stereo system. It was as standard a part of college furniture as a desk lamp. As he strolled from room to room, chatting and hawking his chances, Lavin noted the locations of equipment worth stealing. He and Mikuta waited for a vacation weekend, when few students remained in school, to put the plan into action. Dressed in black, they climbed up to the roof of the dorm and, like trained second-story men, lowered themselves by rope to the ledge of the window of a room they'd chosen. If the window hadn't been left unlocked, Lavin kicked it in. It was the perfect crime done for the most foolish motive: pledge points. The stereos were merely a means to an end, an excuse to play cat burglars. "Afterward we realized we'd gotten carried away. It was kind of ridiculous. We didn't need these things. It wasn't like the ra-ra stuff of stealing the moose head and the poker table from ZBT, then sitting around and laughing when the guys came to pick it up. This was breaking the law, and the fraternity house didn't think it was too cool." Consequently, as soon as the brothers validated the evidence, Lavin and Mikuta carted their cache to a loading dock in a suburban shopping center and made an anonymous call to the Penn police telling them where they could find the sets. Most of them, that is. Lavin couldn't resist holding on to a few of the best components and assembling a first-rate stereo system for his room.

Nobody was more amazed with the success of the stereo caper than Lavin and Mikuta themselves. So they did it again and again on their own rather than as a pledge prank. Mostly they used their rope trick to break into other fraternity houses, not caring much what kind of booty they'd find. Their kick came from the act rather than the loot. Sometimes they even gave away the stuff they stole. They pictured themselves as Robin Hoods with a sense of humor. Once they stole two rear tires and left the car sitting on blocks. It later occurred to them that the owner might not realize his tires were missing, and they drove back to put a note on his windshield so he wouldn't try to drive the car and ruin it. Lavin loved to tell that story because it showed he was really a young man with a conscience.

Fraternity life did more than give Lavin an excuse for breaking and entering. It introduced him to the lucrative profits of the drug trade. In the past, whenever Lavin bought grass, he gave little thought to where it came from or what kind of profit was involved in the sale. Now he started to pay attention to the pounds and pounds of pot coming into the fraternity house in huge laundry bags and leaving neatly packaged in small plastic sandwich bags that would find their way to apartments and dormitories all over campus.

Lavin had come to Penn with two hundred dollars in his bank account and his tuition paid by a combination of scholarships and loans. He didn't need a whole lot of money to live. For entertainment there were dollar movies and cheap meals at a mission near the campus. But he'd been hustling for too long not to spot a good opportunity to accumulate more spending money than he was making at his student job in the library. Moreover, he'd become close friends with a student dealer named Dan Dill, who explained to him the structure of the marijuana business and how easily he could get involved. A born entrepreneur, Lavin recognized the classic economics of supply and demand. Penn was full of buyers like himself, and as long as somebody was going to get rich catering to that market, it might as well be Larry. Here was the ideal extracurricular college activity. It fulfilled all his needs. On a practical level, he could use the money to pay his tuition loans. On a psychic level, he'd get the thrill of dallying in the forbidden world of drugs. And he would never have to buy a joint for himself again.

Since he had no leads to marijuana wholesalers, Lavin talked himself into a partnership with a friend who had a drug connection, which he later appropriated as his own. From the beginning, he established himself as the financier and salesman. Not for Lavin the danger of transporting drugs and money to and from Florida. He'd pay people to take that risk. He'd remain in Philadelphia, where he'd raise the money, arrange the deals by phone, and distribute the product when it arrived. Only once did Lavin venture to Florida himself. He traveled by bus on the theory that he'd be less conspicuous bringing back six suitcases of pot on a Greyhound than on a train, where a courier of his had been busted. Besides, he'd never heard of police dogs trained to sniff pot being stationed at bus terminals. Leave it to Lavin on his one and only Florida trip to meet a strung-out young woman on the bus who, in exchange for a couple of joints, enlivened the dull ride by entertaining him with oral sex in the back seat during the dark night hours while the other passengers slept.

By the end of his sophomore year, Lavin had made more than five thousand dollars selling pot to his friends and was enjoying his role as a big man in the drug culture. One night he was sitting with some of the other dealers in the fraternity when one of them asked, "How much money do you want to make selling pot?"

"I think it would be great to clear ten thousand dollars," Larry answered.

"What, are you crazy? That's peanuts. I'm looking to make at least fifty thousand dollars. Don't you want a nice house someday, or a boat? You gotta think big, Larry baby."

Larry thought the guy was way off base. "We'll never make that kind of money. We'll be lucky if we have enough to get by." But later he began to think that maybe he could do more than get by. "Maybe," he said to himself, "I could have a nice car and no worries. Maybe I could make a fortune with this if I do it right." That's when he started to treat the business seriously. He branched beyond his college friends and started dealing with anybody who could move large amounts of the stuff.

Lavin never expected his business to grow as quickly as it did. It didn't take an accounting class to teach him that the more cheaply he could get the product, the more profit he'd realize. That meant purchasing in volume to get a quantity discount. Since he could hardly have walked into a bank to get a loan, he borrowed money to finance his buys from wealthy classmates and paid them back at ten-percent interest. If none of his friends could advance him money, he'd dip into whatever other till he could find. One summer he ran the sublet program at the fraternity house and used the rent money he collected to cover his drug deals. When his customers paid him, he returned the money. The more pot he bought, the more he found he could sell.

There was never a shortage of customers. It wasn't unusual for him to presell a hundred-pound shipment in a single day. A drug courier might arrive from Miami around noon with giant trash bags full of twenty-pound compressed bricks of pot in the trunk of his car. Larry would take the bricks, break them up with his hands, and separate the product into "buds" (marijuana seedpods) and "shake" (the loose, crumbled bits of leaf), which he'd toss by the handful onto a triple-beam scale. He handled so much he got to know instinctively how many handfuls made one pound, his minimum order. Each pound went into a clear plastic bag, and when the orders were completed, he'd get on the phone and notify his customers. He might take time out for an afternoon class, then return to his apartment to make the deliveries. Before midnight, all the pot would be paid for and a much richer Larry Lavin would be poring over his homework assignment.

Because he was extremely well-organized, Lavin had no difficulty sandwiching his drug business into what was otherwise a very normal college life. After the academic rigors of Exeter, "Penn was a joke to me." He studied in concentrated blocks of time, majored in biologic sciences, and earned good enough grades to be accepted into Penn dental school, one of the country's finest. He held the office of fraternity rush chairman and was urged to run for Phi Delt president, but refused. He claimed he felt it was "immoral" for somebody in that prominent a position to be dealing drugs. If it had just been a question of his doing drugs—smoking hashish, tripping on acid—he'd have had no qualms about taking the offer.

His social life at Penn was as well-regulated as his academic and drug undertakings. In his first days at the school, a friendly upperclassman warned him that the best girls get taken very quickly, and he was determined not to be stuck with second-rate merchandise. Crossing the freshman quad one afternoon a few days later, he noticed a pixie-pretty girl with rosy cheeks, a pug nose, and straight black hair that fell to the middle of her back. She had the look of the women who smile from the pages of the L. L. Bean catalog. He walked by the low brick wall where she was sitting and playfully pushed her onto the grass. They encountered again a night later when she tripped over his inert body on the same quad. It was an unseasonably hot Indian-summer night and Larry had chugalugged more beer than he could handle and passed out from the combination of heat and alcohol. Marcia Osborn surveyed him with her big brown no-nonsense eyes, arched her distinctive half-moon eyebrows, and decided he was attractive but something of a screwball. Not her type.

Marcia Osborn struck casual acquaintances as a rather shy, almost prim young woman, content to strum her guitar and pursue her goal of becoming a physical therapist. She differed from most of the high-powered freshman girls Lavin had met, whose aggressiveness turned him off. Marcia had a more traditional set of values. She had grown up in a small house in a small town in New Jersey near the George Washington Bridge. Dumont was a bedroom community for New York City's blue-collar workers. Despite her proximity to the city, Marcia was not attracted to its glamour. For the most part, she stayed on the Jersey side of the bridge, dutifully attended parochial school, giggled with her older sister in the converted attic bedroom they shared, and became a member of the flag-throwing team in high school. Although money was tight, it never seemed to be an issue for the Osborns the way it was for the Lavins. Marcia's father had had a leg amputated because of vascular disease when she was in elementary school, and he was forced to leave his maintenance job at Rockefeller Center. Thereafter he stayed home. Her mother, Agnes, an intensive-care nurse, became the family breadwinner and managed to send her son to dental school and her two daughters to college.

In high school Marcia made up her mind to be a physical therapist, and after surveying the few schools that had a four-year program in that field, she chose the College of Allied Health at the University of Pennsylvania. The standards for admission were lower than the rest of the university, which suited her perfectly, since she was never a bookworm. If you asked Marcia what she loved, her answer even then would have been: Kids and animals.

Marcia's dorm room attracted a wholesome crowd very different from the boisterous druggies who were Larry's friends. Kids would drift in and sit on the floor while she and her roommate, Patty, sang folk songs. They called themselves the MOPS, a combination of their initials, MO and PS. In time that room became a refuge for Lavin from his pot-smoking, wild fraternity life. As the fall progressed, the two kept running into each other. Each time they'd talk a little longer. Each time they seemed to have more to talk about.

Larry and Marcia, although both products of a middle-class Catholic upbringing, seemed to embody the axiom that opposites attract. He was tall and lean; she was small, round, and soft. He was gregarious; she was reserved. He was a daredevil; she was a homebody. He was fascinated with computers; she liked to knit. Yet each gave the other exactly what was needed. He brought excitement to her life and she brought stability to his. He might have been the sparkler atop the birthday cake, but she was the earth mother who baked it. What began as a loose relationship gradually tightened. By their senior year at Penn they were living together in a rented apartment and planning to get married.

The only thing Marcia and Larry ever argued about was his drug business. Marcia hated it from the start. Although she typically deferred to his dominant personality, she had a streak of stubborn independence and never hid her opinions the way she did her emotions. She wasn't flatly opposed to drugs, and would smoke a joint or do a line of coke at a party. It was the dealing she resented, because it robbed her of Larry's time and attention. She hated the constant invasions of their privacy. Drug cronies floated in and out of their apartment. She implored Larry to quit dealing, and again and again he'd promise her that as soon as he made a specific sum, he'd stop. First it was $50,000, enough to pay off his school loans and upgrade his car from the 1966 Nova he'd bought with the money he'd earned driving a taxi during the summer between his sophomore and junior years. But over the years, whenever he reached the magic number—$50,000, $100,000, $1,000,000—he'd find an excuse to raise the stakes.

"I'd set these goals and they'd just overwhelm my good sense and I'd slide right by them. That I could place them over my relationship with Marcia and push to the limit so many times shows how important the money became to me."

At some deeper level, Larry was as addicted to the excitement of dealing as he was to the money, not to mention the power he had as the supplier of the best grass on campus. And at this point in his drug career, despite all his hard work, he wasn't able to stockpile anything substantial because of his losses. Several times he took everything he'd saved and put it toward a pot shipment that would get confiscated in a drug bust on the trip back from Florida. In the drug business, nobody refunds your losses for undelivered merchandise paid for in advance. Two of Lavin's couriers carrying over one hundred pounds of pot they'd bought for Larry were busted—one in his junior year and one in his senior year. Between the cost of the confiscated drugs and lawyers' fees he paid, Larry was in the hole for nearly $50,000 each time. "It was devastating. I threw myself into the business and worked hard so that I could pay back money I owed to people who were fronting me and build up again." By the time he graduated from Penn in 1977, he had the capability of earning over $30,000 a year selling pot, but all he'd netted at this point was enough to cover his college expenses, provide spending money and a few extras like the $1,700 it took to junk the Nova and move up to an Impala. What he didn't have was $10,000 to pay his dental-school tuition. When he was rejected at Tufts, where he'd also applied, he consoled himself that he couldn't have gone there anyway because they didn't have financial aid.

Actually Marcia was more disappointed at the rejection than he was. She'd been set on moving to Boston and didn't like to deal with change once her mind had been made up. Here was her chance to get Larry out of Philadelphia to a different environment where he wouldn't have drug connections and customers. Instead, just as she had feared, very little was different when Larry entered Penn's dental school in 1977. If anything, the drug dealing escalated. He continued to supply pot to his former classmates as they relocated around the country and brought their new friends into the fold, but he also built up his market in the black community surrounding the university. Added to this base were the customers he began to pick up at the dental school. Word of who's got the good drugs spreads rapidly in a student environment, and one thing Larry Lavin took great pride in was the quality of his pot. With all the socializing that marked the start of a new term in a new school, he had plenty of opportunity to increase his customer list.

The round of dental-school parties that fall followed a typical pattern. There was music, beer, and chips. People stood around, played social geography and, sooner or later, somebody passed a joint. That's how Larry Lavin met Ken Weidler—by offering him a hit at a Friday-night get-together of first-year dental students. At a party that did not include his tight circle of friends, Lavin had a tendency to hang back. He struck people as a nice-enough sort who liked to talk about stereos and electronic gadgets. But with his own crowd he was the center of attraction, the life of the party. This particular night Lavin was among friends and Weidler was immediately drawn into his powerful magnetic field. Larry seemed so together. So sure of himself. So talkative and friendly. He seemed to be all the things Weidler felt he wasn't.

Two tokes on the joint told Weidler he was smoking optimum-quality grass. He and Lavin began trading "where-do-you-get-it" stories and Weidler mentioned he'd had a pot business himself as an undergraduate at a small upstate college. Lavin's capitalist antennae shot up. Here was a potential dealer for his network. Before long they wound up back at Lavin's place on the corner of Forty-third and Osage Avenue, a once-proud West Philadelphia neighborhood of tall shade trees and spacious three-story stone and wood houses on the fringe of the Penn campus. Most of the original residents had moved to the suburbs and their houses had been converted into cheap apartments rented to a mixture of black families, university students, and underfaculty.

Lavin's first-floor apartment was nicer than most—and neater too. There was a fifty-gallon aquarium in the corner of the living room, a black cat named Spooky usually nestled on the couch, and a backgammon board always set up on the coffee table. Larry enjoyed games that gave him the opportunity to take chances, and the combination of his skill and his gambler's instincts made him an excellent backgammon player. He had total confidence in his gaming ability and used the strategy of doubling the stakes whenever the game was very close.

Brushing Spooky away, Larry knelt down and pulled a giant plastic trash bag loaded with grass from beneath the sofa. When Kenny gasped, Larry dismissed the enormous bag with a flick of his hand as if it held leftovers from a much bigger banquet. "This is nothing," he said. "I usually clear out a couple of hundred pounds a week. C'mon with me." As they walked up the block to another apartment, Lavin explained that he fronted many of his customer-dealers, which meant that he gave them grass on credit and they didn't have to pay for it until it was sold. He carried three grades of marijuana. The commercial grade had more green leaves in it. The "gold" was higher quality. The top grade—stuff that would blow you away—cost $2,000 a pound. He sold that for $200 to $250 an ounce. And he also carried hashish. They arrived at the second apartment and Larry ushered Ken into a bedroom where the floor was covered with sheets. There was a triple-beam scale in the corner and piles of marijuana, enough to fill at least three trash bags. More pot than Weidler had ever seen.

"It's great shit," Larry said. "Hey, if you ever decide to go back into dealing, let me know. I'll even front you if that's how you want it." Lavin was a genius at reading people. Whether he was fishing for customers, or cajoling friends to transport drugs, or conning professors about the source of his money, he had a knack for sizing up people and tossing the appropriate bait. Kenny Weidler didn't stand a chance.

Larry Lavin and Kenny Weidler didn't seem particularly compatible. Lavin was supremely self-confident, with a veneer of prep-school sophistication; Weidler was the small-town, ruddy-cheeked boy-next-door. He joked to friends that Hari Krishnas selling flowers in airports always picked him out as an easy mark. The only physical characteristic they shared was their height. Both brushed the six-foot mark, but next to Kenny's athletically tuned body, Larry looked too soft to survive a hard workout. Lavin had the easy grin and canny green eyes of a young man who knew exactly what lurked around the next corner. Kenny seemed boyish by comparison, with innocent blue eyes, auburn curls, and a crooked, almost forced smile. He had grown up in Williamsport, an industrial town in central Pennsylvania remarkable only for its Little League Baseball Hall of Fame Museum. He was the straight arrow, only-and-lonely child of straitlaced Protestant parents and gained whatever attention he could from an indifferent father by excelling as a scholar-athlete. Tennis, football, and wrestling were his sports. He was admitted to the National Honor Society and appeared in the 1973 edition of *Outstanding American High School Students*. To Ken Weidler sports and scholarship could also get him into a good college so he could become a dentist like his dad. Because his parents disapproved of his attending what they viewed as wild high-school parties, he had spent many of his teenage Saturday nights alone watching TV and did little dating. He had friends and was liked more or less, but he wasn't "well-liked." Ken Weidler yearned to be popular, but the best crowd at school looked upon him as a social drag. Not only did he refuse to smoke pot, he avoided any situation where dope was even a subject of conversation.

When Weidler arrived at Muhlenberg College, a small, well-respected liberal-arts school about two hours from Philadelphia, he was determined not to repeat the loneliness of his high-school experience. Other than a single week at summer camp, he'd never been away from home before, and the heady experience of freedom exhilarated him. When someone in the dorm offered him a joint, his previous hostility to drugs snapped like a frayed cord. He took a deep drag and decided that if this was the price to be one of the guys, he was now ready to pay it. Soon Kenny had a small pot habit that he couldn't afford. His parents paid his tuition and gave him some spending money, but he didn't feel right using their money for drugs. Friends advised him to do what so many of them did: get more pot than he needed and sell enough to pay for his own supply. That meant buying ounce bags and selling three-quarter-ounce bags for whatever the full ounce cost him. At first Weidler was hesitant. Then he rationalized an excuse for doing it: marijuana was certainly safer medically than cigarettes. In fact there was no evidence pot hurt anybody. Granted, it was illegal. But so had liquor been during Prohibition. Then the nation saw the foolishness of the law and repealed it. On and off campus, pot smokers were convinced the same thing would happen to marijuana.

Kenny discovered his popularity at Muhlenberg increased with the quality and quantity of the grass he sold. It was "in" to be Kenny's friend, to have Kenny at a party. In an unexpected way, drugs even helped him to grow as an individual. Until then, he'd been very much a clone of his father's narrow perspective. The drug world opened him to other points of view. By his senior year in college he'd advanced from dealing in ounces to pounds. But he was still only breaking even. Unlike Lavin, who, from the start, sold drugs for profit, Weidler aimed only at covering his expenses. He never had a big enough business to distract him from his studies, and maintained a better than 3.0 average, which was high enough to get him admitted to the dental schools at Penn and Georgetown.

Just as he'd left high school determined to get into drugs, Weidler left college determined to give them up. He was entering a professional school and felt that drug behavior wasn't appropriate for a young man about to become a dentist. Besides, he doubted he'd find any drugs at a major university like Penn. That naiveté vanished when Larry Lavin entered his life. Lavin, who attracted people like free hors d'oeuvres at a happy hour, mesmerized Weidler. He was a ticket to the fun house, and his apartment was a great place to hang out, always buzzing with people and activity— especially on delivery day, with customers dashing in and out, exchanging fistfuls of cash for shopping bags of marijuana. Kenny, still mindful of the isolation of his teen years, convinced himself that he had nothing to lose and everything to gain by joining Lavin's enchanted world. He knew drugs would be an immediate avenue for taking him from obscurity to instant popularity, just as they had done in college. He could attract a circle of friends, something he'd never be able to do, like Lavin, on the sheer force of his personality.

Kenny Weidler wasn't a boisterous glad-hander. The only time he got really excited was playing intermural touch football. Too slender for the line, he quarterbacked a dental-school team that finished first in its league for two years running, largely because of his skill. On the field he played an aggressive game, taking charge of the action. Off the field he retreated into the anonymity of just another team player.

That winter, before the snow fell on the campus quad, Weidler was back selling pot. Only this time Lavin was his supplier—and more important, his good friend. Weidler came to look upon him as the big brother he'd never had, the loving father he'd always missed.

Throughout their freshman year, Lavin and Weidler sat in class learning human physiology and managing their individual businesses afterward. Lavin operated like a giant conglomerate, delivering product up and down the East Coast and to large customers from the neighboring black community as well. Weidler ran more of a mom-and-pop operation, selling about a pound of pot a week to dental-school classmates and college friends. Even at that level, he prospered to the point where he couldn't begin to smoke his profits and, for the first time, tasted the addictive flavor of greed. A hundred bucks here, a few hundred there, mounted into thousands hidden away in a box in his closet.

One night in the spring when it was getting warm enough to inaugurate the Frisbee season, Kenny dropped in at Lavin's apartment. Larry had just been given some cocaine as a gift from a pot customer. They laid out a few lines and tried it. It was a different high from pot. Lively and energizing. Whereas good pot can send a smoker off for hours into a languid, private haven, coke is a short, sweet, and intense pleaser.

" 'So whaddya think?" Larry asked when they'd come down.

"Powerful stuff. Makes you feel you could conquer the world," Kenny replied. "From what I read, it's harmless. It shouldn't even be classified as a narcotic."

"I think there's a market for this shit, and it's gonna grow," Lavin said. "There's money to be made with coke. Big money that will leave pot in the dust. I'm gonna invest in some and test the market."

Successful businessmen are the ones who get in on the ground floor of a trend. It would be three more years before *Time* magazine, in its July 1981 cover story, reported that an estimated ten million Americans were using coke with some regularity. By then coke would be established as the preferred stimulant of the rich and famous, the Rolls-Royce of recreational drugs. Lavin, the wily hustler, had sensed the enormous possibilities of coke early on. His sales organization was already in place. He could procure cocaine from his pot suppliers to fill the existing demand and go on to expand his market by weaning his marijuana customers onto coke. The cocaine itself would be a persuasive ally. Almost everybody who did blow once came back begging to buy more.

Here was a big money opportunity for Lavin, with far greater potential than the one he'd already mastered. Granted, the risks were greater, but the stakes were higher too, which for Lavin made coke all the more appealing. His first buy was four ounces. He had no trouble getting rid of it for a tidy profit. Weidler tiptoed into the market with less lofty ambitions. He mentioned to his pot customers that, as an accommodation, he could get them coke if they wanted it. His first sale was only an eighth of an ounce, but he pocketed $150 profit. Soon he would take in another dental student, David Ackerman, to help his branch of the business grow.

Clearly coke was the drug of the future. Within two years Larry would be out of the marijuana business completely and selling nothing but cocaine. In an average month he'd deal three kilos at a profit of $20,000 each and he'd have raised his goal for getting out to a lofty one million dollars. Drugs were already a lot more lucrative than dentistry could ever be.

5

UNIVERSITY OF PENNSYLVANIA
1976

Call it fate that the hostess had just stepped away when David Ackerman and another Penn student walked into the restaurant that spring day in 1976. Relieving her was a willowy waitress with straight shoulder-length black hair, a wistful smile, and dancing dark eyes. Was she Asian? Ackerman wasn't sure, but her exotic good looks attracted him. The college boys had been shopping in downtown Philadelphia and stopped for lunch at La Crêpe, a popular French café.

Suzanne Noramatzu decided the pair looked reasonably pleasant and she seated them at her station. The three bantered back and forth all during the meal, and Suzanne found the short, animated one especially charming. Even sitting still, David Ackerman had an appealing restless energy. It emanated from his lively and inquisitive eyes. He had a trim build and regular features—straight teeth, a good nose, and clear skin. If he'd been taller people would have called him handsome, but at five-foot-seven and with an eternally young face, no matter what his age David Ackerman would always be described as "cute." After the pair left to pay the cashier, Suzanne Noramatzu discovered the note Ackerman had scribbled on a cocktail napkin and slipped under her tip: "If you'd like to do something with me next week, call me at this number. Or, if you are the one who prefers to be called, write to me at this address, David."

She waited a week and wrote him a letter. Ackerman called immediately and asked her to dinner. She suggested an inexpensive restaurant and, under the impression he didn't have much money, she offered to split the check. He said it wasn't necessary and then paid for a movie too. They walked out of *All the President's Men* to find they shared the same political views, which was more important to Suzanne at the time than it was to David. She was the twenty-year-old daughter of a Japanese-American father and a mother of English-Irish descent. Suzanne preferred peace marches to pep rallies and eschewed the stifling conventionality of her suburban Plymouth-Whitemarsh High School for the freedom of an experimental nonstructured school in center-city Philadelphia. Although her grades were good enough for college, she persuaded her parents to let her postpone her higher education and travel instead. Europe became her classroom. In the four years before meeting David she'd explored most of the Continent, financing her trips by intermittent waitressing. That she was so unlike all the girls he knew intrigued David. She had a soft, vulnerable quality and a childlike laugh. That night he asked her out again.

By the summer of 1976 they were living together. Only after David took Suzanne home to his mother's big stone house in Bronxville, an affluent suburban community north of New York City, did she realize how different they really were. His mother, a small, pretty woman who announced her importance by wearing expensive clothes, big gold jewelry, and a large diamond ring, was polite but obviously not pleased. She chattered on about David's former girlfriend, whom she clearly preferred. Mrs. Ackerman knew she had a Jewish mother's prize property: her David was smart, well-mannered, cultured, and rich. Suzanne, on the other hand, was a Jewish mother's nightmare: a Eurasian who dressed like a hippie and hadn't even been to college.

There wasn't a thing in the backgrounds of these two young people that meshed. David was a savvy, sophisticated New Yorker, the product of the liberal, intellectual, upper-middle-class Jewish ethic. His father, a successful dentist, was a warm, unpretentious man whom David adored. As a child, he couldn't wait to grow up and work by his side. "My dad," he'd tell people, "is the greatest. The best." David's mother, a quick, bright housewife, dished out ample helpings of refinement, regularly taking him to museums and children's concerts at the Philharmonic. In return she expected his total loyalty—loyalty that was harder and harder for David to deliver as his parents' marriage became strained and dissolved in divorce while David was in high school.

Caught in the crossfire of his parents' bitter attacks on each other, David protected himself by refusing to take sides. By remaining neutral during these arguments he alienated neither parent, although he felt for both. He was a model child, the favored only son. In his parents' eyes, David could do little wrong, and he was careful to avoid doing anything that might cause them to withdraw their attention. But instead of basking in the praise he garnered, he developed a driving need for affection and commendation that his continued achievements never seemed to satisfy.

In grade school he was the kid waving his hand in the air to answer the teacher's question. At the prestigious and competitive Horace Mann High School in Riverdale, New York, he played tennis, soccer, and golf, belonged to the bridge club, and was captain of the the chess team. Although he scored over 1,400 in his College Boards and placed in the semifinals of the Merit Scholarships, he felt he'd failed because he couldn't get admitted to Harvard and had to settle for the University of Pennsylvania.

The subject of drugs never came up between David and Suzanne until the weekend of July 4, 1976. Philadelphia, birthplace of the nation, was caught in a Bicentennial tizzy. The entire city was in a party mood, and on the campus, at least, the celebration shifted into high gear. At the time, neither David nor Suzanne was a big drinker or drug user. David had smoked some pot in high school but hadn't bought any grass since his freshman year in college. Suzanne mentioned she'd done some coke and it was really fun but expensive. David decided they should splurge. Since they lived in a building full of Penn students, they had no trouble buying two grams of cocaine. The experience was disappointing.

"Nothing's happening," David complained. "How am I supposed to feel?"

"Don't you feel good? Don't you feel happy? Aren't you more alert?" Suzanne prodded.

"Maybe the stuff's bad. If it's supposed to be the superman drug, it's not doing shit for me."

Six months later, in January 1977, they tried it again to celebrate Suzanne's twenty-first birthday. David sent her roses, took her to a romantic restaurant, and afterward gave her two grams of coke. This time they both hit the stratosphere.

The University of Pennsylvania Dental School admitted twenty-one-year-old David Ackerman to the class of 1981 at the end of his junior year in college. He was one of the youngest students in the class. Both Larry Lavin and Kenny Weidler, his fellow classmates, were a full year older and more emotionally mature. David and Suzanne were still living together when he started dental school. She continued to work as a waitress and he poured himself into his studies, as if to prove to the administration that they hadn't made a mistake bringing him in early. So intent was David on his schoolwork that he made Suzanne wear earphones when she listened to music in their apartment to keep the sound from distracting him.

They hardly ever did any lines. Coke was just too expensive, and David didn't want to ask his father to raise his allowance, or take time out from his studies to work at a part-time job. Although his parents had money, he'd always been an industrious kid and worked summers and after school since he was sixteen. He liked to have his own money so he could spend it however he wanted.

With David so devoted to his schoolwork, Suzanne sometimes felt left out. Still, she admired his dedication. He'd known since third grade that he wanted to be a dentist and join his father's practice. At twenty-one she still had no direction. She marveled that even though she was without a college education, David could appreciate her intelligence. He was the first boy she had dated who seemed to respect her mind. If she neglected her own potential, Suzanne elevated David's. She judged him to be the brightest and cleverest person she'd ever met, an opinion influenced no doubt by the fact that she was in love with him. So it came as a severe shock when he told her at the start of his sophomore year that he wanted to date other women. She silently but bitterly packed her things and moved home with her parents.

With Suzanne gone, he moved into a house shared by a group of dental students. Not always easy to live with, David Ackerman could be quirky and temperamental, or generous and chatty. Drugs—a little coke now and then but mostly Quaaludes, which were much cheaper— often determined his behavior. The pills led to his friendship with classmate Ken Weidler.

It was common knowledge at the dental school that you could buy drugs from Ken. Not only pot and coke but also Quaalude 714's, which he bought from Larry Lavin, who got the pills illegally and gave them away to people he owed favors. Ken had two kinds of Quaalude customers, those who took the drug for its own mellow high and those who used it to cut the racing after too many lines of coke. David fit both categories. And to make a little money to finance his coke buys, he occasionally resold the Quaaludes he bought to a friend in New York. Getting close to Kenny was, at first, a way for David to get closer to coke. There'd always be a couple of nearly empty plastic bags of snow lying around Ken's apartment. The two of them would play backgammon with the powdery remains in the bag as the prize. David, a mathematical wizard, usually could figure the winning play and got to scrape up the leavings for a free toot. It was a real treat: pure, uncut, top-quality coke, far better than he could afford to buy.

Weidler didn't mind. He had plenty of other customers in the dental school who included drugs in their weekly budget. While Lavin's trade centered on a diverse crowd which in addition to college students included New England roughnecks and black drug dealers, Weidler catered to his peers. What a bright and talented group they were. In the seventies the University of Pennsylvania Dental School had nearly 3,200 applicants for the 160 spaces in its freshman class. To beat the competition, students had to have impeccable credentials. Those who were admitted fell roughly into three categories: the straight-arrow married students, the singles still into drinking and hanging out in campus bars the way they did in college, and the rich kids. The last set formed the core of Ken's customers. A dental-school professor remembers this particular crowd as "a grasping group who wanted it all and expected to get it right away." Drugs were so openly a part of their lives that the class of 1980 freely circulated invitations to an outrageous graduation party. For $100 per person, guests were promised one gram of coke and an unlimited supply of pot and Quaaludes.

The school's tough admission requirements assured that these drug customers were also academic achievers. They worked hard in class and clinic all week and partied all weekend. The traditional weekend party kicked off at Ken Weidler's late Friday afternoon. Ken was very friendly and invited anybody who needed anything to stop by. He lived about four blocks from the dental school in an elevator building with a doorman, where he had a nicely furnished but not terribly neat two-bedroom apartment. His living room doubled as a waiting room, and since there were usually a lot of people, he provided toys to keep them busy. He had a good collection of jazz records, a large color TV, a Sony Walkman, and board games like backgammon set up for play.

Kenny Weidler wasn't known as a particularly generous guy. Larry Lavin used to joke that Kenny made $150,000 selling coke and saved $151,000, Still, Weidler would thoughtfully leave a few lines lying on the glass coffee table in front of the sofa to keep his patients happy while they waited to see the dentist. In no time, people who barely spoke to each other on campus jabbered like old friends. There was an instant camaraderie among Weidler's visitors, who all knew they were there for the same reason.

From time to time Kenny ambled out of the room he used to conduct business, dressed in jeans, sneakers, and a button-down shirt. Normally reserved in public, he was genial but businesslike as he ushered the next buyer in. There was a couch along the wall and a bathroom off to the side. The shades were tightly drawn and the room dark except for a light on the large desk. A double-balance scale was perched on the desk, and the desk drawers held large plastic bags full of cocaine and coke rocks as big as softballs.

Like any good medical professional, Weidler warmed up the patient before getting down to business.

"Hey, Jack, how ya been? What's happening? How's your requirement going?"

"I had a hard time getting the impression. I had a little bubble at the margin and the instructor made me take the whole thing over again. What a pain in the butt."

"Instructors can drive you crazy. Was it Dr. R?"

"You got it."

"He gives everybody a hard time. Well, whaddya want tonight? This is really unbelievable blow we got this time."

"Well, I'd love to get an eight-ball [a popular 3½-gram buy] but I'm a little tight this week. Just give me a gram."

Whether the orders were small or large, Weidler always had enough coke to fill them. He once quipped that between him and Lavin they could get every dental-school student and faculty member high. Weidler dipped his teaspoon into the coke bag on the table and measured out a gram on the scale. He was very exacting; nobody got more than he paid for. He then took the top sheet from a pile of magazine covers stacked on the desk and cut a piece about two inches square, which he carefully folded into a triangle. With a razor he scraped the coke off the scale onto a piece of paper and carefully funneled the white powder into the neatly folded little paper packages. Weidler's trademark, these triangular packets, were quite famous on campus.

"Here you go," Weidler said, handing over the package. "Need any 'ludes?" Stashed away in his closet were jars of Quaalude 714's, five hundred to a container, that he bought in bulk for one thousand dollars and sold for four dollars a pill.

"No, thanks. I've got some left from last week."

"You know, one of these days we've got to go to a Flyers game together. I've got seats right in back of the bench. You freeze your rear it's so cold, but you feel you're right in the action. That'll be eighty-five dollars." Weidler took the money, smiled, shook hands, and walked the buyer out into his waiting room. "Maybe we'll hook up later when I'm finished." It felt nice to know he was providing a service that gave so many people a good time. "Who's next?"

David was not part of the Friday crowd at Kenny's apartment. They were still just backgammon buddies when Kenny called him one Saturday afternoon with an unusual request.

"Are you doing anything, David?"

"Not much. Why?"

"Could you do something for me? Stop by Martindale's and buy four eight-ounce bottles of inositol. Get a pizza too, and run it all over to my apartment."

"No way. I'm not going to be your gofer. Christ, are you bringing coke in through a health-food store?"

"Don't be stupid. Inositol is just a B-vitamin compound that's supposed to be good for calming the nerves. It comes in powdered form so those health nuts can sprinkle it in their protein wonder shakes. We use the shit for cut. You wouldn't be doing anything wrong."

"Then do it yourself."

David hung up the phone. Five minutes later, Kenny called back.

"You're being a big baby, David. There is nothing illegal in buying four bottles of a vitamin. You won't look suspicious."

"If it's no big deal, why are you asking me?"

"I'm too busy right now. Look, just get the inositol for me, and when you get here there'll be a nice juicy rock waiting for you."

That clinched it. A rock meant uncut cocaine, a chunk of the real thing. It was an offer Ackerman couldn't refuse—just as the scene that met him at Kenny's apartment was a picture he'll never forget. "I walked in and the first thing I wondered was: 'What the hell is Larry doing here? Everybody on campus knew that Kenny was the chief and Kenny was only one of his distributors. I'm barely inside when Kenny flips me a rock. For free. He flips it like it's nothing. I couldn't believe it. Then I notice these kitchen bowls full of coke on his desk and it looks to me like they're filled with boulders. I was floored. All this coke reminded me of things I'd read in *Rolling Stone* about the cocaine parties that rock groups had. I'd never in my life imagined so much coke. I didn't know whether to run or to hang around and do a few lines. They told me to sit down and be quiet, and I watched them, awestruck."

David also took advantage of their hospitable offer and snorted two lines of coke. Until now, the only cocaine he'd had was the cut. This coke was pure and incredibly powerful, and it produced a high that he'd never experienced. "I was instantly exhilarated. My heart started beating very fast. My mind felt incredibly clear and full of brilliant thoughts. I felt great, absolutely great, as if troubles I didn't even know I had suddenly vanished."

His concentration focused like a laser beam, Ackerman watched Lavin and Weidler expertly ply their trade.

The coke arrived from Florida in kilo bags. A "key," as it was nicknamed, was short for a kilogram, which equaled 1,000 grams. Translated from metric weight, there were 28 grams to an ounce.

A kilo weighed thirty-five ounces, a little more than two pounds. Every ounce of uncut cocaine provided Larry with a profit of $350 to $500, depending on how hard he hit the coke with inositol. The cut could expand 1,000 grams into 1,500 grams or even more. After cutting the coke, Larry and Kenny weighed it into varying quantities—ounces for some customers and grams for others—and spooned it into little glass bottles of different sizes which Larry purchased wholesale from a company that supplied them to laboratories. Larry precut and bottled his coke for easy resale on the street. He recognized the value of marketing and packaging, and one of the reasons for his success was his policy of tailoring orders to his customers' specifications.

Customers casually strolled in and out of Kenny's apartment. Anybody who wanted a complimentary toot got one. It was a great working party. The afternoon sped by and they invited David along to a friend's house, where the host supplied free-base—an extremely concentrated and highly addictive version of pure cocaine. "Base" is smoked rather than snorted because it's no longer water-soluble, and when the cocaine vapor hits the brain, it's like a bullet, packed with incredible intensity. Though frightened at first to try it, David was so coked up already that he felt invincible. He took the pipe in his hands, inhaled, and instantly experienced a euphoria more profound than he'd ever dreamed possible. Like the spray from a fire hose, it bombarded his entire body. Never before had he felt so totally relaxed, so completely content. Unlike Larry, who felt comfortable anywhere and could easily mix with people as diverse as hoodlum drug dealers and preppy dental students, David's air of self-assurance was a carefully crafted mask. Under the spell of cocaine, "I didn't have to pretend to be secure and confident because it didn't matter. All I knew was that twenty minutes later when it was over I wanted more. I needed to feel this way as often as I could."

By the end of that day, cocaine had wrapped its arms around David Ackerman in an embrace that would soon become a stranglehold. Eventually the highs would produce pain instead of pleasure. "The bad I'd feel when I didn't have cocaine would be twice as bad as the good I'd feel when I was basing." But in the beginning David Ackerman had no inkling that this wonderful new world he'd discovered would drag him down into a living hell. "When I got home that night I knew I had to have my own bowls of coke. I wanted the rocks to be mine. I didn't want to have to rely on the kindness of others to supply me. From that moment I wanted to have coke whenever I felt like it. And I wanted a piece of that power that came with walking into a disco and saying to a girl, 'Let's go back to my place and do some lines.' "

For a while David managed to satisfy that need by picking up inositol for Kenny and Larry. Kenny soon realized the consuming intensity of David's craving for coke and saw an opportunity to expand his own business. He gave David the standard drug dealer's pitch: go find some customers of your own, and you'll be able to cover the cost of your habit with your profits. Most of Kenny's dental-school trade at the time bought small amounts, a gram or two at a time. David parlayed Kenny's advice into a three-ounce deal with the brother of a girl he was dating. Elated, he and Kenny split the $2,000 profit and celebrated by going out for a steak dinner. David repeated his success with another three-ounce deal with a medical student in Chicago. Apparently David had access to a set of customers very different from the ones Kenny had culled at the dental school. They decided to form a fifty-fifty partnership and pool enough capital to finance bigger buys from Larry Lavin. Weidler contributed $50,000 from his cocaine profits. Ackerman kicked in his customer connections and $5,000 he obtained by applying for a student loan.

Business boomed from the start. There was a lot of bad coke on the local market and Lavin's stood out as superior. By 1980, Kenny and David were buying two or three kilos a month from Lavin at $58,000 a kilo, pocketing profits of $20,000 or more a month. They were soon faced with the same problem as Lavin: what to do with their money? On Larry's advice, they asked Mark Stewart to invest it for them. They'd learned all about Stewart from Larry, who had not yet become disillusioned with the wily entrepreneur and considered him his investment guru.

Mark Stewart was nearly fifteen years older than Larry Lavin and had nothing in common with the Irish Catholic New Englander. Yet the two clicked the moment they'd been introduced in 1979. For all his money, Larry was still a novice college boy who'd never made a straight business deal in his life when he met Stewart. He was mesmerized by the old man's self-confidence and experience as a deal-maker. Lavin had the impression that Stewart was connected with everybody who was anybody in Philadelphia. Stewart might have had plenty of connections, but he had very little cash, a fact he carefully hid from Larry at their initial meeting.

Puffing casually on his pipe, the dapper Stewart asked Lavin, "How much are you looking to invest, Larry?"

"About five hundred thousand dollars to start. Maybe as high as a million later," Larry replied.

Stewart dragged deeply, concentrating on the smoke in a major effort to remain calm and maintain an impression that he attracted million-dollar investors on a regular basis. In truth he thought he'd died and gone to heaven. His heart pounded so furiously he feared a stroke. To a man who'd been cash-poor all his life, Lavin and his drug money spelled opportunity.

At their second meeting, Stewart pulled out one of the expensive gold pens he always carried and handed it to Larry to sign a corporate agreement forming Larmark, their own investment company. He also gave him an interest in some real-estate holdings and a record distributorship.

This was exactly what Lavin needed: a way to explain his income to people at the dental school. He could now say he owned a record company. Stewart immediately printed business cards for Larry, a routine business ploy that not only impressed the hell out of Lavin but also transformed the student into an instant executive. What pleased Lavin even more was the idea that his money would now be working for him instead of sitting idle in a safe-deposit box. Friends of Lavin's sometimes asked him why he didn't just bury his drug profits. "I couldn't bear to do that," he'd answer. "I'm too worried about inflation. You read things about how a dollar ten years ago is worth only fifty cents today. It would bother me to death if my money was buried and not earning anything."

Larry persuaded David and Kenny that it was in their best interest to follow his example and let Stewart launder their drug profits too. From their inexperienced perspective, the glib Stewart had all the business acumen of the chairman of General Motors. They agreed to invest $5,000 a week with him, until by the end of 1980 they'd invested $125,000. In 1981 they gave Stewart another $125,000. In return, they also received legitimate weekly paychecks from one of his companies and glamorous perks that included limousine service and complimentary tickets to sporting events for themselves and their customers.

Kenny and David also made money for Larry by helping him increase his bargaining power. He continued to supply them at his cost as long as they paid in advance and were willing to participate in the risk of any potential loss should the runners sent to Miami to transport the cocaine encounter any problems with the police. There could never be a guarantee that the money Lavin sent to Florida would arrive safely or that the cocaine would make it back.

Between keeping up with dental-school studies and running his burgeoning business, Lavin was too busy to make the trips himself. And it just didn't make sense to take the risks or borrow time from his very profitable selling. He could always find a student or a friend to do his dirty work, someone who needed money to buy drugs or work off a drug debt. And he paid his drug couriers, or "mules," handsomely—anywhere from $1,000 to $2,500 a trip. It was a very tempting proposition for a day's work and an easy way to pay off a cocaine debt.

As one dental student who made a couple of trips recalls, "You'd say yes, partly for the money and partly so Larry or Kenny wouldn't get mad and stop supplying you with coke. They'd take care of all the arrangements, make it real easy for you. Hand you a ticket in a fake name, tell you to hide the money in a gym bag and look for a Columbian guy at the airport in Miami who would come up and ask if you were a friend of Larry's. I remember after I arrived being taken to a nicely furnished apartment full of aunts, uncles, and kids. Lovely people. I couldn't believe how open they were about selling coke. Me, I was sweating bullets. They laid seven bags of coke on the bed and said, 'Pick the one you want.' Then they packed it inside another bag of baking soda to kill the smell and I strapped it across my middle with masking tape. It looked like I had a nice little paunch. They took me back to the plane, and during the flight I removed the package and stuck it in my gym bag. I was scared shitless the whole time."

After a while Larry got impatient looking for different people to make coke runs and persuaded Glenn Fuller, his old school chum from Haverhill, to become a regular courier for him. All during 1979 and 1980, Fuller averaged a trip to Florida every ten days.

Larry's business had just begun to soar. He'd already given $500,000 to Mark Stewart and would double that before graduating from dental school in another year and a half. What had started out as an exciting way to cover his expenses had become a serious enterprise, and Lavin almost lamented the change. "I was running Glenn to the airport one day, and as usual, we're late for the plane and counting money like crazy. I ran some red lights and an unmarked car pulled us over. Real quick I threw my coat over the two hundred thousand dollars in Glenn's lap and talked my way out of the ticket. When the cop pulled away I turned to Glenn and said, 'You know something? This isn't fun anymore.' I realized then that I was in it strictly for the money."

With more time devoted to his fast-growing drug business, Larry decided to take greater precautions. He insisted his mules dress like executives when traveling to avoid attracting attention, and he instructed Fuller to buy some decent clothes. Fuller went on a shopping spree and purchased a wardrobe of $700 suits just to wear on the plane. Like all the rest of Larry's group, he could afford to be extravagant. Fuller even rented a couple of apartments in South Florida, one to stay in and another as a "safe house" to hide drugs. Dealing in million-dollar volume, Fuller wanted a secure place to keep his stash. Not that the "funny talkers" (Fuller's way of describing the Colombian suppliers) ever gave him reason to worry. They couldn't have been more gracious, always stopping by his Florida apartment, offering to take him to dinner or to get him girls.

Fuller also delivered coke to Lavin's New England customers. By 1980 Larry was supplying his old high-school friends as well as college pals who'd settled in the Boston area. Glenn would drive up the Atlantic coast with two or three locked suitcases of cocaine in his trunk, each plastic bag marked with the initials of the person who'd bought it. He'd call from turnpike pay phones and arrange to meet a customer at a bar, a shopping mall, a parking lot, even the highway exit ramp. The buyer would hand Fuller money, and Glenn would hand over the coke and be on his way.

Unfortunately, Fuller was less cautious when delivering coke orders to New England than he was shopping for coke in Miami. On November 14, 1980, he was arrested on the New Jersey Turnpike driving a big black car with Florida tags that had six kilos of Larry's coke in a cardboard box in the trunk and a suitcase full of money in the back seat that Larry had hurriedly thrown in at the last minute. Being the gentleman that he was, Larry hired the best legal talent he could find and paid Fuller's fees. Then, while Fuller was free on appeal because there was some question about whether the police had the right to break into the trunk of his car, Lavin gave him more money to move out to Colorado, buy a house, and keep his mouth shut. Fuller wasn't the first of Lavin's mules to get caught. Between his pot and his coke business, a number of people had been arrested, but not one had ever turned Lavin in. The dentist inspired loyalty and took care of his own.

Even Kenny Weidler made a run to Florida when there was no one else available. At first, the idea of jetting to Florida for an overnight business trip with $60,000 in a carry-on bag seemed thrilling and glamorous. The fear of possible apprehension, however, quickly ended the glamour of the situation. After that first trip he went only out of necessity. When he and David Ackerman became partners, he tried to foist the chore on him. David wasn't particularly receptive, but Kenny persuaded him it would be fun and that he ought to learn the ropes. In the late fall of 1979, the two of them took a weekend off from studies and flew to Florida with $80,000 on the bottom of a soft brown carry-on bag. They packed very carefully, laying packages of money end to end, forming a flat sheet of cash which they covered with clothes. To any of the passengers on the plane, they looked like two young business-men on a vacation. They arrived in Miami, checked into a Holiday Inn, and made a few calls to locate product. A few hours later a Cuban named Paco picked them up and drove them to his home, a ranch in the Hispanic neighborhood of Kendall. Paco led them to the laundry room and opened the washing machine. What might have looked like fine detergent to the untrained eye was actually several kilos of coke. He explained that if the police ever raided his house, he planned to toss in some dirty clothes, turn on the machine, and kiss the evidence good-bye.

Weidler and Ackerman were not yet very sophisticated about pretesting the cocaine. They satisfied themselves of the quality of the drug by doing a few lines in the Cuban's kitchen, and pur-chased one and a half kilos—one for Larry and a half for them-selves. Back at the hotel, Kenny put the half-kilo into David's carry-on bag. It didn't take up much room; he was able to stuff the plastic bag, tightly wrapped with package tape, into one of his sneakers. Still, David was terrified he would be discovered trans-porting cocaine. The two minutes passing through the metal detec-tor at the airport were the longest 120 seconds of his entire life. If you told him then that he'd get so accustomed to carrying coke and money through airports he'd barely break a sweat, he'd never have believed it. In fact, on one of his subsequent trips, Larry, rushing as usual, wouldn't have all the money together in time to pack it neatly and tossed a $5,000 packet of twenties into the side of his bag. The guard at the airport X-ray machine thought David was concealing a brick (a potential weapon) and pulled him aside for questioning. He whispered to her in a hushed conspiratorial tone that it was not a brick but a bundle of bills. He said that he was going to Florida to close a big record deal. She wished him luck and waved him through.

Sometimes there would be so much money to carry that one mule couldn't haul it alone. Once David and Kenny had to take a third person along just to help carry the cash. One of Lavin's new drug connections in Florida, a man named Lester, called Larry and boasted he was sitting with the best coke ever, urging Lavin to fly right down and get it. Larry decided to buy five kilos and sent Kenny, David, and a third mule to Florida with close to $300,000 in cash, most of the money in twenty and fifty-dollar bills. When they arrived, the coke was much less spectacular than promised. By now, Kenny, Larry, and David had been buying pure cocaine for so long they could nit-pick over quality. Was it shiny enough? Did the rocks look like layers of mica when they were broken open? Negative to both. Since they only bought the best, there was no sale. Weidler was furious they'd been brought on a fool's errand. He had a sharp temper when aroused and he laid into the dealer. "You dragged us down here on a Friday with a shitload of money. We missed school. And for what? This stuff isn't the best ever. It sucks."

Weidler called Lavin to report that the deal had fallen through and to complain that he didn't want to cart all the cash back home. Lavin told him to leave it with Lester for the next buy. Before they could leave, however, the money had to be recounted. What a tedious job that was: take the rubber bands off the packages, count five twenties to a hundred, ten packs of hundreds to a thousand; put them aside and start again.

Weidler was getting more upset by the minute. "I'd like to take a baseball bat and bash the side of that jerk's new Mercedes. We'll be here forever." To speed up the process, they decided to weigh the money on the coke scale, but because the rubber bangs weren't all the same thickness, they couldn't get a consistent reading. Weidler lost all patience. "If it's off, it's off. I don't give a damn. Put it in the bags and let's get the hell out of here." Lester was given the uncounted cash, and they flew back to Philadelphia empty-handed.

6

After FBI agent Chuck Reed's pivotal visit to Larry Lavin's dental office in February 1983, the big broad-shouldered FBI agent had no difficulty convincing his superiors to let him focus his energies on building a drug case instead of continuing to investigate the Mark Stewart bankruptcy. One of his first steps was the Phildelphia office of the U.S Drug Enforcement Agency. The agency was housed a few floors above the FBI offices in a building located on the periphery of the Olde City neighborhood where the Lavin ring maintained some apartments.

Reed wanted to see if the DEA had anything on Larry Lavin. They punched his name into their nationwide computer list of suspected drug traffickers, but the search yielded nothing. Reed had them enter Lavin's name in the DEA's computer system and asked them to let him know if it ever came up.

With no leads from the DEA, Reed lumbered off to develop some of his own. He visited the apartment of David Ackerman, another name on the Mark Stewart payroll. His bullying style drew a frosty reception and Ackerman quickly showed him to the door. Reed reacted to Ackerman much as he had to Lavin. Here was one more smart-aleck college boy lying through his teeth.

Reed spent the spring of 1983 interviewing people, looking for leads. This was a case that had an end but no middle or beginning: he knew there was a drug ring, but he'd yet to find drugs or a drug deal. By the summer he had gathered enough information to indicate to the Bureau that the case was too large for a single agent. To Reed's chagrin, he was assigned Sidney Perry as a partner. Perry was a Southerner, two years older than Reed, and also trained as an accountant, newly transferred from the Phoenix office. Reed was more than annoyed. A loner with a Vermonter's reserve, he liked to do things his own way at his own speed. He disliked Sid Perry before they even met. He'd checked out the thirty-four-year-old agent with the bureau grapevine and didn't like what he heard: in eight years with the FBI, Perry had build a reputation for being a crackerjack agent. Reed pegged him as an opportunist. Not the kind of guy Reed could trust. He probably wasn't the least bit creative, and Reed was sure he'd be no fun to work with.

Sid Perry's advance opinion of Chuck Reed was equally un-flattering. He'd done his own checking and heard that Reed was rigid and inflexible, not easy to deal with. Perry, too, had never shared an assignment, and let his supervisor know he was not looking forward to this one.

Perry arrived in Philadelphia at the end of July 1983, took one look at the bearlike, bearded Reed decked out in dungarees and a short-sleeved shirt with his longish straight hair hanging over his collar, and thought to himself: He sure doesn't look like an accountant.

Perry preferred to dress his graceful, muscular body like a profes-sional in a nicely tailored suit or in a herringbone sport jacket. He had wavy dark hair that was just beginning to gray, which he let grow long enough to look rakish without being unkempt. A bristly mustache outlined his easy smile, and his clear blue eyes crinkled at the corners when he laughed, which was often.

Reed and Perry barely had the time to test their assumptions about each other before they were hurled into the casework by an unexpected event. The DEA agent Chuck Reed had visited five months earlier to inquire about Larry Lavin received a similar phone call from another FBI agent in Phoenix. The Western agent was investigating a drug dealer out there named Wayne Heinauer who was said to have bought coke from a dentist named Larry in Philadelphia. Did the DEA know any dental Larrys? The DEA agent didn't, but he remembered being asked the same question by Chuck Reed. The DEA put the two FBI agents in touch with each other. Reed was told there was a wiretap on Heinauer's phone in Phoenix, and if they picked up anything about Larry the dentist, they'd let him know.

Larry Lavin and Wayne Heinauer had known each other at Penn, where Larry had sold pot to Wayne before he'd dropped out of school, moved out west, begun working on the fringes of the rock-music world, and become a major cocaine customer, buying an average of two kilos a month at $70,000 a key. Larry, who always liked to keep current on what was happening to his best customers, would periodically call for a friendly chat. When he telephoned Wayne at 7:45 A.M. on August 23, 1983, he had something more important than chitchat on his mind. He needed to tell Wayne he was selling his coke business and the new supplier, Franny Burns, would be taking over. On his way to his dental office, Lavin stopped at a pay phone—he never made any drug-related calls from his home—and dialed his old buddy in Arizona.

"Hi, Wayne. It's Larry. How ya doing? I thought I'd call and shoot the breeze with you."

"Oh, very good. I've been wanting to give you a call but I thought I'd wait to see how things are going back there for everybody." From previous conversations, Wayne knew about the FBI investigation of Mark Stewart's bankruptcy and Larry's growing fear that he might go to jail for income-tax evasion. They chatted about a bachelor party Larry was planning for a mutual friend and then he brought up the real purpose of the call.

"What I'm basically trying to do is have Franny take over the job I do, which isn't that much. But if there's a problem, ya know, I'm always here, so someone can be reached. Franny's real quick. He answers his beeper in, like, five minutes. He's gonna put up money for buying things down in Florida, which is nice. And he's gonna be changing things with Bruce." By this time Bruce Taylor was running Larry's business and making deliveries. He was notoriously unreliable because he'd go on coke binges that would last for days at a time. In addition to his legal hassles, Larry's other motivation for selling out was his mounting management problems.

"Yeah. Well, we all know how Bruce is. I have a hard time getting a hold of him sometimes."

"Franny's a very smart guy. He doesn't like the fact that Bruce carries things on the plane, ya know. So he's gonna have his father-in-law do it. The neat thing is, the old guy's dying of cancer. He's only gonna be around another year or two. If anything ever happens to him, he's not gonna say anything. So how were the things Bruce brought last time?"

"They look real nice. They're not the problem I'm having. People I used to deal with out here are just dumping the stuff. Selling it for like sixty-five-thousand dollars [a kilo], and I can't compete with the price. I've lost three or four customers and I'm kinda in the hole right now. I'm gonna be a little slow."

"Talk it over with Franny. He does sixty or eighty [kilos] a month. Between our business and his, he definitely gets it cheaper than I was getting it before. If you think it's gonna increase your business, rap with him about it. He'll give you a price break. He'll do anything, know what I mean? He'll send out every week or whatever you want. Things will be more organized now."

"Yeah. Good. Well, just let him know, will ya, that I'm not usually behind like I am right now."

"I told him you hate to owe money." Larry paused. "So how's your legitimate thing going?"

"Well, I had to quit my job in May because my legs are so bad. Probably in September I'll be working for the stagehands' union. Set up stuff for rock-and-roll shows and conventions. That's my bread and butter, the convention business. Then I'm hoping to buy an old house, fix it up, and sell it."

"Rehab and like that?"

"Yeah. I'm even halfway thinking about going back to school."

"I miss it, I'll tell ya. I still wake up in the middle of the night thinking I can't remember where class is tomorrow. Weird, weird things. Ya know, in dental school they don't really push you at Penn. So I might not have shown up for my elective all the time, but I was always worried whether or not I'd get credit and if I needed it to graduate. I still wake up thinking: Am I gonna be able to graduate?"

"I sure know how that works. Say, how's your little one and your wife doing?"

"Just great. Chris is fifteen months old now and he's pretty neat. He imitates everything I do. He tries to drive my car."

"So are your troubles working out or what?"

"Well, to tell you the truth, I think I'm gonna end up going to jail. I've heard the FBI is putting together this tax case, and there's no way of explaining it. They kind of know what's going on behind the scenes but I don't think they can prove it. But I could get a sentence on the tax thing. That's one reason I'm making this move to sell. I can't have people calling me when they can't get hold of Bruce."

"Well, I'm glad for that."

"My biggest mistake was putting money through the record company, which was doing like five million dollars a year, so we didn't think some checks for fifty-thousand dollars here and there would matter that much. If you're ever buying anything, use cashier's checks. What happened was, this singer questioned his revenues, said he didn't get paid enough, and that brought the FBI down doing a whole audit. There was $350,000 worth of checks to me. Like for when I bought my house."

"Oh, boy."

"Then they start looking at everything else I owned, and one thing uncovered another. That's the way it goes. I'm still hoping.

The one good thing is, I've never been in any trouble whatsoever and I think that's gonna help in some way."

"Well, yeah. Hopefully."

"So I'll give you a call every month or so to see what's going on. If you have any problems with Franny, I'm still here."

"Good enough. Thanks a lot for calling."

"Talk to ya soon. 'Bye."

Chuck Reed and Sid Perry listened to the tape of that phone call with mounting excitement. It was an absolute bonanza. In Perry's words, "Almost as good as sex." In Reed's, "It established the case. It's always easy to find out who's who, and what they did. The tough part is getting usable evidence. Up to this point we only had hearsay. Now we have Lavin on tape talking about drugs and identifying his connection with Franny. This gives us the basic players and points us in a direction."

The first thing they had to find out was who this Franny was, since, as the new chief, he'd be the center of action and the one most likely to lead to all the members of the Lavin ring. Without a last name, that took a bit of work. Using phone records from Lavin and Heinauer, they picked up a beeper number registered in the name of Harvey Perry.

The beepers were another of Larry's innovations. He felt that his key people should be immediately available to customers who needed to buy drugs, like doctors who could be beeped by their answering service when patients needed to contact them. Moreover, beepers could be registered under aliases, making it almost impossible for authorities to trace the real owners.

A check on Harvey Perry showed he was the father-in-law of one Francis Burns. Perry, in fact, was the old man with cancer that Lavin had mentioned in his phone call.

Now that Franny had a last name, the agents were able to run him through their various intelligence sources. He was a big, slovenly, round-shouldered man whose weight seesawed between 190 and 250 pounds, depending on whether or not he was dieting for the street hockey season. The twenty-nine-year-old Burns had dropped out of high school in Norristown, Pennsylvania, in the eleventh grade, and began dealing drugs not long after. By the time he met Lavin, his annual cocaine sales reached into the hundreds of kilos, but he never kept written records. His head was his notebook. Burns had unruly black hair, bushy eyebrows, and small eyes that narrowed when he engaged in what appeared to be the difficult task of thinking. He wasn't nearly as dumb as he looked, and was actually quick-witted, but not very smart when it came to keeping out of trouble. His police record included arrests for drug dealing and attempted arson. He'd hired someone to burn down the store of a man who'd been fooling around with his wife. Her punishment was a beating that landed her in the hospital. The issue with Burns wasn't morality as much as proprietorship. He had a stable of girlfriends and liked women who were young but not innocent. His favorite was a seventeen-year-old named Sandy Freas.

Franny Burns had all kinds of idiosyncrasies. He never used drugs, although he made millions selling them. And he didn't put his money in banks or safe-deposit boxes. He either buried it or stored it—as much as a million dollars at a time—in the trunk of his Lincoln Continental or his Toyota. Along with dealing, he always worked hard at some kind of legitimate job. He'd done carpentry, sorted mail at the post office, and supervised the Dairy Queen he owned in a bustling strip shopping center in King of Prussia.

Chuck Reed and Sid Perry passed the early fall of 1983 staking out Francis Burns at his ice-cream palace from the parking lot of a Mexican restaurant across the highway. Their sights were set on the entire ring and they'd decided the quickest route to the greatest number of people was through a massive wiretap that would furnish the leads they needed. Had either Reed or Perry been typical drug-enforcement agents dealing with typical drug traffickers, they might have handled their case quite differently. They'd probably have designed an undercover operation to buy some drugs, and then they would have busted the seller. This case, however, was anything but typical. The pair weren't dealing with the usual street traders. This ring involved dentists. So they decided to take a more creative approach and achieved far more dramatic results when they set out to track the money trail.

To convince a federal judge to grant a wiretap, it was necessary to show a usage pattern on the particular phones they wanted to tap. So day after day Reed and Perry sat sweating in their parked car watching Franny Burns walk out of his Dairy Queen to one of three pay phones in the shopping center he routinely used to return the coded messages left on his beeper. He'd strut purposefully out the entrance and either turn right to the phone in the Pizza Hut or left around the bend to the phone in the drugstore with a video arcade in front of the prescription counter. Sometimes he'd make one call from the drugstore and then walk around to the pay phone in front of the discount department store, jiggling the rolls of quarters in his pants pocket. Each call was noted in their log:

Wed., Sept. 7: drugstore: 11:08 to 11:17. Pizza Hut: 12:12 to 12:20.

Mon., Sept. 12: Pizza Hut: 1:15 to 1:17; 1:30 to 1:43. Department store: 2:10 to 2:30.

Wed., Oct. 5: Dairy Queen phone: 10:06 to 10:16. Drugstore: 11:05 to 11:18.

The agents had no difficulty marking Burns's every move as they sat some three hundred yards away in the parking lot. The inside of the car looked like a high-tech spy station. Mounted on a tripod wedged in the back seat was a camera with a long-distance lens. Perry could just about squeeze between the camera and the rear window to focus the picture. In the front, they had a two-foot-long telescope balanced against the steering wheel that was powerful enough to show whether someone a block away needed a shave. Burns usually did. The surveillance, often the most tedious aspect of policework, continued for several weeks. The agents broke the monotony by getting to know each other. Chuck Reed, the more taciturn, spoke a little about growing up in New England. His suspicious nature kept him from revealing much about his personal life even to his friends. Sid Perry, more open and loquacious, told fond stories about his backwoods boyhood that to Reed sounded like the material for a country-western song.

Perry's mother, one of seventeen children, married his father when she was fourteen and he was twenty-one. Sid, their only child, grew up in his grandparents' farmhouse without the benefits of indoor plumbing. "We lived like you see in the movies. In the winter I'd get a bath on Saturday night. In the summer I'd work twelve hours in the tobacco fields, come home filthy, grab a washcloth and run to the river to take a dip and clean up."

His parents divorced when he was in grammar school but remained close friends. The young Perry was strongly influenced by both of them. His mother taught him to be strong-willed, and also taught him the value of hard work. She was a bartender at a swanky restaurant, and weekends he'd wait up for her until the wee hours so he could count her tips. From his father, who became an antique dealer, Sid learned the value of dreaming. "Friends kid me that I'm always in fantasyland," he told Reed. "I have all kinds of dreams. The way I see it, the worst that can happen is I won't achieve all of them."

Reed just listened, thinking to himself: Maybe this guy isn't so bad after all.

By high school Perry had declared his intention to join the FBI. He'd lived from time to time with an uncle who was an agent and decided, "I wanted to spend my life around people like him. People with integrity and high standards." It took several years to achieve his goal. More interested in sports and socializing than academics, he dropped out of East Tennessee State College at the end of his freshman year to marry his college sweetheart and enlist in the Army. When he returned to school, his priorities had shifted and he made dean's list every quarter, majoring in accounting, since that was the quickest route to enter the Bureau. The day he completed his required two years of field experience, he filed his application and became an agent.

Stuck as they were in tight quarters day after day, Reed and Perry learned they had more in common than they'd ever imagined. Although their personal styles were different, their approach to work was surprisingly similar. Neither tolerated superiors who insisted they do things according to precedent. Just because no agent in Philadelphia had ever gone after a wiretap on public phones was no reason for them not to try.

Perry quickly came to respect Reed's remarkably good instincts and Reed developed enough trust in Perry to confide in him. Hour after hour they leaned back against the upholstery of the car and spun "what-if" strategies. "What if Larry comes to the Dairy Queen? Should we drive by and take a picture? Is it worth the risk of having him put up his guard if he spots us? Should we park a surveillance van in the shopping-center parking lot instead of taking pictures from the car? What if Burns and Lavin show up together? Should we follow them? How far should we go? How long? Should we take the risk they might realize they're being tailed?" Everything they plotted weighed the risk of being discovered too soon versus the importance of getting the evidence they needed.

They found themselves easily bouncing ideas back and forth. One seemed to spark the other, and without their even being aware of it, Reed and Perry forged a bond that over the next three years would make the Lavin case the most important thing in their lives. At every stage they'd bet the next day's lunch check on what would happen. Would they get the wiretap? Would they catch Burns and Lavin exchanging money?

Perry was ahead until Reed said, "I bet you two lunches that when we arrest Lavin, he'll run."

"Nah. Never happen," Sid said. "He wouldn't be that stupid."

"Wrong. He'd think he'd be smart enough to get away with it."

They shook hands. Both were worried the other might be right.

7

UNIVERSITY OF PENNSYLVANIA DENTAL SCHOOL
WINTER, 1980

The music was so loud that Kenny Weidler could barely hear the blonde next to him at the bar. Not that he cared much about what she was saying. He was too intent on soaking up the scene: young girls in clinging dresses gyrating suggestively on the dance floor. Tables with people laughing, drinking. The insistent beat of the music throbbing inside his head. Everything felt so alive, so sharp, so intense. His eyes jumped around the room as he reached into his pocket, cupped his "tooter" in his hand, and drew it under his nose once again. He'd never been in a private dance club like this one, with its jaunty palm trees and glass dance floor illuminated from below with colored lights. He wanted the night to go on forever. He wanted to continue to feel part of this young, successful crowd of guys on the make and girls ripe for plucking. Here he was, the high-school teetotaler not yet out of dental school, right in the thick of the action.

David Ackerman introduced Kenny to the world of private discos, fine wines, and exclusive restaurants. Growing up in New York, he'd been exposed to a life-style that Kenny had only glimpsed in movies and magazines. David dined with his parents at tony eateries like La Côte Basque and danced at Studio 54 while he was still a teenager. Now, with all the money he was making in the coke business, he could indulge the expensive tastes he'd been groomed to appreciate. Kenny, the quiet outsider, was drawn into David's coke-induced revelry just as he'd earlier been drawn into Larry's money-stoked orbit. From business partners, Kenny and David grew to be party partners. Dental school slipped to a low priority; they missed classes and bought the lectures they missed from a note service. Their world turned upside down as they slept away the days and partied through the nights.

By the winter of 1980, cocaine had claimed their absolute obeisance. Their day dawned at dusk, when they got out of bed and dressed for dinner. David, weaned on Brooks Brothers, donned a natural-shoulder navy blazer, gray slacks, and a light blue button-down oxford cotton shirt. He was classically dressed down to his tasseled loafers. Kenny, whose taste was molded at a small-town haberdasher, usually wore a nondescript dark suit. Philadelphia was in the throes of a restaurant renaissance and there were many fine places to eat. They patronized all the best ones—usually without dates—and the heavier David got into cocaine, the more obnoxious a patron he became. One night when the shrimp he had ordered arrived at the table unpeeled, he sent them back to the chef to be shelled. When the chef refused, David marched into the kitchen and threw him a hundred-dollar bill to do his bidding.

The pair's favorite dinner haunt was a classy little French boîte called Maureen's. Kenny, who grew up thinking five dollars was expensive for an entrée, now spent fifty dollars for a dinner without blinking. He would never have admitted it to David, but he was getting a tremendous kick out of eating expensive meals. Since cocaine cuts the appetite, they deferred tooting until dessert and were usually starving by the time they sat down to eat. Their standard fare included two filet mignons each, one with a wine sauce, the other topped with crabmeat and béarnaise. David, the Cordon Bleu expert, took charge of ordering the food, wine, and after-dinner cordials.

Kenny controlled the drugs and the money. He carried a plastic sandwich bag of coke in his inside jacket pocket. If they happened to be relatively well-hidden in a back booth of a restaurant, he might pour some powder into an ashtray, which they sniffed with a straw. When they hit the clubs afterward—and they made the rounds nightly—he'd run his coke sniffer under the nose of a shapely secretary or computer analyst he had his eye on. Done quickly, it looked as if he were flicking a speck of dirt off her face. All the drug-paraphernalia shops sold these little glass bullets that Weidler and his pals referred to as tooters, easily concealed devices designed for sniffing in public. Kenny got so adept he could load one without taking the plastic bag out of his pocket. The bottom portion held a gram of coke, and a little valve released just enough into the top part for a snort. They used the tooter on the dance floor, in elevators, at restaurants, anywhere at all. Often in the men's room, he'd lay out a line which he snorted through a tightly rolled hundred-dollar bill.

It was nothing for both Kenny and David to go through three grams—with a street value of $250 to $300—in the course of one night's club hopping. Kenny rarely danced. He hung out at the bar and picked up girls. In these dark clubs time ceased to exist and coke banished fatigue. Then, all too suddenly, the night would be gone. Too wired to sleep, they'd swallow a few Quaaludes to bring them down and head home toward dawn, promising themselves to get back to their studies. But of course they'd sleep through class, wake up hungry, and reach for the phone. "Maureen's at eight? I'll pick you up."

Larry Lavin never joined Ken and David in their nightly debauches. His business was much bigger and more demanding than theirs. He'd cut down considerably on his own drug use and was living with Marcia, who was jealous of his drug dealing and the time it stole from their relationship. Larry's life centered on school and work. He was as compulsive a student as he was a drug merchant, and rarely cut a class. On a typical day he might dash home for lunch and listen to his message machine while chomping on a sandwich. He'd return the calls, make up a few orders, see some customers, and go back to school a few thousand dollars richer. While he was a highly organized workaholic, he simply didn't have the time to be tidy. And although his life was in order, his money was scattered about the apartment or dumped into the trunk of his car. When a classmate asked Larry one day if he could lend him a few bucks for lunch, Larry had no cash in his pockets and told the guy to walk him to his locker. He opened it and there were stacks of hundred-dollar bills sitting on the shelf. He may not have run up huge restaurant bills, but he had his own way of being flashy.

The dental faculty at Penn viewed Lavin as a capable, if not particularly serious, student. He certainly did not belong to the majority of earnest young dentists-to-be who'd arrive at the clinic well ahead of their patients, professionally attired in neatly pressed lab coats. They'd take their instruments out of carefully organized boxes, line them up meticulously, and study their notes on the incoming cases. Larry, who dressed just short of sloppy, would be more likely to rush in from a drug deal just ahead of his patient with his wrinkled lab coat slung over his arm and his shirttail hanging out of his pants. His tools would be jumbled in a bag, not arranged in a box, and he'd lay them out like he was hastily setting a table. He'd be slipping into his coat while he led the patient to the chair, yet none of them seemed to mind that he was late or a little unprepared. He'd immediately start chattering away, and his friendly, easygoing manner captivated patients just the way it impressed his friends. Ken and David envied and respected Larry for his ability to keep pace with the equally heavy responsibilities of dental school and the demanding coke business.

If Larry Lavin wasn't overwhelmingly devoted to dentistry, he was certainly fascinated by its technical aspects, and his general interest in high-tech equipment extended from electronics to dental tools. He once discovered what he considered a useful little grinding tool in a dental-supply catalog and bought a dozen of them—one for everybody in his lab group. Larry had a reputation at dental school as the young man who had everything—from a top-quality Bang and Olufsen stereo system to professional-level camera equipment. Unlike David and Kenny, who'd adopted the lush life, Larry, influenced by Marcia, maintained a quieter lifestyle, indulging himself only with expensive gadgets—which he willingly shared. When the yearbook photography staff needed a special wide-angle camera lens, he lent them one of his. When a classmate mentioned he was driving to New England one weekend, Larry proffered his radar detector to help him elude speed traps. He was generous with his time and money too. He'd give his dental-clinic patients a lift home in bad weather so they wouldn't have to wait for a bus. Sometimes he'd pay their bills out of his own pocket if there were two modes of treatment and they couldn't afford the more expensive one. Occasionally his largess had an ulterior motive. If he needed to complete a particular procedure as part of a course requirement, he'd pay for it himself rather than miss an opportunity to get the necessary work done. Just as often, he dipped into his own pocket because he liked to be regarded as a super-nice guy.

Super-rich guy was more like it. The dental-school faculty didn't know what to make of this bright, personable student with the extraordinary income. Had he been of a modest nature, his wealth might never have caused so much gossip. But Larry flaunted his affluence, attributing it publicly to his investments with Mark Stewart. He'd brag about the gold record from his recording company, his partnership in the sports arena, his killings in the stock market. He was always offering free tickets to sporting events, reading the Wall Street Journal, and leaving the impression he was attending dental school as a lark. One professor recalls that Larry, as a third-year student, was taking a medical history on a patient and missed the fact the man had a heart murmur. The clinic director thought it was an important enough error to call him on the carpet and assign him a paper on the use of antibiotics to premedicate patients with organic heart disease. Ten days later, a well-researched, authoritative report landed on the director's desk. So impressed was the professor that he sought out Lavin to commend him.

"Frankly, Larry," he said, "I don't understand how you could write such a fine report and have missed something so obvious in clinic."

Lavin explained he'd been particularly flustered that day because he'd just gotten a phone call and found out he'd lost $80,000. The professor stared at him as if he'd just confessed to a mass murder. "Oh, I guess you don't know I'm president of an investment company," Lavin said. "We handle investments for a lot of professional athletes and do tax shelters for executives. Things like that."

"If you've got all this going for you, what the hell are you doing in dental school?" the professor asked.

Lavin smiled that winning smile of his and replied, "Well, I like it, and everybody needs a hobby."

Lavin was easily the most popular student in the dental clinic. The faculty flocked to him for investment counseling. He recommended silver futures and gold mining when gold and silver were skyrocketing, and they all tried to follow his suggestions. He was always a great talker and never at a loss for advice. Men who should have been more skeptical were completely taken in by him. They figured he came from a rich family. He had, after all, attended Phillips Exeter. No doubt he had a trust fund. While it's typical in dental school for the students to look to the young instructors as role models, Larry reversed the norm. The young instructors, struggling to establish dental practices, strove to emulate him. "He and I parked in the same private lot behind the clinic," one of them remembers. "I'd graduated in 1976, and three years later I'm driving a beat-up Renault I can barely manage the payments on. One day he pulls into the spot next to me in a spanking new, exquisite Volvo. I was drooling and asked him how he could afford a car like that. 'Stereos,' he said. 'I sell stereo equipment out of my apartment. It's a very good business.' It sure sounded good to me. Frankly, I was envious and wished I'd thought of it."

Lavin may have worked hard, but he played hard too. His engagement to Marcia made it difficult to go nightclub partying with the boys, so he needed to find another outlet for his wild side. Usually his love for skiing and snorkeling provided the excuse he needed to get away without her. In the spring of their junior year, he decided the boys deserved an all-male "company vacation" during the Easter break and rented two condominiums in Aspen for eight of them—including Weidler, Ackerman, and Mikuta. They planned to visit Glenn Fuller, who was now living in Denver, along the way. Lavin had difficulty pulling himself away from the business, and the morning of their departure he hastily decided to sell off—or, as he called it, "crank out"—the few pounds of coke left in his closet. As the others packed their bags, he called customers on the phone, then mixed and weighed orders. The group nearly missed the plane because Larry made them wait in the airport van in front of his apartment while he closed the last deal.

They arrived in Denver in the early evening and stayed overnight at Glenn Fuller's house before making the plane connection to Aspen the following day. Also sharing the house were three girls, the sisters of Glenn's girlfriend, Patty. Because there weren't enough beds to go around, David chose one of the sisters, Gina, for a bunkmate. A naive nineteen-year-old with straight black hair, a pretty face and sweet disposition, Gina had one salient feature that caught everybody's attention: immense breasts. On a tall, statuesque woman they'd have been appropriate. On little Gina, they were a burden, a conversation piece. Nobody ever remembered her for anything else. Ordinarily David preferred small-breasted women like Suzanne Noramatzu. But Gina was the kind of prize that other guys envied and she was so accommodating besides. As they crawled into bed, he congratulated himself on having lucked out. Larry and Kenny took the other sisters, and by morning it was decided that the girls should accompany them to Aspen.

The intended purpose of the trip was skiing, but David and Larry saw the slopes only twice in ten days. Larry had brought along over a half-pound of phenomenal flake plus a couple hundred Quaaludes. Balancing the two in combination made it possible to do more of each drug and play longer and more passionately in bed. Larry left blow lying around the condo like a hostess puts out bowls of pretzels and peanuts for her guests. Little piles of coke sat on the coffee table, the night table, the kitchen counter, the bedroom bureau. Like the miracle of the loaves and fishes, the supply never ran out.

It never occurred to any of them that what they were doing might get out of control. They were far too caught up in enjoying the wildest time of their lives. The pleasures of the day carried over into the evening. They dined at Aspen's best restaurants and the dinner parties inevitably wound up as coke parties. They made no secret of the fact they had plenty of toot. They got off on letting everybody know what young hotshots they were. As the restaurants emptied of serious skiers, the party people wandered into private dining rooms, the chefs came out of the kitchens, and they all got high. What an incredible trip! Weren't they living the

American dream, throwing around money made brokering a wicked and wonderful commodity that everyone wanted. Nothing was beyond their reach. One afternoon, David and Larry took the girls shopping in a boutique filled with expensive silk lingerie. Gina was much too good-natured to take advantage of the situation and bought only a nightgown. One of her sisters had no such compunctions, and her purchases cost Larry two thousand dollars. David kept the receipt with the playful threat that if Larry ever gave him a hard time, he'd show the bill to Marcia.

The threat may have carried some weight, but the two thousand dollars meant nothing. It was more than replenished the next day when Larry made a call to his buyer in Philadelphia just to check on things. Told there was a demand for coke but nothing around, he immediately got on the phone and pulled together money for a buying trip. With five or six calls he was able to lay his hands on the $160,000 he needed to buy three kilos. He sent one runner to his brother Rusty in New England to rustle up $80,000 and another out to Penn State. In a later call, he gave detailed explanations of how to cut the coke for each customer when it arrived.

David and Kenny joined the action too. David called their worker and instructed him how to handle their portion of the deal. Ever needy of approval, he saw a dual opportunity. "Part of me was showing off to Kenny how well I could operate long distance." By the time they returned to Philadelphia, they'd made over $50,000. It was better than the stock market and just as easy.

They couldn't spend the money fast enough. David, who was infatuated with Gina, decided to bring her back to Philadelphia with him, but there was no space on the shuttle plane from Aspen to Denver. No big deal. They chartered their own.

Money created as many problems as it solved. That spring, shortly after the Aspen trip, Larry came close to being discovered by police over an incident that involved cash rather than coke. As the amount of money Larry sent to Florida increased, it became harder to carry it onto the plane unless the bills were all large denominations. For instance, $100,000 in $100's could be handled in four $25,000 packets, two stuffed into the side of a courier's boots and two in his inside jacket pockets. The trouble was that Larry's customers rarely paid him in hundreds; the average transaction was in fives, tens, or twenties. He was always trying to cajole friends who stopped by his apartment to go to the bank and change his small bills into large ones. "Look,' he'd say, "all you have to do is go up to the teller with the money and say you're going to the casinos to gamble and you want to take hundred-dollar bills." If they balked about being too scared, Larry would tell them, "Before you get to the window, stop and say to yourself, 'I've got balls,' and then hand over the money." That was one of Larry's favorite expressions. He used to tell Kenny whenever he worried about getting caught, "You gotta go for it, Ken. You gotta have balls."

When David and Kenny got tired of doing Larry's dirty work, he hired a thirty-three-year-old divorced dental student on scholarship named Paula and paid her five dollars for every thousand she changed at the bank.

One April day Paula came running into the dental school crying hysterically that she'd been mugged and robbed of over nine thousand dollars. The dean of students calmed her down, called the police, and reported the crime. The following day there was a small article in the local newspaper under the headline "9G Stolen from Woman" which began 'Never carry cash,' warn the traveler's check commercials. It's not bad advice. Yesterday afternoon a . . . woman lost almost $10,000 when her purse was torn from her arm in University City . . . on her way to lunch with her boyfriend, David Ackerman. The money was to pay his tuition at the University of Pennsylvania Dental School." It went on to give a detailed description of the assailant and how she had hurt her arm and head when she fell on the sidewalk.

Two days earlier, Larry had given Paula $30,000 in small bills to change into hundreds for him. The following morning, she stopped by his apartment for her daily run to the bank. Only half-awake, he handed her another $50,000 without realizing she hadn't returned the first $30,000. That afternoon she came crying to him with the story of the mugging, bawling that she'd been robbed of the entire $80,000 on her way to bring the money back to him. He believed her, and in the hope of recovering at least part of the money by reporting the crime to the police, he sent her into the dental school with the tuition fable. David reacted worse to Paula's story than Larry to the loss of his money. He was mortified that she'd implicated him, since he wasn't her boyfriend and he felt she'd made him the laughingstock of the dental school. The students knew if she was carrying any money for him, it had to be drug money. The public exposure not only humiliated David Ackerman but also aroused his already suspicious nature. He told Larry he believed Paula was lying. She'd taken the money herself.

"You're being paranoid again, David."

"If I can prove she stole the money and get it back, will you give me half of it?" he pressed on.

"Right, David. Go find it. Sure I'll give you half." Larry, who tended to trust his friends wholeheartedly, thought David was being utterly ridiculous.

Since they were sharing the same house, it was fairly easy for David to carry out his spying mission on Paula. When she wasn't home, he'd sneak into her room and rifle her things looking for clues. One day he discovered her bank statement, which showed a substantial increase. It also showed that this starving scholarship student had been writing quite a few checks lately. He noticed that her wardrobe seemed to be improving too. But the most damning evidence was his discovery of the safe-deposit key. Now he had her. He reported his findings to Larry and was told he'd attend to the matter.

Shortly after at eight o'clock one morning, a black Delta 88 Oldsmobile pulled up in front of the house where Paula and David lived. Larry hopped out, leaving Glenn Fuller in the front seat and a tough-looking black boxing trainer named Slim at the wheel. He'd brought them to intimidate her in case she tried to deny ripping them off. He roused Paula out of bed and told her he had some policemen with him who wanted her to look at mug shots. She opened the car door, poked her head inside, and said, "These guys don't look like cops to me. What are you trying to pull?"

With that, Fuller jumped out of the car and stuck a gun in her stomach—a .22-caliber Beretta Larry had purchased to protect himself.

"We want the money, sweetheart. The money you stole from Larry. You'd better fork it over or you're history."

Paula screamed and wet her pants.

Lavin pushed Fuller out of the way. "We won't hurt you, Paula. Just return the money."

They allowed her to go inside and change. She admitted taking the money and spending almost half of it. Some had gone to her boyfriend, who was a partner in the deal; some she'd spent on herself and on tickets for a European vacation she'd arranged to take that summer with her boyfriend. What remained was in a bank outside the city. Lavin agreed to settle for that. Despite Fuller's attempt to convince her he wouldn't use the gun, Paula was shaking badly as they drove to the bank. He went inside, holding her hand and posing as her boyfriend to get into the safe-deposit room. Why should they trust her now?

The box yielded $30,000, of which Ackerman got half, leaving Lavin with a net loss of $65,000. He shrugged it off philosophically as he did all his drug losses. Easy come, easy go. It was not in his nature to look backward. Slim drove them all back to the city, and

Larry went to class. Fuller took Paula to lunch, got her drunk, and tried to talk her into sleeping with him.

The Paula incident set the rumor mill grinding at the dental school. Why was a student on financial aid carrying that kind of cash? One professor quipped sardonically, "Doesn't the bursar's office take checks anymore?" The administration contacted university security and learned there was gossip of a drug ring at the dental school, but no hard evidence. Then an anonymous letter arrived at the office of the dental-school dean, Dr. Walter Cohen. Stapled to it was the newspaper clipping about Paula and the admonition that drugs might have been involved. After some discreet questioning of the faculty, the names Ackerman and Weidler surfaced, but the name Lavin leapt out. He talked too much about money, about owning record companies and sports arenas. His income just didn't match his student status.

Dean Cohen took his suspicions up the chain of command to the president of the university and told him that a drug ring, perhaps of significant proportions, was quite possibly operating at the dental school. Whether they were making or selling drugs was unclear. The president set up a meeting with a lawyer from the district attorney's office who he felt would be more discreet than the city police. That meeting left Cohen with the impression the D.A. would conduct an undercover investigation. From time to time, the dean checked back with the president's office and was informed the D.A. was working on the case, which involved a much larger group than originally thought. Cohen was instructed to keep the matter quiet so as not to interfere with the policework and tip off the dealers. In fact there never was any serious investigation at all. An assistant district attorney assigned to the case remembers that university officials couldn't wait to dump what they saw as a hot potato in somebody else's lap and then ignore it. They were distinctly uncooperative. It was clear to the D.A. that the university administration was more concerned with avoiding adverse publicity than breaking up a drug ring. It didn't want undercover cops crawling around the campus and creating headlines. Since the D.A. had no shortage of other drug leads to pursue, the file that might have nabbed Larry Lavin in 1980 gathered dust.

Each time Larry Lavin skirted discovery and walked away unscathed, he got a little cockier. Maybe he couldn't walk on water, but he seemed to have a knack for finding the rocks underneath to support him. His next close call was of another kind. Late one evening, not long after the Paula scam, he and Marcia were watching television in their ground-floor West Philadelphia apartment when two masked black men broke in waving pistols. They threw Marcia on the floor and tied her hands and feet with rope while they forced Larry at gunpoint to turn over his cash and coke. It had been a slow night and he had only $30,000 on hand. Neither of them was physically harmed, but Marcia was badly frightened. She begged Larry again to get out of the business. Wasn't this proof enough that it had become too dangerous? She might just as well have saved her breath. Larry assessed the situation like any intelligent middle-class professional and took the most responsible action he could think of. He moved his operation to a safer neighborhood.

The very next morning he called Mark Stewart and told him to use his real-estate connections to get him a place downtown immediately. One day later Lavin made settlement on a brand-new $150,000 town house not far from the Liberty Bell in an exclusive section of Philadelphia known as Society Hill. He gave Stewart $60,000 in cash and, in return, got a check from one of the Larmark companies to use as his down payment. He mortgaged the balance to avoid suspicion. Even though he was just a third-year dental student he had no trouble getting a $90,000 mortgage because he was earning $50,000 a year on the Larmark payroll and Marcia was making $18,000 working as a physical therapist at the Veteran's Administration Hospital.

Their new home at 4 Willings Alley was part of eight contemporary three-story town houses built around a courtyard. The exterior was designed in keeping with the historical theme of nearby Independence National Historic Park, where the sidewalks are paved with brick and the streetlights are patterned after colonial lanterns. The houses' interiors had soaring ceilings and the kind of fancy architectural details featured in the shelter magazines. Most young couples moving into a home like this would have struggled to furnish it. Larry and Marcia flung themselves into buying expensive Early American furniture and planning their wedding.

Since they didn't belong to a local parish, it took Larry a half-dozen calls to find a nice suburban church where the priest would marry them. Larry was surprised at the trouble he had, since "I can usually talk anybody into anything." Finally he got a priest to agree by telling him that they planned to move to his parish after the wedding.

They were married outside Philadelphia on a Sunday in June 1980. The morning of the wedding, Larry awoke from a restless sleep, stricken with a bad case of cold feet. Was he ready to get married, to give up his freedom? He had everything—looks, personality, brains, and plenty of money. If he stayed single he could live like a playboy. Was it a mistake to tie himself down at twenty-five? He was a rich professional, the perfect catch. He could have any woman he wanted. Was Marcia the right one for him? Yes, she was the kind of woman he wanted to raise his children, but was she exciting enough? Should he have looked for somebody more glamorous, more electric? He made a mental list of her good qualities: she was extremely trustworthy, and in his life that was important. She was also kind and good-natured and would undoubtedly make a wonderful mother and an understanding companion. But could she satisfy his wild side? And how much did that matter? For Larry these weren't emotional questions. He approached them logically, like a trial judge weighing the pros and cons of a case before arriving at a verdict. He had a sentimental streak, sent flowers for special occasions and always chose romantic rather than humorous cards for birthdays and anniversaries, but Larry was a pragmatist. His head ruled his heart. After contemplating his options, he came to what he considered a rational decision and drove to the church.

Although Marcia was a devout churchgoing Catholic, Larry persuaded her to have a simple ceremony rather than the longer and more formal nuptial Mass. Since her father had recently died, Marcia's brother gave her away, and friends say they'd never seen her so happy. She sewed her own gown; it was tailored with very little lace and just the hint of a train. The reception for one hundred or so guests at the Towne House, a popular restaurant, had a band, and the sit-down dinner, like the ceremony itself, reflected Marcia's taste. Everything was nicely done but understated. Larry, who paid for the wedding, would have spent whatever Marcia wanted, but characteristically she leaned toward simplicity.

The bachelor party that Ken Weidler threw at an airport hotel was a lot more exciting than the wedding. Between the drugs and the orgy, they'd made so much noise the hotel told them never to come back. The highlight of the evening came when one of the hookers stepped out of her lace panties in the finale to a sensuous strip-tease she spontaneously performed. Supercharged from snorting the purest coke she'd ever had, she lost her balance and tumbled off the glass coffee table she was using for a stage. In her fall, the spike heel of her sandal broke the table, scattering chunks of glass all over the floor that cut deep gashes in her bare bottom. Lavin did the best he could to stop the bleeding. Glenn Fuller, who'd flown in from Colorado for the occasion, grabbed a camera and took souvenir pictures of the girl's red-streaked rear end, which he showed afterward with obvious relish to friends who hadn't made the party. All the guys thought the accident was funny as hell; so did the girl, who was as high on coke as everybody else and stayed on for hours servicing Larry and the rest of the guests.

The only trace of that kind of rowdiness at the wedding was on the way to the reception from the ceremony. Several of the boys, including best man Paul Mikuta, took a hit from the tooter outside the church and barreled down the two-lane highway three cars abreast behind the limousine carrying Larry and Marcia. Whatever money Larry might have saved on the unpretentious wedding he poured into the honeymoon, a Hawaiian fantasy at the best hotels on three different islands. So powerful was his influence that all of his friends who married after him repeated the identical honeymoon trip on his recommendation.

Back at Willings Alley, Larry quickly set about ingratiating himself with the neighbors, who, like the dental faculty, couldn't understand how the attractive young couple could afford to buy such an expensive house, and assumed he'd inherited money. At the wine-and-cheese gatherings in their private courtyard, Lavin entertained the neighborhood children with his sleight-of-hand and their parents with stories about the sports celebrities he met at the Arena and the rock groups he handled in the record company. Marcia let Larry do the talking and remained pleasantly aloof with little to say. Larry, never one to let a leadership position sit empty, also took charge of the condominium association, which meant collecting money for private trash collections, seeing that the light bulbs in the courtyard were replaced, and the like. Had there been a good-citizenship award, he would have received it.

If Larry Lavin's phenomenal good fortune had not prevailed still another time, he would have left Willings Alley one night in a paddy wagon. He was unaware that a Philadelphia policeman, alerted to Lavin's drug dealings by an informant on the Penn campus, had been keeping tabs on him for years. Dave Grove, a cigarette-smoking, gum-chewing hulk of an ex-marine, belonged to an elite undercover police squad assigned to narcotics. Off and on, he'd been stalking Lavin since his undergraduate pot-dealing days at the Phi Delta fraternity house, but had never been able to nab him with any hard evidence. There were so many big drug cases in those days that a college kid wasn't enough of a priority to use the police department's limited resources for full-time surveillance. Occasionally Grove tried to track Lavin's Volvo, but he couldn't drive fast enough to keep up and avoid being noticed. Lavin drove his car with the same reckless abandon that he steered his life. Once he had coke in the back seat and thought he was being followed. He lost the cop by turning the wrong way down a one-way street, pulling into the exit of a parking garage, and roaring out the entrance.

Lavin was good. Damn good. Grove had worked lots of cases in his career, and the dental student was one of a handful he'd never forget. "He was impressive, a helluva man and a helluva business-man. Many a night I couldn't eat because I'd be so aggravated I couldn't pin him down. When you've got a drug dealer hustling for a buck, he's going to make a mistake. When he's doing it for the thrill like Lavin, he's gonna be much harder to get." Grove lost track of Lavin when he moved away from the campus area in West Philadelphia to Willings Alley, and by sheer serendipity relocated him when his name and phone number turned up in the purse of a girl caught in a drug raid at Drexel, a Philadelphia university about three blocks from Penn. She was a girlfriend of a customer of Larry's and he'd lent her some money to get out of a jam. It took a while for Grove to actually pinpoint Lavin because he had to first break the phone code—one of many devices in the arsenal Larry designed to protect himself. The first three digits of the phone number remained the same, but the last four were subtracted from the base number, 10, 9, 8, 7. For instance, the number 555-3577 would become 555-7410.

Working with his original informant, Grove sat tight until he got word that Lavin was going to receive a drug shipment one night in the fall of 1980. His mustache bristling with anticipation, Grove banged on the custom wood door of the expensive town house.

"Police officers. We've got a warrant to search your house." Lavin answered the door without a trace of surprise. That should have been the first clue. He asked to read the warrant and invited them in, not in the least intimidated by the sledgehammers they were carrying.

"You've got a nice house here, Larry," Grove said. "We don't want to ruin it. Why don't you just tell us where you got the coke hid."

Lavin acted as if they'd suggested he was building bombs in his basement. "I have no idea what you're talking about. You can look wherever you want."

And look they did, from the first floor to the roof deck, while Lavin watched them with an annoyed expression, as if they were keeping him from his favorite TV program. The cops unscrewed the legs of the pool table and removed the moldings along the stairwell. They sifted through closets and drawers and all they found was a single Quaalude. Grove knew he'd been burned and beaten, but he never knew how.

Lucky Larry had triumphed again because a classmate who was

a good friend and customer of Ken Weidler's had a wife working in the district attorney's office. A colleague of hers was privy to a police list of drug-raid targets that included someone from the dental school. In a friendly effort to protect her husband just in case he was involved, the lawyer passed on the information as a friendly tip. She told her spouse, who promptly warned Ken, who alerted Larry. Around the same time, a customer of Larry's was arrested in New Jersey with Lavin's name in his phone book. Between the warning and the bust, Lavin expected a raid sooner or later and moved all his coke to another apartment.

Close calls like this would have unnerved anybody else, but Larry thrived on them. There was something askew in his personality that drew him to danger over and over again. But the fun and games were coming to an end. The Lavin cocaine ring was about to enter a new phase in which security would become much more important. Larry would remain in charge, but everything beneath his command would change.

8

OLDE CITY, PHILADELPHIA
FALL, 1980

The buxom new roommate David Ackerman brought back from
Aspen adjusted easily to life in Philadelphia. On the days he could
marshal enough motivation to attend class, good-natured Gina
explored the city and waited for him to return so they could go out
to dinner or stay home and get high. They were now living a
ten-minute walk away from Marcia and Larry's town house in Olde
City, a fashionable section near the Delaware River popular with
rising young professionals. Larry's tonier Society Hill address tended
to attract those who'd already arrived. Olde City, once a motley
assortment of waterfront warehouses, small factories, and wholesale outlets, was in the throes of being rescued from commercial
oblivion by developers who transformed the abandoned buildings
into chic residential apartments. The Hoop Skirt Factory, the
name of the renovated building where David and Gina lived, had
once been a factory manufacturing the wooden hoops that gave the
swaying motion to Victorian ball gowns. All the renovated loft
buildings with their exposed brick walls, high ceilings, and higher
rents boasted quaint names like the Sugar Refinery and the Wire
Works. Bars where merchant sailors had calmed their sea legs with
a beer and a shot now had hanging plants in the windows, wine
specials, and French menus scribbled on a blackboard.

It was the fall of David Ackerman's fourth and last year in
dental school, and his cocaine addiction had begun to interfere
dramatically with his education. Since the ski trip to Aspen he'd
been doing coke every day, and was on his way to doing lines a
gram long. He was sliding into the addict's abyss of ever-increasing
use. "I was getting to the point where the highs weren't always
wonderful so I was doing more and more to feel good. Then I'd get
so wired that everything would scare me. I'd go to bed swearing I

was finished. Never again. Then I'd wake up so terribly depressed that the only way to get rid of that awful feeling was to do more coke. I felt like a laboratory rat trapped in a cage, pushing the lever every hour for more coke, knowing I was killing myself and unable to stop."

David was hooked on something that was making him wealthy and destroying him emotionally at the same time. From a business-man's perspective, he had the ideal product: a substance that, without the slightest marketing or advertising, created an insatiable demand.

Researchers at the time barely understood what has since been learned about cocaine's effect on the brain. It's now believed the drug distorts the release of brain chemicals called neuro-transmitters that control emotion and trigger pain or pleasure. Constant usage depletes the source of the euphoric rush characteristic of cocaine to the point where there aren't enough neuro-transmitters to meet everyday needs. The starved brain craves coke like a person on a parched desert craves water, and the addict returns to coke, not to feel good, but to keep from feeling bad. Financially David was a beneficiary of the lust that kept his business growing. Personally, he was a victim of that same lust.

One evening while Gina was away in Florida visiting her par-ents, David initiated a conversation with a perky divorced blonde some ten years his senior who lived up the hall. One thing led to another and they wound up in her apartment free-basing cocaine, something David had done just once before. He remembered the incredible rush from smoking cocaine instead of snorting it. She showed him all the smoking apparatus—the butane torch, the glass water pipes—and explained the process for removing the hydro-chloride component from cocaine and reducing it to its purest and most potent form. The customer turned on the dealer. They did a little base, then a little more, until she ran out of coke. David, his craving cranked into high gear, suggested that he had a friend at Penn who would resupply them. They took a fifteen-minute drive to West Philadelphia and came back with seven grams.

The "friend" was David's worker, a dental student whom he and Ken had hired to handle their gram customers. Their enterprise had grown to selling as much as four kilos a month (compared to Larry's four kilos a week) and they no longer wanted to be both-ered with anybody buying piddling $85 quantities. As a result of their expansion, they even hired their own mule, who traveled to Florida along with Larry's mule to carry their portion of the money and look after their interests.

David, panting to do more base, suggested the blonde come to his apartment and show him how to make it. They went into the kitchen and started the cooking lessons.

"We're gonna need a little glass bottle," she said. "Like a spice bottle or something. And some baking soda. Not too much."

"Here. Throw the peppercorns out and use this."

She washed and dried the spice jar and gingerly sprinkled in a gram of coke. "Take some more," David urged. "Put some more in." He spooned in another half-gram.

"That's enough. You have to be careful not to waste it." Having no idea he had an unlimited source of coke, she hoarded the fresh supply like a pensioner with two teabags and a week until his social-security check comes. "Put some water on to boil, will you?"

"How much?"

"Not a lot. Two or three inches."

While the water boiled, she added tap water to the white powder, a drop at a time, swirling the mixture to dissolve it. "You wanna use as little water as you can." She worked quickly and intently. "The thing is, when you put the bottle into the pot of boiling water, you've got to be careful the glass doesn't crack, or it's bye-bye coke. Give me a pot holder. I have to get it out as soon as the coke starts to boil. Are you getting all this?" David, the gourmet cook, committed the recipe to memory. He already knew that this was a dish he'd want to prepare often.

He began getting impatient. "Can't you do this faster?"

She shot him a strange look and held her hand up, pressing her thumbnail against the top of her pinky. "Maybe you're Mr. Moneybags, but I don't waste this much blow. What you want is the vapor. You've gotta watch that this base doesn't melt," she added when she'd finally finished. "Here, take a hit."

David inhaled, and a warm flash tore through his body. His pulse pounded and for a brief but intense few minutes he was bathed in joy. It was the best he'd ever felt, a hundred times more wonderful then any high he'd experienced. At that moment he'd have killed for more. He glanced at the blonde as she bent over meticulously pouring the liquid in the spice bottle through a coffee filter to capture the last little bit of pure cocaine. He pictured her without clothes, her hair falling over his chest as she crawled on top of him and lowered her nipples to his mouth. But he had far too much coke to get an erection and he'd rather have the base than the woman anyway. "Pass me the pipe. And thanks for the lesson."

Free-basing quickly became one of David's favored activities. There were nights he'd exhaust his supply of snow, and without any Quaaludes on hand to help him sleep, he'd become desperate. "I'd usually be in the kitchen because I needed the water to make free-base. When I'd realized I'd run out, I'd get down on the floor and crawl around on my hands and knees looking for a crumb of base that might have dropped. The most important thing in my life at that moment was finding something to get high again. Any little white scrap that caught my eye—a piece of old macaroni, a shred of dried bread—I'd put in my pipe, hoping it was cocaine."

As David Ackerman sank deeper into a world dominated by cocaine, his partner, Ken Weidler, reversed direction, and slowly began his way back to a world dominated by dentistry. When Weidler looked in the mirror, he saw what he really wanted to be—a clean-cut young man in a white lab coat—not what he had become—a dissipated disco denizen selling white powder.

The desire for money and attention that had driven him to drugs wasn't enough to keep him there. Larry had been right all along when he'd told Kenny, "You gotta have bigger balls."

Kenny first realized he couldn't take the heat when the police almost caught him on a federal offense: sending cocaine through the mail. He and David had a big cocaine customer named Tony in California with whom they did a mail-order business. Every week or so they'd send him a pound of coke by express mail and he'd send them his money the same way. The package was usually delivered to Tony with his girlfriend's last name. The return address read Larry Schelling, Fairfax Apartments, Philadelphia. Schelling, a friend of Weidler's who lived in the same building, was the kind of super-straight guy who thought drugs meant aspirin. Ackerman and Weidler played what they considered a terrific practical joke by putting on the package the name of the least likely person they could imagine using cocaine. They stopped laughing when a package mailed to California never arrived. Under an assumed name, David put a tracer on the package. Several days later the Philadelphia police raided Schelling's apartment. They found nothing. Unlike David, who quickly put the incident behind him, Weidler remained badly shaken by it.

The package scare and the Paula episode were the first in a string of events that jolted Weidler back on track. The disco whirl ended when his college girlfriend, the woman he would later marry, moved in with him his final year at dental school. That put a stop to his partying with David, who now had Gina and free-basing to occupy his time.

But by far the strongest blow was dealt by an instructor at the dental school, who liked Kenny and warned him during the summer between his junior and senior years that unless his schoolwork improved drastically he would not be able to graduate in 1981 with his class. Kenny was stunned. "I'd been like a kid in a candystore," he said, "and suddenly I realized candy was making me sick. I'd sown my wild oats and I was finished." He immersed himself in his schoolwork and used whatever outstanding favors he could collect to speed up work on the course requirements he'd neglected. Dental students had to complete a variety of procedures—caps, bridges, root canals, and the like—in order to graduate, and many were long, time-consuming projects. If a little coke to a dental assistant in the lab or someone in the records department could get him what he needed more quickly, so much the better. He was able to buy a half-finished denture to complete from a classmate and drug customer who had already completed his and had an extra one. This practice wasn't uncommon or even dishonest, but partially finished dentures weren't readily available, and it certainly helped Weidler to have the right connections. With those and yeoman effort, he got his dental degree in June.

Extricating himself from the business proved more complicated. He, David, and Larry haggled over how to divide their interest or whether to close down entirely. Kenny wanted a way to keep his capital invested without his having any management involvement. Larry still expected to make a pot of money with Mark Stewart and briefly considered getting out of drugs and moving on to finance. Eventually Kenny and David came up with an alternative that lightened Larry's workload. They agreed on a merger of assets (customers) that would leave Kenny strictly in the role of investor. In this way he would continue to profit from the ring long after he'd stepped down from active involvement, and his earnings over five years would reach somewhere between one-half and three-quarters of a million dollars. All the customers were put in a common pool. David, in addition to receiving half the profits from the customers he and Kenny had developed independently, was given twenty-five percent of Lavin's business in return for assuming total management responsibilities. He was now the only one with time on his hands. At Christmas, he'd been asked by the dental school to take a leave of absence.

The heavier David got into cocaine, the more erratic his behavior, particularly in school. He'd always been flamboyant in an attractive way, but now, with the free-basing, he'd become cocky and obnoxious. Several of his professors observed his personality change with increasing alarm. Here was an extremely talented young man with the aptitude to become an outstanding dentist, unraveling before their eyes, flying into rages and verbally abusing patients. The more savvy faculty members recognized he had a drug problem, but the majority assumed he was having a nervous breakdown. The final showdown occurred at a routine examination in the dental clinic right before the Christmas break. The exam was scheduled from ten until one, with students allotted three hours to repair a cavity with a composite filling. David's patient arrived an hour late, at eleven; he completed the work at 1:15. The professor failed him because he'd gone over the time limit. David thought he was behaving like a Nazi and told him so without mincing words. Granted, he'd gone beyond the limit, but not the time allotment. Had he voiced his complaint appropriately, it might have been heard. Instead, he staged an ugly confrontation and screamed insults at the professor right on the clinic floor. He was told to take a leave of absence. Had he not been so obsessed with maintaining his cocaine connection, he might have reacted like Kenny Weidler and used the warning productively. But it was too late for David.

When he halfheartedly mentioned to Lavin that maybe he should go into a drug rehabilitation program, Larry told him to stop being ridiculous. The news of David's ouster from dental school actually delighted Larry. Ever since the police raid on Willings Alley, he had been concerned that the authorities were monitoring him, and he'd looked for a way to distance himself from the day-to-day operation of the business. "This is great," he told David. "You'll go on the five-year dental-school plan and you'll be a millionaire by the time you graduate." Lavin assumed a chairman-of-the-board role and David became chief operating officer. He tried using Gina as his executive assistant but she wasn't sharp enough to satisfy him. The only woman he could depend on was Suzanne Noramatzu. They'd had minimal contact during their two-year separation. The first time she'd seen him was early that fall, when he called her to stop by so he could pay back a $300 loan she'd forgotten about. As he peeled off three crisp hundred-dollar bills from a pile, he said, "I'm selling cocaine, Suzanne, and I've got a lot of money now. I don't want to owe anybody anything." Suzanne was shocked. She had never pictured her Ivy League lover as a drug dealer. David introduced her to Gina and asked her to take his new playmate to lunch or out shopping because "she doesn't have any friends in Philadelphia."

David telephoned Suzanne a second time around Thanksgiving when Gina was in Florida visiting her sister. He said he was hungry, wanted to go out for dinner, and that she should pick a place she wouldn't normally be able to afford. She chose an exclusive French restaurant where they rolled up a $150 tab. Afterward he invited her back to the Hoop Skirt Factory for a cocaine dessert and, in a pensive moment, said, "Remember, Suzanne, the food we ate just now is much better than cocaine." It seemed to her he was trying to keep something in perspective, but she didn't realize what it was.

The call that would give Suzanne the direction her life had lacked until then came shortly after New Year's Day, 1981. She had been working as a cocktail waitress, taking private French lessons and some introductory college courses at Temple University. A number of men had drifted in and out of her life since David, but they were just dates. None of them filled the shoes of the man she still loved. When David said, "I need you to come work for me, Suzanne, I don't have anybody I can trust," she found it impossible to refuse. He complained that Gina was very young and sweet but utterly without ambition. All she wanted was to get married and have babies. Suzanne agreed to help him and David insisted she rent an apartment near him that same day. He was, as always, impatient. She met with a local realtor that afternoon who showed her an apartment around the corner from David's for $440 a month. "If you like it, take it," David said. That afternoon she gave the agent $880 in cash and took the key, telling him not to bother to clean the bathroom, she'd do it herself.

What was supposed to be a part-time job turned into a twenty-four-hour on-call life-style. In the beginning, Suzanne leaned on David to rationalize their illegal activity and he had no shortage of convincing arguments. "Do you respect John Kennedy, Suzanne?"

"You know I do."

"Do you respect Robert Kennedy?"

"Of course."

"Well, we're like the Kennedys."

"What are you talking about?"

"Their father made their millions bootlegging liquor. But they were good people and we're good people. They were nice. We're nice. The government was wrong with Prohibition and they're going to realize they're wrong about drugs. This is 1981. It'll all be legal in ten years and we'll be rich. And just like the Kennedys, nobody will care how we made our money."

They decided the real reason for the government's antidrug hysteria had nothing to do with morality and everything to do with its inability to collect taxes on the enormous profits the drug business generated. Suzanne drew on her liberal politics and announced that they had a right to do what they wanted and the government shouldn't be controlling private lives. David assured her he'd read all about drugs in his medical textbook. Coke wasn't a hard drug like heroin. It was as harmless as pot, only more fun and more expensive. The endless debate on the pros and cons became more meaningless as the daily routine of the business consumed their attention. Cutting cocaine, packaging it, and counting money developed into routine activities. David restructured and expanded the operation and Suzanne took over the bookkeeping. Soon dealing seemed like a perfectly normal way to make a living.

Larry had already reached the same conclusion. He took the position that they were operating a service business in a profitable marketplace. Society had created this demand for drugs, and the circle he moved in had given its stamp of approval. The worst he could be accused of was having the foresight to step in and take advantage of an existing need.

As to the danger of cocaine, Larry was convinced there wasn't any. He never came in contact with street junkies shooting up in filthy abandoned houses. "When I was selling drugs, I never met anybody who'd destroyed his life with cocaine. All the magazines we were reading in college quoted studies that said cocaine was not addictive. There was no evidence then it was killing people. In the years I dealt, there were maybe one hundred deaths attributed to cocaine. Why, there's nothing you can name that doesn't cause more deaths than that. Gall-bladder surgery kills 3,500 people annually; car accidents, 40,000; cancer, 400,000. That may be a cold way of looking at coke, but compared with the thousands who die from Valium, I don't believe cocaine is that awful. I don't think I was responsible for anybody dying or I would have heard about it." From his privileged perch, drug deaths were something that happened to people in ghettos, not to his customers.

9

OLDE CITY, PHILADELPHIA
1981

If an economist were to chart the growth of Larry Lavin's cocaine organization, he'd single out 1981 as the year the business exploded. With David Ackerman at the helm and the base of operations moved from the Penn campus to the residential neighborhood of Olde City, sales jumped from an average of two to three kilos per month to ten to fifteen kilos mailed or hand-delivered to thirteen states. As the ring's college and dental-school customers graduated and relocated all over the country, they continued to buy coke from Lavin and frequently increased their orders by becoming dealers themselves. The scope of the market now included Pennsylvania, New York, New Jersey, Massachusetts, New Hampshire, Vermont, Maine, Ohio, Florida, Arizona, Maryland, Illinois, California—and Canada. Bigger orders meant more money. On the organization's books, which kept track of each partner's current equity in the business, David Ackerman's share was listed at $1 million; the no-longer-participating Kenny Weidler had $650,000, and Lavin hovered at the $1.5-million mark. In a single week Ackerman could make as much as $20,000. Lavin's portion was even higher. He estimated that by the end of 1981, after deducting his expenses and losses, he'd netted at least a million. Over the next three years he got even richer as the monthly sales volume increased to twenty-five kilos at profits $10,000 to $20,000 per kilo, depending on variations in the wholesale market.

Much of the credit for the expansion of the business belonged to Ackerman. With Kenny out of the picture, trying to catch up on his studies so he could finish dental school on time, and Larry busy investing and laundering his millions in cocaine profits through Mark Stewart, David acted as chief operating officer. Despite his addiction to cocaine, he displayed as much talent for management as he had for dentistry.

One of David's earliest innovations was to minimize the organization's risks by spreading both the coke and the money it brought in among five apartments (at an aggregate rental of $3,000 a month) similar to the one at St. Charles Court in Olde City that he'd leased for Suzanne Noramatzu. In case of a problem with a rough customer that might lead to a robbery attempt, he didn't want all his assets in one place. Plus it made sense to reduce the evidence that might be seized in the event of a police raid. David was also concerned about the convenience of his customers. He took pains to choose attractive apartments in chic neighborhoods where the comings and goings would blend inconspicuously with the activities of local residents. And he realized how important it was for his upscale clientele of stockbrokers, dentists, lawyers, and businessman to feel safe stopping by to pick up their orders.

Two of the apartments—Suzanne's and another where one of her girlfriends was installed—served as combination residences and sales offices. They were simply furnished and each contained, hidden in the bedroom closet, a safe filled with up to a million dollars in cash.

The other apartments served as mini-factories for compounding and packaging cocaine orders. They remained uninhabited and unfurnished except for a few standard items: a safe, a large glass dining-room table for a work surface, a refrigerator stocked with beer and soda for the workers, and paraphernalia for cutting coke.

Breaks—breaking down cocaine by adding inert filler to cut the purity, increase the quantity, and lower the unit price—took place once or twice a week when product arrived from Florida and was delivered to the factory. Lavin didn't run an ordinary buy-and-sell, wholesale-to-retail outlet. He functioned more like a specialized boutique. What made his organization unique was the way he customized his orders to customer preferences, offering several grades of coke at varying strengths. This required a highly structured and efficient operation.

The typical Lavin ring break employed four or five people who each had assigned tasks. The sifter, for example, stood at a long metal folding table set with a giant sieve and several mixing bowls. This job often fell to Suzanne. She'd empty a kilo—a little over two pounds—of coke into the sieve to separate the shake (cocaine powder) from the rocks. These chunks of coke, produced in the process of converting paste to powder, were a highly desirable commodity because buyers believed they represented uncut cocaine. In reality this was not necessarily true, since rocks could also be manmade from cut coke.

After Suzanne or another worker sifted off the powdered cocaine, the rocks left in the sieve had to be sorted according to size—big ones the size of baseballs in one bowl, medium ones about the size of eggs in a second, and chips in a third. While Suzanne sifted and sorted, another worker would be fluffing the filler in the blender. Usually inositol was used to cut the strength of the coke, and the trick was to aerate it just enough to remove some of the vitamin compound's natural shine while taking care not to grind it to a finer powder than the coke itself or the two would have had an incompatible texture.

The next step was weighing the shake and the rocks to figure the percentages required to make up individual orders. When Lavin ran the show in West Philadelphia, he weighed coke on the same triple-beam scale he'd used in his undergraduate marijuana business. That was not accurate enough to satisfy David, who switched to more exacting electronic digital readout scales that cost over $2,000. He believed in quality control and felt the organization's reputation rested on consistency. He drew from his background as a gourmet cook and recast the formulas for preparing orders into easy recipes that any novice could follow. These were written on posters tacked to the wall of each factory.

There were recipes for standard orders and for custom blends. The standard menu offered a choice of an ounce priced at $1,400, $1,800, $2,000, and $2,300, depending on the percentage of coke, filler, and rocks. A $1,400 ounce (there are 28 grams to an ounce) consisted of 11 grams of rock, 7 grams of shake, and 10 grams of cut; a $2,300 ounce had no cut at all. Prices varied somewhat, depending on special deals that Larry made. Some smaller customers paid a $50-an-ounce premium. And others, like his sister, Jill, who was a major New England customer, got a $50 discount. Generally Larry's profit ran to twenty-five percent—$350—on the $1,400 ounce, which accounted for over eighty percent of their sales. The $1,800 ounce brought a $550 profit; the $2,300 ounce of pure coke, the least demanded, had a $700 profit built in. The dealers who bought drugs from the Lavin ring resold them at another markup, and a kilo that cost Lavin $58,000 could wind up with a street value of three times that figure.

In addition to the basics, the ring provided custom specialties. One customer liked his order packaged in glass bottles, a marketing device Larry introduced early on and later dropped. As the sales volume soared, the organization switched to easier-to-fill plastic zip-lock bags and offered the bottles only on request. Other customers might be less interested in packaging than in content, preferring big rocks or small rocks or a particular combination. One wanted his $2,000-an-ounce product with twenty-two grams of regular rock and six grams of "nicky" rock, a special manmade item fashioned from adulterated cocaine.

Creating manmade rocks was a trade secret the organization learned from their Latin suppliers in Miami. It took a team of two trained workers to produce them. They'd begin by spreading a pound or so of shake on the glass worktable, with or without a cut, depending on what they needed. Using an ordinary house-plant spray bottle filled with methanol, one team member dampened the coke while the other mixed it using two plastic loose-leaf binder sheets. At just the right saturation point, the coke would turn yellowish and they'd grab handfuls at a time, squeezing their fists into tight little balls for about three minutes for the rock to congeal. They always wore rubber gloves so there'd be no handprints. At first they baked the rocks they made in conventional ovens, but Larry wasn't happy with the uneven results. He came up with the idea of using heat lamps that pulled down over the tables. The rocks hardened in about four hours and had to be turned periodically so they'd dry evenly. Finally the rough edges were smoothed by hand, then weighed and added to the orders which were bagged, tagged with the customers' names, and left in the safe until delivery to the sales offices for pickup.

Breaks lasted anywhere from several hours to all night, depending on how much coke was being handled. It was painstaking work but it seemed more like a party because everybody got high by doing lines or simply from breathing the coke dust which filled the air like a fine mist of talcum powder.

Once David had organized the breaks into production lines, he turned his mathematical talents to restructuring the books. Larry had a tendency to be loose about money and kept simple records on a yellow legal pad with the customers' names on the left-hand side and a running total of their current debt on the right. David was far more fastidious and, in addition to keeping more accurate customer records, developed an elaborate accounting system which included a running tally of his, Lavin's, and Weidler's mounting equity as the business grew. By 1981 the principals were being credited with profits of $10,000 to $50,000 a week.

It was during this period that the trio began to turn money over to Mark Stewart regularly. Ultimately three million dollars in profits from the Lavin ring found their way into the promoter's slippery hands. One of Suzanne's weekly chores was to carry a brown paper bag full of cash to the record-company office, some of which Stewart supposedly invested and some of which he sent back in paychecks.

The boys' relationship with Mark Stewart was actually fairly complicated. They needed him to launder money and provide legitimate checks for major expenses like the beautiful old stone home with a swimming pool in suburban Philadelphia Kenny wanted to buy when he got married. Weidler transferred a $105,000 down payment from the coke business to Stewart, who washed it through his companies and gave Kenny a check to use at settlement.

At an other level, Stewart was a link to a financial world that was more interesting to David and Larry than the pedestrian business of dealing drugs. These boys had attended a university that boasted one of the country's foremost academic business institutions, the Wharton School. Many of their college friends who hadn't gone on to law or medicine had gotten MBA degrees and were using their talents in banking and commerce. This group of college graduates entered an economy that had turned from manufacturing to service and was generating much of its income not by producing goods but by manipulating investments. To their generation the primary mark of achievement was money. Cut off from using normal investment channels by their illegal activities, the dentists sank millions into Stewart's Byzantine empire because they were obsessed with having their money make more money. The cash became as addictive as the cocaine. In fact, Larry's investments with Stewart compelled him to work harder in the coke business because once he gave money to Mark he felt it was no longer his and had to be replaced. David, while somewhat less obsessed on that score, quickly caught on to the potential of investment or "unearned" income, constantly reinforced by Stewart's injunction, "Your money's gotta work for you." Kenny escaped the Mammon mania somewhat because, by backing away from the business, he had less cash to play with.

From the start of their association, Stewart had found the dental students eager to learn the intricacies of the business world. In time he would teach his young protégés, especially Larry, now to inflate the value of properties and manipulate figures to influence loan officers at banks. Stewart would tell people how impressed he was with Lavin's thirst for information of any kind. "Larry wasn't a quick study but he was an avid researcher. I remember when we got into the music business how he read everything he could. Once he digested it, he not only retained it but also compounded what he'd learned and talked about it like he was an expert."

None of Larry's or David's investments ever paid off like the cocaine business, but that didn't stop them from putting money into one scheme after another. As they became more financially sophisticated, they stopped sending money to Mark and moved in other directions. Both of them bought a couple of condominiums in the city and at the seashore for short-term rental incomes and long-term investments. David purchased a half-dozen discount second mortgages and also deposited $100,000 in an Israeli savings bank while on a vacation there because it accumulated interest at a much higher rate than banks paid in the United States and, more important, wouldn't be reported to the IRS. The glitter of precious metals also attracted their avaricious eyes and together they bought twenty thousand ounces of silver at nine dollars an ounce. Silver immediately plummeted to four dollars an ounce. They held on to it for a year until it rose and they could unload it at a break-even point. David's $70,000 in Krugerrands turned out to be more prudent than Larry's investment in a gold mine that wasn't worth the paper shares he got for his cash.

Larry was luckier throwing dice at the Atlantic City casinos than with any of his investments. His high had always come from taking risks, not from taking drugs, and casino gambling was a perfect outlet for him. Rarely was he reckless with money except at the gaming tables. He'd wager thousands—and usually win. The very first time he played craps he won $1,200. David gambled too, but usually lost. Not that it mattered. All those greenbacks piled up in the safes looked to him just like Monopoly money. Whenever he was in the mood, he'd stuff five $5,000 packs in the inside breast pockets of his navy blazer and drive or take a stretch limo down to the casinos. Sometimes he brought Suzanne along and booked a suite at Harrah's or the Golden Nugget. He played both craps and baccarat, betting $5,000 on a single card or roll of the dice. One night he lost $50,000, but a few lines of coke back in the room made the loss seem inconsequential.

David was obsessed with running the drug operation in a businesslike manner and he introduced an elaborate record-keeping system so that he could tell at a glance the current status of both the company's coke and its cash. In the apartments where cocaine was stored there were inventory sheets of lined notebook paper with the coded names of the customers, the amounts of cocaine they purchased, and the prices they paid. A typical sheet might have 17,000 at the top, which referred to the current number of grams of cocaine in the safe. An individual entry could read: Paul M . . . 1,000 . . . $60,000. Paul Mikuta was the customer's name; 1,000 referred to his order of 1,000 grams (which equalled one kilo of coke); $60,000 was his price. Dealers like Mikuta and Billy Motto were considered preferred customers of the organization, and because of the huge quantities of uncut coke they purchased, they were permitted to buy coke at just $2,000 over cost. For everybody else who bought uncut kilos, the price was $76,000, or $18,000 over cost.

David's inventory sheets monitored how much coke the organization had in stock and where it went. There were also cash balance sheets that recorded payments from customers going into the safes and withdrawals for business expenses (airfare, rent, payroll, food, cars). Larry and David could dip into the well for whatever they wanted—a new BMW, a house in the suburbs, a weekend in the Bahamas, gold Krugerrands, call girls for a bachelor party, or gambling in Atlantic City.

In addition to the company records, individual customer accounts were recorded in a small black book which listed the buyer's name, the amount of money paid each time a purchase was made, the amount of cocaine received, and the balance due. The job of collecting all the information from the different accounting sheets belonged to Suzanne, who was, in effect, the company bookkeeper. She entered the data on a master record divided into several columns: the customer's name; the amount of real grams purchased (before the addition of cut), the wholesale cost, the actual sale price, and finally, how much profit from each sale went to Larry, David, and Kenny (based on which customers they'd contributed to the merger). David instructed her always to write the profits in pencil so she could erase her figures if she made a mistake. Larry was skeptical at first as to whether Suzanne could manage the books, and she was quite proud when he later complimented her on the neatness and accuracy of her records.

Customers were never identified by last names. That would have been too dangerous if the apartments had been raided and the books seized. Instead of last names, the organization used locations. Billy Motto, for example, became Billy South Philly because that's where he lived. There was a Billy New England, a Brian New England, a John Tampa, and so on. The number of customers in the book never rose above fifty, with perhaps a dozen of them accounting for eighty percent of the business.

The makeup of the list changed on a regular basis as the customers changed. For example, Larry began selling cocaine to Dan in dental school. After graduation Dan moved away and stopped buying, but told Larry about somebody to whom he resold coke. Then that buyer switched directly to Larry and brought along his brother, who lived in Maryland. Rich stopped using coke but had a cousin whom he supplied, who now got his coke directly from Larry. David had a customer, Milt, from Chicago, who graduated from medical school and ended the relationship. There were former marijuana customers who returned years later to buy coke, and small buyers like Priscilla, a former New England schoolteacher, who, divorced and broke, decided to get back on her feet by dealing cocaine. She put up her wedding ring as collateral on her first buy and slowly became one of Larry's biggest customers, purchasing as much as nine kilos at a time for over a half-million dollars.

New England was prime territory for the Lavin ring because Larry had friends and family there he could depend on. His sister, Jill, had been the person who turned him onto pot and he repaid the favor by turning her onto cocaine. She developed a substantial business with Larry as her supplier—and a bad cocaine habit too. His brother Rusty toyed with drugs but never became a heavy user. Larry's bait to draw him into the cocaine business was money.

The ideal sales situation in the coke business has high volume and few customers—and is structured like a pyramid. Larry Lavin, the source, sat on top of his pyramid, or ladder, as it was also called, and people moved up the rungs closer to him as the size of their orders increased. Every one of his customers had a ladder of his own, and so it went on down until the cocaine reached the last street sale. The common goal of dealers all along the line was to build volume and decrease customers, because the fewer people you dealt with, the less exposure you had to those who could finger you if they got arrested.

Larry encouraged his customers to grow along with him. In early 1981 the organization sold in quantities varying from a quarter-pound to several kilos; ultimately Lavin would eliminate all but the kilo-or-more buyers.

Most of the names on the customer-account sheets showed a running debt because Larry believed in extended credit. He routinely fronted coke to dealers who would cut it and peddle it to smaller buyers and then pay him back out of their profits. The organization liked keeping customers in debt because it meant they had to increase sales to meet their payments. Frequently this practice got out of hand because Larry allowed certain old friends to pile up enormous debts—as high as several hundred thousand dollars—before cutting off their credit. His own brother, Rusty, was a debtor. As was typical of so many recruits, it was a debt to Larry that got him into the business and kept him there.

In 1980 Rusty owned a small trucking company that hauled heavy equipment and parts around New England. His credit rating would never have impressed a banker, so when he needed $14,000 to buy a special engine, he asked his rich brother, Larry, for a loan. Unable to repay it, he began to do cocaine errands for Larry in lieu of cash payments. Couriers like Glenn Fuller would drop off a suitcase of cocaine at Rusty's house and he'd make the local deliveries. Then he began collecting money and driving it down to Philadelphia. Eventually he developed some small customers of his own and added Fuller's after his drug bust on the New Jersey Turnpike.

Rusty was always short of cash, and the fastest way to get it was working for Larry. "That kind of easy money had tremendous power," Rusty said. "I wanted to build my business so it would take off; I wanted a nice house and nice things for my wife and kids. I couldn't put my hands on thousands of dollars unless I did deals for Larry."

Several people in the organization viewed Rusty more as a deadbeat than a productive worker. Once when he was holding $100,000 in his house that was supposed to be delivered to Philadelphia, he called Larry, declared he'd been robbed, and the money was gone. Several people thought he was lying. Larry believed him and wiped the money off the books.

Whether it was his brother or anybody else, Larry was never very forceful at collecting. Goons and brass knuckles weren't his style. He believed "if you overwhelm people with friendliness, they'll want to live up to their obligations." This forgiving attitude extended far beyond his immediate family. One afternoon a female courier bringing money from a major customer in the Penn State area arrived at Larry's Willing's Alley condominium distraught to the point of tears. It seemed she'd stopped for lunch on the turnpike and when she returned to her car, the hatchback on her Celica had been forced open, and the $50,000 was gone. Larry calmed her down and went out to inspect the damage to the car. There wasn't a scratch on it. He sent her back to Penn State, called the customer for whom she was working, and both agreed she was obviously lying. When confronted, she explained she'd just been diagnosed as having cervical cancer and needed the money to pay for her surgery. Larry told her to keep $15,000 and return the rest.

This almost naive trust came from a feeling Larry had that "if you don't screw people, they won't screw you." While that philosophy helped his business grow, it also created massive losses. He estimates that at least one-quarter of his profits were written off the books as bad debts. His typical way of handling deadbeats was to knock them off the ladder and assume their biggest and best customers directly. That accomplished two things. He kept the outlet open and he increased business because once new customers gained access to a primary source of high-quality coke like Larry's, they usually bought more than they'd been getting before. Over the years Larry lost millions from bad debts that he simply canceled. But he was making so much that the losses hardly mattered, and there were always new customers waiting in line. He had a gift for recruiting people into his network. He knew just whom to lure with money and whom to lure with coke. There was nothing accidental in his technique. He explained it succinctly to Suzanne: "You let the line with bait out. They take a little nibble, then a bite. Then you roll them in and they're hooked."

Managing this growing enterprise required a dedicated work force. There was no difficulty at all filling positions for drivers and couriers. In college it had been easy to find drug users who needed cash. Several of these workers followed Lavin downtown after graduation, lured by fees of up to $2,000 to drive coke and money back and forth between Philadelphia and Miami and $500 for flying a package out to Colorado or Chicago. Once people became accustomed to the easy drug money, it seemed to override any fear they had of breaking the law. The organization recruited workers in much the same way it boosted sales—by applying a little basic psychology. Everybody had some kind of problem. The organization simply had to identify it and present a solution. With Willie Harcourt, for example, the Achilles' heel was a large unpaid drug bill.

Harcourt was a college dropout with aspirations of becoming a writer. He had curly reddish-blond hair, sun-bleached eyebrows over quick blue eyes, and was built like a linebacker. He was a small-time dealer who bought coke from the organization and, because of the mismanagement of his partner, ran up a $10,000 debt for which he was held responsible. David offered Willie the opportunity to reduce his debt by coming to work for the ring. He began as a part-time courier flying on all-expense-paid trips to California to deliver cocaine and bring back money. He was paid anywhere from $250 to $1,000 a trip (depending on the number of West Cost deliveries he had to make), which was far more than he could earn at the little café he managed. David soon recognized Willie Harcourt's dedication to the business and his ability to work with people, and wanted to train him for management. He dangled the possibility of investing in the record company with Mark Stewart, and that brought Willie into the fold. The guy who had been scraping to make ends meet now had money to burn. He never went anywhere with less than $1,000 in his wallet and dined out in first-class restaurants at least three times a week, indulging his penchant for rare cognacs so expensive they often brought the dinner check to $500.

Hiring workers was easier than keeping them. This was particularly true for those who took part of their pay in cocaine instead of cash. The more drugs they did, the more unreliable they became, and some had to be replaced. Whenever the ranks thinned out, David sniffed among his acquaintances until he found someone new whom he judged ripe for recruiting. He was always full of grand promises at the outset but weak when it came to delivering on them. Typical was the situation with a chef named Gary who worked at one of David's favorite restaurants and harbored a dream of someday opening a place of his own. When Gary broke his hand and couldn't cook for a while, David offered him a one-year deal to come into the organization at $1,000 a week plus a paid apartment with a storage safe. At the end of the year Larry would give him a $50,000 bonus, enough to make a down payment on his dream restaurant. When the year was up and it came time to collect, Gary went to Larry for his money. Larry told him flatly that David had had no right to make promises in his name and sent him back to Ackerman, who pointed to a $50,000 debt on the books owed by a customer in Ohio and said, "That's your bonus. If you want it, go collect it."

The hub of operations was Suzanne Noramatzu's apartment. In addition to keeping the books—which she was instructed to burn in her fireplace as soon as the debts recorded in them were all paid, since there was no reason to save them for Uncle Sam—her responsibilities included taking telephone messages for Larry and David, meeting with customers, and joining the entire crew for the marathon cocaine breaks when product arrived from Florida. An average business day began about noon, since she usually saw customers in the evening and then she and David stayed up until the wee hours snorting cocaine. Suzanne, with her gentle manner and lilting laugh, was an ideal hostess. Because customers usually stayed around for at least fifteen minutes to lessen any suspicion aroused by people running in and out of the building, Suzanne served them beer or soda and chatted brightly about their families, a fishing trip they'd planned, or the quality of tomatoes in their garden. The benign quality of her relationships enabled her to ignore the sleazy aspects of drug dealing. "I wasn't like those sinister people you see on TV," she says. "Our customers were mostly Larry's friends. Sometimes they brought me flowers or a bottle of wine. It wasn't like I was dealing with people who sold dope to kids on the street."

Working with people she admired, like David and Larry, raised Suzanne's self-esteem. For the first time in her life she felt capable, competent, and bright. "I was responsible for all the safes. One night I was sitting as caretaker of one million dollars and I thought to myself: They trust me. These highly intelligent, accomplished, successful people gave me all this responsibility. It really made me feel good."

The job of counting the endless flow of cash also fell to Suzanne and it occupied so much of her time that she had to find someone to do routine chores like marketing, taking clothes to the cleaner, buying money orders to pay rent on the apartments, paying parking tickets, and purchasing plastic bags and inositol for the cocaine breaks. She hired a friend from her waitressing days named Christine, who quickly became part of the gang and was installed in one of the apartments.

Christine, caught in the right light, could look rather pretty but was actually quite plain. Of average height and build, she had pale skin, shoulder-length straight sandy hair, and square cheekbones that showed her Slavic ancestry. Both girls were extremely well-paid for their work. In addition to living rent-free, Christine's salary rose from $500 to $1,500 a week as her duties increased. That was in addition to easy access to cocaine.

Suzanne's salary started out similar to Christine's but rose to $500 for every kilo the company processed at a break, which by the end of the year amounted to over $100,000. She also was supposed to receive a $50,000 bonus, which, like Gary, she never saw. Larry withheld the cash and entered it on the books in what he called an F.S.—forced savings account. David liked to goad the other workers by pointing out how rich Suzanne was. When she complained that it embarrassed her, he said it was his way of giving them an incentive to work harder so they could become rich too.

Cash had to be reckoned up on a daily basis. Night after night, Christine and Suzanne would sit cross-legged on the floor sorting bills into piles of five, tens, and twenties. Billy Motto's money was the messiest to straighten out. "Street money," they called it, because he didn't have any carriage trade peeling fifties from snakeskin wallets. His customers paid in fives and tens, crumpled in their pockets. Billy had to be taught to smooth out the bills, separate the fives from the tens, and arrange them heads-up in neat stacks. David was a stickler about how the money was to be sorted and bound. He felt it was unfair to burden his Cuban suppliers with mixed-denomination money to put through their counting machines. So the girls counted each denomination into $1,000 packets held together with a single rubber band. Five $1,000 packs were then stacked together and wrapped with two bands, one crosswise and one lengthwise, to form the $5,000 bundle that was standard with drug traders. It was a tedious, boring job—and a relief, when the work ended, to lay out the relaxing lines of white powder. Sometimes the girls would snort by themselves; sometimes they'd wind up across the street with David, who was temporarily living alone, having shipped Gina back to Denver with a $5,000 going-away gift; it had become too much trouble to sneak out on her to visit Suzanne. David always had a cache of coke and Quaaludes in his apartment. He, Suzanne, and Christine would often do lines until their inhibitions disappeared and then climb into bed together for a friendly three-way romp.

By now David was snorting anywhere from three to seven grams of coke a day and his drug abuse was slowly transforming him into a caricature of his worst personality traits. The workers referred to him as Fagin after the greedy Dickensian villain.

David's instructions had to be followed to the letter and no one dared question them. He became imperious and demanding, exploding into a temper tantrum when his rules were broken. If cocaine arrived from Florida at midnight, he insisted on having the break immediately rather than waiting until morning. Workers would complain, "Why the hell do we have to do this now?" He'd answer, "Because I say so." And that was the end of the discussion.

David wasn't particularly eager to get the job done. What he wanted was the cocaine. "I'd only insist on having breaks right away when I'd run out. I had an insatiable lust for cocaine. When I wanted it, I had to have it. I didn't care what people thought of me. I only cared about getting coke. Nothing else mattered. At the same time, I didn't want anybody to know the extent of my addiction. I had become a closet user. Getting an order made up on my demand was a way to get into the supply without asking for it directly."

The more he lost control of himself, the more David tried to control his workers. He wanted to be able to communicate constantly with Suzanne, and sent Willie Harcourt to Florida to get a set of the expensive, high-powered walkie-talkies he'd seen the Cubans using. As soon as Willie delivered the gadgets, he gave one to Suzanne, admonishing her to leave it on at all times, and took the other to his apartment. A few hours later he tested her to see if she'd done as she'd been told.

"Suzanne. Suzanne."

"Yes. I'm here.

"Good. I'm coming over." He walked out of his apartment. "I'm in my hallway now. Can you hear me?"

"Yes. Fine."

"I'm in the elevator." A minute or so passed. "I'm in the street." Next she heard, "I'm in your elevator." And then he was at her door, grinning his cute little smile and reminding her for the moment of the lovable guy he sometimes still could be.

David's tongue-lashings of his assistants usually drew Larry away from the dental school to Olde City to play peacemaker.

The first time Suzanne met him, she was struck by how ordinary he looked. "I thought to myself: Is this the famous Larry Lavin? I had pictured him larger than life, brilliant, handsome. He looked like just another nondescript WASP dental student in those awful neon-green golf slacks he wore. Could this be Mr. Big?" When she told David her impression, he warned her, "Watch out or you'll fall under his spell like everybody else. He'll charm you and he'll use you. He'll ask about your family, how your parents are. He's great at conversation. He can talk to anybody about anything. You'll feel he really likes you. But he's a master manipulator." Suzanne had a hard time believing David because Lavin's easy-going style quickly won her over. He was a great talker and the clearinghouse for organization gossip. Things always livened up when Larry was around.

Larry's visits were always fun if for no other reason than that he provided such a contrast to David. He was as nonchalant about the dangers of the coke business as David was paranoid, and he repeatedly said, "The risks aren't legal. They're financial." Larry openly courted detection by doing things like leaving a message on his answering machine at Penn that said. "We're breaking now and can't come to the phone. At the sound of the beep, put your orders in." David, on the other hand, acted as if his phones were perpetually tapped. Larry might call the apartment and ask, "David, did Paul pick up the two keys yet?" Annoyed by his indiscretion, David would respond, "Lawrence W. Lavin is speaking. He lives at Willing's Alley and attend Penn Dental School." And he'd hang up.

As David's coke habit increased, so did his paranoia about getting caught, and he was always looking over his shoulder. He'd grow a beard, then shave it and grow a mustache, then shave it and go back to the beard. When he traveled, he used an alias or made reservations in Suzanne's name. Whatever he bought, he paid for in cash. He slyly tucked away some of the company's financial records among his private papers because he thought they might someday come in handy as bargaining chips to offer the authorities. Once a customer made the mistake of bringing some strangers to the apartment. Not only did David bar them from entering, he angrily dragged the buyer inside and roundly chastised him. "You know the rules. You are *never* to bring anybody here. *Never* ever let anyone know where this apartment is. You ought to know better! Don't you ever do this again!" Some of this nervousness rubbed off on Suzanne, and she brought it up one afternoon when Larry stopped by and they were discussing a customer in Baltimore who'd just been arrested.

"What if he tells the police, 'I got it at Suzanne's'?" she asked.

"He's not gonna say that," David answered. "Besides, everyone likes you."

"That's not the point. We're not friends."

"If they point the finger at anyone, it will be me," David insisted.

Larry laughed at both of them. "Suzanne, tell him the person everybody knows is me. Look, Glenn got busted and Dick got busted. Did either of them roll over? No. Would you give up David?"

"Of course not."

"Would Willie give you up?"

"Probably not."

They went on and on through their list of customers and reassured her that she needn't worry about being betrayed by anybody in the organization. Anybody except the one customer they feared, the one they suspected had mob connections—Billy Motto. Hadn't he brought her a gun one day as a gift and told her a girl handling drugs and money needed protection? "Leave it on the coffee table. Youse don't have to use it. It'll just send a message." Billy Motto. He had a heart of gold. And lead in his jacket pocket. He was the organization's best customer but his ring was very different from theirs. He didn't deal drugs to college boys; he sold to people who cleaned college dormitories. In some ways he was an even bigger success than Larry Lavin because he had started with so much less. Billy Motto was a story all by himself.

10

SOUTH PHILADELPHIA
1981

"This is the operator. I'm sorry to interrupt but I have an emergency call from a Dr. Martino trying to get through to you."

Suzanne laughed to herself. Billy Motto was at it again. "Thanks, operator. I'll hang up right away." A moment later the phone rang. It was "Dr. Martino."

"Hi, Suzanne. Is David there?"

"No. He's probably still sleeping. It's only eleven. I just got up myself."

"When's the stuff due back from Florida?"

"Sometime this afternoon."

"Beep me as soon as it gets in, will ya? So how ya doin'?"

"I'm fine, Billy. I'll call you when it gets here. 'Bye."

Toward evening Willie Harcourt drove in from Florida with ten kilos of cocaine double-bagged in a locked suitcase in the trunk of his car. As soon as the product was unpacked and locked in the safe of the vacant apartment, Suzanne called Billy's beeper. They'd just started using new beepers, a little bigger than a deck of cards, and she was careful to punch in the correct numbers. With the old ones you simply dialed the beeper number from your phone and when you heard the tone, you left a message: Please call Suzanne. With these new gadgets you dialed the beeper number from a push-button phone, waited for the beep, then hit the number of the phone you were using and hung up. As soon as Suzanne's number appeared on Billy's beeper screen, he called her back.

"Hi, Suzanne. Did it get in?"

"About an hour ago."

"Did you get a look at it? Is it real good?"

"David says it looks great."

"Are you going to be there in an hour? I'll be over."

"Fine. See you then."

An hour later the security buzzer rang at the front gate of Suzanne's apartment. Motto was as dependable as the sunrise. He bounced into the apartment and flashed a smile that sent the heat up ten degrees. The code name Billy South Philly described Motto to a tee. He had that Italian working-class neighborhood written all over him. His speech. His swagger. The way he leaned in close and touched you when he talked. Even his clothes, which came from the most expensive men's boutique in Philadelphia, still looked like they'd been borrowed from the wardrobe department of *Saturday Night Fever*—white suits with pastel shirts open at the neck to show off gold chains, or black suits with black silk shirts open at the neck to show off gold chains. Even his sweatsuits had a designer label. Billy's philosophy was: As long as you can't show the money, you might as well spend it.

Suzanne went into the kitchen to prepare Billy's favorite drink, a mix of orange juice, strawberries, and bananas whirled together in the blender. He was a fitness nut who jogged six miles a day and worked out at the gym to keep a pasta bulge from collecting on his small, lithe frame. Meanwhile he and David went to the other apartment to examine the coke. David took the ten bags from the safe and spread them on the table. Billy was a produce huckster and liked to have a selection of coke to choose from. As a kid he'd hawked vegetables from the back of a truck, and he picked his cocaine the way he picked the best strawberries or the plumpest tomatoes. He looked at each bag to assess the shine. He rubbed the coke between his fingers, smelled it, and finally took out teaspoon and a little spray bottle of methanol to test for purity. He dipped the spoon deep into one of the bags—you never tested from the top—and sprayed a fine mist of methanol over it. Only pure uncut coke would dissolve completely. The powder instantly turned to liquid. "*Marone* David. You done it again! Very nice stuff." Billy chose two kilo bags and David initialed the bags BSP to indicate they belonged to him. Later Billy would send one of his workers with $120,000 in a gym bag to pay for it and pick it up. He never carried coke or coke money himself. In fact he rarely used cocaine. It gave him gas.

Billy Motto was the Lavin organization's biggest and most unique customer. When Lavin was a kid cutting lawns, Motto was already sniffing glue and drinking wine stolen from the state store. He grew up in the neighborhood immortalized in the film *Rocky,* an area of tiny, tightly packed row houses squeezed into narrow congested streets where kids played a game called halfball with a sawed-off broomstick and rubber ball cut in half. You were considered a success if, before you died, you made enough money to buy a new Cadillac. The best food in the world was macaroni swimming in Mama's homemade gravy (nobody ever called it sauce); the only wine you drank was the color of the pope's easter robe and it came from jugs that Uncle Vito corked in his basement. There wasn't much else but wine and macaroni at Billy's house. His parents were too poor for anything but peasant food, the kind of poor that caused Billy to stuff cardboard in the worn soles of his shoes and paint the bottom black. He told the bill collectors that swarmed around the house that his dad had moved to Florida in the hope they'd leave them alone.

Billy's father was a hustler whose income depended on the season. He sold whatever he could pick up cheap enough for resale—produce the big vendors passed over, suits that "fell off the back of a truck," trees at Christmas, plants at Easter, flowers outside the cemetery on Memorial Day. A womanizer, a deadbeat, and a loudmouth who referred to anybody he didn't like as a "fuckin' crumb," Peter Motto was also a guy with a heart as big as a ten-dollar pizza. He was the fellow you called in the middle of the night to come out and jump-start your car if it broke down. Billy adored him. "He never took me to no ballgames, but he taught me street wisdom. He hugged me and kissed me and loved me to death."

Love wasn't enough to keep Billy from drugs. He took his first shot of speed with three other twelve-year-olds crouched in the weeds of the dead-end street. He was scared to death. One boy held his arm straight out. He turned his head away so he wouldn't see the other boy stick the needle in his vein. Weeeeeeaw. Billy was gone and all he wanted was more of the same. By junior high he was smoking marijuana every night, selling nickel bags of pot on the corner, and showing up for school just often enough to keep from being expelled. He spent most of his time in the boys' room with the school counselor banging on the door yelling, "I know you're in there smoking," while Billy would be sticking a needle in his arm hoping he'd finish before the door opened. He fell further and further behind in class. "After a while it got so embarrassing when the teacher called on me that I just stopped trying. The trouble with a bad reputation is that you gotta live up to it."

Billy never made it to high school. By eighth grade he was breaking into houses and stealing money to support a $100-a-day heroin habit. His dad dragged him from one detox center to the next, sneaking in meatball sandwiches to fatten up his skinny ninety-nine-pound pimply-faced son. Billy would come out, stay clean for a few weeks, and start shooting up all over again. He couldn't bear disappointing his old man, so he'd scrape his arm against a concrete wall to make a scab to hide the needle marks. One night a group of his buddies mixed some goofballs—the lethal combination of heroin and morphine. Billy shot one too many and overdosed. The boys carried him to their car, drove to the nearest hospital, and dumped him on the steps. They dared not take him inside because they could be charged with murder if he died. Had someone not come along and discovered his abandoned body, that's exactly what would have happened.

Luckily, Billy got sent from the hospital to a residential rehabilitation program called the Bridge, located on a farm far from the city streets and the corner drug dealers he so faithfully patronized. He stayed two years. The Bridge's patient teachers taught him how to read and do math. The therapists taught him that men could be sensitive without being wimps and "how to treat a girl as more than a lay." At eighteen he was released and told not to move home because his brother was a drug addict. He found a little room and tried to catch up on the life he'd missed, the normal life of high-school football games and making out in the back seats of cars. "I'd never been further than Atlantic City. I wanted to kiss blonds, buy a convertible, and go to Florida at spring break." What he needed was money. He worked days in a funeral parlor and nights as a hospital orderly. "I used to copy the spelling from others to fill in the charts." He wanted to be a Big Brother because he thought his experience could help a kid, but he wasn't able to fill out the application properly so he never handed it in.

Whenever he had any free time, Billy helped his father at a fruit stand he'd opened in downtown Philadelphia. It was a time when street vendors began to appear on every corner of the commercial district. They did a brisk business with secretaries shopping at lunch or stopping to pick up vegetables for dinner on their way home. Whatever they didn't sell, Billy peddled at cut rate to the nearby coffee shops and luncheonettes. He hustled anything he could lay his hands on, from watermelons to cheap wristwatches to long-stemmed roses. One stand became two and then they added a truck with a regular route. For the first time in his life Billy had money in his pocket. He vowed that whatever he had to do, he was never going to be poor again. When he hit the exacta at the racetrack, he took his $200 winnings, bought a pound of pot, broke it into ounces, and sold it. Soon he had two businesses. One sold produce; the other sold grass. Both flourished. Before long he was buying not one pound of pot but twenty or thirty.

Billy's supplier was a kid named John from West Philadelphia, whose father owned a campus hangout. Whenever there was no marijuana downtown, Billy could depend on getting something from John. One afternoon Billy approached John for twenty pounds. He didn't have that much on hand and took Billy to *his* source. "In the living room is a guy in Levi's and one of those shirts with the little alligator. He's got on boat shoes and white socks. We haggle over the price. I give him six thousand dollars. We shake hands and I leave. I don't know anything except that his name is Larry." A year later, in 1978, John skipped town and Billy needed pot. He remembered Larry and left a note on the apartment door: "Larry, I'd like to get together with you. Maybe have lunch. Call me at this number." A week went by before Lavin returned the call and told Billy that he was no longer selling pot. He only dealt now in cocaine.

In Billy Motto's mind cocaine was a drug for Hollywood movie stars, not the streets of South Philadelphia.

"What's it cost?" Billy asked.

"One hundred a gram," Larry answered.

"Christ! A hundred bucks! People down here don't have that kind of money. I'll never be able to sell it."

"Sure you can. Pretty soon nobody will be buying pot. Everybody will want cocaine and you'll already have a corner on the market. You've got to start to think differently. Coke is so much easier to conceal than pot. Why carry an elephant on your shoulders when you can carry a mouse in your pocket?"

Billy's skepticism was no match for Larry's salesmanship. "I was a street kid. He was a dental student. I wanted to be successful, to be somebody like him. Here's this professional telling me that coke is no big deal. It ain't heroin. It's cool. It's fashionable. You don't deal with dope fiends. You deal with classy people." And Lavin didn't demand cash in advance—as in a department store, you'd shop and pay later. Larry, the wily entrepreneur, was more interested in building his business than worrying about debts. Billy agreed to take four ounces, and months passed before he unloaded all of it. But when he did, he came back for two more. Actually he had an ulterior motive. What Motto really wanted was the name of Lavin's pot connection in Florida. He offered to fly to Miami, buy the pot for Lavin, bring it back, and let Larry sell it to him. Larry agreed to give him the source if he'd make a coke trip to Florida.

Larry handled all the arrangements. Billy had never even made a dinner reservation, let alone flown on a plane or rented a car. Nor had he ever seen $60,000. When Larry handed him the money he was to carry the next day his hands shook.

"Is it gonna be all right, Larry?"

"Yeah, Billy. It's gonna be all right."

That night before the trip, Billy's father advised him to take the money and disappear. "I'll cover for ya, Billy. He'll never find ya." Billy wouldn't hear of it. Lavin trusted him, and something told him that trust would someday be important. The next day Billy boarded the plane with the $60,000 stuffed in his socks and tucked in his underwear. He checked into a Holiday Inn near the University of Miami and made his call as instructed. Soon two Spanish-looking guys appeared. They took the money and the car he'd rented and came back the next day with the cocaine. On the way to the airport, the driver leaned over and told Billy, "Listen, I can sell you coke direct. You don't need Lavin." Billy told him to get lost. He had his own code of loyalty, and cutting out a guy who'd done him a favor wasn't part of it. Billy recounted the incident to Larry on his return. It sealed their business relationship and marked the beginning of a friendship that would make them both very rich.

Lavin taught Motto how to live like a gentleman. Billy was an excellent student. "The first time I went to Vegas I couldn't read the menu in the fancy restaurant. In my neighborhood, nobody knew what Château Lafite Rothschild was. I ordered a buck-and-a-half bottle one night in this Italian place and I tell my dad, like I learned from Larry, 'Ya gotta let it breathe.' Dad reaches for the bottle and says, 'It can breathe in my stomach.' " Soon the maître d's at Philadelphia's nicest restaurants were greeting Billy by his first name and looking forward to visits from the big tipper. Larry showed Billy the difference between flash and class. He told him to trade in his Cadillac. It was a pimpmobile. Buy a Volvo instead. Billy did, a black one with tinted windows. And two vintage Corvettes, one turquoise and one white.

There were some things Billy just didn't understand. "The college boys tried to tell me how I should clean my money. They'd talk about gold and silver and securities. It was way over my head. I'm a kid who can't count two-four-six-eight and I'm tryin' to figure a way to deal with hundreds and thousands. I didn't have no accountants to do this for me. And I couldn't put it in the bank and save the deposit slips." What he could do was protect it in safe-deposit boxes or have his workers buy certificates of deposit for him in their names. Or he could spend it.

After having been a pariah in the neighborhood, growing up as a drug addict, Billy desperately wanted to be liked and accepted, so he bought his way into people's hearts. When a deaf child in the next block needed a special teletype machine to enable her to use the telephone, Billy paid for it. He bought a blind boy a pony and sent a substantial check to a little girl he saw on a telethon pleading for money for a liver transplant. A neighbor's teenage daughter had a pockmarked face from a bad case of adolescent acne. "Take her to the skin doctor," Billy said, "and send me the bill." You did Billy a favor and he wanted to pay you back. He'd send a personal trainer to your house to help you get in shape. Mention that you love Streisand: "You got two tickets complimentary front row when she comes to town." There were times Billy felt remorse for the way he made his money. "I'd go to church and confess I was selling drugs. Somewhere in my heart I knew I was wrong but I couldn't stop."

Billy didn't restrict his expenditures to other people. He spared no expense outfitting himself exactly like the models in one of his favorite magazines, *Gentleman's Quarterly*. The one thing Lavin never taught Motto was how to dress. On his own, Billy developed a taste for $45 cashmere socks and $500 suede pants. "I wanted to be like him, but I never wanted to look like him in those baggy jeans with his ass hanging. He was Ivy League. I was Rock-and-Roll. He was ballgames. I was racetrack. Larry pulled me out of the ghetto. He gave me my dream."

What did Billy give back? Money, for one thing. Good times, for another. He was open and generous and his energy woke up a room. Motto was a human battery charger, and fun to boot. He did a devastating imitation of Al Pacino in *The Godfather*—which was his favorite movie until *Scarface* came along.

Lavin, an avid television fan of shows like *The Gangster Chronicles,* associated Billy with the glamour of organized crime. According to local legend, South Philadelphia's modest row homes, with their plastic flowers in the front windows and their custom wrought-iron railings on the front steps, produced two kinds of celebrities: singers like Fabian and Frankie Avalon and crime bosses like Nicky Scarfo and Angelo Bruno. If you came from South Philly and your name ended in a vowel, it was assumed you knew people in the Mafia or had a cousin who did. Although Billy Motto's name never appeared in any government investigation of organized crime and he never personally exhibited any kind of violent threats or behavior, he was Italian and a drug dealer and, for Lavin, that was close enough. A spate of mob murders swept Philadelphia in the early 1980's and Lavin liked to drop hints that Billy had "connections."

Lavin genuinely liked and respected Billy South Philly and viewed him as something of a protégé. Ackerman, on the other hand, merely tolerated him. Billy felt that David treated him like a fruit-and-produce huckster. "He saw my money but he didn't see me." Yet, when it came time for Billy to expand his business and buy uncut kilos that he could break down himself, it was David who taught him to do it.

Larry, looking to grow, convinced Billy he'd make more money buying uncut kilos rather than ounces, because they'd sell to him at a better price. To sweeten the deal, he promised that David would teach him their formulas for breaking coke. Instead of buying it precut, he would learn how to premix the formulas himself.

What Billy lacked in education he compensated for in zeal. Week after week he'd come to Suzanne's apartment for his business lessons. David would sit with him at the dining-room table with a yellow pad and a calculator. They started with basic fractions. What's an eighth? What's a quarter? Then it was translating pounds into grams. On his pad David wrote the equations and drilled Billy over and over.

"One pound is how many grams?"

"Four-forty-eight, and with the bag, four-fifty-six."

"A half-pound?"

"Two-twenty-four."

"Four ounces?"

"That's . . . lemme see, a quarter pound is 112 grams."

"Right. What's an eighth of an ounce?"

"Four-point-five grams."

"Try it again."

"Shit. Wait a minute. It's 3.5 grams."

When he finally had the fractions committed to memory, David moved to word problems to teach him how to make up the formula and price the product.

"The cheapest ounce we offer is for $1,400. If you're making a $1,400 ounce, how much rock, how much shake, and how much cut would you use?"

Billy chewed on his lip. "Uh-huh. That would be ten grams of rock, five small ones and five big ones; ten grams of shake, and eight grams of cut."

"Now, suppose you've decided you want to make $76 profit per real gram, and you've got somebody who's willing to pay $1,800 for a higher quality than he gets at $1,400. How would you figure the percentage of cut to real coke?"

That was a tough one. David had to go over it again step by step. "You divide $1,800 by $76 per gram, which gives you 23 ⅔ grams of pure coke plus 4 ⅓ grams of cut."

Billy pounded the table in frustration. Division and multiplication. He always mixed them up. Over and over he'd say to David,

"Quiz me again. See if I got it right." He had difficulty with the math, but the drill helped, and so did the calculator. When he'd mastered the numbers, David took him to a wholesale restaurant-supply house in Olde City to buy an electronic digital scale and commercial-size bowls and sifters. Now he was on his own. He'd pick up his one or two kilos when they arrived and take them to a workhouse—usually the dining room of a sidekick who'd been told to send his wife out to visit her mother. Compared with the elaborate breaks of the Lavin organization, Billy, at that time, ran a mom-and-pop operation. He'd lay out his formula sheet and, with two helpers, separate the rock from the shake, add the cut, weigh up the orders, and double-bag them. Every few minutes Billy would pause to make a phone call to a customer to arrange a pickup time. Following Larry's example, he increased his volume by encouraging those under him to increase theirs. "Buy a little, an eighth of a z, break it up and sell it to your Quaalude and pot customers. Tell 'em you'll get 'em more at a good price and good quality."

Lavin's customers rode in BMW's and Porsches to pick up their coke and take it back to snort in their elegant suburban homes or the private bathrooms of their well-decorated offices. Billy's buyers walked over on their way home from the factory or drove used Eldorados. He had a street trade of pimps and junkies and two-bit dealers who cut the coke again and sold it to schoolboys and salesmen for their weekend parties. It was rumored Motto paid the Mafia protection money so they'd allow him to keep his small annex of their gigantic drug trade. Violence may have been foreign to Lavin, but to Motto it was as a fact of life. In South Philly, everybody kept a baseball bat in the trunk of his car—just in case. Billy preferred to think of himself more as a lover than a fighter. His idea of a perfect evening was to sit on the sofa holding hands with his common-law wife, Angela, while they ate popcorn and watched a movie on television. He dealt with brutality by hiring workers who carried switchblades next to their pocket combs and kept brass knuckles in the glove compartments of their cars.

Billy's chief enforcer was Nicky Bongiorno, a sleek, lean-and-mean six-footer with coal-black hair and penetrating eyes whose idea of fairness was chasing a car that tried to cut him off until it stopped at a light, then grabbing the baseball bat he kept in his back seat and breaking all the guy's windows. One night the two of them stood at a bar in a restaurant popular with Philly's young hip crowd when Billy, who could be quite chivalrous, got into an altercation with a fellow who'd insulted his female companion. They exchanged a few four-letter epithets and the guy swung at

Billy. Nicky, without blinking, smashed the glass he was holding against the bar and drove its jagged edge into the assailant's neck.

Billy didn't need to carry weapons as long as he had Nicky's wild temper, his arsenal of pistols, his sawed-off shotgun, and his readiness to use any of them to deliver messages when customers didn't pay their drug debts. One such unfortunate fellow received a visit from Billy and the boys at his apartment. Standing at the door when he opened it were Billy, Nicky, and five henchmen. He didn't have to invite them in. Two carried guns. Nicky held a broken baseball bat in his hand. He had wanted to bring a pistol but Billy told him to leave it home for fear that if he had it, he'd use it.

"We want the money," one of the guys snarled, pointing his gun directly at the debtor's head.

"I ain't got it," he began to blubber. "I can't pay you until I get the money Joe owes me. I got nuthin' here. You can look."

Billy said nothing and quietly nodded to Nicky.

"That's bullshit," Nicky barked, and smashed his bat over the man's head. "We don't want your excuses. We want our money." To make absolutely certain he understood, Nicky filled the kitchen sink with water, and grabbing him by the hair, dunked his head in and out as if he were rinsing dirty laundry. "You've got to the end of the week," he said, and threw the limp body on the floor.

Billy nodded again, the signal it was over, and they all marched out.

The worlds of the dentist and the dropout were very different except for the commodity they shared. Somehow, Motto's drive made more sense than Lavin's. He had begun his journey as an ex-addict with no education and a burning desire to rise out of his poverty. What more natural role model could he find than a bright, successful, well-schooled young professional? What a thrill it was for the junkie whom people once crossed the street to avoid to hobnob with the likes of Larry Lavin, to brag about "my friend, the doctor." Indeed the dentist taught the dropout well. After Billy South Philly met Lucky Larry, he was making a million dollars a year. He might have worried about going to jail, but he never had to worry about money.

11

FBI HEADQUARTERS, PHILADELPHIA
SUMMER, 1983

August 1983 was especially hot and muggy in Philadelphia. On every corner within whistling distance of the Liberty Bell, a water-ice vendor hawked brightly colored grape and raspberry cups to tourists looking for a momentary respite from the oppressive humidity. Chuck Reed watched them from the window of the FBI headquarters, a block from Independence Hall. Only a month had passed since Sid Perry arrived to join him on the Lavin case and the agents were still mired in the tedious stage of amassing the evidence required to get the court's approval for the wiretap on the Lavin organization. On Reed's desk sat a stack of subpoenaed phone-company records. He'd been cross-referencing numbers all morning in an effort to trace a pattern of calls between Larry Lavin and Franny Burns. It might be sticky outside, but Reed needed to get out of the office. He took off his tinted aviator glasses, wiped the perspiration from the bridge of his nose, and decided to take a ride out to King of Prussia to see if there was any action at Burns's Dairy Queen. Perry was out interviewing somebody, so he went alone.

The lunch crowd had already left the Casa Maria restaurant, and the back lot where the agents always parked was deserted when Reed pulled his black Buick into his usual spot. He sat for a while waiting for Burns to come out of the Dairy Queen and head for a phone booth or maybe his car, in which case Reed would tail him to see if he could catch anything interesting. A half-hour passed with no sign of Burns. Reed had developed the patience required for this tedious aspect of FBI work. He'd learned that, sooner or later, watching and waiting pays off. And this day he had to wait only another half-hour until a familiar silver BMW 733 turned off Route 202 and into the Casa Maria lot. It was Dr. Larry Lavin.

Reed ducked under the steering wheel so that his face was not visible as the BMW drove by. Lavin parked about fifty feet away. Before the dentist had even turned off his ignition, Reed jerked his car into gear and drove around the block into a bank lot on the other side of the restaurant where he could see Lavin without being observed himself. It was crucial to Reed that neither Lavin nor Burns suspect they were being followed. Should they spot Reed, they'd be likely to change their established patterns, rendering the evidence so assiduously assembled for the wiretap request completely useless.

Reed only had to wait five minutes before Burns, chauffeured by his seventeen-year-old girlfriend, Sandy Freas, pulled up alongside Lavin's BMW. Franny Burns, dressed in a T-shirt and shorts, hopped out carrying a package wrapped in brown paper. He got into Lavin's car and they talked for about fifteen minutes. When he got out, he was no longer holding the package. Clearly he wasn't presenting a birthday gift. The package was either coke or money. Reed wrote it all down in his notebook: time, date, place, action. He couldn't wait to tell Sid. This was the first time Burns and Lavin had been observed in a face-to-face conversation. The FBI was a step closer to getting its wiretap, and Reed was very satisfied that his urge to get out of the office had paid off so beautifully.

All the FBI's activity during the summer and fall of 1983 was directed toward gathering evidence to convince a federal judge to grant the wiretap they needed to bring indictments against the Lavin ring. Wiretaps are very difficult to obtain. Reed and Perry wanted to prepare their Title III request affidavit with such compelling information that there'd be no way the judge could refuse it. One source of information came from surveillance, sitting for hours in a parked car watching Burns and other suspects who kept getting added to the case. Other information was delivered through the pen register, an electronic device that provided a printed record of all the numbers dialed from a particular phone and the duration of the individual calls. Pen registers had been placed on some eighteen different telephones, including Lavin's, Ackerman's, Weidler's, and the pay phones in the shopping center where Burns's Diary Queen was located. The data obtained were sent to the Bureau for analysis. Printouts showed the agents who was calling whom and also helped flesh out the cast of characters by providing new leads.

When a phone number registered repeatedly, the agents subpoenaed the phone company for background on the subscriber. In whose name was the phone registered? What did the recent toll-call records of the subscriber show? Phone-company records led to other computer checks. Police records. Motor-vehicle records. Property records. Utility bills. Employment records.

Little by little, personal profiles emerged and suspicions were either aroused or confirmed. With the Lavin organization, the warning buzzers went wild. Nearly all the phone numbers led to people who were either unemployed or going to school but living in fancy apartments and driving expensive foreign cars.

When a person began to look particularly interesting, Sid or Chuck might drive out to his home, park nearby, and watch the traffic in and out the front door in hope of finding another piece to add or fit into their expanding case. And when it looked like the person might be helpful as a source, the agents knocked on the front door themselves. In the early stages of an investigation, the FBI paid two kinds of visits to ask for assistance. One type was to people they had no intention of prosecuting—friends, neighbors, and witnesses. On these calls, the agents were polite, professional, and noncoercive. In the Lavin investigation, the agents made almost no visits to peripheral sources after the initial bankruptcy-fraud-investigation stage. Instead, Reed and Perry dropped in on people they had every reason to believe they might ultimately prosecute. Typical was the chat they had with a friend of Larry's named Steve, who surfaced through the pen register.

Steve was the custodian of an abandoned Nike missile base outside Philadelphia which had been used to store nuclear warheads during the Vietnam war. His job drew Sid Perry's attention. Perry had been a missile electrician at a Nike site in Germany during his Army service. He knew the layout of bases like this and suspected the now-empty underground bins would be an ideal place to store cocaine. Maybe Steve would like to tell them about it.

Despite the vast resources of the FBI, frequently the most valuable asset in an investigation is the criminal who decides to further his own cause by cooperating with the government. While there will always be an occasional example of honor among thieves, it's an axiom of policework that most suspects will sacrifice their fellow suspects to save themselves. Flipping suspects, or offering an opportunity to cooperate in exchange for favorable treatment, is a dependable weapon that has become as routine a part of an FBI investigation as the search warrant. It was the real purpose of Reed and Perry's call on Steve. A bit player like Steve might provide information that could save weeks of digging elsewhere. Reed and Perry drove out to the Nike site hoping to convince Steve it was the right time to come to the service of his country.

This FBI pair made an effective team when it came to flipping suspects. Some people respond when confronted with a hard-nosed approach and others bend under the right stroking. Chuck naturally played the heavy and Sid played Mr. Nice, the agent you could trust. It wasn't a planned strategy; it just happened to accommodate their personalities. Reed, gruff and threatening, scared people. He had one basic approach: tough. Perry, relaxed and charming, adjusted his style to the situation and used whatever strategy would get him what he wanted. If force were needed, he was capable of applying it.

One of the toughest decisions for agents in Reed and Perry's situation is choosing the right time to flip a suspect. It's a little like playing poker. Occasionally agents will bluff, intimating they're holding more incriminating evidence than they really have. More often they go in with a full house or at least a pair of aces in their hand. They may flash their badges, chat for a few minutes, then hit the button on a tape recorder and play thirty seconds of a phone call of the suspect placing an order for cocaine. Then they'll turn off the tape, smile, and say, "What would you like to do about this?" If their evidence is weaker, the offer may be more subtle. The trick is not to give away the store, not to bargain to the point where the suspect gains so much by cooperating that he doesn't get the punishment he deserves. The other risk agents carefully avoid is the accusation of entrapment. There's always a defense lawyer lying in wait to undermine the government's case by accusing the FBI of buying cooperation by offering suspects immunity.

Ultimately, how much the government offers depends on how much the investigation will benefit by the information gained. At this stage in the Lavin case, nobody was given anything more than an insinuation that, down the line, there might be an advantage for having helped. That's all Reed and Perry dangled in front of Steve, and for him, it wasn't enough. After introducing themselves and telling him that they already knew he was associated with Lavin, Perry laid out the future scenario.

"In two or three months, Steve, there's going to be an indictment, and you're a part of it. If you decide to cooperate now . . . well, then later on we'll make a decision as to exactly what you'll be indicted for."

Then it was Reed's turn. "That would determine how much of a prison sentence you'll be exposed to. Have you read much about prison, Steve? The showers aren't a lot of fun."

Back to Perry. "If you decide to cooperate, we would let the judge know that you helped, and then, of course, it would be up to him."

It's usually at this point that people either crumble or say, "I'll have to talk to my lawyer." Steve opted for his lawyer and showed the agents the door. They left only mildly disappointed. Whatever happened at interviews like this, the government still held all the winning cards.

August 1983 was a busy month for the burgeoning Lavin case. First there was the FBI wiretap on Lavin's Arizona customer and old school chum Wayne Heinauer, identifying the critical Lavin-Burns connection. Two days later another Heinauer call delivered the man who would ultimately develop as the weak link that broke the organization chain.

Bruce Taylor had joined the Lavin ring a year earlier when he moved to Philadelphia from New England to work as a bodyguard for a drug dealer Larry would ultimately hire to replace David Ackerman as manager of the business. The thirty-year-old Taylor didn't need the intimidation of a dark alley to frighten people. He was scary enough in broad daylight. It wasn't his build so much—at five-foot-ten and 160 pounds he wasn't particularly big or muscular. It was more the way he looked and nervously jerked his arms and legs. Taylor, a black-belt karate expert, gave the impression that it would take very little for him to cross the line from dangerous to crazy. His long thick dark hair fell into a natural part that drew a fine line smack between his bloodshot brown eyes to the back of his head, and a menacing Fu Manchu mustache covered his thin lips. The most important thing in Bruce Taylor's life, next to cocaine, was his motorcycle. He had a tattoo on his forearm of a wheel hugged by a pair of wings emblazoned with the name Harley-Davidson.

Although Lavin tried to dress him up in a suit and tie, Taylor preferred the standard uniform of an outlaw biker—black motorcycle jacket, black pants, and black boots—and he reinforced his tough-guy image by leaving a pistol or a sword from his collection lying somewhere in his home where it could be seen. Taylor hardly seemed the sort Larry Lavin would entrust with his affairs, but the dentist accepted his limitations because Taylor was extremely loyal and, initially, a very hard worker. Given the gun collection and the karate in the biker's background, Lavin's support was typically self-serving. "I thought it best to stay friendly in case Bruce ever got pissed and considered ripping me off."

Even before Larry Lavin's wiretapped call to Phoenix, Chuck Reed and Sid Perry already knew something about Bruce Taylor from information furnished by the Phoenix bureau agents who had observed Taylor delivering cocaine to Wayne Heinauer. In an active investigation like the Lavin case, the FBI will leapfrog from fact to fact, attempting to form a clear picture from a vague sketch. The Phoenix data strengthened their own findings on Taylor drawn from the pen registers on Lavin's and Burns's phones that identified him as a frequent caller. A month earlier, the Philadelphia agents had traced Taylor to an apartment on the fringe of another city neighborhood undergoing renewal, an apartment they knew was important for coke deliveries. Reed had done a couple of surveillances on Taylor and then lost track of him when he abruptly disappeared. Only much later did the FBI learn the reason he had moved elsewhere.

One night on his way home, Taylor drove the wrong way down a one-way street and was stopped by the police, who recognized that he was high, handcuffed him to the squad car door, and searched his car for drugs. They tried to get him to open a portable safe they found in the trunk, but Taylor lied and said he didn't have the combination. It contained two kilos of cocaine, enough to get him in serious trouble. The police settled for the ounce of coke they discovered in a bag in the glove compartment and hauled him to the station while they analyzed the powder. A short time later a lab technician came into the area where Taylor was being held and dangled the bag of cocaine in front of his face. "This is pretty pure stuff," he said. Bruce nodded. "Why don't you just keep it," he offered. The technician disappeared with the coke and shortly afterward Taylor was released without being charged. He assumed the technician had filed a false report on his lab test and pocketed the bag of blow. Smart enough not to stick around and strain his luck, Taylor moved out of town, rented a house using the alias Bruce Gorman, and installed a phone under a friend's name.

It would have taken the FBI weeks to trace him all over again through the pen registers, so Reed and Perry were particularly pleased when Taylor surfaced in a phone call to Heinauer on August 22.

"Hello, Wayne. How ya doin'?"

"Good, Bruce. What's happening?"

"Not too much. Hey, I'm gonna show tonight."

"Okay. Very good."

"Hey. I looked at them. They look fuckin gorgeous." Bruce had been taught by Lavin never to mention the word "cocaine" on the telephone. Wayne understood that he was referring to the kilos he'd be bringing, and if they were gorgeous, that meant they were full of rocks.

"Yeah. Why don't you double it, then. If they're really good-looking, I can do something with them here."

"Okay, now, this is the story. I'm bringing an old man with me."
Taylor had just been informed by Franny Burns, who was in the
midst of buying Lavin's business, that his father-in-law would be
making deliveries in the future and Wayne would be buying coke
from Burns instead of Lavin. "I think they're gonna take the run
away from me and give it to this old guy. If he gets caught, he's too
old to go to court. He might even die before the court date can
come up. So I'll see you tonight, my friend."

"Right. Do you want me to get you a room and stuff like that?"

"No, just see if you can book me a flight out around midnight."

"All righty. What about for the old guy?"

"Ah, fuck him. He might want to rest, being an old buzzard."

"Okeydoke."

"Thanks a lot, my brother. See you sometime tonight."

When Bruce Taylor and the old man, Harvey "Pop" Perry,
landed at the Phoenix airport, the FBI was waiting. They tailed the
pair to Heinauer's, waited while they transacted their business, and
followed them back to the airport, where one of the agents stood
behind Taylor in the ticket line in order to eavesdrop on the flight
information, which he called back to Philadelphia.

The following morning, there was a welcoming committee at the
airport, composed of Sid Perry, Chuck Reed, and five other agents,
but when the Eastern flight arrived, Taylor and Franny's father-in-
law weren't on board. Fortunately, the Phoenix agent had overheard the alias Taylor was using, and a quick airline-computer
check revealed they'd changed planes in St. Louis and would be
flying in on Piedmont after lunch. As Taylor and Pop walked off
the plane there was an agent sitting in the terminal waiting area,
his face hidden by a newspaper. He had a tiny microphone pinned
to his lapel, an earpiece in his ear, and the body of a walkie-talkie
strapped to his waist under his jacket.

"Subjects coming off the plane. Subject number one. White
male with dark hair wearing black pants, black jacket, and carrying
a black shoulder bag. Subject number two. Older white male.
Beige pants and a short-sleeved shirt. Heading toward security
checkpoint."

Seated in a phone booth near the security checkpoint was Sid
Perry, outfitted with another walkie-talkie. He picked the pair up
as they passed in front of him. "Subjects observed heading across
Concourse D." Perry left the phone booth and, walking about
twenty-five yards behind them, continued to report their movements to the agents stationed at the various exits. "Subject One
turning off to baggage-claim area. Subject Two heading toward

parking garage. I'll follow Subject One." Perry got on the escalator several steps beyond Taylor, tailing him through the claim area to the taxi stand out front. "Subject One boarding Yellow Cab number 37816. Departing now." Another agent in an unmarked car parked by the only road leading out of the airport turned on his engine, pulled into the traffic far enough behind the cab not to look suspicious, and followed Taylor to his new residence, an unpretentious postwar rancher in a lower-middle-class suburb called Newtown Square about forty-five minutes from downtown Philadelphia. The lost Bruce Taylor had been found.

Meanwhile, another group of agents picked up Pop, who'd apparently forgotten where he'd parked his car and meandered from one parking garage to the next until he finally stumbled on his faded green 1973 Olds and climbed in. The FBI wrote down his tag number but didn't waste the time following him, since they could get all the information they needed from a motor-vehicle check. Chuck Reed turned to Sid Perry and, with a wicked little grin, chortled, "These guys are dead."

Both Taylor and Pop could have been arrested on the spot, but that would have been a fatal mistake. It was much too early for the FBI to tip its hand. These guys were more valuable out on the street where they could lead Lavin into deeper trouble.

12

MIAMI, FLORIDA
SPRING, 1983

David Ackerman considered himself a seasoned traveler. Having stayed in some of the world's best hotels and dined in its four-star restaurants, he was not easily impressed. When he arrived in Miami Beach for a business meeting with his Cuban suppliers, however, and stepped into the marble entrance of the Governor's Suite atop the Fontainebleau Hilton, its $1,500-a-day grandeur left him speechless. A marble staircase with brass rails rose majestically to an upper floor with four bedrooms, including a master suite that opened onto a marble bath with a step-down Jacuzzi spouting water from gold faucets shaped like swans. The penthouse was wrapped by a balcony overlooking the ocean and the palm-shaded beach sixteen floors below. Elegantly decorated with white Italian Provincial furniture trimmed in gold, the suite included a baby-grand piano, a pool table, and a full kitchen. Adjacent to the dining room was a powder-blue ballroom dominated by a crystal chandelier that glittered in the bright Florida sun. The Latins were every bit as good as the Americans at flaunting their cocaine dollars.

In the spring of 1981, Larry Lavin decided that at $58,000 a kilo, he was paying too much for cocaine and he sent David to Miami to negotiate a better price with Pepe and Paco, their current suppliers. Pepe, a thin and slight copper-colored man, was fun-loving and hot-tempered, and kept a gun tucked in the back of his pants. He was a refugee who'd spent two days on a raft escaping Castro's Cuba, and was quick to admit that the Mercedes, the expensive suits, and the custom-built home he'd bought with profits from his prosperous drug business more than compensated for whatever hardships he'd endured at sea. Pepe managed the business end of the operation, while Paco, a heavy, big-boned Colombian with a menacing scar on his face, served as chief of security, supervising a troop of guards armed with an arsenal of machine guns.

David had developed an excellent working relationship with the Cubans and on one buying trip to Florida when he brought Suzanne along, he stayed at Pepe's home. Around midnight, Pepe, who spoke reasonably good English with a singsong Spanish inflection, announced that he was going out to do the deal.

"David, I am leaving you in the house with my wife and children. Here, there can always be trouble. If something happens, do you know how to use this?" From under the bed he pulled a machine gun, which David eyed as if it were a cobra he'd rather die than touch. "It's easy. You just spray it in the air like so." Pepe gave David precise instructions on how to load a clip of ammunition. David nodded, pretending to pay attention while, in truth, he was so frightened he didn't absorb a word.

While Pepe was off negotiating, David and Suzanne stayed awake doing lines of coke. By dawn, they were wired. Suddenly a noise outside the house startled them. Footsteps padding in the dewy grass. A smothered cough. David's face turned white.

"Go see what it is," Suzanne hissed.

David tiptoed down the stairs, as a picture of himself lying on the floor riddled with bullets played in his imagination. "My God. How did I ever get into this? I'm not a killer. I'm a dental student. I never touched a gun in my life. I don't even like war movies. My mother will die when she sees the headlines: 'Dentist Murdered in Miami Drug Deal.' "

Evaporating, with each step he took downstairs, was the power and invincibility he'd felt the day before trading with the Cubans. He reached the first floor and inched past the sofa and up to the side of the window. His heart racing, he flattened his body against the wall and moved the curtain just enough to see a gardener dragging the hose across the front lawn as he prepared to water the flowerbeds.

The memory of that visit was far from David's mind as he sat with the Latins in the Fontainebleau penthouse. David could just as well have closed the deal in a parking lot, but Pepe liked doing business in style. What the Lavin organization proposed was cutting out their middleman, a fellow named René, and dealing directly with Paco and Pepe. In a mixture of high-school Spanish and English, David explained that he didn't trust René, whom he suspected of shorting his orders, nor did he like the way René operated. He took too many unnecessary chances David felt.

Pepe had a simple solution. If René was cheating the customers, he deserved to die.

David suggested he'd be satisfied is he could simply bypass René and do business directly with his bosses at a lower price. The deal they finally cut in the opulent penthouse suite was a price reduction of $2,000 per kilo if David would increase his order from the present twenty keys a month to fifty, a savings of $100,000 on the order. That meant the Lavin ring would have to raise a whopping $2.5 million in a thirty-day period. The Latins operated strictly COD. Fronting coke may have been a gentlemanly enterprise in Philadelphia but it wasn't in the cutthroat drug scene in Miami.

It had taken Larry Lavin and his cohorts several years to work their way from buying from Miami street dealers to buying from big Latin wholesalers like Paco and Pepe, who in turn bought their cocaine directly from the Colombians. At first, Larry made his wholesale buys over the phone. After a while, he'd send a buyer to shop for the best coke. He insisted on high rock content and high shine. Price was a consideration but quality was always more important. Larry liked to boast to his customers, "You can't get better coke anywhere." By 1980 Willie Harcourt, the young ex-restaurant manager, was Lavin's primary shopper, traveling to Florida three to five times a month. He had no steady reliable source and cultivated a number of different dealers, some American and some Cuban.

Larry and David received frequent calls from Florida. "C'mon down. The weather's sunny," meant that good shiny coke was available. Or Larry and David would call from Philadelphia. "How's the weather? I'd like to come down for five days," meant that five kilos were needed. When Willie Harcourt arrived in Florida he'd work the street to see what was around, or contact recommended brokers who would take him to three or four places to examine product. He was always worried about being caught by the cops or robbed by the cocaine cowboys, and his fears were increased by the working conditions. It wasn't unusual for him to be frisked at the door of a supplier's or to be required to test the coke at gunpoint.

In this oppressive setting, Willie had to be absolutely certain he was purchasing coke untainted by cutting agents. Initially he carried a "hotbox," an electrical device about twelve inches long and five inches high with a metal surface and a temperature dial. If he liked the looks of the coke, he plugged the box into a wall. Reaching deep into the bag where the cut was most likely to be, he'd scoop out one-fourth teaspoon of coke and put it between two small glass slides like a lab technician smearing a blood sample. If the sample melted at 75 to 100 degrees, the batch was considered poor quality, beneath Lavin's standards. Good, uncut coke melted into a clear and clean liquid at 150 degrees. If it became smoky or black or if it melted at two different points, it had been cut and he'd pass.

Another purity test involved immersing the powder in methanol, a poisonous alcohol that dissolves cocaine. As Lavin's shoppers became more knowledgeable, they preferred to run this test with Clorox because it was more accessible than methanol. Willie Harcourt would finely chop the coke sample with a razor blade, being careful not to contaminate the cocaine with body oils on his fingertips. He'd fill a tall clear glass with Clorox and sprinkle a pinch of the chopped coke on the top. If pure, the cocaine would spread as it hit the surface, then float for ten or fifteen seconds before sinking slowly in a milky white trail, dissolving before reaching the bottom. Cutting agents will cause different reactions. Quinine stays on top; sugar cuts trail down quickly and don't dissolve completely; amphetamines leave little pebbles in the glass.

Clorox was the perfect test for someone with Lavin's medical training. When Franny Burns came along, he had no patience with anything this clinical. He imitated the Hispanics by rubbing the coke into the web of skin between the thumb and forefinger on his left hand. If it was pure, his body oil would absorb it like expensive vanishing cream. If any grit remained on his skin, he knew the coke had been cut.

Testing methods were just one of the things that changed as Lavin's organization blossomed. As the quantities of coke and money traveling back and forth increased, it became necessary to find more sophisticated means of transporting them. Before 1981, runners flew back and forth hiding cash and drugs in their clothing and their baggage. New mules were lectured on how to pack their carry-on bags by layering packages of cash under a tennis racket, a blow drier, sneakers, shoes, magazines, and books—typical vacation gear likely to look perfectly normal to the guard studying the screen of the airport X-ray machine. Boots were especially popular for packing because of the amount of storage they provided. A kilo bag of cocaine is about the same size as a two-pound bag of carrots, and one pair of boots could easily conceal a couple of kilos. Black garment bags were another excellent hiding place because all the clothing pockets could be filled with coke or cash and the bag itself lent the mule the aura of a traveling businessman.

Larry had a tendency to be late getting money to his mules before their journey south, and on one summer trip Willie Harcourt had no time to properly pack the last $150,000. He simply stuck the money in every pocket of his pants and jacket and dashed for the plane. It was hot and sticky when he arrived in Miami. Figuring he'd look suspicious wearing a jacket on such a muggy day, he went into the men's room, removed his coat, and put all the cash in his bag—all but the wads of fifty-dollar bills in his rear pockets, which he'd forgotten about. He couldn't understand why people were whispering about him as he walked through the airport until he heard a little boy tell his mother, "Look at all the money sticking out of that man's pockets."

By the spring of 1981 when David Ackerman negotiated his fifty-kilo-a-month price discount, the organization had already switched from flying to Florida to driving. In the beginning, Willie rented cars on an as-needed basis. Then he decided he wanted his own vehicle and one afternoon took $15,000 from the company safe, walked into an automobile agency, and bought a brown Buick Electra off the showroom floor as casually as if he were purchasing a shirt. By now the organization had four regular drivers plowing the route between Philadelphia and Miami several times each month with coke or money in locked suitcases in the trunk. Normally the cars traveled in pairs, one behind the other, linked by radio communication so that in case of an emergency like an accident or breakdown the precious cargo could be transferred to the second car and sent safely on its way. Obviously it was not a wise idea to tow a damaged car to a repair shop with maybe a million dollars in cash or huge quantities of cocaine sitting in the trunk. Pepe, the expert in such matters, suggested they ought to have a contingency plan. If cops ever pulled over the first car, the jam car, as he called it, should be trained to distract the law by speeding past at 100 mph or jamming into the police car as if by accident. David nixed the idea. It was a bit too TV cops-and-robbers for his taste.

Eventually the teams of drivers would be replaced by a down-on-his-luck attorney who'd moved to Florida and opened a fruit-juice-extract company which wasn't setting the world on fire. Desperate for cash to pay his debts, he began ferrying coke and found himself nauseated by the telltale smell seeping from the trunk. Cocaine in large quantities has an odor similar to ether. He came up with the ingenious idea of packing the plastic bags of coke in airtight number-ten metal cans, which conveniently accommodated exactly one kilo of cocaine. He bought a special machine to seal the lids and packed the odorless cans six to a carton the way his juice extract was shipped. He always had a few cartons of real extract in his trunk along with the cases of coke, and business cards in his pocket in case authorities stopped him for any reason. On one winter run he got stuck in a snowdrift and required police assistance to tow him out, but there was no reason to suspect he was anything but a legitimate businessman with a trunk full of orange extract from the Sunshine State.

The organization's new fifty-kilo-per-month arrangement was inaugurated in May 1981. By the end of that month they'd made two buys of eight kilos each and one of sixteen, which left them eighteen kilos short of their goal. By pressuring all their regular buyers for advance orders and emptying the safes in every apartment, David managed to pull together enough money to complete the commitment. Somebody suggested taking a picture of the cash mountain to commemorate the landmark occasion of their having amassed almost one million dollars, but David, paranoid as always about leaving evidence, wouldn't allow it.

Willie Harcourt reached Florida on May 31, the money bundled in suitcases, and spent all day selecting his coke. He intended to drive back with eighteen kilos of the sixty that Paco and Pepe had available. Returning to his motel room—only David got the Fountainebleau treatment—he put on a pair of rubber gloves as a precaution against leaving fingerprints and carefully repacked his large Samsonite suitcases. He slipped each kilo plastic bag of coke inside a larger plastic bag filled with baking soda to absorb the smell and sealed the package with masking tape. Placing a folded bath towel between the layers of bags to keep them from sliding around, he closed the suitcases and laid them in the trunk of his car along with the usual camouflage tennis rackets and scuba gear. Anxious to return home as soon as possible, he left immediately and drove nonstop. Toward dusk the next day, he alerted David via walkie-talkie that he was on the New Jersey Turnpike and would be arriving shortly in Philadelphia.

The eighteen-kilo shipment was the largest single delivery the organization had ever received and David decided it called for unusual security measures. Instead of working as they normally did at one of the factory apartments, he concluded they'd be safer going somewhere they'd never been before, and arranged through Paul Mikuta to conduct the break at a town house in suburban Philadelphia. When Harcourt's car pulled up in front of the Olde City apartment headquarters, David, with his walkie-talkie, was waiting in a car with Mikuta, while Suzanne and Christine, her assistant, sat parked in a car behind them.

"Willie, it's David. Can you hear me? Over."

"Shoot."

"This is the plan. The girls will follow us. You wait a few minutes and I'll give you instructions by radio how to get to the rendezvous spot. I don't want a caravan with the cocaine car. It's too dangerous."

"What kind of stupid fucking nonsense is this? I've been driving for twenty-six hours and I'm beat. I've gotta take a nap before we break."

"There's no time for that. Just keep your set on and do what I tell you."

The first two cars headed out the Schuylkill Expressway, past Fairmount Park toward the Main Line. Suddenly David's car veered off the exit and made a U-turn back toward Philadelphia. Thoroughly confused, Suzanne followed and wound up in front of her apartment, exactly where they'd started. It seemed David had lost radio contact with Willie because the walkie-talkies weren't functioning properly, and his elaborate plan had to be scuttled. Eventually Willie returned to the apartment and the three cars drove together to a fancy suburban town-house development of cluster units scattered on several acres of beautifully landscaped grounds.

The azaleas were still in bloom but the group was far too irritated to notice. David was annoyed they'd wasted so much time with the damn walkie-talkies. Willie was exhausted. Suzanne felt sick; her head throbbed and her body ached. Christine was nervous. She'd never been to a break before but looked forward to snorting free coke and earning the $100 an hour David had promised to pay her. Paul was simply being irascible. He opened the front door with his borrowed key, helped bring in the suitcases and the drug paraphernalia, and impatiently urged Willie to unpack the coke.

Willie spread the eighteen bags on the sofa in the upstairs den and David divided them according to customer preference. He chose Billy Motto's coke first and then set aside the whitest of the lot for the airline pilot who liked his coke very white because he added a lot of cut and the whiter the coke, the less the cut showed. Willie took a bag for his private customers and Paul selected what he wanted for himself and said good-bye. As soon as Mikuta left, the break began. The bedroom was really too small for the four of them to work and the cramped space only exacerbated everybody's frayed tempers. Suzanne and Christine unpacked the gear and arranged it as best they could—the digital scale on the coffee table; the bowls, sifters, and plastic bags on top of the dresser with the cut alongside them. The bag with I drawn on it in black marker contained inositol. The other, marked E, which stood for "enhancer," was filled with a cutting agent they'd concocted themselves when a dental-school customer of Larry's repaid a debt by supplying a drum of lidocaine, an anesthetic compound that gives off a slight numbing sensation similar to coke. By mixing one part lidocaine with three parts inositol, they'd created a superior custom cut.

With everything laid out, Suzanne sat on the floor and began to sift the coke. She kept stopping to wipe the perspiration from her forehead. Something was definitely wrong with her.

"David, I'm feeling hot. I bet I have a fever."

"It's just the coke, Suzanne. You know coke raises your body temperature."

"No, this is different. Feel my forehead."

Christine gave her an understanding look. "I'm hot too, Suzanne. Is it always this warm? I guess I shouldn't have worn a turtleneck."

"Oh, Christine, that's my fault. Why didn't I warn you? And look at me in this black jumpsuit. I'm covered with shake. I should know better than to wear black to a break. This stuff gets all over everything, even inside your ears."

"This is great," David moaned. "Now I have to listen to the girls discuss what kind of clothes they should wear to the break. 'What do you think, Christine, the white pants with the yellow shirt or my gold lamé?' Will you cut the crap and tell me what the shake weighs." He sat next to Suzanne, his computer in his hand figuring the percentages for the orders to be filled. She was as good as useless and Willie was being a royal pain in the ass, every ten minutes threatening to leave:

"I'm telling you, David, I'm shot. Beat. Dead. You get it? Over twenty-six hours of driving. I'm not a goddamn animal. I want a shower and I wanna sleep."

"Let Willie go, David," Suzanne begged. "Look at him."

"This is none of your goddamn business, Suzanne. Just stay out of it. I'm running this, and we need Willie."

"Yeah, well, you don't need Suzanne," Willie retorted. "She's gonna pass out and spill the coke all over the floor. Then you'll get what you deserve."

Christine, who had no idea what she was supposed to be doing, interrupted them. "Could you two stop fighting and show me how much inositol goes in this shake? How do I mix it together?"

Soon they were all covered with cocaine dust. It was in their eyes, on their clothes, seeping into their pores, bombarding their brains with every breath. Suzanne was sorry she hadn't brought the surgical masks the boys sometimes wore. She was light-headed to begin with, and now she was buzzed besides. If only David weren't being such a slave driver. If only he'd let her and Willie take a little nap. Even the coke wasn't helping Willie stay awake. Why didn't David just let him leave? Their shouting only made her head pound more. It was getting so hard to breathe. So hot. She unzipped her jumpsuit. A little air. Just . . . a . . . little . . . air.

"Oh, my God, Suzanne," Christine screamed. "She's passed out." David panicked. Suzanne's face was flushed and her forehead burned under his touch. He carried her to the other bedroom, found a bottle of alcohol, and poured it over her body, rubbing frantically. She must have had a 104 temperature. "Christine, turn the air conditioning on. Maybe that will cool her down." In her agitation, Christine turned on the heat by mistake and the bedroom became a steambath. "You'll kill her, you idiot. What the hell is wrong with you?"

Christine began to cry. Embarrassed and hurt, she considered taking off with Willie, but her loyalty to her girlfriend and her desire to earn $100 an hour deterred her. Eventually Suzanne's fever broke and she fell asleep. At that point Willie went home to bed, leaving Christine and David alone to break the remaining kilos. They worked through the night and into the next morning, when they drove home to Olde City with all orders neatly filled in small bags. Christine was $1,200 richer. David, on the other hand, was faced with an unexpected problem.

He'd met the challenge of buying fifty kilos in one month, despite Larry's skepticism that he'd be able to do it. But he'd made the mistake of building the volume without increasing the number of customers. When June came along, nobody needed coke because they'd overbought in May, and the month passed with no trips to Florida and no breaks. By July supplies were low again and David set out to repeat another fifty kilos. He had difficulty raising the money and by the last week in the month it looked as if he'd be unable to meet the deadline. But somehow he managed to scrape up $100,000 for the last two kilos and, with great relief, rushed it to Miami on July 31. Paco and Pepe delivered the coke but refused the rebate, claiming David had misunderstood them. Their discount offer stood only as long as he did fifty kilos *every* month, not simply on any month he managed to buy that much. Never mind that he'd be spending over two million dollars between May and July. They insisted on fifty kilos per month or the deal was off. David hung up the phone in a fury. Feeling like he'd been knocked down by a sucker punch, he locked himself in his apartment and applied free-base to his psychic wounds.

David Ackerman's 50 kilo milestone and subsequent disappointment coincided with a far happier event for Ken Weidler and Larry Lavin—their graduation from the University of Pennsylvania Dental School. In May 1981 Dean Walter Cohen presented their diplomas with a great deal of personal frustration. He'd had strong reservations about granting medical degrees to two suspected drug dealers and voiced them. He'd been told that as long as the suspected students met their academic requirements, their moral character was not a graduation issue. Since the police had never produced any concrete evidence that the boys had committed a crime, Cohen's hands were tied. The early 80s were a confusing time on college campuses. Universities, like Penn, frightened of being slapped with lawsuits for denying civil liberties, scrupulously followed the letter of the law, and neither Lavin nor Weidler had been charged with breaking it. While Cohen resented being forced to graduate a couple of *suspected* drug dealers, he was, at the same time, relieved he would no longer have to worry about the scandal that would erupt if the ring had been revealed while the two were still enrolled. Ken and Larry had no idea what was going through the dean's mind as he shook their hands and presented their diplomas. Despite heated debate among the top brass at the dental school, Cohen had followed orders and sent the boys off into the world with the best possible criminal cover: professional credentials.

Ken went to work almost immediately. He'd learned about a small dental practice for sale in South Philadelphia from a dental-lab owner acquainted with his father. His parents gave him the down payment as a gift. Having no knowledge of his independent income, they assumed he needed the money and didn't have the credit to borrow it. He loved going to the office and found dentistry as fulfilling as he'd anticipated, although not as financially rewarding. The practice was small, just three days a week from noon until seven. The $15,000 or so per year he earned certainly wasn't enough to keep him in the style to which he'd become accustomed. He continued to withdraw several thousand a month from his equity account at the drug business, and even more for special purchases like an $18,000 Saab turbo and the $105,000 down payment on a splendid home with a pool and beautiful grounds in the old-money, low-key suburban neighborhood of Villanova.

The house was for his wife and the baby they were expecting. Ken had married his college sweetheart the August after graduation. Her parents gave the wedding at a hotel in North Jersey and it was a lovely affair except for some annoying details. David Ackerman, the best man, was so coked out he never made it to the church and the minister conducted the ceremony with a substitute in his place. When David finally arrived at the reception, he was forgiven only because he brought enough coke to get all of Ken's friends so high between cocktails and dinner that they never ate a thing. Ken's wife's parents couldn't understand why so many of the guests ignored the beautiful buffet they'd ordered. The cocktail-hour chitchat resounded with boardroom repartee. Mark Stewart prattled about a record contract he'd just signed, big things on the horizon for Larmark, perhaps expansion into TV. Larry Lavin expounded on tax write-offs and capital gains. A dental-school classmate and customer listening to them recalled feeling like a thirteen-year-old at a family dinner, awed by the conversation of rich uncles conversing in the obtuse language of big business. He was immensely impressed and fleetingly thought: I'll be damned. They're going to get away with this.

Lavin, in fact, had temporarily abandoned dentistry for the razzle-dazzle world of stocks and bonds. After graduation, he felt more secure about his financial skills than his dental ones. When he couldn't immediately find a practice that suited him, he decided to buy one of the 505 seats on the Philadelphia Stock Exchange. It cost $65,000 and was paid for with a check issued by Bank Leumi from the Mark Stewart Real Estate Escrow Account. The clerk at the Exchange who handled the application remembers Lavin "because he had beautiful teeth and a wonderful style." Lavin taught himself what he needed to learn for SEC approval as a broker/dealer by watching videotapes at home. He then flew to Washington and passed the qualifying test. In his mind he figured the Exchange seat would be, at best, a career change and, at worst, an investment he could resell. After about two months on the floor, trading as Lavin Options Inc., he opted for dentistry and transferred his trading power to a friend on the floor who, over the next two years, lost close to $60,000 of Larry's money. Lavin sold the seat in early 1984 for $125,000, ostensibly breaking even on his flier as a trader. More important than the money, the seat had served as another cover to explain the young Lavin's luxurious life-style to his Society Hill neighbors.

The major event in the lives of the cocaine trio that fall of 1981 was the burning of the Martin Luther King Arena, which they treated as just another of Mark Stewart's stupid mistakes. Initially they'd been swept up in Stewart's grandiose plan to revitalize a decaying sports arena, currently being used as a warehouse for a lumber company. The building stood about fifteen blocks from the University of Pennsylvania in a run-down, mostly black residential section of West Philadelphia. Back in the forties and fifties the Arena had been the only indoor professional sports palace in the city, hosting boxing and wrestling matches and, in particular, drawing huge crowds for roller derbies. It was eclipsed in 1966 by the

Spectrum, a much bigger, splashier, ultramodern sports and entertainment center built at the other end of town with plenty of space for parking. Stewart envisioned restoring the Arena to its former glory, renaming it for Martin Luther King, and targeting its attractions to the black marketplace. He figured he could stage sports and music events at a fraction of what it cost downtown at the Spectrum by staffing the place with nonunion labor. He convinced Lavin that the Arena would not only make money but also be another source for laundering, because Lavin and his drug partners could all go on the payroll.

Stewart bought the Arena for $200,000 and poured another $300,000 into refurbishing the plumbing, the electrical system, seats, and decor. He was able to obtain a mortgage by using as collateral the certificates of deposit that he'd purchased with the $500,000 that Larry had given him when they formed their Larmark Corporation. Larry personally invested thousands more to cover additional remodeling expenses. As it turned out, Stewart was accurate about his ability to attract events, but the events never attracted the crowds to support them. He even acquired a minor-league basketball team, the Philadelphia Kings, and expected fans to ignore the lack of parking and flock to watch the Kings play at the Arena while the first-rate Philadelphia 76ers weren't even selling out at the Spectrum. The boxing matches Stewart booked through another of his companies, Impact Promotions, fared better than the basketball team but the gate receipts weren't nearly enough to cover expenses. Stewart kept turning to Larry for cash to meet payroll. Lavin would dip into his drug profits and messenger over up to $10,000 at a time. So persuasive was Stewart that Lavin would walk into his office yelling that he was through supporting "this fool enterprise" and wind up emptying his pockets all over again.

"Air conditioning. The place needs air conditioning." That was Stewart's response to Lavin's complaint that the King Arena was a bottomless pit. Dealing as he did in the fast profits of cocaine, Lavin did not have the patience to wait out the two years Stewart now estimated it would take to turn the business around. Tired of Stewart's excuses, he began to pressure him to return some of his money by getting the CD's released from the bank. That was possible only if Stewart could satisfy the loans they covered, and the only way Stewart could get his hands on such a sizable amount of cash was through some kind of miracle. Or through an insurance claim on the $1.4-million-dollar policy he'd taken out on the King Arena. The more Lavin pushed for his money, the more desperate Stewart became.

It's unclear who actually hatched the plan to burn down the King Arena. Stewart, clutching for a lifeline to pull him out of the financial mire threatening to drown him, swears that Larry suggested the torching at a meeting, perhaps as a joke. Ackerman says he heard about the plan right before it occurred, from either Larry or Mark, and told Ken Weidler to watch the TV news the night it was to happen. Afterward Suzanne overheard Larry and David discussing the fire. Larry said he was angry with Stewart for burning the Arena and Suzanne's eyes widened.

"That's arson, isn't it?" she asked incredulously.

Larry laughed. "Well, you certainly don't mince words, Suzanne." Then he abruptly said, "I don't want to talk about it anymore." The subject was closed. No one could anticipate how badly the ill-conceived arson would eventually burn all of them.

After the attempted arson that autumn, David began to slip further from reality, locked away for days at a time in his apartment with his free-base pipe and his hallucinations. When he emerged, it was often to go on a wild spending spree. Whatever David craved, he craved in excess, whether it was coke, women, or beautiful things. His safe was crammed with money and he'd reached a point where grabbing a pack of thousands of dollars had no more significance than reaching for a Kleenex.

One chilly afternoon when a cold wind hinted at the winter to come, he and Suzanne went out to pick up her new $24,000 BMW 528. She'd only worn a light jacket that day and he decided on the spur of the moment that she needed a fur coat. When they couldn't choose between a mink and a fox, he bought both coats and a muskrat jacket besides. In just a few hours he spent $12,500— $8,000 for a Black diamond mink coat and $500 for a hat to match, $2,000 for a muskrat jacket, and another $2,000 for the fox coat.

David loved to take Suzanne shopping and drape her lithe, long-legged body in clothes he selected. His personal style ran toward conservative elegance, and when they walked into an exclusive restaurant, he wanted his girlfriend dressed to complement his expensive attire. He saw to it that alongside the jumpsuits she favored, her closet included tailored wool suits and Albert Nipon dresses. He filled her jewelry box with a $1,200 gold-and-tourmaline necklace, a $1,000 strand of cultured pearls, and a $7,000 Rolex watch. He bought three more of the Rolexes, one for his mother, one for his father, and one for himself.

On a stroll one winter afternoon with Suzanne, David wandered into a craft gallery and walked out the owner of a $7,000 desk. The gallery manager remembers the couple with perfect clarity: Suzanne wore a mink coat and matching hat and handled David with an amused tolerance. She was very bright and outspoken and wanted to know what made the desk worth $7,000 and how could a young American artist command this kind of price? David, while not an educated collector, said he liked buying beautiful things. The desk certainly met that criterion. It was hand-carved with curved legs in an art-nouveau design. "It was apparent to me," the gallery director recalled, "that the purchaser had an eye for quality, was open to learning more about the fine-crafts movement, and had the potential to become a serious customer. He told me he was a dentist, but had an interest in a record company, which explained why he was paying cash. He commissioned a chair to go with the desk for another $2,500 and, when negotiating the terms, behaved like a sensible businessman, understanding what was a fair profit for the gallery without trying to squeeze too much. He was a bit arrogant perhaps, but on the whole quite likable."

David could also be overly possessive. He and Suzanne had an argument after Labor Day about an affair he suspected she was having. Included in his general paranoia was a specific obsession that she was cheating on him. It wasn't the sex itself that bothered him. The threesomes with Christine had shown him Suzanne had a lively, free-wheeling libido. What disturbed David was the possible humiliation of being the victim rather than the perpetrator. Suzanne wanted to go away by herself to put a little distance between herself and David's increasingly threatening irrationality.

"I'll take you away," David insisted.

"Let me go alone. I need to be by myself," Suzanne begged.

He persisted; she relented and off they went to Hawaii, flying first class and staying in first class hotels—the Hyatt Regency in Maui, the Kahala Hilton on Oahu, and the Moana Keya on Hawaii.

Whenever David and Suzanne traveled, all the bills were paid in cash and the reservations and tickets were in Suzanne's name. David carefully erased any trail he thought the IRS might follow. When Suzanne questioned him about what might happen if Uncle Sam pursued her, David assured her that was highly unlikely. "If anybody's getting audited, it will be me they investigate. Don't worry, Suzanne, if anything happens to you, I'll be here to take care of you." And because she loved him and trusted him, she believed him.

But David could no longer be trusted for anything. He'd break appointments or simply not show up. He'd refuse to answer the phone or the door, infuriating people with his unpredictability. Customers would call and leave messages, workers would telephone asking for instructions, and he'd be off in a cocaine daze. There were times he'd promise himself he was finished. No more coke. He'd be perfectly lucid, and except for his aggressive behavior, almost normal. He became adept at acting the old David for his father. And when he was too high to pretend, he'd call and postpone their dinner dates by saying he had a business appointment, which his father regarded as a perfectly legitimate excuse. After all, David, he thought, was a record mogul and sports promoter. David would disappear for days on a coke or free-basing streak, inhaling as much as an ounce a day of cocaine and going as long as a week without sleep.

He'd lock himself in his apartment, insulated from a reality he could not face, alternately exploding with exhilaration and cowering with fear. When it got very bad, the itching would start. It drove David crazy. From his knees to his feet he felt as if he were covered with an unbearable case of poison ivy. He'd claw and scratch until he bled and scabs covered his legs. He even visited a dermatologist, hoping the doctor would diagnose some skin condition, but he could find nothing wrong. Even worse than the itching were the hallucinations. The dark, high-ceilinged, windowless bedroom of his apartment had exposed-brick walls that horribly changed into the stones of a medieval dungeon. Only another line of cocaine could free David from this prison. There was no other release. "I'd swear off again and again, but I couldn't stop. It was like having a gun to my head."

And always there was the paranoia that the police were watching him, that their powerful telescopes could pierce the protective wall of his brick womb. Ten times an hour he'd dash to the window to look for them. Every stranger walking the street below was a plainclothesman; every car that drove by an unmarked vehicle sent to spy on David Ackerman. Dawn would come and he'd cry for sleep, but without Quaaludes it was impossible to quiet the rage and shut away the pain. He'd crawl into a corner and curl up in a ball, drowning as the awful depression of a waning coke binge washed over him. *David. David. Stop this. You're killing yourself.* Waves of self-hate tortured his dreams. But he was in a free-fall without a parachute, knowing he'd crash and unable to do anything about it but lay out another line to make the misery go away.

By Christmas David's cocaine-corrupted world had become intolerable. At night he'd flail around the bed unable to sleep, even when he wasn't doing coke. By day he was too depressed to get dressed or talk to people. His compulsive, erratic behavior had driven Suzanne into an affair with one of the workers. She'd made a fool of him and it mattered not that he deserved it. He was always accusing her of sleeping with other men and this time he was right. A coke whore. Well, he'd show her. He'd *marry* her. Maybe if he made a commitment to something, to their relationship and their future, he could pull himself back together.

He planned an exquisite dinner party for New Year's Eve, a black-tie affair in a private room at his favorite haunt, a charming French restaurant near the waterfront called La Truffe. He spent hours with the chef planning the menu, which was handwritten as a souvenir for each of the twenty guests. The meal began with oysters and beluga caviar. A casserole of french truffles with asparagus completed the appetizers. The entrées included a lobster ragout, foie gras in an herb vinaigrette, and smoked fillet of venison. Next came a salad-and-cheese course, followed by a dessert of white-chocolate mousse with fresh strawberries, passion-fruit sorbet, and assorted petits fours. Seven exquisite wines accompanied the meal, including a 1978 Meursault, a 1947 Margaux, a 1934 port, and a magnum of Cristal champagne.

Larry and Kenny and their wives were invited to the party, but because Marcia hated David, Larry begged off. Kenny, who felt strongly about spending New Year's with Larry, the person in the world he most admired, also declined so they could be together. But it was a hard choice. He knew he'd never eat or drink like that again at someone else's expense. The dinner bill came to $25,000; the tip alone was $5,000.

The night before the party David asked Suzanne to marry him. She remembered the boy she had loved before he turned to cocaine, the boy who wrote the note on the napkin, the boy who would always be her first true love. Somewhere in this difficult man, that boy still lived, and she accepted his proposal. He called the guests and told them the New Year's Eve party had become an engagement party and he asked his father and stepmother to join the celebration. It was a dazzling evening. David introduced the organization workers to his father and stepmother as executives of the record company and the two accepted the description unquestioningly. David then made a beautiful toast to Suzanne as he slipped a four-carat diamond on her finger. The ring had belonged to his grandmother, and the corners of Suzanne's almond-shaped brown eyes glistened with tears.

David made another important announcement later that evening in private to Willie Harcourt as he gave him a $5,000 bottle of hundred-year-old cognac as a holiday gift. David told Willie he was moving out of Olde City and turning over to him the daily operation of the business. Ever since the disappointment last summer when the fifty-kilo discounts with Paco and Pepe turned sour, killing the thrill of engineering special deals, David's interest in the business had been waning. What he didn't tell Willie was that he secretly hoped by distancing himself from the cocaine supply and the hands-on activity, he would be able to conquer his addiction. There would be kicks and spurts of David at the helm over the next several months, but New Year's Day 1982 effectively marked the end of the Ackerman era. Soon David would be gone completely and Larry would be back in charge, holding the reins by himself.

13

FBI HEADQUARTERS, PHILADELPHIA
CHRISTMAS, 1983

At ten A.M. on December 19, 1983, Judge Norma Shapiro of the United States District Court for Eastern Pennsylvania granted the FBI approval to conduct one of the most extensive wiretaps ever undertaken by the Philadelphia office. Until twenty years ago wiretapping had been an almost routine FBI investigative tool, and there were few criteria to meet in order to get permission to tap a phone. With the revelation of civil-rights abuses in the sixties, the Warren court decided that electronic eavesdropping was a personal intrusion, too easily misapplied by law enforcement, and ought to be more stringently regulated. In 1968 the standards for granting a wiretap were tightened considerably, demanding that four requirements be satisfied before a federal judge could give the green light. First, it had to be proven that there was probable cause to believe a crime was being committed. Second, that a bug or a phone tap would produce information about the crime. Third, that normal investigative procedures, like surveillance and flipping witnesses, had been tried and failed or weren't tried because they were too dangerous or unlikely to succeed. Last, the agents had to show why they thought the place to be bugged or the phone to be tapped would provide information about the suspected crime.

Under the law, wiretaps cannot be used for certain types of crime, and the list of crimes excluded from the statute is longer than the list of eligible felonies. Mail fraud, bank fraud, and check kiting, for example, are ineligible, whereas investigations involving counterfeiting, kidnapping, and drugs may employ eavesdropping. Wiretaps are very carefully monitored by the judiciary and carry a thirty-day limitation, which can be extended only with special permission. The presiding judge receives a weekly progress report from the FBI and can cancel the tap early if he or she decides the objective has been reached.

Two hours after Sid Perry and Chuck Reed got their permission, the project they'd been working on for five months was under way. The agents had prepared for the wiretap flawlessly, fully aware from the beginning that they couldn't depend on drawing a judge from the conservative "law-and-order" ranks who'd view electronic snooping more leniently and give approval on the basis of suspicion. As it was, they wound up with Shapiro, a liberal judge who demanded black-and-white documentation why the tap should proceed. They submitted a 185-page affidavit. Weeks and weeks observing Franny Burns hop from pay phone to pay phone, endless hours sitting in a parked car taking note of the traffic in and out of certain homes and apartments, information generated by the telephone pen registers which indicated what telephone numbers Lavin and his colleagues were calling—everything was included. This particular affidavit was so thorough it received kudos at each required stop along the chain of command—FBI headquarters in Washington, the Justice Department, and finally the federal court. Even defense attorneys, who normally subject wiretap affidavits to intense scrutiny, looking for reasons to prevent the evidence they produce from being used in court, found this one to be impenetrable.

Most federally approved wiretaps involve eavesdropping on a single telephone. Four phones is considered a significant drain on manpower, which made the Lavin operation noteworthy for its size and scope—eight telephones, six of them public phones located in Franny Burns's Dairy Queen and the shopping center around it. The residential phones excluded Lavin's—because the pen registers indicated he never made drug-related calls from his home—as well as Weidler's and Ackerman's for the same reason. At this point in the investigation Weidler and Ackerman were too removed from the day-to-day business to provide evidence. Instead the private phones chosen belonged to Franny Burns and Bruce Taylor, both men whom the agents had ample reason to suspect would be fonts of information. Burns, the buyer of Lavin's business, stood at the center of the current operation. If they could nail him, his link to the trio would help the FBI prove the conspiracy theory that was central to their winning the maximum drug penalty under law. Conspiracy as outlined under the drug-kingpin statute is the only drug charge carrying major penalties that allows the government to indict dealers without catching them with drugs in their possession. Taylor, by then the point man for pickups and deliveries, made and received calls from everybody involved. He could lead the FBI to the ring's as-yet-unidentified customers as well as provide additional evidence against those who'd already surfaced.

The long, narrow, and windowless FBI wiretap room is located in a maze of nondescript Bureau offices that occupy one floor of the massive William Green Federal Building in downtown Philadelphia. There are twelve identical work stations, one for each phone, so that unrelated taps can proceed side by side. Every section has a Formica countertop inset with a pen register, the electronic device that records the time and number dialed and the duration of calls on a continuous roll of white paper similar to that used in adding machines. The work stations also have a double set of reel-to-reel tapes mounted on the wall, with a small cassette tape recorder installed above them. For the thirty-three-day duration of this wiretap, the reels were changed daily, one sealed immediately and sent to Judge Shapiro, who was overseeing the operation, the other kept by the FBI. The cassettes went to Reed and Perry for use in their investigation.

As soon as an incoming or outgoing call activates the phone being tapped, the entire system kicks on automatically and the agent on duty slips on a pair of headphones to determine if the call is drug-related. The court requires that agents decide immediately whether the call is pertinent to the purpose of the wiretap. Calls to lawyers cannot be recorded or overheard, nor can agents eavesdrop on personal conversations. If on the public phone, for example, the agent hears something like, "Daddy, this is Sue. Can you pick me up?" he must, by law, immediately shut off the tape. When the pen register shows the call has been completed, the system is then reactivated.

All through the 1983 Christmas holiday until the twentieth of January, a rotating squad of a dozen FBI agents worked around the clock in the windowless wiretap room, listening to thousands of phone calls. To familiarize themselves with the case, they had all read the federal affidavit and been provided with an inch-thick computer printout listing names and phone numbers of people known to be associated with the conspiracy. When an important call came through, they were under instruction to notify Perry or Reed, who remained on twenty-four-hour alert. Of the hundreds of calls related to the conspiracy, a handful had special significance, and two of those calls occurred on the night of January 7, 1984.

Bruce Taylor's phone rang at 8:33 P.M. Earlier in the day he'd called Lavin at his dental office and left a message that he needed to talk to him about his oral surgery. That evening, Lavin returned the call from a pay phone at a Sunoco station.

"Howdy," he said when Bruce picked up.

"How you doing?" Bruce replied, obviously glad to hear from him.

"I could be doing better. I was fucking around in my hot tub and you know the stupid stakes people use to hold tomatoes, well, I turned the wrong way and cut one of my eyelids. Sliced it right open a couple of hours ago. It looks like someone punched me. I'm all black and blue."

"You can say somebody nailed you. You pulled the wrong tooth."

"Yeah. It's weird. What's up?"

"I lost some books and I need a coupla numbers off ya."

In the course of selling his business to Burns, Lavin had arranged to turn over to Taylor the under-one-kilo customers. In his typically disorganized fashion, Taylor misplaced some of the phone numbers. In response to Bruce's request, Lavin took out his equivalent of a a little black book: a pocket computer where his customer information was stored. He then proceeded to give Bruce a long list of names and phone numbers—complete with area codes. The dozen leads that were dropped in the FBI's lap left Reed and Perry drooling.

"Anybody else before I turn this thing off?"

"No, that's it. Hey, you wanna hang on just a second? My beeper's going off." While Bruce was talking to Lavin, Burns punched his identifying code into Bruce's beeper and left his phone number. "That's Franny," he told Larry. "I'll call him later."

Larry replied that Fran had been complaining about how hard it was to reach Bruce, who had become notoriously unreliable because of his cocaine addiction.

Taylor got defensive. "I can't fucking believe this. I sat here and said, 'Now listen, if you've got a bitch with me, then tell me. At least fuckin' bitch me out. Don't send me home fuckin' not saying nothing.' "

"Well, he hadn't heard from you in a long time and he asked me what your debt was as if I was responsible for you. I said, 'Fucking A, man, what are you asking me for? I gave away the best customers, and I'm out.' "

Bruce said he'd gotten his debt down to $84,000 and Larry asked, "What's he charging you now?"

"I got him down to forty-four." (Bruce was paying $44,000 a kilo, over twice what it was costing Franny, who rarely cut his coke to order the way Larry did and instead just marked up his wholesale price fifty percent. By late 1983 there was a glut of coke on the market and the wholesale price of a kilo had dropped to an all-time low of $19,000, with a street value of $50,000. The Colombians would gradually manipulate the price back to a higher level by drying up the supply, but coke would never again reach the $58,000-a-kilo height that Lavin paid in 1981.)

"That's good," Larry replied, and urged him to push for less.

"Yeah. I pushed for forty but he stuck at forty-four."

Suddenly Larry remembered something else he wanted to tell Bruce. "BSP [Billy South Philly] called the other day to get the number where to get methanol. He was sending his guy Nicky out for an extra five-gallon bottle." This bit of information intrigued the FBI who'd not yet heard of Billy Motto. Who was BSP? Obviously a big dealer if he was buying methanol in large quantities.

Bruce then began to complain about how lousy business was, that some of his customers had moved away and the rest were "penny-ante." "You know that snake Rob beat me for eleven-two [$11,200], and I told him no more credit. From now on, it's up front."

Larry sympathized and shifted the conversation from business to pleasure. "So did you ever close the pool for the winter?"

"Sure," Bruce said. "I had to. The people next door are the noisiest fuckers, but they moved to Florida for the winter."

"The people on the other side of the big tree?"

"Yeah, the old people. They had nothing to do. Retired. They just sat there and fucking watched all day."

Larry then admonished him to be more careful about attracting the wrong kind of attention. "Well, you know, if you're still living there next year, you ought to have somebody in to cut the lawn, to keep up appearances. Make it look good. These people where I live are all into this stuff. The big scene now in my neighborhood is cutting down trees. They're having a tree service in every day. They're nuts. They can't leave their places alone."

Bruce seized the opportunity to brag a little about his own life-style. "Fuckin' A . . . I just had a portable Jacuzzi put in. It's fucking great. I got it downstairs near the pool table. I'm living down there now. I shut off the upstairs. There was more fucking drafts up there. Jesus, you could fly a kite in the living room."

Larry was more interested in the Jacuzzi than the drafts. He advised Bruce how to take care of the pump and the blower system, then wanted to know whether the hot tub was made of redwood and how much it cost. "What is it, six or seven grand?"

"No, no, twenty-eight hundred. My savings. Life savings. I bitch and complain. I'm a fucking miser. I tell you, I'm getting to be a fucking squirrel."

Larry laughed and told him that after a while he'd get tired of using the Jacuzzi just like he got bored with his hot tub, that now he was into exercise. "Hey, I got a gym set with all these weights and shit, like a Universal. Marcia gave it to me for Christmas so I've been working out every couple of days. I'm trying to get in shape for when I go to jail."

"Yeah, you gotta be in shape," Bruce told him. "Otherwise you'll be fucking walking bowlegged. Just fucking nail the first person you see. The first person that gets close to you, fucking beat him."

Larry laughed again. "I was reading the other day in the paper they gave this guy two years for $180,000 tax evasion and the judge lets him off on appeal 'cause it turns out this judge had married the guy's lawyer." This tipped off the FBI that Lavin still had no idea they'd shifted their investigation from tax fraud to drugs.

"By the way," Bruce asked, "have you heard from Frank?"

"Yeah. He owes Franny eighteen grand and he owes me sixteen-five." (Larry's deal with Franny allowed him to collect his accounts receivable, and he was having difficulty getting people to pay their debts now that he was no longer dealing.) "I'd just like my money, that's all. Especially after Glenn calls me up the other day and his lawyer wants twenty grand." (Lavin was paying Glenn Fuller's legal bill for his bust on the New Jersey Turnpike.)

"That motherfucker. It never ends, does it?"

"I'm telling you, Bruce, stay with your good people and don't take too much risk on the ones that always owe you money. If you've got a chance to make some money, put it away."

"That's what I'm doing."

"All right. Good talking to you."

"Yeah, it's been real good. Fucking A, take care now. Let me know if anything new develops."

"This is our once-a-month call now, ya know. Not too many calls anymore," Larry cautioned.

"I got it."

"See you later."

Perry and Reed could barely contain their excitement as they listened to Larry and Bruce talking. For the first time, here was Lavin recorded in Philadelphia discussing his drug business, his problems collecting money owed him, the works. They could see the jury hanging on every word as they played the tape in court. And then there were all the names and numbers he'd given Taylor. What a motherlode! Before they'd even had a chance to recover from the impact, Taylor's phone rang again. This time it was Franny Burns.

"Yo there," Bruce says. "Hang on a second till I turn this fuckin' stereo down. Okay."

"You're at home, right?" Burns asked.

"Yeah. Good news? Same place?" Bruce wanted to know if Burns had cocaine for him and whether he should meet him as usual in the parking lot of the Sheraton Hotel in Valley Forge. In a typical transaction, Bruce would park his white Mazda among a group of cars where Franny would be able to find him. They'd chat for a few minutes. Then Bruce would walk over to Burns's battered blue Datsun, lean in the window, drop some money in the car, and pick up a package of cocaine.

"No. I have a small problem. I've been staying here for you and three other guys and I can't get where I wanna get because I don't know where the fuck Sandy's at. I didn't forget you." Burns meant that instead of spending the New Year's holiday in Florida, he'd stayed in Philadelphia to service his customers, but the delivery was delayed because he couldn't locate his teenage girlfriend and courier, Sandy Freas.

"No problem."

"Here's my program. Tomorrow I'm going to Caesars to see a football game on a thirty-six-foot screen, like early in the morning. You did tell me you had three hundred level tickets left, right?" Franny, who never uttered the word "cocaine" over the phone, was asking Bruce if he still had three hundred grams of coke on hand.

"Well, that's what I did say, but 144 tickets I got rid of." Bruce had sold 144 grams.

"Can you hold out to Monday?"

"Oh, baby!"

"You'd really help me out a lot. I mean, I'm trying [to get the coke delivered]. We're not gonna lose nobody, right?" Burns was worried they'd lose a customer because they couldn't provide product.

"No."

"I mean just till Monday."

"Okay. For sure?"

"Definitely."

"I hear you. Have a good game."

"Yeah. Now, listen. Monday call me late, like about three in the afternoon." Franny liked to get his drug business finished in the morning so he could be at his house when his children came home from school.

"Very good. We'll do it right then. I'll hang on to the tickets."

[In this exchange, "tickets" now refers to "money" rather than "cocaine."]

"I'll talk to you then."

"Thank you, my friend."

This call was almost as good as the one with Lavin because it provided hard evidence of Franny and Bruce conducting drug business. On a continuing-criminal-enterprise, or CCE, charge, conversation alone would be sufficient evidence to prove a relationship.

About a week later, another call between the two, also spiced with code words for cocaine, strengthened the case even further. The agents were certain that when the U.S. attorney got to court, he would surely point out to the jury that there'd have been no need to speak in euphemisms if Burns and Taylor were selling shoes.

"Hi, Fran. How ya doing? I'm just checking in like I promised."

"Did you try to call me between last night and today?"

"Yeah, I called you this morning about eleven-thirty."

"I just got the fuck up. [It was now dinnertime.] I fucking went to sleep last night and never woke up."

"Holy shit. A coupla beers, huh?"

"No, that wasn't it. I didn't sleep for like two days."

"Yeah, I know the feeling well." Bruce would sometimes do cocaine jags that kept him awake for days at a time. Franny, on the other hand, rarely did any drugs at all.

"Not that way. I was beat from doin' things. I'll explain when I see ya. So what you did think of the last girl?" Here Fran was speaking in code again and Bruce understood that "girl" referred to the last kilo he's purchased.

"Ah, very good chick [coke]. Very good chick. Compliments on her looks and everything."

"Good. Good. I like that."

"It's those cosmetics. She knows how to wear 'em." Bruce was complimenting Franny that the cocaine was very shiny and full of rocks.

"Listen, what's the case with Willie New England?" Franny wanted to know about a big customer Larry had given to Bruce whom he had wanted.

"He's mine. But I'm having trouble with the one Brian cut my throat on. Slit me from ear to ear. That was one of my better ones, too. One every week." Brian, another of Bruce's customers, was trying to steal a pound-a-week buyer who owed Bruce money. "It's the same guy I told you about who lost [bought] half an elbow [a pound of cocaine]. Well, he broke his elbow and he owed me for setting his arm. And I ain't been able to make contact with anybody." Bruce wanted Franny to know that he was having a problem collecting his money.

"Do you know where he lives?"

"Sort of. I got a chick that knows, and we're gonna go up there to see if his cast is off and everything."

"Do you need some help? I can send a few guys with you. Nice-size guys."

"No, but I appreciate it."

"Do you think Brian will try to steal Billy from me?" Burns feared he might lose Billy Motto. "Fuck him. Do you know where Brian lives?"

Taylor laughed, knowing exactly what was bothering Burns. "Yes, I do."

"Don't talk to Larry about it." Lavin would disapprove of sending in muscle to handle a problem. "Just keep it—"

"—between me and you."

"We'll sit down and talk next week. All right, Bruce?"

"Okay. Take care, my friend."

Bruce Taylor's telephone never would have been such a gold mine for the FBI if he'd followed Lavin's example and conducted his drug business from pay phones as he'd been taught. But Bruce was a lazy drug addict who deluded himself that listing the phone in an alias was enough protection. Bruce used as many as twenty grams of cocaine a day. Then, in a hyper state, he'd telephone people and spin out the fantasies the drug induced. The day before Christmas he made one of these paranoid calls to his brother-in-law in New Hampshire.

"Hey, listen up. I got to talk quick. I'm supposed to be hit tonight. Shot. His name is David Ackerman. A-c-k-e-r-m-a-n. So if I go down, make him pay. I might have to hang up instantly on you. Got that? A-c, I think it is, k-e-r-m-a-n. Jewish. Family's out of New York, but he's in Philly. Call Greg in Anchorage, Alaska, to make the hit for you. He's listed, you know, in the phone book. Give him ten grand. Thanks a lot. 'Bye."

Fifteen minutes later, Bruce called his friend Greg, in Alaska himself, jabbering grandiose delusions a mile a minute, characteristic of a cocaine jag, his disjointed thoughts connected by a meandering thread that only he could follow.

"Hello, Greg. Hey, you motherfucker. What's up, buddy?"

"Hey, Bruce. What the fuck you up to?"

In the family room of their home in Virginia Beach, Lavin, a warm and devoted father, snuggles with his baby daughter, Tara, and son, Christopher. A third child, Kelly, was born after the FBI captured the fugitive dentist.

Shortly after graduating from dental school, Lavin paid $240,000 for this five-bedroom colonial home in Devon, an exclusive Main Line suburb. Within months he added an Olympic-sized swimming pool and a greenhouse with a hot tub.

While hiding as a fugitive in Virginia Beach under the alias Brian O'Neil, Larry Lavin built this handsome custom home in the affluent neighborhood of Middle Plantation. He explained his wealth and unemployment to his new neighbors by saying he'd sold his computer company and was living off his investments.

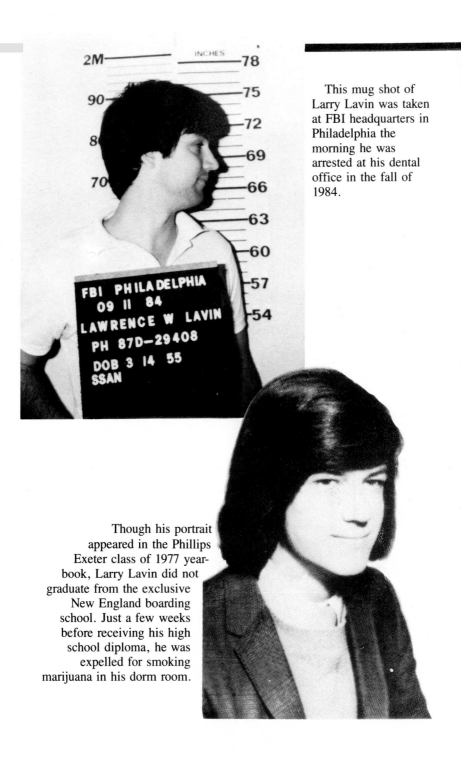

This mug shot of Larry Lavin was taken at FBI headquarters in Philadelphia the morning he was arrested at his dental office in the fall of 1984.

Though his portrait appeared in the Phillips Exeter class of 1977 yearbook, Larry Lavin did not graduate from the exclusive New England boarding school. Just a few weeks before receiving his high school diploma, he was expelled for smoking marijuana in his dorm room.

In the fall of 1982 a boyish Larry Lavin romps in the autumn leaves with his infant son, Christopher, and Rusty, the family dog. His Main Line neighbors thought Lavin made his money as a record company entrepreneur and were shocked when they learned the affable young dentist masterminded a huge cocaine ring.

Lavin's main diversion in exile was fishing and scuba diving. Here he poses with his son, Christopher, in front of the $75,000 speedboat he bought and equipped with an additional $7,000 worth of electronic gadgets.

In 1981 at the height of its operation, the Lavin ring operated from chic apartments in Olde City, an upscale, gentrified neighborhood near the Philadelphia waterfront. There were several units rented in this building and used variously to store cocaine, make up orders, and deliver to buyers.

Suzanne Noramatzu lived in the right-hand corner apartment on the third floor of this building with a view overlooking the Quaker Meeting House. Most of the ring's customers came here to pick up their coke and mixed easily wth the rising young professionals who rented in the building.

The canopy in the left-hand corner marks the entrance to the building where David Ackerman rented a loft apartment of exposed-brick walls and high-beamed ceilings. It was here that Ackerman freebased for the first time and often locked himself away on coke binges for days at a time.

Billy Motto, the South Philly street kid who became Lavin's largest customer and good friend, mugs for the camera seated in one of his favorite possessions. Motto bought the vintage Corvette and several other cars, including a Cadillac and a Volvo, with his drug profits.

Billy Motto grew up poor and loved spending money when the cocaine business made him rich. Here he parties at a Las Vegas casino in 1982 with his best buddy, Nicky Bongiorno, who, after a bad falling out with Motto, aided the FBI in arresting him.

Assistant U. S, attorneys Ron Noble and Tina Gabbrielli happily face reporters outside the courthouse after the jury has returned a guilty verdict in the Billy Motto trial. (Courtesy of the *Philadelphia Inquirer*)

The gig is up. Just hours after the FBI's relentless manhunt closed in on him at a Virginia Beach marina, a newspaper photographer caught a shackled Larry Lavin leaving the district courthouse led by a federal marshal. Lavin had just been denied bond and was on his way back to Philadelphia where he would soon be sentenced to 42 years in jail. (AP Wide World Photos)

"I don't know. About five foot now. That's my dick."

"Is it in the way?"

"It's like it weighs 145 pounds. Hey, you want to retire? Now, listen up, I can only say it once 'cause I might be overheard. I'm going to be hit. Blown right away. I want you to seek revenge for me. My brother-in-law will call and give you the name."

"What's going on? What's the problem?"

"Competition. Big-league. Christ sakes, I'm up in the two-million bracket. What time is it up there?"

"About seven-thirty."

"Is that right? I got no idea what time it is. I got all my windows painted black so I don't know if it's daylight or dark. So will you do it?"

"Yeah, sure."

"Fuckin' A. Guess what I'm gonna do. I'm buying a boat and gonna cruise the world till I drop dead. I ain't kidding. I'm buying a fuckin' yacht. Why don't you come down here and work for me?"

"I can't. I've got a family."

"Bring your family. I'll pay you fifty G's a year. You gotta be on your toes, though. You don't get high. Only get high on your own time. Not when you're working. Your job would be to see that nobody gets closer than six feet to me. I hire bodyguards to watch my bodyguards."

"Sounds like paranoia will destroy you."

"You try carrying a fucking ten mil a week and see how paranoid you get. Hey, I'm worried."

"It sounds it."

"You know, I got a truckload of delightfuls too."

"It sounds like you got a few of them pumped into you."

"No. I don't have a habit. I just do twenty-eight inches of snow a day."

"A day! That's a lot."

"Other than that, I wonder why I weigh 145 pounds. Okay, my friend. I'll give you a buzz later."

Sometimes Taylor would get maudlin when he was high and he'd call his sister in New Hampshire, looking for sympathy. She'd believe the absurd tales he wove, intertwining fact and fiction until it was impossible to tell one from the other and all that remained was a pathetic portrait of a full-blown addict.

"Hello, gorgeous. I love you. How ya doing?"

"I love you too, Bruce. I'm good. How's Opie?"

"He's dead. Cat leukemia. Will you send twenty-five dollars in our name to the Leukemia Society for Opie Taylor?"

"Sure I will."

"He was my best friend. I gave him leukemia. The cat caught leukemia from me, believe it or not. My poor Opie. My best fucking friend. My white blood cells all went south. I have an extremely rare form of very active leukemia."

"My God. Are you getting transfusions?"

"I've had two. My body rejects everything. Right now I'm carrying three broken toes, a broken little finger, numerous rashes."

"Are you sure you don't have herpes?"

"No, I checked that right off the bat. Hey, did you get my Christmas card?"

"Yes, we did, but it wasn't your handwriting."

"I can't write. I shake too much. I can't fucking sign anything anymore. Listen, I want you to get me a German shepherd. A trained German shepherd. I need a dog bad. I need extra ears."

"How the hell am I gonna get you a German shepherd down there from New Hampshire?"

"You get me a German shepherd and I'll fucking send a limousine for him."

"I don't know, Bruce. You make me worried. I know you're not okay. I wish I could do something for you. Why don't you come home and go back to living like we used to?"

"Nah. I like what I'm doing. I love it. Nobody's making me do this. Besides, I want to be remembered, and I still got so much to do. In twenty fucking generations from now when they're all sitting in their castles from my millions, they'll know who their fucking Uncle Bruce was. I'm leaving you everything in my will. Don't tell my wife."

"No. No. You're my kid's Uncle Bruce. You're my brother and that's all I want."

"I'm starting to fall asleep. I'm going to go."

"Listen, I love you. Take care."

"I just dropped the phone. I love you all. 'Bye."

Monitoring eight telephones was the main thrust of the wiretap operation but not the only activity. There was an outside phase too, consisting of three agents from the Bureau's surveillance squad who were specially trained to follow cars in traffic and make clandestine observations. This team moved into a hotel in the King of Prussia area not far from Burns's Dairy Queen for the month of the wiretap so they could be dispatched at any hour of the day or night when a phone call provided information of a meeting Reed and Perry wanted to document with photographs or eyewitness reports. The FBI believes in covering all its bases, on the outside possibility that if wiretapped evidence is deemed inadmissible in court, they'll have surveillance information to substitute.

The tap picked up dozens of calls in which Bruce and Franny made delivery arrangements. The surveillance team was sent to cover them. If a customer called and told Bruce, "I'll be by around three for a six-pack," Sid Perry would call the team immediately. "We're expecting a pickup of six ounces of coke at Bruce's house around three this afternoon. Get the tag number and a description of the occupant and the car." The purpose was to find out who the customer was by running a search on the license plate and building a profile from there. On slow days when nothing spicy came over the phones, Sid and Chuck might ride out to King of Prussia themselves to generate action, or, as they call it, "tickle the wire." That's why, one snowy morning in early January, they were parked at eight A.M. in separate cars linked by radio in front of the apartment house where Sandy Freas, Burns's teenage girlfriend, lived with her seventy-eight-year-old grandmother. Sandy did a lot of errands for Franny and they never knew where she might lead them.

After a half-hour or so, Chuck decided to leave Sid and drive to another building where they knew Burns maintained a stash house, but they didn't know which apartment it was. Maybe Chuck might catch something happening over there that would help him identify it. About nine, Sandy, wearing tight jeans and a burgundy leather jacket, bounced out to her Cutlass. "She's leaving," Sid radioed to Chuck. "I'm following her." He tailed her to the Pennsylvania Turnpike, and that's where the trouble started. Still new to the area, having been there only since the summer, Sid was unfamiliar with the territory and unable to give Chuck any clue where Sandy was racing at eighty miles an hour with his car about a quarter-mile behind her.

"Where do you think she's going?" Chuck radioed.

"Damned if I know," Sid answered.

"Well, where are you now?"

"On the turnpike."

"Yeah, I know. But *where* on the turnpike?"

"I haven't the slightest idea. When I get to a sign, I'll let you know."

By then it was too late. Sid lost Sandy at the tollbooth when she turned south and he headed north. Meanwhile, back in his car, Chuck tried to imagine: If I were Sandy, knowing what I know about her habits, where would I go? Given the direction he surmised she was coming from, based on Sid's sketchy information, his hunch was the Howard Johnson's restaurant where she and Burns often made drug-related calls from the bank of outdoor pay phones. He radioed Sid to meet him in the motel lot across the street from the restaurant, and by the time he arrived, Sandy was inside drinking coffee with Franny Burns. Soon Burns emerged and walked to the phones, rubbed his hands together to warm them, dialed, and hung up. A few minutes later the phone rang. Reed and Perry were wondering whom Burns had beeped, when the radio in the car went off. It was the agent back in the wiretap room telling them that Burns was on the phone with Bruce Taylor. Hot damn. What a piece of good luck: an eyewitness report of a recorded call.

"Hello," Franny said, careful not to identify himself by name.

"Hello. How are you doing?" Bruce answered.

"God damn. I thought you fucking died."

"Hey, I . . . uh . . . I been waiting for you to call."

"Did Larry just call you for me?"

"No. No. I just saw you beep in. This is the first time I seen you beep." This little exchange would provide a nice piece of evidence in court. Why would they use beepers if they didn't have something to hide?

"Nah. I called before. I waited. I waited. I waited. God damn."

"This is the first time your number came across." Bruce was lying. He'd been on a drug binge and too removed from reality to return calls.

"Let's set up a time to meet and we'll go over everything."

"Yes. Yes. Very good idea. How about early this evening? I'll give you a buzz by, say, six-thirty. If not, buzz me. You ain't gotta worry about me. I always pay my debts. I'm on time."

"I haven't had it this high before." Franny wanted the $100,000 Bruce owed him.

"Don't get nervous. It's not high but it's been higher. I really gotta talk to you anyway. I need worries [coke]."

"Okay, I get pissed I can never get hold of ya. I'm in contact with everybody and I'm always wondering how people are doing and what's going on and where everything's at and we never got together. That's my problem."

"It was simply timing, 'cause I was ready. Christ sakes, I had the old lady stay up all night and recopy a new set of books so I could show you I had my own and maybe drop off a set." Bruce's wife had prepared a set of drug ledgers for him to give Franny as proof he wasn't cheating him.

"That's not my main concern. It's like I didn't know if something happened to you. If you got popped. I gotta know what's going on." Franny didn't trust Bruce and only dealt with him at Larry's insistence. Bruce's addiction made him too careless and Fran worried that he'd get arrested and blab everything he knew to the feds.

"No way. If I get popped, I'll scream loud enough and everybody'll know. I keep a low profile, that's all. So I'll see you tonight."

"Okay. Great, great, great. 'Bye."

As soon as Burns finished the call, his father-in-law, Pop Perry, drove into the restaurant lot to pick up Sandy, who left her car and went off with him. Sid sent the surveillance team after them but they lost the car in heavy traffic. He and Chuck followed Franny in his car, but he was speeding as usual and they lost him too. No big deal. They'd already gotten more than they'd hoped for when they started out that morning. This was the first time they actually saw Burns talking on the phone with Taylor. In addition to the tape of the call itself, they now had a positive identification of Franny that verified his recorded voice. It was an irrefutable piece of evidence, just the kind of thing Reed and Perry knew they'd use later on to bring Burns to his knees. Although it wasn't yet lunchtime, their day was made. Just a few more lucky breaks like this one and they'd have probable cause to pull a raid on Bruce Taylor's house, shut down the wiretap, and let Dr. Lavin find out that tax evasion was the least of his problems.

14

DEVON, PENNSYLVANIA
1982

The year 1982 broke colder than average for Philadelphia, with February temperatures dipping below zero. With his cocaine business more or less completely run by managers, Larry Lavin had the time—and money—to leisurely pursue the more traditional activities of a twenty-seven-year-old husband and father-to-be, and he began to look for a new home.

The Lavins had none of the financial restraints of typical first-time home buyers. With money to burn, the young couple could live wherever they wanted. Since neither of them was comfortable with ostentation, they bypassed the flashy new-money enclaves and chose a Main Line suburb about forty minutes from the city that whispered its affluence as only an established neighborhood can. The area of Devon into which the Lavins moved was about twenty years old, new enough to have long curving streets without sidewalks, but old enough for the shrubbery to have matured. In negotiating the purchase of a house on Timber Lane, Larry told the owners that if they lowered the recorded price, he'd pay them the difference in cash under the table. They refused, and although he could easily have paid the full $240,000 in cash, he put $132,000 down (the check for settlement was laundered through Mark Stewart) and mortgaged the rest so as not to attract undue attention. He was, after all, just a newly graduated, yet-to-practice dentist.

The two-story, white-brick, five-bedroom house had a colonial flavor both in its design and in its decor. The young couple had some decorating assistance from Ethan Allen, the upscale classic store where they bought most of the furniture, but the taste reflected in the house was clearly their own. The formal living room to the left of the center entrance hall was painted Williamsburg blue to match the blue of the Oriental carpet they laid over the hardwood floor. Marcia sewed the swag-and-jabot draperies for the windows herself out of a dark blue cotton fabric dotted with flowers the color of persimmons. One could tell this handsome room was decorated more for show than use, because the fireplace hadn't a trace of ash.

The rest of the house had a more homey, lived-in feeling, especially the well-equipped eat-in kitchen with its mustard-colored wallpaper, and the cozy paneled den to the right of the foyer, where the Lavins spent most of their evenings. Larry wasn't much of a reader. His favorite author was Ernest Hemingway. By the end of college he'd gone through everything Hemingway had written, but after that he was too busy to read much more than professional dental journals and financial tip sheets. The only newspaper he read was *USA Today*. What Larry enjoyed was winding down with a VO and ginger ale after work in front of the television set. *It Takes a Thief* was one of his favorite shows, along with *St. Elsewhere* and *Hill Street Blues*. And he was addicted to the nighttime soaps *Dynasty* and *Dallas*.

Most nights, Marcia would be curled up next to him on the sofa, occasionally reading a Sidney Sheldon novel but more often doing needlepoint or knitting an afghan, with their cat, Spooky, at her feet and their dog, Rusty, a Labrador retriever, nearby. When Marcia had mentioned casually one day that she might like a dog, Larry, who loved animals, put her in the car before she could change her mind and drove to a nearby mall, where they bought the Lab from a pet shop. They named him Rusty because of his auburn color, not after Larry's red-haired brother.

Upstairs, Larry converted one of the five bedrooms into an office, where he kept his computer and displayed his gold record. A quick peek at the trophy was a requisite stop when he showed the house to neighbors. It reinforced his explanation of his income from record producing. The master suite was also impressive, with its own dressing room and bath, where Larry had a telephone jack installed next to the tub. The telephone was Larry's lifeline and it was normal for him to be on the phone for two or three hours a night. When he worked outdoors in the yard, neighbors noticed he was always talking on his portable phone. A picture in his dental-school yearbook shows Larry cupping a phone to his ear. And his patients swore he could drill teeth and talk on the phone simultaneously. His conversations combined business and pleasure. Larry loved to gossip.

Larry had an organization rule that all drug-related calls were to be made from pay phones. He was the only one permitted to break that rule because he had a collection of electronic gear to foil surveillance of his home phone. From an ad in an airline magazine he'd come across a New York company that specialized in spy equipment—everything from bulletproof BMW's to sophisticated phone scramblers. He visited the showroom and returned home with $25,000 worth of fancy gadgets for himself and his friends.

The one he used most often was the remote briefcase phone, a device that was illegal in the United States and sold with a caveat "for overseas use only" that Lavin promptly ignored. The device was similar to a portable phone, but it had much more power. The idea was to disguise the origin of calls by routing them through a phone located in another place with a number listed in someone else's name. Lavin paid a friend $250 a month to install a receiver and antenna in his office, which was located about two miles from Timber Lane at the top of a hill where the reception was excellent. Larry installed another antenna in his attic and ran a wire to an outlet in his den. When he wanted to make business calls from home, he'd open the black vinyl briefcase, plug the sleek phone into its jack, and dial. If his call were being traced, it would show up as originating from the office, not from Lavin's home. It was an excellent ruse because the FBI did pick up some of these calls on their pen-register checks, but they didn't realize at the time what Larry was doing.

Larry also had a way of delivering incriminating messages over the phone without using his voice. For five thousand dollars each, he bought two special sets of transmitters that had originally been developed for use in hospitals to allow doctors to sign long-distance prescriptions. Each unit consisted of a pair of white boxes about fourteen inches long and four inches high containing a receiver, an adapter, and a special message pad with an electronically wired pen. On a regular telephone, Larry would call the person who had the matching part to his device. When he wanted to say something risky, he'd announce, "Let's couple." They would then both place their receivers into the adapters. Larry could write a message on his pad and it would quickly appear exactly as he'd written it on the pad at the other end.

Then there were the three briefcase scramblers. They would garble voice transmissions over phone lines, and only an unscrambler on the other end could decode the conversation. Larry gave one to Billy Motto, who could never quite figure out how to use it. It was full of switches and dials, one of which showed a change of current on the line indicating when a phone might be tapped. This was the kind of gadgetry Larry loved to play with, but Billy had no patience. The scrambler could be used on either a pay phone or a private phone as long as both parties had the gadget.

Like the written-message box, it was activated by the "Let's couple" signal.

Larry also bought Billy a special wristwatch to warn him if he were being secretly taped. The watch had two red lights; one gleamed in the presence of a hidden recorder and the other responded to a transmitter. It was a cumbersome device with a wire that went up his sleeve into a buried antenna. Billy didn't like the watch either because it picked up all sorts of other signals in its magnetic field and gave off misleading information. Larry tried to explain to him that the watch was just as valuable turned off. He used his for the psychological effect of unnerving anybody who might be thinking about wearing a wire against him to help the government, but actually he preferred a little blue box about the size of a beeper that he carried in his jacket pocket. It simply began to vibrate when a conversation was being recorded.

The Lavin house was large and lovely, but the grounds were the real showpiece. A big screened-in porch in the rear off the kitchen looked out on a vast expanse of land full of flowering trees and shrubs that stretched to a stream leading to a pond where the local children skated in the winter. At first the neighbors got nervous when the Lavins added an Olympic-size swimming pool and a greenhouse with a hot tub. It looked like they might be a wild young couple given to throwing noisy parties with crazy people from the recording industry. But nothing like that ever materialized. The Lavins lived quietly in much the same style as the other people on the block who were old enough to be their parents. Larry actually used the pool to swim laps every day during good weather. It turned out he was simply into home improvement and poured a fortune into a house that didn't need a thing when they bought it. One major expenditure was the solar-energy panels he installed on the roof. He bragged how much he saved on his heating bill, but the system wound up being nothing but a constant source of aggravation. It never worked properly.

Larry's proudest project was turning the lower level of the house into a magnificent recreation room. Because of the way the land sloped in the back, what would have been the basement was actually a ground-level room opening onto the pool area. With the help of a few drug customers, Larry custom-paneled the room in inlaid strips of alternating light and dark wood and fashioned a large bar in the same design. His father had built furniture as a hobby, so woodworking came rather naturally to him. There was a pool table in the center of the room with a plastic reproduction of a Tiffany shade hanging above it. The remodeling didn't cost nearly as much as it would have if Larry had used professional carpenters, because he paid his helpers with cocaine.

Their first Christmas on Timber Lane, Larry and Marcia ingratiated themselves with the neighbors by dropping in on them to deliver holiday greetings and cranberry loaves that Marcia had baked. The neighbors describe Marcia as plain and pleasant. She wore very little makeup—a dab of eyeshadow and a lick of pink lip gloss—just enough to complement her wholesome looks. Although the neighborhood wasn't particularly close-knit, there were parties at holiday times to which the Lavins were invited. They would always make an appearance, but never reciprocate. "Marcia was an old-fashioned girl, the sort of unassuming person you'd forget after you met her," one neighbor recalls. "But Larry was self-confident and mature for his age. Very much at ease with everybody. Usually he talked and you listened. That way you never got to ask him any questions."

After resigning her job as a physical therapist at the local veterans' hospital right before their son was born in the spring of 1982, she spent the time she wasn't caring for the baby on craft projects. She needlepointed decorative pillows and made calico wreaths for the house. When friends began to have babies of their own, she crocheted crib blankets as gifts. Most of her clothes she sewed herself, favoring the country prints and shirtdresses popularized by Laura Ashley. Larry brought his suits, several at a time, off the rack at an upscale men's clothing store in downtown Philadelphia. He had his shirts custom-made and hand-laundered at the local dry cleaner. Larry saw himself "as kind of a bright dresser," and while his suits were conservative, his sportswear was loud and at home on the golf course.

Marcia was as quiet as Larry was gregarious. But when they were alone together, she was quite assertive. She repeatedly asked him to stop dealing drugs and spoke of his cocaine cronies scornfully. "What a jerk that guy is. . . . How can you trust someone like that?" Still, they were a close, affectionate, hand-holding couple who never had loud, horrible arguments like David and Suzanne did. Marcia would have what Larry called "her little temper tantrums" if he was really late for dinner or fell asleep at the table when she finally got him to take her out to eat without another couple along. They got along so well because Marcia had the intelligence to keep her husband challenged and the common sense to let him rule the roost.

Larry Lavin, drug dealer and thrill-seeker, had a strong conservative streak and believed that tradition played an important role in people's lives. He supported organized religion, and although he'd lost his faith, he'd occasionally accompany Marcia to Mass on Sunday. After graduating from dental school, he accepted the position of co-fund-raiser for his class. One day he met with the other agent to write contribution requests to the rest of the graduates and remarked that what he most liked about Penn and Exeter was their sense of tradition. Marcia fulfilled that need at home. He understood that beneath her quiet surface was a strong and self-sufficient woman who loved him loyally and unconditionally but who would have been much happier as the wife of a suburban dentist than a big-city drug dealer.

Although Larry managed to keep his drug enterprise separated from his family life, Marcia would have gladly foregone his millions for his undivided attention. The money that was so important to him had only minimal interest for her. She didn't care for expensive clothes or fancy jewelry. When she did shop, she frequented factory outlets, and she continued to clip grocery coupons every week just as her mother had taught her. Agnes Osborn, Marcia's mother, was a widowed, plump, retired intensive-care nurse who moved to a Spanish-style town house complex five minutes from the Lavins' to be close to her daughter. Mrs. Osborn was the most frequent guest on Timber Lane. Larry liked his mother-in-law and appreciated having her around to keep Marcia occupied. His parents visited on their shuttles between Massachusetts and the Florida condominium their son bought for them.

Larry had a huge circle of friends and acquaintances and thrived on the adrenaline of people and parties, whereas Marcia had a limited set that included her brother and sister and a few college girlfriends from Penn. Just about the only people from Larry's drug world that she permitted into their private life were the Weidlers.

Larry vented his need for excitement by going off on outings with the boys. For a while he was interested in golf and bought himself a $900 set of clubs, which he used when playing an occasional nine-hole round. He wasn't much of a golfer and cared little about the game. When he did enjoy was wagering on every hole, and, in fact, much preferred a day in Atlantic City to an afternoon on the links. On the pretense of a gambling excursion, Larry, with Kenny, Paul Mikuta or a couple of other guys, would drive to the shore, rent jet skis for the afternoon, gamble at the casinos, and cap off the day with call girls and some coke. Larry rarely used any drugs at home because they reminded Marcia of that aspect of his world she abhorred. Recreational sex was another story. The boys loved their wives and would have considered anything like a mistress or an affair a genuine betrayal. But hookers were okay. They didn't view extramarital sex as cheating, so much as boyish high jinks.

Larry was raised in an outgoing household where there was always an extra plate on the table for dinner or a party to look forward to, and it bothered him that Marcia wasn't more sociable. When he brought drug cronies home, she barely gave them cursory acknowledgement. When it came to asking neighbors in, he was more likely to proffer the invitation. Although much of their backgrounds was similar, in this respect they were dramatically different. Her people had been reclusive and suspicious. When Marcia was a child, her father used to slip a two-by-four plank across the inside of the back door every night to keep out intruders.

While Larry was perfectly content to spend most of his evenings in the den watching TV with Marcia, it disappointed him that they rarely entertained at home, other than having a few friends over in the summer to use the pool. The one big party they gave annually for twenty close friends on New Year's Eve was held in the elegant restaurant of a center-city hotel. Before their first child, Christopher, was born, Marcia agreed to one or two vacations a year, usually in the Caribbean so Larry could scuba and snorkel. But after Christopher came in May 1982, it was hard to pry her out of the house. For the first six months of the infant's life, they went nowhere because Marcia couldn't conceive of leaving him with any baby-sitter but her mother. When they finally did take a jaunt to Bermuda, they brought the baby along.

Christopher Lavin was a healthy seven-pound baby. Neither Marcia nor Larry had a preference for a boy or girl, but Larry was pleased when his firstborn turned out to be a son, so he could do all the things he wished his own father had done with him. Larry refused to have the child named after him. He hated it when people had to be called Junior or Senior to tell the generations apart. Besides, he had never liked the name Lawrence. It sounded stodgy. For a while it seemed that every name he did like, Marcia objected to on the grounds she knew somebody with the same name she didn't respect. Finally they agreed on Christopher because it had no such negative associations. Larry wondered fleetingly if, being like he had been, Christopher would be mistaken for Jewish because of his last name.

Larry celebrated Christopher's arrival in his own inimitable way. When the baby was two days old, he left the hospital early on a Saturday evening feeling terrific. He had a beautiful son. He was married to the best wife and mother in the world and he was going to be the best father. He hopped into the BMW and made the hour ride back to Timber Lane in forty minutes, speeding as usual.

He pulled into the driveway of his empty house with his plans for the night already hatched. The birth of his first child simply had to be shared with his friends. He pulled out the pocket computer that held his phone numbers and began to dial. First he called a contact and ordered two call girls. "Send them out by cab," he said. Then he rounded up a few ounces of cocaine—he didn't keep any at home—and eight of his good friends. The girls arrived at 9:30 and Larry gave the cabdriver $100 to wait for them outside. By then the boys were already high and raring to go. They sent one girl upstairs to the bedroom for anybody who wanted one-on-one, and had the other strip and join them in the hot tub, which nestled in the greenhouse among the flowers Marcia had so carefully cultivated. It was quite a celebration. Larry demonstrated his tonsorial talent by shaving the girl's pubic hair. The cocaine in combination with the sensual arousal of the hot tub made for incredible—and exhausting—group sex. By midnight they were all wiped out and the party was over.

But the trouble was just beginning. A day or so later one of the guests who'd once had a case of veneral disease began experiencing familiar symptoms. He immediately saw a doctor and his blood test showed he had an infection. Meanwhile some of the others, Larry included, were running fevers. Larry's temperature soared to 104 and he thought it best to shoot himself with penicillin to kill whatever it was he'd caught from the hookers. He bought the antibiotic and a syringe at the drugstore and locked himself in the bathroom to inject it. Somehow the needle bent in his buttocks, giving him a sharp pain. Marcia, who was now home from the hospital, wanted to know what he was screaming about. He gave her a lame excuse and managed to yank the needle out.

It might have ended there had the fellow with the VD symptoms not felt so terribly guilty that he confessed to his wife every lurid detail of the party. It so happened that she'd been in the hospital along with Marcia giving birth to her own child. Furious with Larry, she called to let him know in colorful terms exactly what she thought of his perverted celebration. He calmed her down and persuaded her not to tell Marcia, but that was the last time Larry entertained at home.

By the spring of 1982, Larry had been out of dental school nearly a year and his diversionary activities were wearing thin. The drug business was running smoothly in the hands of his managers, and the stock-exchange seat he'd bought as an alternative to dentistry turned out to be less interesting than he'd anticipated. Since Christmas, when he'd hired another trader to handle his account, he'd had very little to do with it. There was nothing left to improve on the house, and even the real-estate-investment company he formed, L Inc., didn't come up with enough deals to occupy his time. Ever since he'd realized he wasn't going to get rich investing with Mark Stewart, he'd been tinkering with real-estate deals. He'd bought a few condominiums and rehabilitated a house on the New Jersey shore. What he wanted to do down there was get involved in government-subsidized housing where the casinos would undertake some of the financing as part of their required commitment to create moderate and low-income housing. But the program was taking too long to get off the ground. Then there was an apartment renovation across the river in Cherry Hill, New Jersey. He'd met with the mortgage bankers, but the deal didn't coalesce despite the fact that he had amassed enough assets to show a financial statement of one million dollars. Larry spent a lot of his time on these projects—scouting out land and office buildings, talking to bankers, lawyers, and developers—but the action never fully satisfied him. What he missed was dentistry.

He started looking around for a suitable practice to buy and finally found the situation he was seeking in the for-sale column of the local paper: a small, underdeveloped dental office in a working-class section of Northeast Philadelphia near the city's Holmesburg prison. He bought the practice for·$75,000 and immediately made Ken Weidler the gift of a half-partnership. Larry felt rusty after his time off and needed Kenny, who'd had a year of hands-on experience, for a security blanket and also to share the time. They split the hours. Lavin worked Tuesday, Wednesday, and Thursday afternoons and evenings and every other Saturday. Kenny, who still had his own office in South Philadelphia, worked Mondays, Fridays, and mornings.

There was nothing Larry liked better than getting a project off the ground. He transferred the same energy into the dental practice that he had poured into the drug business, completely immersing himself in every aspect. He hired the girls to clean teeth and run the office. He set up his computer to devise record-keeping systems. He read books on productivity and had ten thousand advertising fliers printed and distributed through the neighborhood— with a coupon offering a free dental examination. He was having such a good time that he claimed if it hadn't been for Marcia and Chris he never would have·gone home. This was the perfect enterprise for him because it combined all the things he liked to do: work with people, tinker with tools, and manage finances.

Larry had a special gift for making people feel comfortable by turning them into instant peers and confidants. Whether it was a poor white welfare patient, a fellow dentist, or a hygienist who worked for him, he treated them with equal importance. He could mix effortlessly in any crowd, sink or rise to anybody's level, and converse on any subject from current events to new trends in dentistry to the cause of a recurrent nightmare. Whatever the topic, he'd become totally absorbed in the conversation. His mood was always upbeat and his enthusiasm contagious. He simply had to share in exquisite detail everything he'd learned about a new dental material or a new computer program he'd just discovered.

He also happened to be excellent at his profession. Larry had very good hands and a gentle touch. He could talk dental technique for hours and was fascinated with the newest gadgets and the latest innovations in the field. Bonding, a new cosmetic technique to resurface and recontour teeth, was just coming into popularity and he couldn't wait to master its use. When new materials came on the market, he liked to experiment with them to see how they compared with what was already available. He once made a patient two sets of dentures—one with a vinyl base and one with an acrylic base—and charged him for only one, on the promise that the patient give him feedback on which fit better.

He was totally involved with his work and worried about his cases after the office closed. It wasn't unusual for a man with an emergency root-canal problem that Dr. Lavin had worked on in the afternoon to get a call from the dentist late that evening just to see how he was doing. Larry understood basic human psychology and used it instinctively to his advantage. He recognized that people judge a dentist's ability more by his personality than by the quality of his work, and he liked to say, "You give a little attention and you get a lot more back."

His chairside manner captivated both children and adults. Most parents have to drag their kids to the dentist. Larry's young patients would come bounding into the office begging him to do the scarf trick. He had a full repertoire of card and coin tricks, but the perennial favorite was the hollow thumb stuffed with a red scarf that fit over his real finger and made it seem as if the scarf were being pulled out of his finger. Originally Larry wanted to specialize in children's dentistry, but to his surprise he found he enjoyed talking to adults more than entertaining kids. He was so easy to relate to that women patients would prefer to discuss something as personal as an impending hysterectomy with Larry than with their uncommunicative husbands.

Larry and Kenny made a balanced team, although Kenny's

approach to patients was very different. Kids didn't take to him as well because he acted like the traditional sit-still-or-this-is-going-to-hurt disciplinarian. And the younger female patients and office girls preferred Larry's free-wheeling geniality to the more formal doctor-patient or doctor-employee attitude that characterized Ken's style. Weidler's fans were senior citizens who felt he was respectful and caring, and they usually requested to be seen by him.

By this time Kenny was totally removed from the drug business and dependent on his two dental offices for his entire income. He wanted to make his fair profit and frequently argued with Larry, who continued to rake in enormous amounts from his cocaine operation and was content to do dental work at cost or even *pro bono* rather than let his chair remain empty and his hands idle. Ken refused to work on people who couldn't pay the established prices for fillings or dentures. Larry was willing to create a sliding scale and take whatever the patient could pay. He was in the enviable position of being able to deflect the greed that drove him to excess as a drug dealer from his professional life, where he actually had difficulty collecting fees from his patients, about forty percent of whom were on public assistance. Even with Larry's lackadaisical collection policy, the practice netted $100,000 by its second year. But for him it would never be more than an engrossing hobby and a source for petty cash. He looked at Ken's half of the profits and said, "I don't understand how people can live on fifty thousand dollars a year."

One afternoon in midsummer Larry had a visitor to the office who sparked a flurry of curious stares from the young hygienists. It was obvious by the way he dressed that this visitor wasn't from the neighborhood or a preppy pal from college. He was wearing a white silk suit with a black shirt open at the neck and lots of gold jewelry. He strutted like he owned the place. And when he smiled, the staff found themselves smiling back. Billy South Philly had arrived.

Larry greeted Billy warmly, and proudly showed him around the office. He explained every piece of equipment, what it did and how it worked. Billy hopped in the chair and Larry gave him a shot of laughing gas and cleaned his teeth, establishing a monthly ritual. Larry explained Billy South Philly to his aides as somebody with whom he did a little loan-sharking. Now that Billy Motto could afford to indulge himself, he'd become a fanatic about personal grooming: manicures, pedicures, facials, massages, haircuts twice a week. A plastic surgeon had removed the tattoo and needle marks from his days as an addict. He'd even gone to modeling school because he thought it would be fun to parade in fashion shows in designer clothes, although he was actually several inches too short for runway work. His stumbling block turned out to be the speech class where the teacher told him he'd have to stop talking with his hands and get rid of his "youse-guys" patter. "So I leave and what happens? Along comes the movie *Rocky* and a guy gets famous yelling 'Yo, Adrian' and talking just like me."

Billy hadn't stopped by the dental office that day on a social call; Larry had summoned him. About six months earlier, Motto had crossed swords with David Ackerman and taken his cocaine business elsewhere. He didn't like the way things were being run in Olde City. There was too much hysteria, too many people moving in and out, too little of the Lavin touch. He'd paid Larry twenty thousand for the name of a source in Florida and had been buying direct. It was an arrangement Billy didn't particularly like. For one thing, there were too many risks, and for another, his organization wasn't set up to run back and forth to Miami. He preferred to pay Larry a little extra and have him shoulder those burdens. Besides, Billy missed the dentist's friendship.

The feeling was mutual. Motto was not just a loyal customer who could be depended on to pay his bills; he was, in Larry's view, "a super-nice guy." Larry told people, "If everybody in the drug business were as decent as Billy, there'd never be any problems. Here's a man who knows the meaning of respect. I'd loan him any amount of money he asked me for."

Larry sat Billy down to bring him up-to-date on the management changes the organization had undergone in his absence. To begin with, David Ackerman no longer had anything to do with the daily business, having moved to an apartment in the suburbs with his fiancée, Suzanne Noramatzu. His replacement, Willie Harcourt, was also gone. He'd resigned in June after a heated argument during which David accused him of cheating. Nobody under Larry was ever as responsible or organized as Larry himself was. The managers all got too greedy or too sloppy. Then customers like Billy would call him and complain that there was a problem with a debt or that deliveries were late or that the person currently in charge was unreliable. That's when Larry would step back in and pick up the reins. He was the consummate businessman, bending over backward to keep everybody happy, accommodating where others commanded. He realized that in the drug trade you always walked a tightrope, and anybody you screwed badly enough would eventually get even—in a lethal way. Years later, Larry's drug associates would look back on Larry's management style and describe him as a user and a master manipulator. But in those days their favorite adjectives for him were "charming" and "charismatic."

The first order of business after Harcourt bowed out in June 1982 was to find a new manager. Larry turned to his New England roots and found Brian Riley a big, rough-looking fishmonger with a wall-eyed stare who'd been introduced to the organization years earlier when he began buying cocaine from Larry's sister—his ex-girlfriend, Jill Lavin. In the intervening years, Brian Riley got passed from Jill directly to Larry and became a courier for Northeastern deliveries. Larry originally moved him to Philadelphia to assist Willie Harcourt, and now chose him as Harcourt's replacement. Riley moved the headquarters from Olde City to another popular yuppie neighborhood on the other side of town near the Art Museum. He also brought in Bruce Taylor, the New England motorcycle freak with a black belt in karate and a fondness for handguns, to work as Brian Riley's bodyguard and take over his New England delivery route. Eight months later, Taylor would have Riley's job.

Lavin's second order of business during the summer of 1982 was to renegotiate the price he was paying for cocaine. He called Paco and Pepe up from Miami for a summit meeting in the suite of an Atlantic City hotel-casino. They argued for six hours. Despite Larry's threat that he had an alternative source and would not stay with them unless they improve on the current $55,000-a-kilo figure, the Latins would not budge, and that was the end of their relationship. For the next several months Lavin would buy some of his cocaine through an old friend from his pot days now operating in Miami and some from an unknown supplier funneled through his college roommate, Paul Mikuta. That unknown supplier would turn out to be Franny Burns.

Convinced by Lavin's persuasiveness that he'd have none of the personality clashes with Brian Riley that he'd encountered with David Ackerman, Motto happily returned to the fold and slipped back into his old buying patterns. Arriving with one or two of his bodyguards at the stash house whenever a shipment came from Miami, he'd carefully choose his kilos by dipping into each bag with his spoon and spraying the coke with methanol to test for purity. Depending on what his huckster's instinct told him about the quality, he'd set aside as many as six kilos of uncut coke at a time. Then he'd leave as quickly as possible.

Always wary of a potential bust, Billy never lingered where drugs were kept any longer than he had to. Another of his personal quirks was to avoid riding in a "dirty" car—one that contained either drugs or money. After making his selection, he'd drive off in his spotless Volvo—the one he had had outfitted with an electronic control on the dashboard that, activated by a paperclip, would automatically raise the steering wheel to reveal a compartment just big enough to hide a small pistol. His workers would return with the money and take the coke back to Motto's "factory." They drove Billy's yellow Cadillac that had been fitted with two switches in the back seat, one on the floor and one by the window. When the buttons were touched simultaneously, the armrest lifted, revealing a secret compartment with space to store fifteen to twenty kilos of cocaine. It was just like the old days, only Billy felt more confident knowing that Larry was running things instead of David.

By late 1981, nothing David Ackerman had planned seemed to have gone the way he'd expected. He'd been booted out of dental school, had become increasingly addicted to cocaine, and lost his opportunity to build the volume of the cocaine business as he'd promised Larry he could do. Maybe 1982 would be different.

After his extravagant New Year's Eve engagement party to Suzanne Noramatzu, he'd handed the daily management of the business over to Willie Harcourt and moved away from Olde City with his fiancée, hoping he'd be able to gain control over his cocaine addiction. The plan didn't work.

Suzanne, whose habit wasn't as bad as his, had no desire to give up cocaine, and he lacked the will to cut down on his own. His personal life was falling apart and his work life was suffering as well. Although he installed a phone line in his new apartment just for drug transactions and examined Willie Harcourt's books and records on a weekly basis, he hadn't been paying very close attention: the books were riddled with discrepancies. He continued to go on paranoid drug binges and refuse to return phone calls, leaving workers stranded on cocaine runs waiting for his instructions.

By the time Harcourt bowed out, Larry's patience had just about been exhausted. He was fed up with David locking himself in his apartment incommunicado, doing cocaine for days at a time, and felt he no longer contributed anything worthwhile to the business. As a manager David had become useless. His original customers had long since been absorbed into the organization and Brian Riley was now handling Harcourt's duties. David no longer had any real function, but Larry kept him around long enough to teach Riley the formulas and take him to Miami on a buying trip to show him the ropes. When autumn came and Riley had been sufficiently trained, Lavin decided it was time to buy Ackerman out.

It was a long and ultimately acrimonious parting. First, Larry established his own equity in the business at $1.1 million and David's at $700,000, so there was no question of who could afford to buy out whom. They worked out a complicated payoff that included $300,000 in silver certificates, and bonds placed in David's grandmother's name. The rest was to be doled out in weekly $5,000 payments. As 1982 was winding down, Larry called David to his home in Devon and in an angry encounter told him he would not pay the remaining $400,000 he owed him. Larry pulled out the books and claimed the assets and liabilities of the business were off by $250,000, for which he held David responsible. (David suspected that Brian Riley had stolen the money, but he had no way of proving it.) Larry then pointed to a $100,000 customer debt accrued under David's stewardship that was obviously not going to be collected and deducted that amount too. There were additional customer debts that Larry blamed on David. They traced back to the fifty-kilo-a-month transaction when David, overloaded with more coke than he could sell, flooded people with "fronted" coke they were never able to pay for. It tidily added up to $400,000 and Larry declared it settled his debt to David.

Ackerman might have handled his ouster better had his relationship with Suzanne not been deteriorating at the same time. They were both using too much cocaine, although David was by far the more compulsive of the two. "Drugs had turned us both ugly," he recalls. "We weren't getting along at all. We were into hurting each other. Suzanne had been the sweetest, nicest girl you could ever imagine, but she wasn't anymore." Nor was David any longer the lovable charmer who'd scrawled the note on the napkin six years ago. Their plans for marriage were withering, and their life together was punctuated by shouting matches that sometimes escalated into fistfights. Suzanne would seek refuge in her parents' house and David would come to fetch her, insisting she return to their apartment. At other times David, paranoid that she was cheating on him, would order her to leave. Once, in a fury, he telephoned her younger sister, Kim, and told her to come and get Suzanne. When Kim arrived to drive Suzanne home, it was past midnight. David had snorted another line and changed his mind. He chased the girls down the hallway to the elevator, loudly imploring Suzanne to forget what he had said, he hadn't meant it.

"Okay, you three, just quiet down." Their shouts had attracted the attention of the apartment security guard, who had no intention of getting involved in a domestic squabble. He just didn't want the other residents to be awakened. "This is a respectable building. Go have your argument somewhere else."

David glared at the guard, his right hand tightly squeezing Suzanne's wrist so she could not flee. "Right. Right." He lowered his voice. "Just leave us alone. We'll settle it in a minute." He leaned in close to Suzanne and whispered, "You're not leaving. I won't let you go."

When Kim tried to separate them, David sank his teeth into her arm. She let out a howl. "Suzanne, the crazy son of a bitch bit me." As she tore her arm out of his mouth and pushed him away, David turned back to Suzanne, grabbed her, and pushed her against the wall of the open elevator.

"Get off me, you bastard," she shrieked, "or I'll throw this ring down the elevator shaft." The threat of losing the $25,000 family-heirloom engagement ring frightened him sufficiently to relax his hold on her, permitting the sisters to escape into the elevator and out into the starless night. The next day David once again cajoled his fiancée back home, but this would be the last time his apologies had any effect.

Around the Christmas holiday Suzanne went off to do some shopping and David headed down the shore for a quick gambling trip to the casinos with some of the money Larry had given him in the buy-out. It was not one of his luckier nights and as his losses mounted, he raised his bets until he was $75,000 in the hole. Already high on coke, he decided to console himself with a call girl and, in his distorted drug state, had the audacity to drive her back to the apartment he and Suzanne shared. Suzanne awakened in the morning to find the two of them half-naked entwined on the couch and her fur coats tossed on the floor. She was furious. Suzanne was no stranger to kinky sex, but somehow the sight of David, her husband-to-be, in the arms of a strange woman was the last straw. "Who is this?" she shouted. He claimed the call girl had been hired by a friend whose wife discovered them in bed, and he'd brought her home because she had no place to go. That ridiculous excuse further enraged Suzanne. Not only had David betrayed her, he was insulting her with a bald-faced lie. She packed her things and left for good. When David trailed her to her parents' home, all he returned with was the diamond ring.

David's therapist pointed out that he might have subconsciously used the call girl as a means of getting out of a destructive relationship. Maybe the therapist was right, David thought. He'd certainly been on target about a lot of other things since David began seeing him in late 1982 after he finally recognized that if he didn't get some kind of help, he'd probably kill himself. In the beginning David treated his therapy as a game. The psychologist laid down ground rules about his drug use. First, he wasn't allowed to come to his appointment high. He broke that rule once or twice and the therapist charged him for the visit but wouldn't treat him. Realizing that he was wasting his own money, David abstained on treatment days. The next rule prohibited him from doing coke a day before the appointment and a day after. That was a little harder.

The painful struggle to kick his habit would have been easier if David had told the doctor the truth about the severity of his addiction. The therapist would probably have checked David into a twenty-one-day drug rehabilitation program and gotten him the help he most needed. Unfortunately, David revealed very little about the extent of his cocaine usage to the psychologist because he'd been warned by a lawyer to downplay his drug problem—if he ever got indicted, the information could be used negatively in court. It was lousy advice but it did force David to concentrate instead on working out the emotional problems that contributed to his coke abuse—his overwhelming need for praise and approval, his lack of self-respect, and his compulsion to overachieve. He learned how drugs had been useful in muzzling the anger he'd felt toward his parents after their divorce, and he finally put to rest his power struggles with his mother. As David straightened out his personal problems, he gradually weaned himself off drugs. His most destructive relationship, cocaine, died slowly, punctuated by fewer and fewer relapses, each one marked by shorter binges— until the night that literally scared him straight.

Suzanne had been gone several months and David was dating a nurse named Linda who knew very little about his past. One night she mentioned that she'd never tried cocaine and David thought she deserved to have this special experience. He called Bruce Taylor, who met him on his motorcycle in a McDonald's parking lot and sold him a half-ounce. Back in his apartment, David laid out the glistening white lines on the black Formica kitchen counter, rolled up a bill, and showed Linda how to snort. They did one line, then another. By the end of the first hour, David was far ahead of her and already flying. He suggested they stop for a while.

Linda, who still showed no signs of being high, sat down on the living-room couch and suddenly began to flail about as if she were having an epileptic seizure. Her arms and legs beat in the air in wild, jerking movements. Her eyes became round and glassy and the frozen look on her face made the uncontrollable motion which afflicted her limbs seem even more bizarre. The fit lasted no more than twenty seconds but it seemed to David like three hours. Her spasms stopped as abruptly as they had started. Before David could let out his breath, Linda turned blue and collapsed against the back of the couch. Too horrified to move, he watched her skin fade from blue to ashen gray and realized she was no longer breathing.

"Linda, Linda, wake up. Wake up!" he screamed at her. "Don't die, Linda. Oh, please, don't die."

His mind raced: What should I do? Should I call an ambulance? Can't do that, I'll get busted. But I have to do something. I can't let her die. CPR. That's it. I've seen it on television. He laid her down on the couch and started pressing on her chest. "Shit. Is it two breaths in and one breath out? Or three in and one out?"

Whatever he was doing, it wasn't working. As he pushed down on Linda's inert body, she sank into the soft cushions. Never in his life had he been in such a state of panic, icy cold, too frightened to sweat even. Between the coke he'd snorted and the fear that he had a corpse on his hands, his own heart was pounding so fast and hard that he was sure he was going to die along with her. "Oh, God, Linda. Linda. Please. Please open your eyes. The floor. I have to move her to the floor." He rolled her off the couch onto the floor and started the CPR again. "C'mon, Linda. Just one little breath, just one."

And miraculously she responded, opened her eyes, and smiled as if she had awakened from a delicious little nap. "David. You look awful. Is something wrong?" He was shaking so badly that his teeth were chattering. He couldn't believe it. She didn't know what had happened to her. But David did. It was the coke. He knew he had to get rid of the coke before he needed more. He ran into the kitchen, took what was left in the bag, and flushed it down the toilet. Then he scrubbed the counter and vacuumed the rug. No coke. No more coke. No coke ever again!

That David finally succeeded in conquering his addiction almost on his own was a testimony to his extraordinary desire to clean up his life and return to dental school. Penn wasn't eager to have him back, but when he reapplied in May 1983, the professors who opposed his reentry had no concrete evidence to block it. Only the same rumors and suspicions about the Lavin ring that had been circulating for the last three years. When David produced a letter from his therapist stating that he'd overcome the problems that had caused his dismissal, the administration readmitted him.

Almost as punishment, he was given a heavy and exacting caseload and his performance astounded everyone who remembered the brash, know-it-all Ackerman of two years earlier. The braggadocio was replaced by an appropriate self-confidence. Complex techniques came easily for David because he was very talented with his hands. He told friends he'd felt that he'd really changed as a person and especially regretted "how nasty I've been to women." A professor who taught the reformed David remembers him as a student who was one of the best in his class and only wanted to get better. "Picture thirty to forty students in clinic working on patients, with maybe a half-dozen of us in the faculty observing them. The majority would politely approach us and ask, 'Could you please check this when you get a minute?' David was part of a smaller, more impatient group who didn't like to waste time waiting. He wanted to be as productive as possible without cutting corners. His work was very high-quality. I genuinely liked the kid." As a result of his diligence, David was able to finish his two remaining years six months ahead of schedule and score in the highest percentile on his licensing examination.

David's broken engagement to Suzanne started him in a new direction but left her as aimlessly adrift as when they'd first met. She wandered in and out of a few meaningless affairs with workers on the fringe of the Lavin ring in order to keep her coke-supply lines open. Then, to the total shock of everyone in the organization, she ran off to Las Vegas on the spur of the moment in August 1983 and married Bruce Taylor.

Until the week before they eloped, Bruce was supposed to marry Suzanne's younger sister, Kim, with whom he'd been living. The wedding was planned for Valentine's Day in the Virgin Islands. Kim met Bruce hanging around Suzanne's Olde City apartment, where he'd occasionally stop to pick up orders. When Bruce moved to Philadelphia they started dating, and Kim attempted to help him with his coke business the way Suzanne assisted David, but she didn't have anywhere near her sister's capabilities.

Bruce's sister-swapping was a surprise to everybody, including Suzanne, when he impulsively asked her to marry him. She'd been alone with him only a few times. Once he gave her a ride on his motorcycle; once they went to dinner and he took her to see Elizabeth Taylor and Richard Burton who were appearing together in Philadelphia in a Noël Coward's *Private Lives*. Apparently in that brief time she glimpsed a lovable side of Bruce that he kept fairly well hidden from the rest of the world.

The Bruce Taylor that Suzanne grew to love was one of eleven children raised on a New Hampshire farm, ridiculed by the other kids in his class for having to milk the cows before coming to school and for smelling of manure. His gun-toting, tough-guy biker act was the only way he knew to gain respect, and when he came to Philadelphia he played it to the hilt. Next to Dr. Lavin and David Ackerman, he felt even more like a country bumpkin. If they were, at least, afraid of him, he thought, he'd have some kind of status. With Suzanne, that bravado was unnecessary, and he wasn't embarrassed to be tender and loving. He regularly bought her a gift to mark the monthly anniversary of their wedding day. He'd gather wildflowers in the field and present her with a bouquet. He even served her breakfast in bed.

Suzanne describes herself in those days as "very impulsive and out for a good time. I didn't think much about why I did things or what they meant." This may explain why she spontaneously agreed to marry a boy who was her sister's beau and had advanced to a similar position in the organization as her ex-boyfriend, David Ackerman. Ever since her breakup with David, she'd missed the excitement of being in the thick of the cocaine intrigue, and Bruce certainly provided some of that.

As soon as she said yes to the proposal, they flew first class to Las Vegas, checked in at Caesar's Palace on August 13, and were married the next day by a justice of the peace. They'd left so quickly she hardly had time to pack, and her wedding attire ended up being a black-and-pink silk blouse with black jeans. Afterward she shopped for clothes at the hotel. Not long after the ceremony, they were desperate for a fix and had exhausted their cocaine supply, so Bruce hired a Lear jet to fly them to Phoenix, where they picked up some from Wayne Heinauer.

Mr. and Mrs. Taylor honeymooned for five days in the Nevada desert and returned to Philadelphia to take up residence under the alias Mr. and Mrs. Bruce Gorman in a modest split-level rented in Newtown Square, an unpretentious neighborhood in the western suburbs. Suzanne took over the job of managing her husband's accounts while he ran Dr. Lavin's drug operation. The business from which Taylor was drawing anywhere from $20,000 to $40,000 a week was too big for the two of them to handle alone, and within days after they'd settled into their home, Bruce moved in a young helper named Karen who had previously been working for him as a courier, delivering drug packages to about three dozen New England customers.

Bruce trained Karen, a petite, well-proportioned blond, the way Larry had trained him. He taught her how to hide the coke inside old sneakers so it wouldn't show in the airport X-ray machine and to dress like a lady when she traveled by plane so she wouldn't attract attention. She was instructed that if she ever saw a police dog coming toward her in the airport, she should put down the coke and walk away. A policeman with a German shepherd on a leash actually did approach Bruce once in an airport. Taylor, fearing the dog had been trained to sniff drugs, immediately dropped his suitcase and walked to the other side of the waiting area. Only after the policeman left did he retrieve the luggage.

Karen continued transporting cocaine after becoming a housemate of Bruce and Suzanne, and also answered beeper pages and mixed orders. Bruce paid her a little extra to be nice to "the boss," which is what he called Larry Lavin. Increasingly Bruce was getting so high that he couldn't talk to the dentist and needed Karen to cover for him. Larry was easily hoodwinked. He didn't socialize with Bruce, so their contacts were infrequent and orchestrated by Bruce to take place only when he was clearheaded enough to function.

Larry hadn't the slightest idea that Bruce had become a hard-core junkie. Depending on what was on hand, Bruce gulped Quaaludes and Valium, shot speedballs, and tripped on acid. On one of those journeys, he hopped on his motorcycle and roughed up a woman in a neighboring town, who called the police and had him arrested for attempted rape; the charges were later dropped.

Bruce's drug of choice was cocaine. He snorted it, smoked it, ate it, and even dissolved it in water and injected it directly into his veins as many as thirty times a day. By the time he married Suzanne, although he never injected drugs in her presence, he was using anywhere from five to twenty grams of cocaine daily, enough to fill a dozen teabags and more than enough to drive him to the state of hysterical paranoia revealed in the phone conversations taped by the FBI in January 1984.

Suzanne's coke habit had escalated from the daily gram or two she snorted when she lived with David to three or four grams a day. She had her share of paranoia too, most of it directed against Karen, who, upon returning from a delivery in Vermont one crisp day in October with $21,000, was brusquely told by Bruce to pack her bags and get out. Later Bruce called her to explain that Suzanne felt she was trying to come between them and had forced him to banish her from their home.

15

PHILADELPHIA
JANUARY, 1984

It had snowed the night before. The five FBI agents, dressed in jeans and ski jackets, slid on the icy path that led from Ashley Road some twenty feet down a steep incline to the ranch house where Suzanne and Bruce Taylor slept peacefully, totally unaware that their lives were about to be destroyed. Two of the agents crunched through the deep snow to the back of the brick-and-stucco house. There the land leveled off sufficiently to accommodate a swimming pool, which, like the rest of the place, looked seedy and unkempt. They walked under a rickety porch onto a concrete patio and tried to peer inside, but couldn't see anything because the windows had been painted black. One of the agents glanced at his watch to make a note of the time for his report. It was 9:30 A.M., January 17, 1984. Then, stationing himself by the rear door, he spoke into his walkie-talkie. "Back door secure."

The three agents who'd gone directly to the front of the house responded, "Ready to enter," and pounded on the door, shouting, "FBI! Open up!" They waited the requisite two minutes. No answer. One agent raised the sledgehammer he'd been carrying and swung it against the front door, bursting it open with such force that it slammed into a mirrored wall, shattering glass all over the floor. Gingerly making their way around the glass, the agents entered a combination living-dining room that looked like it had been furnished for a bordello. There were red velvet draperies on the windows and zebraskin shades on the lamps. In the corner near a table and chairs that badly needed refinishing stood a plastic fountain, and in place of a chandelier there was a mirrored globe that showered little bits of colored light all over the room. Parked in the center of the room was a Harley-Davidson motorcycle, its hand-polished chrome gleaming in the dim light. Again they shouted, "FBI!" Again there was no answer.

While one agent covered the scene with a shotgun, the other two quickly swept through the rest of the rooms on the unheated first floor. The kitchen sink was stacked with dirty dishes, and in a bedroom, clothes were strewn about. Bruce Taylor's used drug syringes littered the floor. There were holes in the flimsy fiber-board walls and dents in the doors and furniture. The destruction was the handiwork of Bruce and Suzanne, who often had violent arguments, but instead of assaulting each other, vented their anger by kicking a door or punching a wall.

Convinced that the upstairs was empty, the agents cautiously inched their way down the stairs to the lower level, a long narrow room that contained a pool table and a hot tub. Beside the pool table was a stack of wrapped, undelivered Christmas presents, and on top of the table, a beeper was going off, sending its incessant bleep-bleep-bleep into the still morning air.

Again the agent yelled, "FBI!" and called to another agent upstairs, "Come down here and cover me with the shotgun," as he headed across the room toward two closed doors at the rear. Standing to the side of one of the doors with his body flattened against the wall, he stretched his arm out and turned the handle, pushing the door open. The room was empty. He repeated the same thing at the second door and this time heard muffled voices, but because of the blackened windows he couldn't see who was talking.

Suzanne heard the agents before Bruce did and thought she was having a nightmare. The night before, she'd been at a nearby mall shopping for Christmas presents for Bruce's nieces and nephews. During the holidays they'd been too busy selling and snorting coke to buy gifts. Instead, they were planning to drive to New England and deliver their presents to the family in person. When she got home, they started doing lines and stayed up for hours wrapping and talking. It must have been nearly dawn when they'd come down sufficiently to get to bed, so she was in a very heavy sleep when the words "FBI" and "shotguns" pierced her consciousness. Groggily she shook Bruce to wake him, thinking the house was being burglarized. It took only a minute or so to realize she was wrong. Through the open bedroom door she could see the rest of the agents coming down the stairs. Thump. Thump. Thump. So many legs, she thought. Like the Rockettes.

The agents formed a semicircle outside the bedroom door. "FBI. Get down on your knees and crawl out."

"Get down," Bruce whispered to her, but she was damned if she'd crawl on her knees for anybody. They weren't going to humiliate her.

There was no response inside the pitch-dark room. One of the agents, careful to keep himself out of any potential line of fire, snaked his arm around the wall beside the open door into the bedroom itself and flipped on the light switch, suddenly exposing the naked bodies of Suzanne and Bruce sprawled across their king-size water bed. A gun lay on the floor beside them. "Stand up," the agent ordered, and this time they both obeyed. A female agent took a sheet from the bed and handed it to Suzanne to cover her slim body. This is it, she thought. I'm going to prison for a long time. And it fleetingly occurred to her: I got what I asked for.

"Are there any other guns or narcotics in the house?" the agent asked, pointing to a black box on the floor near the bed. Bruce stared dumbly, too loaded with drugs to fully comprehend what was happening. The box was opened, revealing five plastic bags of cocaine and a .22-caliber pistol. Already the raid showed signs of being very successful. Suzanne was permitted to slip into a black jumpsuit and Bruce pulled on a pair of jeans. They were taken upstairs to the living-room couch and given a quilted white comforter from the bed to keep them warm. The couple were so debilitated from drugs that within minutes they'd fallen back to sleep. Meanwhile, the FBI began the arduous task of completing its search.

The federal wiretap on Bruce Taylor, Franny Burns, and the eight pay phones he used was authorized to run until January 20. The raid on Bruce Taylor's house on January 17 was an intentional strategic move on the part of Chuck Reed and Sid Perry to stir up the pot before the tap ended, create some confusion, and see who would call whom and ask what. They were now ready to tip their hand to Lavin and observe his reaction. The secondary purpose of the raid was to accumulate hard evidence. In a case this big, the FBI wanted overwhelming odds in its favor when it went to trial.

From the phone tapes presented to the court to get permission for the search, it was obvious that Taylor was dealing drugs from his house. That made him a logical target for a raid. Two other warrants were issued that morning as well: one for the apartment of a Drexel University student named Michael whom the tapes had identified as Taylor's top deputy, and one for an apartment in Valley Forge where they believed Burns stashed his coke. Reed and Perry, fairly certain of what would be found at Taylor's house, sent a squad of agents trained for break-ins on that raid and went themselves to Burns's suspected stash house, where the outcome was more in doubt. Their morning turned out to be a bust. The college apartment yielded nothing significant and the tip led to the right building but the wrong apartment. Angry and disappointed, they drove out to Taylor's house to try to improve their luck.

They arrived about 10:30, an hour or so after the raid, to find Suzanne and Bruce fast asleep on the living-room couch. The team of agents, bolstered by the addition of staff from the other two raids, had increased from five to seventeen, plus five clerical employees. The search for narcotics and other evidence kept them all occupied for the next four hours. Short of tearing the walls down, they went over the house with a fine-tooth comb, frequently commenting to each other about what a mess the place was and how hard it was to believe that people with so much money could live like such slobs.

Everybody had an assigned task. One agent stood watch over Suzanne and Bruce. Others searched and took photographs. One group laid out everything that would be taken back to headquarters on the pool table and filled out exacting inventory sheets, since every one of the hundred or so items from the house had to be cataloged.

The evidence fell into several categories. There were drugs and drug paraphernalia: one black-handled strainer; one wooden-handled strainer; seven metal bowls of various sizes with white residue; one silver spoon with white residue; several straws coated with white powder; various plastic bags with unknown white substances; two electronic scales, serial numbers B50345 and 3206012; one green pillbox with unknown substance; a black-and-white compact with white-powder residue; two packs of rolling paper; dozens of syringes; one bottle labeled "Aspirin" containing thirty-three pills; nine capsules of unknown substance; one Motorola beeper model A40BGB4661B; one NEC radio page #122036. . . . All the unknown substances and white-powder residues would be turned over to the FBI lab for testing. Some of the powder showed up as cocaine, some as inositol.

Then there were personal items, the most sentimental being a black Halliburton-zero briefcase, serial number 266192—the case that Dr. Misery, as Bruce was sometimes called, used to carry cocaine and which he referred to as his good-luck charm. It bore the gold initials L.L. and had been given to him by Dr. Lavin, who collected fancy briefcases and told Bruce at the time he presented the gift that it was special because he'd made his first million dollars out of it. The government also took a 1983 appointment book; a Band-Aid can containing a cigarette lighter and a coupon for a road map; a plastic coated binder containing bank statements; a traffic citation for Bruce Taylor; stationery and envelopes from the Bellevue-Stratford and the Four Seasons hotels; motor-vehicle registration for a 1982 BMW, a driver's license and pass-port for Suzanne Noramatzu; a Harley-Davidson wallet containing two expired licenses to carry a pistol, a group insurance card for Bruce Taylor, a sex-show coupon; a black camera case with boom mike extension; a TWA boarding pass in the name of B. Winus from Philadelphia to Phoenix, 8/22/83; a Temple University grade sheet for Suzanne Noramatzu. One of the personal items they decided not to take was the monogrammed cue stick Bruce had given Suzanne after teaching her how to play pool.

A number of weapons were also confiscated: an unassembled H&R model 929 .22-caliber revolver, a J. C. Higgins model 88 .22-caliber revolver, nine .22-caliber cartridges, one Beeman preci-sion airgun and a box of pellets, one Gerber knife with shield serial number C4034 S, one German World War II dagger, one Buck 110 knife.

A separate contingent of agents collected financial and drug records and counted money. There was $3,000 in cash scattered through the house, loose bills lying about like scrap paper. Bruce refused to give the agents the combination to the black safe in the kitchen, but they found the numbers they needed scribbled on the back of a business card. Inside was $84,920 wrapped in green Christmas paper. The safe weighed about five hundred pounds and they worried how they were going to haul it up the slippery path to the street without falling on the ice.

Chuck Reed and Sid Perry hadn't planned on making any arrests that day, but the quantity of cocaine discovered in the house changed their minds. However, first they needed approval from the Justice Department. They didn't want to use Bruce's phone for this confidential call because of their own wiretap on it, so they had to drive to a nearby pay phone to call the U.S. attorney.

"How much cocaine would you want to authorize an arrest?" Perry asked him.

"At least a kilo," he replied.

Sid went back to car. "We're on," he said to Chuck. "They want a kilo and we've got at least a kilo and a half. Bruce is in shit up to his lips."

On the short drive back to the house they discussed the best strategy for giving Taylor the chance to flip before arresting him. Should they soft-pedal the trouble he was in or scare the hell out of him? Few suspects realize how critical to their future it can be, when given the opportunity, whether or not they cooperate with the FBI. With all the tools law enforcement has at its disposal, the best one for convicting crooks is still other crooks. And what the FBI doesn't get willingly at first, they'll probably get under duress later on. As Sid Perry puts it, "We win or we win. If a suspect helps us, we get what we want. If he lies, we can crucify him in court with his false information. And if he says nothing, we'll say at his hearing that we gave him the chance to cooperate and he refused. It's pay now or pay later."

When they walked back into the house, Bruce was sitting up on the couch, shirtless, huddled under the quilt. It was so cold he could see his breath in front of his face.

"Can I take a leak?" he asked.

Perry walked him downstairs to the bathroom. The tub looked like it hadn't been scrubbed in months. There were holes in the tile, and used syringes, wadded-up paper cups, and dust balls all over the floor. Perry thought to himself that he'd sooner use the bushes outside than this toilet.

Bruce relieved himself and said, "I need a shot of insulin. Is it okay?"

"Sure," Perry answered. "Do whatever you have to."

Taylor told people that he was a diabetic, a blatant lie he even sold to Suzanne to hide the fact that he frequently injected cocaine because of the terrifically potent rush it gave him. He thought he could fool people into associating the needles lying around the house with diabetes rather than drug addiction. Actually, the insulin was a part of his drug abuse, since it had the effect of bringing him down when he was extremely high. Perry watched Bruce take a syringe of insulin from the medicine cabinet, remove the blue cover, and pull down his jeans. He stuck the needle into his left buttock, rubbed the spot with his hand for a minute, and pulled his pants back up. He did it as routinely as brushing his teeth.

While Sid Perry was downstairs with Bruce, Chuck Reed moved in on Suzanne. Her name had surfaced during the arson investigation as David Ackerman's girlfriend and he'd visited her around the same time he'd dropped in on Larry Lavin's dental office. Like Lavin, she'd refused to cooperate. It seemed to her now that he enjoyed throwing back in her face what a mistake that had been.

"See, Suzanne, you wouldn't be here now if you'd listened to me before. Well, I'm giving you a second chance. Tell me about Larry and Franny." Chuck Reed made Suzanne feel like a six-year-old being scolded by an authoritarian father. She hated him passionately. He made her feel dirty.

"This is serious. Do you realize how serious this is?" he pressed on aggressively.

She averted her gaze and whispered, "Yes."

"Larry doesn't care about you. He's sitting in his hot tub and not caring one bit about Suzanne Taylor."

She continued to stare at the floor, thinking it would be easier to keep silent if she didn't look at the contempt on Reed's face. He realized this wasn't going any better than their first encounter. Maybe he'd have more success with Bruce. As soon as Sid brought him back upstairs, Chuck said coldly, "C'mon, Bruce, we want to talk to you," and they led him to the back bedroom and shut the door. Reed motioned for him to sit down and stood in front him, allowing the sheer bulk of his body to send a threatening message.

"We paid a visit to Suzanne some time ago. We wanted her to cooperate and she turned us down. 'Fine,' we said. 'We'll be back.' You see, we kept our promise." Reed spoke in an emotionless voice, trying to impress Bruce with the gravity of his decision.

Perry crouched down on his knees so that his warm blue eyes could look directly into Taylor's vacant brown ones. He was totally different in style from Reed, who couldn't separate a criminal from his crime. Perry never humiliated or intimidated the people he questioned. He spoke from a position of strength, yet he appeared to be inviting Bruce's cooperation without striping away his dignity. Partly it was the softness of his Southern drawl. Partly it was his philosophy of treating suspects politely until they gave him a reason to withdraw his innate good manners. "We've got your coke, Bruce. We've got your drug records. We have pictures of you in Arizona with Wayne Heinauer. We know all about Burns and Lavin. You're in a lot of trouble and this is your chance to cooperate and help yourself." He briefly outlined what he might be able to do for Bruce if the coke dealer decided to help the government.

Bruce kept blinking at them: Reed slightly taller and bearlike, his eyes inscrutable behind tinted steel-rimmed glasses; Perry taut like a panther, his wavy gray-flecked hair curling rebelliously over the collar of a businessman's suit. The agents in turn watched Bruce struggling to make a decision. His brains appeared to be so fried from cocaine abuse that the simple act of thinking required serious effort. Over and over he asked them, "Will it be good for me? Will it really help me?" He nervously rubbed his hands together. "I just don't know. Larry's got a long arm." Just as he seemed on the verge of opening up, he requested to talk to his wife. Reed called in Suzanne and they left the couple alone for five minutes.

Suzanne could see Bruce was badly frightened. She sat down beside him and he clutched her against his quivering cold body, stroking her long dark hair. He grabbed her hand and squeezed it so hard it hurt. "They want me to make a deal," he whispered. "If we give them Franny and Larry, I'll only get fifteen years."

"What did you tell them?"

"Nothin' yet. They asked me if I was afraid of Larry and Franny." It wasn't Larry he feared. He had no doubt, though, that if he turned Fran in, Burns would have him killed or maimed for life as casually as he'd order juice for breakfast.

Suzanne was silent, remembering all the conversations with David and Larry when she was worried that somebody might squeal on her. They'd talked about loyalty and friendship. "No deals, Bruce," she said firmly. "No deals."

He softened his grip and hunched over. "Yeah. Right. No deals."

The agents returned and sent Suzanne back to the living room. Bruce looked at them with dead eyes. "No. I can't. He'd kill us."

Perry put his hand on Bruce's shoulder and in his Southern drawl said softly, "You made the wrong decision."

Around two that afternoon the search was completed. The agents didn't spend any time cleaning up afterward as they normally would have, because the house looked no worse than when they had arrived. Suzanne was handed the inventory sheets to sign.

"Do I have to?" she asked.

The agent smiled politely. "Yes, ma'am. You do."

There was just one item left on the agenda. Reed touched the sleeping Taylor on the arm to rouse him. "You're under arrest."

Bruce, his face pale and expressionless, said he needed another shot of insulin for his diabetes. When he returned from the bathroom, he kissed Suzanne lightly on the cheek and told her, "Call your uncle as soon as possible." Then he extended his hands for the FBI to slip on the cuffs and lead him to a waiting car.

Perry and Reed handed Taylor to another pair of agents for the routine booking and bail hearing and headed back to the Bureau with mixed feelings to assess the day's work. The Taylor raid had been quite fruitful, not so much for the amount of coke found as for the drug records that substantiated the conspiracy charge and provided several new leads. But the other two raids had been failures. There was no place for that bleak word in their vocabulary. They were hungry for total success and anything less than a perfect score was unacceptable. Maybe they could still squeeze a little more out of the day's events. Instinct told them to pay a follow-up call on the college student whose apartment they'd raided that morning, the kid Bruce Taylor called Howdy Doody because he looked like the all-American boy.

Michael had met Taylor through Kim Noramatzu. He functioned

for Bruce much as Bruce did for Larry—as a primary worker. Although Michael didn't buy or sell drugs, he made phone calls, carried cocaine, recruited customers and mules, and helped mix orders. He knew everything about Taylor's business, and since most of Bruce's customers had been bequeathed to him by Larry, Michael held a ball of wool that could roll out information. Reed and Perry found him sitting on his couch looking so shaken they knew immediately he'd turn like a leaf in the wind. This time when they left his apartment they had company on the way back to the Bureau: their first cooperating witness. It hadn't been a disappointing day after all.

Left alone at home, Suzanne wandered from room to room trying to sort out what to do next. All the Christmas packages bought and wrapped the night before and ready to be taken by them to new Hampshire this weekend lay open on the floor, the bright wrappings scattered all around. How sad, she thought. How very, very sad. Finally she picked up the phone and called her sister, Kim, who'd long since forgiven her for stealing her fiancé. She'd barely said hello when Kim blurted out furiously, "You won't believe what happened today. The FBI went to Michael's apartment!"

Suzanne had even more shocking news of her own. "Well, guess what? They just took Bruce out of here in handcuffs. Look, I want you to call our uncle and tell him what happened." Kim understood she was referring to Larry, whom Suzanne didn't want to call herself. He'd insist on hearing everything that very minute and press her for the smallest detail. She didn't have the strength to handle that kind of interrogation right now.

Kim immediately phoned Larry at his dental office and told him about the raid. Just as Suzanne had predicted, he couldn't wait to question her. As soon as Kim arrived at the Taylor house, she convinced her sister to speak to Lavin directly. She placed the call and put Suzanne on the line. It was 5:30.

"How ya doing? Are you pretty good?" Lavin asked, his voice masking the gravity of the situation. "I tell you what. They've already been there so I don't think it makes any difference if you just tell me what happened." Something told Larry it was probably a mistake to talk to Suzanne on the phone, but he had to find out how much the FBI knew. His instinct was accurate. The FBI was recording the conversation, surprised at the casual tone of the exchange. The two of them might just as well have been discussing a television program.

Suzanne thought to herself how typical Larry's reaction was. He could never wait for anything. David would have been so cautious over the phone. He'd probably have talked about the weather. "Well, what do you want to hear?" she asked. "We woke up and there were about twenty of them running around with shotguns. They had a search warrant. It was that same Charles Reed. Remember him?"

Did he ever? The bastard! He had known that guy would be trouble the minute Reed left his office a year ago. But until today Lavin had looked upon Reed as a dumb gumshoe, a guy with a gun, a badge and no brains. Larry had figured that if Reed and Perry were so smart, they wouldn't have had to spend a whole year putting the investigation together. Lavin, comfortably smug in his own sense of superiority, had read the signals all wrong. He'd mistaken for bungling the FBI's painstaking and methodical creation of an airtight case. Slowly it was beginning to register that these two might be more formidable opponents than he'd anticipated.

"When did all this happen?" he asked Suzanne. "Early this morning? What time?"

"They started around ten and left around three."

"Geez. All day?"

"I didn't know until the moment they left they weren't gonna take me. They mentioned a couple people's names and they found some cocaine and some money. I called his lawyer. He spoke to Bruce and said first they wanted a quarter of a million bail, and they reduced it to twenty-five hundred."

Larry laughed. "That's a big move. So how much of each thing do you think they got? A rough guess."

"Oh, about eighty-five."

"Eighty-five thousand?" he asked, raising his voice nervously.

"Yeah, and about a pound of the other."

"And did they take all kinds of paraphernalia?"

"Yeah."

"I imagine what they'll do is dump any cut they got into it and call it all one thing." Nobody ever expects the government to abide by the rules.

"Let's see what else they took. . . . Pictures of me and David, and anything that was written to me from David."

"So that's nothing, right?" Larry was more interested in how they had discovered Bruce. "Can you figure any way they knew to go to your place?"

"They said they had photographs of Bruce and someone named Wayne from about a year ago."

Larry's heart started to beat faster. "Someone named Wayne, you say. Oh, my gosh. Did they mention any state?"

"Yeah. It's out there. They said they've been looking at him for a while."

"Oh . . . my . . . gosh. A year ago." And all this time he'd thought he had only tax problems. Now he realized they'd been watching his drug deals for at least a year. This was much worse than he'd imagined.

"So what did Bruce do this whole time?"

"Me and him slept on the couch."

"Did they hassle you?"

"No. I wouldn't look at them when they talked, so they went away and took Bruce off into another room and tried to make a deal, but he wouldn't."

Larry seemed relieved at that, but eager to find out how much they had on him. "So they talked to him about me and David or other people? As far as making a deal, was it us they were talking about? Did you recognize any other names besides David and me?" How much could they possibly know?

"Your other friend. I don't really know him."

"Does the name begin with an F?"

"Yeah."

"Unbelievable." They had Franny too. He breathed a heavy sigh. "Well, is there anything I can do?"

"You can lend me some money." Suzanne was virtually penniless at the moment. The FBI had taken every bit of cash in the house.

"Okay. I'll come see you tonight after I finish at the office. Wait. I don't know how great an idea that is. Maybe we should meet up the street. It's just so unbelievable they would watch him for a whole year. What's your number there so I can call you?"

"I don't know." All their incoming calls came via the beeper and the phone was used only for outgoing calls, so Suzanne had never bothered to learn her phone number. Bruce had written it down somewhere, but she had no idea where.

Larry barely heard her answer. He was stunned by what Suzanne had been telling him. "So they definitely mentioned those names, huh? I wonder what happened out there with Wayne? Did they get intimidating with Bruce? Tell him he was going away for a long time and that kind of stuff?"

"Oh, yeah."

"Well, it will be interesting to see what the lawyer says. What he thinks is the worst they can do." Larry, from experience, recognized that the justice system could sometimes be manipulated by a good lawyer. Maybe they'd discover flaws in today's search warrant. Who knew what legal maneuvers might yet save them.

"I'm just surprised if they had pictures that there weren't more names," he mused, wondering if there was anybody he should warn. "I'm sure they grilled Bruce downtown all day. But he's smart enough. He's been through all that. Isn't that your feeling?" He was worried Bruce would crack. Burns believed that Bruce was the weak link in the organization. He'd always said if Bruce were caught, he'd run far and fast. Was Bruce planning such a move right now in jail? "Well, I guess I'm gonna have to drive over there later. I'd hate them to have a picture of me just driving in. They could add that to their album." He laughed at his little joke. "Listen, did all the neighbors see what was going on?" Even at a time like this, Larry worried about maintaining appearances.

"I don't know," Suzanne answered. "I haven't been out."

"Well, I'll drive over later. Is your beeper working?"

"No, they took it."

"That too? How about phone books and sheets with debts and stuff?"

"I think so."

"Geez. This is unbelieveable. I'll try to be there by nine. Don't go anywhere."

"I can't. They took my keys. 'Bye."

Finishing with his patient was just about the last thing Lavin wanted to do when he hung up the phone, but he was in the middle of fixing a bridge and couldn't stop despite the fact that it was difficult to concentrate. Later that night, he came to see Suzanne as promised and gave her $3,500—$2,500 for Bruce's bail and the rest to tide her over. They again reviewed the day's events, step by step, and discussed the options a lawyer might present. Larry was as pragmatic as always and treated the matter almost mundanely. He'd been through all this several times before, hiring lawyers, negotiating pleas. There had been Glenn Fuller's drug bust on the turnpike and at least three other workers who'd been caught with cocaine. This looked worse than the earlier arrests, but it was too early to tell. He was just a little uneasy about Bruce. Could he depend on him to keep his mouth shut?

The answer was no. On the way downtown that afternoon, the agents were hungry and stopped at McDonald's to buy hamburgers for everybody, including Bruce. He complained he had a broken wrist and asked them to loosen his handcuffs, which they did. He felt awful. Separated from Suzanne, he'd lost whatever resolve she'd been able to transfer to him. All he could think about was jail . . . years and years of jail . . . alone . . . no drugs to make him feel better. With very little prodding, he began babbling.

He bought his coke from Burns and Sandy, who worked for Burns. Burns would call him on his beeper, leave the number where he was to call back, and he'd go to a pay phone to return the call. He'd been told by Burns never to use the same pay phone twice in a row. He'd bought two kilos of coke from Burns a week ago and the money they'd found in the safe that day was money to pay Burns. Could he have a cigarette? He normally bought on credit because he didn't have a whole lot of cash and still owed Burns another sixty thousand dollars. Would the government like to make a deal with him? If they'd drop the charges, he'd give all kinds of information about Larry and Fran, even get Fran to deliver ten kilos of coke to an undercover agent. What else did they want to know? Burns and Lavin both had "muscle" and they might hurt his wife, Suzanne. Franny used his father-in-law to deliver drugs but probably didn't pay him much. He cut his coke about one-third before he sold it. The gun the FBI found in his living room had been there since he moved. It wasn't his. How about another cigarette?

The sun was setting when Bruce ran out of steam. He was arraigned and taken to a cell in the Detention Center until someone arrived to make his bail. Later that evening, he was permitted to call Suzanne.

The phone startled her. Larry had just gone and she was deep in thought.

"Collect, from Bruce," the operator said. "Will you pay for this call?"

"Sure," Suzanne answered. "Hi, baby, how are you?"

"I'm lousy. I'm sick. Oh, baby, I miss you. Are you gonna get down here and get me out in the morning?"

"I was thinking of coming down tonight so I can be there tomorrow, 'cause it's gonna snow."

"Yes, do that. Oh, God, I love you."

"I woulda come down today but they didn't call me until four-thirty. I'm so sorry. I miss you and I love you."

"Oh, God. Tell me."

"I love you."

"Tell me again."

"I love you. I love you. I love you so much."

"Listen, bring plenty of cigarettes when you come 'cause I ain't had a fucking cigarette. They won't give me any. Fucking lunatics up here."

"I bet. They, did the lawyer say how it looked or anything?"

"He said it don't look that bad, but he always says that. The law says I'm gonna get at least ten years."

"Don't listen to them."

"I ain't. Fucking Chuck Reed. What an asshole. He said to me, 'Your wife set you up with us.' I told him to fuck off."

"Why didn't they take me?"

"They said they're gonna arrest you later, but I think he's talking through his asshole, because you could be running."

"Arrest me later, huh?"

"Yep. Oh, God, I don't wanna hang up. I love you, baby. See you nine tomorrow. Did you find the car keys?"

"No, they took all the keys, my driver's license. They took everything. Telegrams. Letters. Photographs. They took bankbooks, passports. Everything."

"How will you get here?"

"Take a cab."

"You know how much I love you. I'm sorry. So sorry. Listen. Is there anything they missed? Did you find any you-know-what?" Bruce was desperate for a fix and told Suzanne where to look for some cocaine that he had hidden. "Down on the shelf where I keep the tools. Near the Epsom salt. Go see if that little package is there. The little silver thing the cartridge came in. Go take a look and see if they got that."

Suzanne put down the phone and returned shortly. "I can't find anything."

"It wasn't there?"

"No. You meant near the Epson salt in the back, right?"

"Yeah. In the washing-machine room on that shelf. Near the rug cleaner. Not in the cabinet, but on the shelf. Right above the opener, behind my tool bench."

"Wait a minute. I'll look again." She ran back to search some more. "Nope. Nothing there."

"Well, see if you can get hold of something tomorrow. Fix me a blast in the morning. A big one."

"Well, I don't know . . ."

"If you can't, you can't. You're sure there's nothing?"

"I'll look some more later. I know I didn't look so good."

"I miss you."

"What's it like there? Can you sleep?"

"It's horrible. It's all niggers, about thirty of them. I'm naked. They took my clothes."

"Oh, Bruce. I'm so sorry."

"Yeah. It's horrible. So I'll see you tomorrow about ten."

"Nine. I love you."

"Forever," Bruce said softly.

"I will love you forever," Suzanne repeated, and hung up the phone. Her eyes were wet.

16

By the time Billy Motto heard about Bruce Taylor's drug bust it was stale news, and he was too far away to be terribly concerned about what effect it might have on him. The same Christmas in 1983 that the FBI launched its wiretap operation, Billy South Philly moved to Florida with the intention of getting out of the drug business and starting a new life. His common-law-wife, Angela, was pregnant and he was tired of living with the constant fear of getting caught. His plan was to remove himself from the business and let his brother, Vincent, and his right-hand man and enforcer, Nicky Bongiorno, run things for him. Maybe that way he could live a normal life and break the cycle that was consuming him. "I was hung up on the entourage, the people. When you got money to spend, everybody caters to you. But I could never get enough to fill the hole inside me. I kept reaching for more—bigger drug deals, more girls, more cars, more everything."

A drug connection of his in Florida helped him find a $1,200-a-month home in a development called Boca Greens on the outskirts of Boca Raton. It was one of those upscale communities pictured in so many Florida real-estate brochures: sand-colored stucco ranches with dark wood trim artfully spaced on wide streets that wind around golf courses and artificial lakes. Each house was lushly landscaped with bougainvillea and palm trees and had its own pool in the backyard. There were golf carts parked in most of the driveways, driven by cheerful retirees in Bermuda shorts. It couldn't have been more from different from the narrow, crowded, noisy streets of South Philadelphia. Motto signed a year's lease and installed a pool table in his living room to make him feel more at home.

Billy was so accustomed to having the people on his payroll

handle his day-to-day chores that, left on his own with Angela, he had no idea how to get the phones hooked up, the electricity turned on, or even what size sheets to buy for the beds. His drug connection helped with all that too, and also found a health club nearby where Billy could expend some of his nervous energy in exercise. But after a month lifting weights and sunning on the beach, Billy South Philly was bored and restless. He didn't like the reports he was getting about his business either. His brother, Vincent, was extending credit to the wrong people. "That Vinnie," Billy used to say, "he's like Fredo in *The Godfather*. He's got to try to outdo me, like Fredo tried to outdo Michael, and it ain't gonna work." By February Billy was back selling drugs, commuting between Philadelphia and Florida, busier than he'd been before.

His business had really exploded when Larry passed him on as a customer to Franny Burns. Fran believed in stretching his customers' credit to the limit and pushing extra keys on dealers, figuring the more they had, the more they'd sell. Billy was a perfect example of how effectively this could work. Through Franny, he had access to larger quantities of coke than he'd ever been able to buy from Larry, and he began wholesaling uncut kilos along with the $1,400- and $1,800-an-ounce blends he was already handling. That brought his monthly total as high as thirty kilos, or over one million dollars—which didn't include his ongoing marijuana business. Unlike Larry, Billy never stopped selling pot when he got into cocaine, and he moved anywhere from 500 to 900 pounds of grass a month. In some ways, the pot business was a real nuisance. The weed was bulky to transport and the smell made it difficult to hide. Although Billy considered the profit of $100 a pound "goof-off money" compared with the $10,000 a kilo he was making with cocaine, he couldn't walk away from the cash. In that regard he was exactly like Franny Burns.

Even the danger signal raised by the FBI raid on Bruce Taylor's house didn't drive Burns from the drug business. It simply made him a bit more cautious. In the months following the Taylor bust, he and Lavin had endless meetings to assay just how much the government actually knew about their activities, what they could do to contain the case against them, and how they could keep it from spreading to New England, where Jill and Rusty Lavin were certain to get caught in the net. From talking to Bruce and Suzanne, Burns learned his name was definitely included in the government's file, that the FBI was aware of his coke sales to Wayne Heinauer in Phoenix, and had photographs that probably included his father-in-law making deliveries out there. Larry thought they ought to get in touch with Heinauer to see what information he might add. Since it was too risky to call directly, he attempted to make contact through mutual friends in upstate Pennsylvania. When that failed, Franny placed a call from a phone booth and, speaking in a muffled voice, offered the Phoenix dealer money to pay for a lawyer if he should need one. The financial aid was actually Larry's idea. From the time he'd started selling pot, he felt a responsibility to assist his cohorts when they got in trouble. It wasn't purely altruistic. Larry was also protecting himself, since he firmly believed, "The more you help someone, the less likely he is to betray you."

That was the main reason Larry continued to support Bruce Taylor, fearing that if he cut him loose, Bruce might become angry and try to get even. When Bruce expressed some willingness to disappear for the right price, Larry tried persuading Franny, who was now supplying him, to foot the bill. But Taylor's price tag for fleeing was $100,000, and Burns was unwilling to part with that much cash. He didn't trust Bruce, even with a payoff, to keep his mouth shut. They finally settled on paying his lawyer's fees. Burns put up $15,000, Lavin $5,000.

As the short days of winter lengthened into spring, Larry became increasingly preoccupied with his own situation and his plans for the future. Immediately after the raid on Taylor by the FBI, Marcia attacked Larry with her I-warned-you-to-get-out routine, and he countered that he *was* out, since he'd already sold the business to Burns. He still thought that he might get away with just facing the tax-evasion charge. But the more he talked to people who were being interrogated by the FBI, the more he realized he was in very deep trouble.

In the worst of all possible scenarios outlined by is lawyer, Lavin could be indicted for "engaging in a continuous criminal enterprise," which is the most serious drug charge in the government's arsenal, carrying a minimum prison sentence of ten years and a maximum of life without parole. He dismissed this as highly unlikely and expected he'd be charged under a drug conspiracy statute.

That charge offered him three choices.

The first and most logical option was to plead guilty to the conspiracy, which had a ten- to fifteen-year maximum sentence. Given the state of prison overcrowding, he'd probably serve only a third of that time, and if he gave the government a million dollars, maybe he'd get nothing more than probation. At first the thought of prison and the violence he'd heard took place there frightened Larry, but long talks with Franny Burns, who'd served seven months on a drug-possession conviction, convinced him that the men who had problems in jail were the ones who engaged in sex and gambling, and he'd had enough of that already. He worried far more about coping with a total state of boredom. Franny told him there were times he'd sat in his cell and cried because he missed life so much. "You know what's the biggest problem about jail, Larry?" Fran used to say. "You can't go out for pizza." And, in a way, that summed it all up, the waste of endless days with nothing to do. Not to mention the recognition that, for Larry, being locked away meant that he'd lost the game.

Larry's second choice was to cooperate with the government in exchange for a sentencing deal, but he rejected that from the outset. It was inconceivable for him to consider turning against the people who were his closest friends and relatives.

The third option was to take his wife, his son, his money, and run.

Unable to predict the government's plans for him, Lavin decided to lay the groundwork for a future in exile under a new identity in case he needed one. By sending away for a variety of pamphlets and books advertised in the back of the magazine *High Times*, he gradually built up a library of information on how to survive as a fugitive: *New ID in America, Guerrilla Capitalism, How to Get the Degree You Want, Directory of Mail Drops in the United States and Canada, ID for Sale: A Comprehensive guide to the Mail-Order ID. Industry, The Paper Trip I and II: For a New You Through a New ID.* With his typical diligence, he devoured the books and became an expert on creating bogus identities, a process that began with securing phony birth and baptismal certificates for himself and his family. Billy Motto's henchman, Nicky Bongiorno, connected Lavin with a printer who, for two hundred dollars, ran off a stack of blank, simulated documents by whiting out the personal information on Larry's original birth certificate and Marcia's baptismal papers. He did the same thing with Larry's official grade records from the University of Pennsylvania, another form of identification Lavin wanted, should he, for some reason, need to prove he'd been to college.

Finally Larry designed and ordered seals to give the documents an official stamp, confident from all he'd read that nobody ever checked to see if a seal was genuine. Previously when he'd required real corporate seals for his businesses, Lavin's Options and L's Inc., his lawyer had obtained them for him, and he assumed that only lawyers could order the kind of seals he now needed. With typical thoroughness, he created a phony law firm for himself by having cards and stationery printed in the name of McDermitt and Sullivan on Lancaster Pike in Malvern, Pennsylvania. The address was actually that of a public mailbox company. Armed with his new business card, he arrived at the place that made the seals, only to find that the clerk wordlessly handed him a standard form to fill out and didn't even ask who he was or what he did. Just to be safe and cover his tracks, he used the McDermitt name and address anyway.

The other activity that kept Larry so busy that spring that he had no free time to play golf with Kenny Weidler was converting the money he'd laundered into investments back into cash. This time he wasn't leaving any paper trail for the FBI to follow. From the sale of his stock-exchange seat, his real-estate holdings under L's Inc., and other checking and savings accounts, Larry accumulated several hundred thousand dollars in the bank. He couldn't withdraw the cash clandestinely because of a banking regulation that requires reporting any currency transaction over ten thousand dollars to Internal Revenue. Getting a check for the entire sum didn't solve the problem either, since there was nowhere he could cash an amount that large without drawing unwanted attention. His solution was to remove the money piecemeal by cashier's check, then drive to the casinos with $20,000 to $40,000 in checks and deposit them in the casino bank for chips. He'd gamble awhile, cleverly moving from table to table. Later he'd give his chips to a friend to exchange for him into cash, which he squirreled away in safe-deposit boxes. Sometimes he lost a little on the transaction, but more often he won. Lavin was an astute gambler who didn't believe in luck. He carefully played the odds and was never too emotional not to know when it was time to walk away.

At the same time Larry was preparing for the possibility of fleeing, he was actively involved in orchestrating the flow of information and its content to the FBI. One means of accomplishing that was to make certain his old customers and dealers had their stories coordinated if Chuck Reed or Sid Perry came to visit. One buyer in particular Larry needed to reach was a South Jersey lawyer, and the intermediary for contacting him was Michael, the college student who delivered coke for Bruce Taylor. What Larry didn't know was that Michael had agreed to cooperate with the FBI back in January after they'd raided his apartment. He'd given permission to have his calls recorded by the government. (Consentual telephone recordings, unlike secret wiretaps, can be easily obtained, since they require only the approval of the local FBI bureau chief and the U.S. attorney.) Under the FBI's direction, Michael had been calling several Taylor contacts and casually chatting with them about Larry and Franny, piling up more ammunition for the government's case. It was an unexpected bonus when Larry himself rang up Michael one morning and simply said, "Hi. Can you call me?" He purposely didn't use is name, but Perry and Reed, listening on the line, recognized the voice. "Sure," Michael answered, "I'll go to a phone booth," and he did—with a hand-held device to record the call.

A breakfast meeting to concoct a cover story explaining Michael's frequent visits to the lawyer was set up at Olga's, a popular South Jersey diner. The FBI considered fitting Michael with a body wire to record the conversation, but decided against it, fearing Larry might frisk him. Instead they sent a surveillance team to follow Lavin's BMW from Philadelphia across the Ben Franklin Bridge out into the Camden County suburbs where the diner was located at a busy traffic circle. Two agents were sent into the diner to eat breakfast at a booth next to Michael and Lavin; another parked not far from the entrance to take pictures.

When the lawyer pulled into Olga's lot, he drove right in front of the agent who was holding the camera ready to snap the shutter. The sight of the camera was enough for the lawyer to keep his foot on the gas pedal and steer his car back onto the highway.

A short while later he telephoned Lavin at the diner and told him somebody was outside taking pictures. He and Michael paid for their coffee and left, unable to find any photographer outside, because the FBI agent, realizing he'd been spotted, had put the camera way. Michael convinced Lavin that the lawyer was being paranoid about security. They got back into the dentist's BMW and headed for the nearest pay phone, which happened to be in the gas station across the street that Sid Perry had chosen for his observation site. Instinctively Perry ducked under the steering wheel to hide from Lavin. It didn't occur to him until later that the two of them had never met face-to-face. Lavin parked and walked to the outdoor phone. He reached the lawyer at his office and instructed him to create a phony client file in Michael's name to show the government they had a legitimate business relationship. Later, Perry would subpoena the pay-phone record to verify the call. He now had another piece of evidence against Larry, as well as the name of another customer to add to the indictment.

The Bruce Taylor raid marked a pivotal point in the FBI case. No longer would Perry and Reed be gathering information for purely investigative purposes. Henceforth they would be targeting specific people to charge with crimes and building cases for trial. Until now, it had been difficult persuading people to cooperate. That would change with the indictments, which the agents knew from past experience, were powerful tools for yielding cooperation. The impact of being arrested, fingerprinted, and brought in front of a judge to respond to charges had a way of loosening tongues. Originally the agents planned to indict thirty people in their first round of arrests, but on advice from the U.S. attorney, they narrowed the field to the fourteen strongest cases, which still left them with an enormous amount to do.

The FBI operates on the theory that all the work pertinent to readying a case for actual trial should be completed prior to asking a grand jury for an indictment. If the suspect chooses to plead guilty when charged and there is no need for a trial, so much the better. But the possibility of not having to go into a courtroom doesn't discourage them from fully preparing for a trial in advance. For each of the fourteen people the government expected to indict, there would have to be detailed and conclusive proof to support the charges. That meant furnishing dates, times, and places of meetings to buy or sell drugs, facts to confirm the structure of the conspiracy and how it operated, witnesses to corroborate allegations, hard evidence like taped phone calls, phone records, surveillance photos, articles taken in searches, and the like. All during the spring of 1984, Perry and Reed sorted through the mountain of information they'd collected, assembling data to present to the U.S. attorney. Then the legal and the investigative arms of the U.S. Justice Department sat together as a team reviewing each defendant individually and weighing whether they had a strong enough case to proceed to trial.

Merely having witnesses report on this or that event wasn't going to convince a jury. Many of the people the government would be putting on the stand were dope dealers themselves, and for their words to be accepted as truth, it was crucial to establish a pattern of credibility in their testimony. If, for instance, a witness would be testifying that he attended bachelor parties at a casino hosted by Lavin where cocaine was readily available, Perry had to have casino room records in Lavin's name to corroborate the statement. If the witness claimed that Larry called him four times a week, Perry needed phone records to prove he was telling the truth. Then, when that witness reached the point in his testimony where he said he bought coke from Lavin and the government had no proof of that transaction, chances were a jury would believe him because it had been shown that everything else was accurate.

By the summer of 1984 the FBI was ready for the courts. There are just two ways the United States can bring indictments against private citizens. One is the established grand-jury process in which the government spreads its goods before a group of the defendant's peers, hoping they'll agree there is sufficient evidence to charge that defendant with a crime. The other is called "an information," in which a defendant waives his right to a grand-jury proceeding by pleading guilty before an indictment is delivered, usually for the purpose of arranging a plea agreement. There was a brief time after the Taylor raid that it seemed Franny Burns might take the latter route. His attorney looked at the barrage of charges his client faced—tax evasion, drug dealing, attempted arson of a competitor's ice-cream store—and thought he might be able to wrap them all up into a reduced sentence if the Dairy Queen owner cooperated with the government. They met to arrange a possible plea bargain, but the demands Burns made to examine the evidence behind the government's curtain were too great and, rebuffed, he decided not to take a plea. He left the meeting particularly angry at Chuck Reed, who acted as if he had God on his side.

The task of presenting the FBI's evidence to the grand jury fell to Sid Perry. Whenever there is a choice of agents who are able to testify, the government prefers to use one for the grand jury and use the other for the trial. The purpose is to keep as much pretrial-discovery information as possible out of the defendant's hands since, by law, it's not required to release to defense attorneys the secret grand-jury testimony of any witness unless that same witness is scheduled to take the stand again in open court. Another advantage to using separate agents is that it reduces the risk the defense will be able to weaken an agent's credibility by catching him in a that's-not-what-you-told-the-grand-jury memory lapse. Finally, there was a purely practical reason for choosing Perry to go before the grand jury. Reed had very little courtroom experience and this was an ideal case to cut his teeth on because there was so much evidence to back him up.

Over the summer, Perry, nattily attired in a gray checked suit, white-on-white shirt, and dark tie, sat in the federal-grand-jury witness box six different times, some days as long as five hours straight, spinning the government's tale of a cocaine conspiracy that started at the University of Pennsylvania Dental School and spread across the United States. Not for a minute did he doubt the outcome. Before a case gets to a grand jury it has to be approved by many levels of the U.S. attorney's office, which presents it, as well as the local FBI chain of command.

The Lavin file sailed through. On September 9, 1984, the grand jury issued fourteen indictments against Dr. Larry Lavin, Francis Burns, Bruce Taylor, Suzanne Noramatzu Taylor, her sister Kim, Burns's girlfriend, Sandra Freas, and a mix of small customers and workers. At the government's request, the indictments were sealed. There are always reporters hanging around the grand-jury room, and it wouldn't do for the defendants to learn from the morning newspaper that they were about to be arrested.

Neither Sid Perry nor Chuck Reed slept very well the night before the arrests. A combination of nerves and excitement, although more of the latter, kept them tossing fitfully until their alarms went off. Neither was worried that something could go wrong. Perry compared it with the night before a vacation when something you've carefully prepared for and looked forward to for a very long time is about to happen. He rose at four A.M., an hour earlier than usual, and skipped his routine predawn two-mile jog. It was too early to tell how warm the day would become, and he dressed in a tweed sport coat that, by the heat of midmorning, he'd be sorry he'd worn. He ate no breakfast and stopped, as he always did, at McDonald's to pick up a container of coffee, which he drank as he drove the forty minutes from his home in a lakeside New Jersey community to the Philadelphia FBI headquarters just off the Ben Franklin Bridge. He loved it when things got hectic and a day was crammed with more things than he could possibly attend to. It wasn't the caffeine that was making his heart beat faster than normal.

Reed awakened at five A.M., too jumpy to eat. His head was full of the day's possibilities. Would they get keys, address books, the location of Burns's stash house? As he pulled the trousers of his tan summer suit up to his thickening waistline, he thought of the satisfaction he'd soon have pointing his revolver at the man he'd been stalking for so many months and smugly smiling as he said, "Good morning, Fran. You're under arrest." And wouldn't it be sweet to see smart-aleck Dr. Lavin in handcuffs? It was going to be a terrific day.

By six A.,M. the fifty agents comprising the arrest teams had assembled at the Bureau and reviewed their final instructions. It had already been decided to park and wait for each of the defendants to reveal himself rather than have the agents flush them out of bed. If, by nine A.M., they hadn't been apprehended, then the FBI would go hunting.

Larry Lavin left his house earlier than usual on the morning of September 11 because his partner, Ken Weidler, was going to fill a cavity that had been bothering him. He dressed casually, as he always did for work, in a white Lacoste shirt, yellow poplin slacks, and soft leather loafers worn without socks. Lavin expected to be arrested sooner or later; still, that didn't lessen the shock when he eased into the parking area next to his dental office and saw the two cars waiting for him. Instinctively he shifted into reverse gear, but the agents blocked him before he could back out of the driveway. Suddenly there were six guns aimed at his head and men yelling, "This is the FBI. Keep your hands up." The scene reminded Larry of bad television. "Here I've got the car running with one foot on the clutch and one on the break. If I can't put my hand down to slip into neutral I can't get out and the car's going to slip into gear and somebody will get hit. They're beating on the glass with their guns, motioning me to keep my hands up, and I'm trying to explain what I have to do. The whole thing was so stupid. It was just like the FBI to lie in wait for me and play cops and robbers."

It took just a minute for the surprise to wear off and for Lavin's mind to turn to practical matters. What lousy timing, he thought. Tucked into his briefcase was the phony church seal he'd used to validate the baptismal certificates sitting on his desk at home. Now they were all worthless. He'd intended to toss the seal into the dumpster behind his office just in case the FBI was searching the trash collected at his house. Now they'd get that along with all the other things in his briefcase—a receipt for money he'd loaned the Florida fruit-extract dealer who delivered cocaine to him and Franny hidden in large juice cans; his Casio pocket computer with all his customers' phone numbers, the receipt for a mail drop he'd planned to use if he fled, his address book, and God knows what else. He'd played perfectly into the FBI's hands. To maximize the evidence they could seize at his arrest, they'd purposely chosen to grab him at his office rather than his house, figuring correctly he'd be more likely to have his briefcase with him. They also wanted the opportunity to impound his car and inventory the contents. Anything that smacked of being connected with criminal activity could be confiscated as government property.

Lavin wondered for a minute where Chuck Reed was. It never occurred to him that Reed's absence had been deliberately calculated to deliver a message, a little slap in the face that said: You think you're such a big deal, but you don't deserve my attention. I have bigger fish to fry. In planning the arrests, Reed and Perry had decided that Larry's would be the least exciting. They were certain he wouldn't fall apart or give up any startling information, so they sent in the second team—"like Reagan sends Bush when it's not important enough for him to show up" was the way Perry put it. For them it was more fun to drop by the room at headquarters where Lavin would be detained and wave hello. The arrest proceeded exactly as the agents had expected. Lavin was calm and uncharacteristically reserved. He even refused to give his name. "Can I tell my office I won't be in today?" he asked.

The arresting agents told him he could call when they got downtown, put him in handcuffs, and shoved him in the back seat of their car. The only time he opened his mouth during the ride was to ask the agents if they could possibly loosen his handcuffs. Following his lawyer's advice, he was careful to give no personal information. The blank expression on his face revealed nothing of the maelstrom inside his head. "My mind was racing a million miles a minute, thinking of every possibility. I'm wondering: Who else did they pick up? Who are they going to indict? Is there any problem with Marcia? I'm not frightened at all, more like concerned about all the things I have to do."

Chuck Reed was waiting for Franny Burns to leave his house when he got the news that Lavin had been arrested. But he was too involved in capturing Franny to gloat. At seven A.M. under a clear, cloudless sky, he'd joined five other agents at a shopping mall, and in a three-car caravan they'd driven to the development where Burns lived, just a stone's throw from Valley Forge National Historic Park. Reed drove his car down Franklin Lane, turned right, and right again, parking out of sight on the dead-end street. The other agent positioned his car at the opposite end of the same street so that no matter which way Burns went, his route was blocked. A third car stood nearby for assistance should it be needed. Franny Burns, for one thousand dollars a month, rented a four-bedroom brick colonial in this pleasant family neighborhood where all the streets bore the names of men who'd signed the Declaration of Independence. He lived on Paine Circle in a house like most of the others with a border of hedges set against a manicured front lawn.

The clock in Reed's car read 8:50. The agents had been sitting well over an hour, having arrived early in case Burns did not follow his usual pattern. Reed passed the time relishing the stunned look he expected to see on Franny's face when he snapped the cuffs on him. Would he crumble and talk? What would they find in his car? Would he play his poor-little-me role? The agent wiped the perspiration gathered under the fine straight hair that fell on his forehead. He'd played every scenario in his head at least twice and now he was getting restless. He called the FBI on his radio. "Let's flush him out." An agent downtown telephoned the local King of

Prussia police and gave them Burns's unpublished phone number with instructions to tell him his Dairy Queen had been burglarized.

"Something's not right," Burns said to his wife when he hung up the phone. In the past when there had been trouble at the store, the police had called Burns's mother because he had an unlisted phone and didn't like to be bothered at home. He was uneasy as he jumped into a pair of baggy nylon jogging shorts, covered his sagging belly with a T-shirt, and lumbered out of the house to his car. He didn't bother to brush his teeth or comb his hair. As soon as the agents heard his engine kick on, they started their cars and the four autos converged within seconds at the mouth of the Paine Circle cul-de-sac. Burns was instantly surrounded by six men shouting, "Freeze. Don't move. You're under arrest." He slowly let out the clutch of his 1978 Toyota and almost ran over one of the agents. Two others yanked open his car door and dragged him out. He looked dumbfounded and fixed his black eyes in a meaningless stare as they read him his rights, locked the cuffs on his wrists, and pushed him into a car for the trip downtown. By 9:30 it was all over.

Burns's car was also confiscated, but it didn't yield anything as important to the FBI as Lavin's. There was a toolbox with $1,000 in the trunk and a Tupperware container with $112 in quarters. When asked later why he carried so much small change, Burns shrugged and muttered, "I make a lot of pay phone calls."

More productive were the search warrants executed at Burns's mother's home and his Dairy Queen. The government was looking for clues to explain how he laundered money and, also, for drug paraphernalia. They took some business records from the ice-cream store and found hidden in his mother's basement a machine gun, a shotgun, drug scales, and a pile of papers. A week or so later, while examining the carton of papers, Reed suddenly let out a whoop. On a green accounting sheet, written in Larry's handwriting, was a list of fifteen customers, their code names, phone numbers, and credit lines. Not one of the names was familiar, not even "Priscilla New England" with her $200,000 credit limit. These were all new leads, plus another piece of evidence linking Burns and Lavin. Sid Perry described it as "better than sex in the afternoon."

The person Sid Perry chose to arrest was Sandy Freas, on the outside chance that she might flip and take him to Burns's stash house. He and two other agents (one female, in case Freas had to be body-searched) had been sitting patiently in their car since 7:30 outside the garden apartment where the teenager lived with her grandmother. At nine, when Sandy still hadn't appeared, Perry got out and rang the bell. She came to the screen door with her shaggy shoulder-length brown hair partially rolled in curlers.

He nodded pleasantly. "Hi, Sandy. How are you? Do you remember me?"

"Yes," she said sharply. How could she forget? He'd been by last winter trying to get her to talk about Fran.

"Fran's been arrested, Sandy. You're under arrest. Can I come in?"

She opened the door and stepped aside, saying nothing while she toyed with the curler in her hand. Perry stood directly in front of her and in a serious yet friendly voice said, "You know, when we talked before, I asked for your cooperation. I won't be coming to you anymore after this. We're going to take you downtown now where you'll be fingerprinted and photographed. Then you'll go in front of a magistrate for a bail hearing. It won't be very pleasant, but you could make things a lot easier on yourself. What do you think?"

Her response was like the blast when a freezer door is opened. She may have been a teenager, but she was no innocent kid. And after sitting next to Franny in a Miami hotel while he negotiated coke deals with a Colombian balancing a rifle on his lap, this guy in a business suit was hardly her idea of frightening. "I'll give it some thought," she said, making it clear to Perry she wasn't the least bit interested. He allowed her to remove the rest of the curlers, handcuffed her, and drove her downtown. The other agents impounded her car, a beat-up Cutlass, and found Sandy's purse. In it were her address book and Billy South Philly's phone number scribbled on a piece of paper.

The only arrests on September 11 that did not go according to plan were the Taylors'. Since the previous spring, Suzanne and Bruce had been living with one of his relatives in New Hampshire, trying to keep a low profile. A phone call from Suzanne's mother telling them Kim had been arrested earlier that morning gave them advance warning that the FBI was on its way. In fact a team of agents had already started out after them and discovered that the house they occupied belonged to someone else, which meant the FBI needed a search warrant to enter. While the agents were getting the warrant, Suzanne and Bruce slipped away in their white Mazda, leaving the black BMW in the driveway for the agents to seize. A day later the Taylors surfaced in Philadelphia and turned themselves in, a move regarded by the government as a clever bail ploy. Now their attorney could go before a magistrate and argue for a lower bail on the basis that they'd given up on their own free will, which showed they could be trusted and had acted in good faith. The maneuver succeeded. Bruce's bail was $100,000; the $10,000 he actually had to post for his freedom came from Franny Burns's pocket. Suzanne's bail was set at $35,000 and she was sent home on her own recognizance without paying a penny.

Larry Lavin arrived at FBI headquarters before Franny Burns. He was strip-searched, fingerprinted, and photographed. Although it was only midmorning, he already looked like he needed a shave. He found the procedure more bothersome than embarrassing. "I dealt with this like everything else that had gone wrong. It was just one more thing I had to endure."

The government allowed him to make two phone calls. One was to his office and he was uncharacteristically brief. "Something's come up and I won't be in today." The other was to Marcia. After telling her what had happened and ascertaining that she was all right, he told her to call his lawyer and find the deed to the house.

"I'm gonna need bail. We may have to post the house. Marcia, I'm really sorry all this happened. I love you very much."

Although the sun was shining into the kitchen where Marcia held the phone, a cold chill swept over her. "I love you too, Larry. Don't worry. Whatever happens, I'll be here for you." She carefully replaced the receiver and wondered how much time she had left before beginning to pack.

After his calls, Larry was led to the eighth floor of the Federal Building and detained in a classroom that the FBI used for in-service training. It was there that Reed and Perry dropped by to say hello. Perry introduced himself by saying, "Hi, I'm the one you always say is the nice guy." Reed looked as smug as ever. Larry thought of how Reed had called him on the phone months earlier to come in and be fingerprinted on the tax case. "Make sure you wear dungarees," Reed had needled him. "I'm gonna see that you get good and dirty."

After Franny Burns joined Larry at the FBI, they were taken together down six floors to a holding cell in the federal marshall's section of the same building. It was Lavin's first taste of what his future might be like. They paused in front of a locked iron door which was electronically opened to admit them to the cellblock. Slowly they walked down the four-foot corridor past the line of identical cells until they were locked together into a twelve-by-fifteen-foot space with a toilet, a sink, and benches built into the wall. Larry was too preoccupied to pay much attention to his bleak surroundings. He was worried about what his bail would be and whether he'd be released. "I just sat there thinking of all the things I had to do for myself and for the business. Somebody had to tell people not to call the beepers or show up with money. The idea of making a deal wasn't even a remote possibility. I'd already made up my mind that I couldn't turn in my family and friends."

Lavin stared at Burns sitting across from him. He liked Franny. They'd both made a lot of money selling drugs, yet he considered it unfair that they'd been charged with the same crime. "Franny was a bigger threat to society than I ever was. He hurt people." Lavin saw himself as a decent guy and a good dentist who'd conducted his business like a gentleman and rarely even threatened anybody. He didn't deserve the same fate as Burns, and he wasn't going to stick around to get it.

At his bail hearing, Lavin stood before the magistrate listening to the charges against him, forty-four counts rolled into what he had most feared: the drug-kingpin statute. His worst-case scenario had been realized. He'd been indicted under an 848 for a continuing criminal enterprise. The minimum he would have to serve in jail was a full ten years without parole; the maximum was life without hope of parole.

The government requested $250,000 bail, but the judge reduced it to $150,000, claiming that Lavin was a professional man with no prior criminal record and posed no risk to the community. Larry had no trouble raising the ten percent, or $15,000, necessary for release, and was a free man by the afternoon. He was acutely aware that his freedom was only temporary. Two weeks later he was indicted by another grand jury for four counts of evading $545,000 in taxes on income of $1.12 million that he had failed to report between 1979 and 1982.

Franny Burns's thoughts as he sat hunched over opposite Larry in the stuffy cell were not of flight but fight. He was a different kind of conniver, a man who knew how to strike a bargain and finesse a deal. He tried to convince his friend that cooperating was the most sensible route.

"You're kidding yourself, Larry. They already know everything, so who are you protecting? You think Bruce isn't going to talk? Come on. I'll bet you ten thousand bucks. He's not going to jail for ten years. Don't you see the handwriting on the wall? Sooner or later, everybody's gonna flip. The only smart thing is to cut a deal."

Larry disagreed. "You're wrong Franny. It would hurt people if I talked. I can't do that. I just can't."

"You don't have to hurt people. You can fake it. I'm gonna

pretend to set up my suppliers in Florida, but I won't really do it. I'll buy forty keys and put it in a room somewhere instead of turning it over to the feds. You're smart. You can figure a way to make it look like you're cooperating without really doing it."

But Lavin was cut from a different cloth. He'd rather match wits with the FBI than make a deal with them. He posted his bail and left Franny behind to plot what he could give the government and what he might get in return. Burns had a night alone to mull over the question, because he was unable to meet his bail figure right away. The government wanted Burns's bail set at $500,000 and argued that because of his criminal record there was a risk he might flee. The judge reduced the request to $250,000 but the ten percent Fran would have to post was more than he had lying around the house. It took a day for his wife to get down to one of the casinos in Atlantic City where he kept huge sums of money to gamble—and to hide from the government—and withdraw the $25,000 to bring her husband home.

The next morning, shortly before Burns's release, the government received an anonymous tip that he'd be moving large amounts of coke and money out of his house on Paine Circle. The FBI quickly sent a surveillance team to watch the house, while Reed hustled around getting a search warrant approved. He had not yet arrived with the warrant when Burns's father walked out the front door and got into his car. One of the agents decided to follow and stopped him on the highway, using a law that allows a person to be detained if there's reasonable suspicion he's aiding or abetting a crime. The old man agreed to have his car searched, not realizing it contained something far more valuable than cocaine. In a purple flannel Crown Royal liquor bag on the floor under the dashboard were Franny Burns's beepers. Without the beepers he was helpless. He had no other way to communicate with his customers or, more important, his Colombian sources. Bereft of them, he had nothing to trade with the FBI. By arrangement the Colombians would call Fran's beeper when they had coke to sell, leaving a number where they could be reached. If they beeped twice and he didn't answer, they'd know something was wrong and stop calling. The relationship would be severed.

It took Burns only twenty-four hours to realize that he'd lost his biggest bargaining chip, and getting the beepers back quickly was critical to any deal he might hope to make with the government. He and his lawyer came to the FBI on September 13 offering to cooperate and delivering three kilos of coke as a show of good faith.

Larry found it terribly amusing when he learned that Franny had flipped. They'd had so many talks in recent months about which people would talk, and Franny was always telling Larry that he'd be surprised how weak people were and how quickly they crumbled under pressure. What irony that the toughest of the lot, the only man in the conspiracy who'd actually served time in prison, was the first one to save his skin by double-crossing his friends. Actually Burns's cooperation worked to Lavin's advantage by keeping the FBI so preoccupied with a Columbian drug bust Franny was arranging for them in Miami that Reed and Perry were too busy to pay attention to the dentist's travel plans.

17

MIAMI, FLORIDA
NOVEMBER, 1984

Franny Burns may not have finished high school, but he thought he was smart enough to outwit the FBI. In exchange for allowing his calls to be taped, wearing a wire to entrap his former customers, and trying to set up a drug bust in Florida against his Colombian suppliers, he negotiated a plea agreement with the government that reduced the maximum number of years he faced in prison from sixty to nineteen.

He was trading his cooperation for the government's support when he stood before a judge for sentencing. But Franny did not intend to play it straight with the FBI. Instead, he decided if he was going to jail, he would go as a rich man—which would require some tricky maneuvering. Huge drug debts were owed to him at the time of his arrest, and he had every intention of secretly collecting them behind the government's back. To accomplish his goal meant making the FBI believe he was fully and honestly cooperating, while convincing people who owed him money that he was lying to the government and protecting them.

As the leaves turned in the weeks after his arrest, Burns met regularly with Chuck Reed and Sid Perry in a motel room the agents rented in the Valley Forge area near his home so they'd have a place to talk and to tape the calls he answered from his beeper. In addition to hours of interviews, filling in the who, what, when, and where of his dealings with Lavin, Burns placed several calls to Florida trying to arrange the drug buy that would deliver his Colombian source to the FBI. His contact was a man he knew as Alex, who would beep him when he had cocaine to sell. Throughout October, Alex was having difficulty amassing the quantity and quality of coke Burns wanted to buy. Finally, after several attempts to put a deal together, Alex beeped Franny in the beginning of November to tell him he was ready. Franny responded to the message from a pay phone in center-city Philadelphia and taped the call with a small device supplied by the FBI that suctioned onto the receiver.

He began by whispering into the recorder, "I'm returning a call to the Colombians. I'm calling from 555-9825 and the number I'm calling is area code 305-555-9797. I'm at the corner of the alley at Fifteenth and Spruce and it's about four-thirty."

In Florida the phone was picked up by a Hispanic woman named Edith who worked as an interpreter for Alex. She would translate everything Franny said into Spanish and then translate Alex's responses into English.

"Hi," Franny answered. "You might have to talk a little louder because I'm on a highway in Philadelphia."

"Okay," Edith answered. "How's your kid?"

"She's doing good. She went to school today." Franny's daughter had been sick with the flu.

"That's good. Alex says everything is going to be solved for tomorrow, and since you can't come down on Sunday, can you come on Monday?"

"That would probably be good. Then I can be with my wife and kids all weekend. But like I said, I gotta get outta there and be home by six."

"No problem. Everything will be ready for four tomorrow."

"Just tell him to give me a beep over the weekend to be sure. Is he certain for Monday, because I can get my uncle to call me and say he needs me to come down. You know what I mean?"

"Right."

"In other words, he's sure about Monday? Because I'm running out of excuses and I have to to tell my wife something." Franny had already made two recent trips to Florida and the product wasn't there. He had led the Colombians to believe his family was unaware of his drug business and he couldn't fly back and forth just to take a sunbath.

"Well, everything is here. He's just waiting for them to give it to him."

"I don't understand. Don't they trust him: He's like family to them guys."

The operator broke into the call. "That will be another forty-five cents, please." Franny put more change into the phone.

"It's not they don't trust him. It's because of security."

"Tell him this is the same bullshit we went through during the summer. I got people telling me it's gonna be here. My other guy is waiting. I mean, I'm cracking up. I live at pay phones. I don't wanna do that no more. Is it in or are they waiting for a plane?"

"No, everything is here. They haven't given it out to anybody yet. Alex said to tell you this example. It's like the truck full of newspapers and he's the newspaper boy but they haven't started to give the papers out yet."

"Well, tell him to make sure he looks at the stuff first, because he knows what I like."

"He says he'll take care of you like always."

"Okay. Then we're set for Monday. Have him call me Sunday. Maybe noontime. Definitely have him get hold of me Sunday."

"All right."

"Okay. I'll see you then. 'Bye."

As chatty as Burns was while betraying the Colombians, he seemed to suffer severe memory gaps when it came to discussing his local drug-dealing clientele, particularly one Billy Motto, about whom he seemed to know surprisingly little. At this point the FBI had only minimal evidence on Motto, and he remained a shadowy figure in this phase of the investigation.

Reed and Perry began to suspect that Burns was double-dealing when they realized he was giving information only on dealers who were far away—in Florida or New England—while he seemed evasive about his Philadelphia customers. His duplicity really didn't bother them. Reed knew that "he might start out screwing the government but he'll end up screwing himself." He'd seen it happen again and again. A cooperating witness thinks that by selectively withholding information, he can prevent particular co-conspirators from getting caught. The government uses other evidence to indict those people, who, to save their own hide, almost invariably testify against the very person who tried to protect them.

The agents didn't even bother to object when Burns asked to be taken into the witness-protection program, claiming his family's life was in danger because the Colombians would know where to find him and had a reputation for vicious paybacks. They considered his request totally unnecessary, part of a defense strategy geared toward showing the sentencing judge the great risk he was willing to undergo in order to cooperate. No matter. Eventually, they knew, Burns would get exactly what he deserved for lying to the feds. Meanwhile, the FBI would play his game and milk him for whatever information they could.

That did not include data on Billy Motto, who was aware of Burns's arrest and his cooperation. Burns believed it was in his best interest to keep Billy South Philly out of the picture at least long enough to collect the substantial drug debt he owed him.

And it was in Motto's best interest to meet his financial obligation, in the hope the payment would serve as hush money to keep Franny from putting the finger on him to the FBI.

The two met in October to discuss their separate agendas at one of Motto's favorite health spas, the Philadelphia Athletic Club, in a large, once-handsome building that had long ago been a luxury hotel and now reeked of chlorine and sweat.

Motto was standing in the lobby when Burns arrived. As Franny lumbered toward him, Billy held his index finger to his lips, warning him to keep silent. The message was clear. Motto wasn't talking until he could be certain Franny wasn't wearing a wire. Billy chatted affably with the receptionist about a reservation for a massage and then motioned for Franny to follow him down the steps toward the pool. They went into the locker room. Billy tossed him a pair of gym trunks and silently watched him remove his clothes. Then he also stripped, put on a swimsuit, and they both jumped into the pool.

"So how you doin'?" Billy asked, treading water.

"I'm all right. Could be better," Franny answered in his husky voice.

"So what's going on? Have they asked about me? What are you gonna do?"

Billy wanted information; Franny wanted money. After Burns solemnly promised not to talk about Motto to the feds, Billy agreed to deliver several hundred thousand dollars through Larry Lavin, which seemed safer than meeting again. They got out of the water, dried off, and parted company.

It was not only the money Billy owed him that made Burns reluctant to talk about Motto to the FBI. Although he'd never done anything violent or even alluded to "having the right connections," both Burns and Lavin *believed* Motto had ties to organized crime and feared what retribution he might exact if crossed. Lavin was always careful not to ruffle the wrong feathers, but in Billy's case he wasn't being merely cautious. He genuinely liked the audacious Italian and respected what he'd built on a foundation of poverty and drug addiction. Lavin thought he could help Billy elude prosecution by starting rumors that would frighten Burns and other potential informers into silence. So he made a point of telling people, "I'd kill myself before I'd testify about Motto. I'd sooner walk out on my front lawn and slit my wrists. That way at least I'd know how and when I was going to die."

The key figure in Franny Burns's plot to have a fortune waiting for him when he eventually got out of jail was Larry Lavin, whom he desperately needed to run his collections. The dentist was the only one with the right contacts. Nobody else could convince his former customers—who knew of Franny's indictment—to pay the debts owed him on coke he'd fronted for them. To placate Larry, Franny downplayed his role as government informant with the lie that he was "going to fabricate a deal in Florida, put some dope in a house, and let the FBI get it so they think I'm cooperating."

Larry bought Franny's story and agreed to be his intermediary. Never one to let opportunity slide by, he recognized that while he was collecting Franny's money, he could pick up some of the cash owed to him as well. In mid-October Lavin arranged for Motto to meet him in a hotel room at the Resort's casino. Billy arrived at dusk, strolled in, and emptied $500,000 from a canvas gym bag onto the bed. It briefly crossed Larry's mind to put the money in his own kitty instead of delivering it to Franny, but his peculiar sense of honor prevented him from stealing. Besides, he felt guilty having dragged Fran into this mess. If the FBI hadn't been investigating Lavin when he sold his drug business, they'd never have stumbled onto Burns.

Larry and Billy talked for a while, and the dentist confirmed that he expected to flee toward the end of the month, assuring Billy he'd carefully considered his options and laid foolproof plans. "I wouldn't go if I didn't think I could get away with it," Larry said with his usual confidence.

Billy kept pacing back and forth, shaking his head. The last thing in the world he could imagine was cutting himself off from his family. He thought back to the beginning of their friendship, when Larry had sent him to Miami to buy dope. How green he'd been. How unsophisticated. How scared. But now the fear he felt wasn't for himself. He turned to Larry, his mouth dry, and asked him the same question he'd asked on the eve of the first Florida trip, the one that changed his life.

"Is everything gonna be okay, Larry?"

The phrase from the first Florida trip Billy had made for Larry had become a kind of private joke between them, and now it carried a very special meaning. Larry swallowed hard and smiled. If he doubted the outcome, his steadfast green eyes never betrayed a trace of concern. "Everything's gonna be okay, Billy," he answered in the broad new England accent that ten years in Philadelphia hadn't softened. They shook hands and never spoke face-to-face again.

Francis Burns stepped off the Eastern flight from Philadelphia and blinked behind his dark glasses at the intensity of the mid-

morning Florida sunshine. Tall and broad-shouldered with bushy
black eyebrows seemingly painted in heavy strokes of charcoal
above his small dark eyes and too many gold chains circling his
neck and his wrists, he looked exactly like a television version of a
dope dealer. He tossed his blue blazer over his arm and rolled his
shoulders to loosen the white shirt already sticking to his sweat-
soaked chest. Was it the temperature or his nerves? He'd made
dozens of these trips over the last five years and bought hundreds
of kilos of cocaine. But this was the first time he'd be doing a deal
for the FBI instead of for himself. He wasn't nervous; he was
scared to death. If anything went wrong, the Colombians would
kill him.

Chuck Reed and Sid Perry followed him off the plane to the
car-rental counter, where, as instructed, Burns rented a white
convertible, one that wouldn't look too flashy but would be easy
for the FBI to follow. He drove to a shopping center five miles
south of the airport, where the FBI team had already assembled.
For what seemed like the hundredth time, they reviewed the plans:
visit the Colombian stash house, check the product, leave as he
always did, and go to the nearest pay phone to call his "uncle,"
who would then bring the money to pay for the coke. Only this
time his "uncle" would be Uncle Sam.

The FBI had its own scenario, directed by Ken Parkerson, a
forty-two-year-old, tanned, Georgia-born agent with a receding
hairline, who'd been brought to Florida to work in narcotics because of a knowledge of drugs he'd gained as a Navy medic.
Parkerson's cast of forty-five consisted of an arrest-and-search
team, a SWAT team of ten agents stationed about two miles from
the Colombian stash house, and a surveillance team poised to track
Burns both on the ground and in the air. They were a lot more
comfortable in their roles than Burns was in his, having performed
them dozens of times before.

Chuck Reed and Franny Burns remained temporarily with the
surveillance team while Sid Perry left with Ken Parkerson for their
stakeout position in Kendall, one of the Miami bedroom communi-
ties that had sprouted in the sixties when Dade County began
expanding and eventually became a haven for Spanish-speaking
émigrés. Their destination was Stratford's—a run-down bar in Hollywood Hills, popular with local agents for a sandwich, a beer, and
a game of shuffleboard. There were two pay phones in the parking
lot next to the bar, and Franny Burns carried both numbers in his
pocket. It was to one of these phones he'd call his "uncle" and set
the operation in motion. The arrest-and-search-team cars pulled in
close by and parked behind a stucco church painted a bright
Florida orange.

As soon as Parkerson turned off the engine in his gray Chevy, Perry jumped out to check the pay phones and make sure they were working. Parkerson stayed in the air-conditioned car, attentive but relaxed. Drug raids down here weren't as exciting as pictured on *Miami Vice* but they were a lot more routine policework than in Philadelphia. Perry was noticeably edgy. He had little confidence in Burns and worried that something would happen to prevent him from finishing the deal. There was a reasonable basis for his concern, since they'd already been through two false alarms. The first time the FBI brought Burns to Miami his contact hadn't been able to pull together fifty kilos for him to buy. The second time, Burns arrived at the stash house only to discover the product hadn't been delivered, and he left empty-handed. The agents worried that Alex, Burns's Colombian source, might have suspected he was being set up. But he continued to call Burns's beeper and they decided their suspicions were unfounded.

Actually, the postponements worked to the FBI's advantage by identifying the stash house for Parkerson and opening other avenues for him to investigate. He anticipated making inroads into the Colombian network by tracing the ownership of the stash house, but it belonged to a law-abiding middle-aged American couple who'd raised their children there and recently moved to a fancier neighborhood. Unable to sell their home because of a glut on the market, they rented it to what they thought were two nice young college girls. They had no idea the girls worked for Alex, who, much like Larry Lavin, used needy students to maintain his cover. Some of them signed leases for stash houses where they never lived, but, in return for a few hundred dollars, gladly paid the monthly rent with money Alex supplied. Others purchased his beepers so they couldn't be traced to him. He then leased under phony names the shortwave lines they required.

Periodically Ken Parkerson drove by the house looking for activity, hoping in vain to catch someone moving drugs in or out. Usually the shutters were drawn tight and the house was empty. Sometimes he spotted a car in the driveway, but the license plate always wound up being registered to a false name, and the car, if followed, never took him to a warehouse or a residence inhabited by Colombians. He had to be careful not to hang around too often and hazard alerting Alex. This was one of those times in policework when it made more sense to back off than to risk blowing the arrest. Finally, the first weekend in November, Alex beeped Franny that he had a large shipment of coke and was ready to do the deal. The FBI hastily coordinated its operation, which was fairly simple to do since the two false alarms had been like dry runs. The agents knew exactly where to go and how to conceal themselves. On Monday, November 5, when Franny Burns arrived at the Fort Lauderdale airport, everything was in place.

As soon as Perry and Parkerson satisfied themselves the pay phones outside the bar were in working order, they radioed Burns to put the plan in action. Sid was hungry and went inside for a fish sandwich, which he ate in the car while they sat and waited for Burns's call. The sun was just past its midday point when Burns steered his convertible onto I-95, trailed by a seven-car surveillance team and a plane circling in the air. The government wasn't taking any chances on losing him. He exited at Hollywood boulevard and, just as he always did, drove past the rows of palm trees into the Hollywood Mall to use a pay phone inside the main entrance. He dialed Alex's beeper and hung up. Within minutes the phone rang, telling him to go back outside, where two Colombians were waiting to meet him. He wiped his damp forehead and walked into the heat. Two young men greeted him. Both were college students employed by Alex, one as a translator and the other a lookout. Juan, the translator, joined Burns in the convertible while Aymer got back in his car and led the way, unaware that the FBI was following at a discreet distance and relaying their every move by radio to Perry.

"Subjects turning right at Forty-sixth Street into Hollywood Hills." The stash house was located in a community of pastel-colored ranch homes in the $100,000 range, where the saplings planted twenty years ago had grown into tall flowering fruit trees shading the small but tidy front lawns.

"Subjects at the corner of Johnson and Garfield, turning left."

"Subjects parking at 4306 Garfield. All are out of the cars and entering the house."

The modest tan ranch house had brown shutters and a patio next to the front door with a decorative cinder-block border. Burns walked in without knocking, and acted as casually as he could, despite the fact that his heart was pounding like a drum.

"How ya doin'?" he said, extending his hand to Alex.

"Hello to you," Alex answered, using just about his entire English vocabulary. The Colombian was of medium height and weight, with a broad chest, a bad haircut, and a mustache that drooped like the curves of parentheses around the corners of his mouth. He looked like a peasant. In fact, he was a prosperous middleman who imported coke into Miami from two large Colombian drug cartels.

Burns was anxious to do his business as quickly as possible. With Juan translating, they went directly into a back bedroom, where

Alex slid open the closet door, revealing stacks and stacks of cardboard cartons about sixteen inches long and eight inches wide, sealed with masking tape. He hoisted a couple of the cartons onto a table, slit them open with a knife, and took out the one-kilo plastic bags of cocaine. Usually Franny tested every kilo, but today he opened only a few of the bags and rubbed a little white powder into the web between his thumb and forefinger. When it was absorbed without a trace, he said he'd take it and waited while Alex weighed each of the fifty bags on a digital scale to make certain Burns got his full fifty kilos. The two assistants packed the coke into a Sears lawn-mower box which happened to be handy since they'd just bought a mower. Franny left by himself "to call his uncle," who supposedly would bring the $1.7 million to pay for the coke and pick it up for transport to Philadelphia.

Perry jumped when the pay phone rang. He hadn't expected the call so quickly. The words tumbled out of Burns's mouth so fast he had trouble understanding him. "Christ, they've got *tons* of coke. Tons! They want me to take some back north for another customer. I'm tellin' you, there's a lot of dope there. Good stuff. Really good. Don't let them get away."

"Okay. Where is it?"

"In the closet in the back bedroom."

"How many people are there in the house?"

"I think three or four. I heard some noises behind a closed door. Maybe somebody was in the room."

"Were there any guns?"

"I didn't see any."

"Fine. We'll take over now."

As soon as Burns had left the stash house, the surveillance squad ordered the other support teams into the neighborhood. Sid Perry hung up the phone and radioed the signal to move in. The SWAT team sprang into action. They'd obtained a blueprint of the house from the realtor and had the advantage of perfecting their plans in advance. Two cars pulled into an alley in back of the residence and two parked in front. Using the cars as cover, ten men wearing dark gray-blue coveralls and bulletproof vests with "FBI" emblazoned across the backs and on the visors of their baseball caps jumped out. Among them, they carried enough firepower to level the entire neighborhood: 870 Remington shotguns, M16 rifles, and 357 Magnum revolvers. Burns had told the agents that some of the times he'd dealt with Alex there had been armed guards present. Having no idea whether they'd meet that kind of resistance today, they came fully prepared. As it turned out, they were armed for elephants to catch a mouse. Burns was such a longtime customer that Alex had come without any weapons.

Crouching behind an old Buick station wagon standing on the grass of the backyard, a bilingual agent raised his bullhorn and shouted in both Spanish and English: "This is the FBI. The house is surrounded. Come out the front door with your hands over your heads."

They waited three minutes. When there was no response, the agents in the alley edged their way along the left side of the house to a porch enclosed with jalousies and smashed the glass panes of the door. "Don't shoot. Don't shoot," screamed the young translator in English. "We're coming out."

The three of them marched out of the house holding their hands high in the air. The SWAT team clamped cuffs on them, patted them down for concealed weapons, and turned them over to the arrest team. Their job was finished. Within fifteen minutes the house was secured, seventy kilos of cocaine were confiscated, and the three Colombians were on their way to jail. A smug Franny Burns was on his way to the airport, confident he could have no more trouble with the FBI now that he'd delivered what he'd promised.

To the disappointment of the Miami bureau, the raid yielded nothing more than the coke, a single dealer, and two insignificant workers. It was a typical dead-end Colombian arrest. Unlike Cuban dealers, whose attitude toward law enforcement tends to be similar to Americans'—which means there's a good chance they can be turned around when apprehended—the Colombians maintain an unbreakable code of silence. Far more than the law, they fear their fellow dealers, who exact cruel revenge on the families of colleagues who talk to the police. The only information Alex revealed was that his real name was Diego Arbelez and he had a small jewelry business. He'd been arrested and deported once as an illegal alien and had sneaked back into the United States. Any expectation he might lead the government to other customers or dealers was soon dashed. His two beepers found in the house never buzzed and the FBI was certain that within hours of his capture, another Colombian had picked up his customers. Except to his family, he no longer existed.

The Arbelez arrest proved to be an even greater disappointment for Sid Perry and Chuck Reed. During the two-week period they'd been shuttling back and forth from Philadelphia to Miami, concentrating on the details of the Florida operation, a much more important cocaine dealer had taken advantage of their distraction and slipped away.

Dr. Larry Lavin packed up his cash and his family and sneaked out of Philadelphia to begin a new life under a new name in a location that might be anywhere in the world.

18

DEVON, PENNSYLVANIA
FALL, 1984

None of Larry Lavin's close friends were surprised when he fled, since he had openly talked about his plans long before absconding. At a thirtieth birthday party for Franny Burns in Atlantic City in August, shortly before they were both arrested, Larry chatted about how to set up a phony identity and invest money under a false name. He even gave one of the guests a pamphlet titled *New ID in America* and told him not to worry about returning it because he had more copies. But even though all his friends had been forewarned that Larry was leaving, only a handful knew exactly when he'd go.

Larry Lavin was a thrill-seeker. He had a compulsion to walk the edge and thrived on the excitement of walking the tightrope between crime and respectability. More than once he told Kenny Weidler, "I can't stop living like this. It's just something in me. I can't help it." Occasionally in the past, through carelessness, he'd lost his balance, but he always managed to pull himself out of danger. Ironically, having survived his brushes with authority—the youthful snowmobile heist, expulsion from Exeter, the FBI tax-evasion investigation—strengthened his belief that he was invincible. Special. The laws and rules made for other people did not apply to him. His slip this time was different. He'd fallen into a space where there was no safety net, no hope of emerging unscathed. He'd lost the game and was going to jail. Rather than accept defeat, he took the one outside chance he had for a stand-off. It was a long shot, but that made it more challenging. Larry never doubted that with the proper planning, he had the wits and the guts to pull it off. And take his wife and son with him.

What worried him was whether he'd have the emotional fortitude to completely sever all ties with the rest of his family and his friends. He saw himself as a cool, rational thinker, yet he had deep feelings of attachment and the real pain of leaving was getting cut off from people he loved. He'd always been very close to his family, and so had Marcia. It seemed particularly cruel to deny grandparents the joy of watching their grandchildren grow up. On the other hand, it would be just as damaging, in his eyes, for his family to suffer the shame of having their youngest son sent off to jail.

Fortunately, his parents were away on a trip when the arrests hit the paper, and their only source of information about the case was what Larry told them. He'd already informed them that he was likely to be indicted by the IRS for what he described as "problems stemming from loan-sharking." When he went home to Massachusetts to say good-bye, he never mentioned the word "drugs." He told them it appeared he would get a several-year jail sentence for his tax problems, and he couldn't bear to be locked up that long. He was going to get new identities for his family, and they might never see each other again. Pauli Lavin wept and told her son that it was wrong to run. His father, Justin, supported his decision. Having felt wronged by a system that robbed him of his shoe business, he bitterly damned the government and the FBI and wished his child Godspeed. There were no recriminations flung at Larry, no denunciations of his actions. How could his parents be angry? Larry had never been anything but a devoted son who'd been supporting them financially for years. They'd miss him and their grandchild terribly and they'd miss his assistance too. Only after Larry disappeared did the Lavins finally discover the truth about their son's legal problems after a friend sent them a newspaper clipping detailing Larry's flight and his monumental drug dealing.

There was no chance of hiding the truth from Marcia's mother, who lived in Philadelphia and read about Larry's problems in the newspaper. She had difficulty reconciling the story with the devoted son-in-law she knew. Marcia tried to persuade her to flee with them. Agnes Osborn mulled over the invitation and refused. She said she was too old, too set in her ways for such a major change, and also unwilling to lose contact with Marcia's brother and sister and their children.

Larry briefly considered going by himself and leaving everybody behind. Night after night he and Marcia sat in the den trying to choose the best road map for their future. She was three months pregnant with their second child. Maybe it would be better if he left alone? To Marcia that wasn't even a remote consideration. She'd married him for better or worse and would stay by his side forever. Larry thought back to the morning of his wedding, when, in a rare spasm of indecision, he'd questioned whether Marcia was the right girl for him. He remembered reviewing in his mind the qualities she possessed that were most important to him, and what stood out had been her loyalty. He had never anticipated how critical that would someday be to their relationship.

Once it was decided they were fleeing as a family, the Lavins began to consider where to go and what would be best for their children. A friend recommended Ireland, since the native language was English and, at the time, the Emerald Isle had no extradition treaty with the United States. Marcia nixed that idea immediately. Her children were Americans and deserved to be raised here, not as aliens in a foreign nation. Besides, they didn't have passports with their new identity. Both of them felt they'd be more likely to draw attention living abroad as émigrés than settling in a community where they'd be just like everybody else. That was one of the reasons they chose Virginia Beach.

The Lavins had briefly visited there years earlier when they were unable to book rooms in colonial Williamsburg. Larry liked the area because it was on the water and he'd be able to pursue his passion for water sports. Moreover, its proximity to several naval bases made Virginia Beach a popular way station for transferred military personnel, so he and Marcia would have no trouble blending in as another young suburban couple. Since it was only an afternoon's drive from Philadelphia, it was probably the last place the FBI would expect them to be. And what made it especially appealing was the fact that, since it was a resort town, Larry could rent an apartment in advance by telephone. He was not about to arrive, a hunted man with all his worldly possessions in a U-Haul, and begin to look for a place to live.

He located a local real-estate agent, called her and introduced himself as an American professor who had been teaching in London for the last four years. That eliminated the possibility she'd contact his former landlord for a reference and credit check. He explained that he wanted to spend his sabbatical in Virginia Beach with his family, described the kind of apartment he was seeking, and said since they were all presently on the road touring, he couldn't leave her a phone number. Instead he'd call from time to time to check her progress. Larry, a creative liar, never had difficulty inventing a cover story. This one secured him a lovely furnished high-rise condominium. Over the phone.

Kenny Weidler tried fruitlessly to talk Larry out of leaving.

"Cop a plea, take seven years and get it over with," he advised. "If they ever catch you, you're history." Larry replied that he simply would not and could not do serious time.

"Then think of your family, of Marcia."

He already had. "If we gain even one more year together with nobody harassing us, it will be worth it."

Kenny pressed on. "Do you realize you'll have to change your whole personality if you leave? You'll have to stop walking on the edge. My God, if you get a traffic ticket, that will be it. They'll lock you up and throw away the key."

"You're right, Ken. Changing will be the hardest part. But I can do it."

Kenny believed him and envied him too. He knew that eventually he'd also be indicted and would have to face the same problems. "How can you think you can just make all of this go away?" he asked.

"I can," Larry answered. "But don't think you can do the same thing. You worry too much. You couldn't put it together. You don't have the balls." Larry understood Kenny better than Kenny did. That's what made Larry such a treasured friend and why Weidler dreaded the future without him.

In mid-October Larry learned from Franny Burns that the Colombian drug bust he was setting up in Miami was scheduled for the last weekend of the month and he decided to time his departure to coincide with it, figuring the most logical time to flee was while the FBI's attention was diverted.

Suddenly there was so much to do. Since the FBI at his arrest had confiscated the phony church seal he'd used to "validate" the baptismal certificates he'd printed, he had to order a new seal and have new certificates printed with another name. This time, instead of Scared Heart Church in Bradford, Massachusetts, he used St. James Church in Haverhill. But the printer made an error and spelled "Haverhill" as "Havorhill." It was too late to have the forms redone, so Larry made a small tear where the O appeared, which made the certificates look much-handled and, as a consequence, more authentic.

He still hadn't collected all the money people owed him. There were drug debts, some of which he might as well kiss good-bye, and a $500,000 outstanding loan to a guy who'd gotten him into a gold mine that had turned to dross. One-half to two-thirds of the ten million dollars his ring had made between 1979 and 1984 had come his way and a lot of it was long gone, spent in bad investments and good times. Of the remainder, maybe a half-million dollars was tied up in real estate—his house on Timber Lane, his Willing's Alley town house, the investment condos at the seashore. He couldn't sell any of them without creating suspicion. Nor could he recover the $75,000 invested in the dental practice. That would be his gift to Kenny. His BMW and all his expensive gadgets couldn't be sold either, so while his net worth on paper, including money owed to him, was nearly three million dollars, he'd flee with only the $1.6 million he could convert into cash and leave the rest behind—a cheap price for his freedom.

While Larry devoted much of his time to accumulating cash, Marcia spent every spare minute with her mother and Christopher, hoping the two-year-old would remember his grandmother and feeling awful that the baby inside her would never see this woman she so dearly loved.

Larry's biggest concern was the dental practice. He had confidence in Kenny's professional skill to handle his routine cases competently, but he stewed over certain patients on whom he was using advanced techniques that Kenny was unfamiliar with and would now have to finish. Moreover, Weidler knew practically nothing about the business end of the practice and had difficulty learning the most basic bookkeeping, such as employee payroll-tax deductions, as well as how to operate the computer where Larry kept all the records. It was typical of Larry's compulsive nature that he needed to tie up all those loose ends, and of his professionalism that he'd be troubled about improperly discharging his responsibility to his patients. Just as he'd convinced himself earlier that he couldn't leave the drug business because his dealers and their families depended on him for their livelihood, he now worried about patients who relied on him for their dental care.

He considered many of his work connections friends, especially the girls in the office. Actually they were more like family, and they threw a farewell party his last night in the office. The fellow from the dental lab who stopped by daily to make deliveries brought the champagne, and everybody, including Larry, got a little teary. Anybody else might have been cautious about keeping his departure date a secret. Not Larry. He trusted his staff completely, like he trusted all the people close to him. It was a trait Marcia had once teased him about, warning him that one day he'd trust the wrong person.

Larry was still at the office party when Ken arrived, as arranged, around ten o'clock at the house on Timber Lane to make his good-byes. At first glance it was hard to tell the occupants were vacating. So much of the furniture still remained in place. Over the last several weeks Larry and Marcia had been packing some of their clothes and precious knickknacks into footlockers, which, along with cartons of breakable items like stereos and lamps, had been put into storage to be loaded into a truck on moving day.

Marcia made a special point of taking as many of Christopher's toys as possible so he'd feel some sense of familiarity in their new home. One item they left hanging on the wall of Larry's study was his gold record. There'd be no need for that kind of cover in their new life.

While they waited for Larry, Marcia and Kenny talked in the den. She'd had dinner that night with her mother, and the difficulty of their parting showed in the redness around her usually bright brown eyes. Larry had already made his good-byes to his mother-in-law with words of apology and promise.

"I'm sorry I have to do this, Mom," he told her when he dropped a sewing machine off at her apartment.

"It's all right, Larry," she said, trying to hide her hurt. "I just can't understand why this had to happen."

He shrugged his narrow shoulders. "I promise you this won't be the end. You'll see Marcia and Chris again. You can count on it." In his mind he believed he'd figure out how to sneak them back in the middle of the night for a surprise visit.

Larry had made the same vow to Marcia. In the meantime, Kenny offered that he'd look after Mrs. Osborn and help her if she needed anything. Marcia thanked him. Beneath her distress, Kenny sensed her priorities were clear and her resolve strong. The welfare of her husband and family took precedence over everything else; her mother would have to adjust to their absence and find new activities to fill the void their leaving created. Marcia did not appear nervous, and sat with her hands folded in her lap. It was the only time he could remember seeing her in her den when she wasn't doing some kind of needlework.

"Are you sure you're doing the right thing?" he asked for the last time.

She smoothed the short dark hair that lay across her forehead and replied with an answer she'd obviously spent a considerable amount of time contemplating. "If we get a year or two of peace, it will be worth it."

Kenny had difficulty making small talk. He felt he was paying a condolence call, and, in a way, he was. After tonight, Larry would be as good as dead, and the ache in his stomach already told him how lonely he'd be. I wanted to spend the rest of my life doing things with Larry, he thought. Sure, there'll be other guys to play tennis and golf with, but whom will I confide in? Whom will I go to for advice? Nobody but Larry had all the answers.

It was getting on to midnight when Larry finally arrived and told Marcia there was a bigger rental truck available than he'd anticipated, and they could take a few more things. They selected one table that Larry's father had made, another with an inlaid top that had a turquoise fish in the center, a plant stand, and a small corner étagère. He and Ken put the pieces in their cars and drove to the Sheraton Hotel in Valley Forge to meet Rusty Lavin, who'd driven down from Massachusetts in a rented van that was to serve as a decoy to throw the FBI off Larry's trail.

Rusty was annoyed when Larry showed up with Kenny. He felt the flight should have been kept as a private family matter and didn't trust any outsider, particularly Weidler.

The three men slid into a dark corner booth in the hotel bar. Kenny ordered a manhatten; Larry a rusty nail. Rusty drank Scotch, which did little to calm his nerves. He was scared for Larry and for himself and Jill too. From the moment Larry had been arrested, he'd wondered when their turn would come. Like Kenny, he'd had numerous conversations with his brother, trying to change his mind, to find another lawyer, to search for another loophole. He'd even tried to dissuade Marcia, despite the fact they'd never had much of a relationship and he'd always found her "a tough girl to get close to." Her response to his plea had been cool and pragmatic. "This is only another page in another chapter of the book of Larry Lavin," she'd said prophetically. It seemed to Rusty she'd begged and begged Larry to stop and then given up and accepted their fate.

Only Larry seemed relaxed and upbeat. Rusty remembers his "acting excited, like somebody ready to go off on a vacation." He joked and reminisced a lot. About dental school. About the bachelor parties. About the fabulous ride they'd had on the cocaine train. But not about the crash. The only serious note came when they spoke about the future. He told Rusty to take whatever he wanted from the house, and said, "It's too bad that you may have to go to jail for a while. I'm sorry." Turning to Kenny, he expressed some anxiety about how his partner would react to his indictment when it came. Larry feared that under pressure from the feds, Weidler would roll over.

"Honestly, Larry, I can't promise what I'm gonna do until it happens. I just don't know," Weidler said.

It was not the answer Larry had hoped to hear. Nevertheless, he advised him, "Once I'm gone, you might as well go ahead and blame everything on me."

Finally at two A.M., the waitress brought the check and told them the bar was closing. Larry paid and they all walked into the parking lot, just tipsy enough to hide their real feelings. After loading the furniture into one of the rental trucks, Kenny and Larry shook hands.

"We'll see each other in the future. I promise," Larry said, and he truly believed it. He'd read about fugitives who suddenly popped up for brief encounters with their parents and friends as they walked into work or out to mail a letter. While he hadn't formulated any concrete plans on when and where he'd appear, he had every intention of seeing the important people in his life again. "Sometime when you least expect it, I'll knock on your door and walk right in."

"I'll miss you," Kenny said.

"Yeah. Well, don't do anything stupid. I'll call you tomorrow at the office."

As they were driving out of the parking lot, Larry lowered his car window and yelled, "Hey, Ken, did you know that our Allentown buddy is ready to ask his wife if his girlfriend can move in with them?" How like Larry to toss a tidbit of gossip at a time like this. Kenny's heart felt like stone, but he laughed because he was supposed to.

At seven o'clock Saturday morning, October 27, Rusty drove the decoy truck to the storage company, loaded it with the thirty or so footlockers that contained Larry and Marcia's belongings, and returned to the Sheraton lot to transfer the things to Larry's U-Haul. Later Rusty would go to his brother's deserted home and take what he'd been promised: the blue Oriental carpet and the grandfather clock from the living room. He'd put them in his truck and drive back to Massachusetts.

Meanwhile, on Timber Lane, Marcia, carrying Spooky the cat, and Larry, with Chris in his arms and Rusty, the Labrador retriever, padding alongside, piled into a rented car as casually as if they were going on a weekend trip. Tucked in Larry's wallet was a Massachusetts driver's license with his picture and the name of a friend who had donated his license to help Larry. Earlier Larry had flown to Boston, where Rusty picked him up at the airport and drove him to a motor-vehicle office. Posing as the longtime friend, Larry claimed his wallet had been stolen and his license lost. He produced identification and left with the document he needed to drive without fear of being identified if for some reason he were stopped by a cop. Purposely missing from the wallet were Lavin's credit cards. He'd given them to friends in New England, who'd been instructed to use them for small purchases to throw the FBI further off his trail. He planned henceforth to pay all his bills in cash or by checks written on his new identity. Once established in Virginia Beach, he'd unpack the phony birth and baptismal certificates and begin to build a dossier of identification under his assumed name.

In the car on the way to get the truck, Marcia and Larry tried to reassure each other there was nothing to worry about, although they both knew differently.

"It's going to be fine," Larry said. "We're gonna be all right." He patted Marcia's knee over and over as he spoke.

"I know," she said, "Everything will be okay." And she told herself she meant it as she squeezed his hand.

"You have to start practicing calling me Brian from now on and get used to thinking of yourself as Marcia O'Neil. In a few hours we'll be Mr. and Mrs. O'Neil. It will be just like we got married all over again."

Larry had chosen the name Brian O'Neil from the file of a patient in his dental office. If, for some reason, he ever needed a legitimate birth certificate, he thought it wise to base his identity on a real human being whose background could be verified rather than a fictitious character. He also wanted a name that sounded unmistakably Irish. With all remnants of their past erased, maybe a strong ethnic link could provide some sense of belonging. At the least, with a name like O'Neil, he'd no longer be mistaken for a Jew.

At the parking lot, Larry gave the car keys to his brother, Rusty, so he could give the rental car back to the Philadelphia agency. Then he, Marcia, Chris, and the pets got into the U-Haul. Two days later Larry would drive the truck to Washington, D.C., where he'd meet a friend who would return it.

Larry headed south for the New Jersey Turnpike, confident that he could build a new life. He actually viewed the future with a sense of adventure. He was an old hand at survival. Hadn't he been taking care of himself and everybody else since he was a kid? What hurt so terribly were the good-byes, and the awful realization that he might never see any of his circle again. That's what brought the tears to his eyes when he hugged his brother in the parking lot. He could cope with just about anything but living the rest of his life isolated from his family and friends.

In midmorning, about halfway to Virginia Beach, Larry stopped at a pay phone to call Kenny as he'd promised. He was breaking the cardinal rule of a fugitive: Don't look back.

"Is everything okay?" Kenny wanted to know.

"So far, so good."

"Are you sure you're not being followed?"

"Positive."

The purpose of the call was to discuss a set of dentures Larry had left for Kenny to complete that had been made with one of the new experimental materials with which Kenny had no prior experience. Larry satisfied himself that his partner understood what needed to be done and finished the conversation.

"Take it easy."

"I will, Larry. Good luck. Love to Marcia."

Larry sounded cool as ever and completely in charge. Kenny hung up the phone and returned to work. Overcome by a deep sense of loss, he found it hard to concentrate.

Sunday afternoon, October 28, a day after the Lavins fled, a small gray cat was hit by a car on Timber Lane and left to die on the sewer grate in the street at the foot of their driveway. A neighbor thought the cat belonged to Barbara Eisenhower, daughter-in-law of the former President, and telephoned her to come outside. She ran over to check and was relieved to find the cat wasn't hers. Soon a small group of people had gathered around the limp ball of fur. It took but a minute for the conversation to switch to the Lavins.

Ever since Larry's arrest, the majority of the neighbors had felt betrayed and angry that the young dentist had brought a touch of scandal to their neighborhood. Only one woman had come by to chat with Marcia and say how sorry she was about what had happened. Larry tried to downplay the news by telling the man next door not to believe everything he read. However, most of the group were virulently antidrug and there was little sympathy now for Larry despite the fact he'd been universally liked.

The main topic of those gathered around the cat was the flurry of visitors at the Lavin house over the past two days and the unusual amount of traffic in and out of the driveway. One neighbor had recognized Mrs. Osborn and assumed that Marcia was entertaining relatives. (It hadn't been a family dinner going on inside. Marcia had invited her mother, brother, and sister to pick through the contents of the house and take whatever they wanted.) Another neighbor thought the trucks had belonged to one of those rock bands from the record company Larry once owned, because of the grungy guy driving it. (That would have been Rusty moving out the clock and the carpet.) Others were suspicious because they thought they'd seen a van in the driveway in the middle of the night.

Barbara Eisenhower suggested calling the FBI to alert them that Larry might be running away. One of the men in the group squelched that idea. "I'm quite sure that's unnecessary. The FBI must be watching his every move. They probably know all about this already."

The perception of the FBI as the ultimate watchdog is one of the Bureau's most widely accepted myths. It simply isn't possible to

justify the expense of round-the-clock surveillance without supporting evidence. Chuck Reed had always felt that Larry Lavin
would run when cornered. His release on bail was like handing him
an exit visa. If Reed were a gambler, he would have bet a year's
salary on what his intuition told him was going to happen. But
believing something he couldn't prove gave him no leverage downtown and no reason for the Bureau to put Lavin under constant
observation. On his own time Reed would occasionally drive an
hour from his home to Timber Lane to reassure himself that Lavin
was still there. There wasn't much else he could do. This was a
large, complicated case and most of the agents' current energy was
consumed by the bust Burns was setting up in Miami.

Originally the raid was scheduled for the last weekend in October. Franny Burns was to take his kids to Disneyland in Orlando
earlier in the week and fly into Fort Lauderdale to meet Reed and
Perry on Friday. Before they left, an informant tipped them off
that Lavin would be fleeing the following Tuesday. No problem.
They'd be back by then. They flew down to Florida on Thursday,
and at the last minute, things fell through because the coke shipment hadn't arrived from Colombia and the buy was postponed for
at least another week. At that point Reed and Perry had been
working a string of twelve-hour days and they were exhausted.
When they reached home they took a calculated risk that they
could safely take the weekend off and zero in on Lavin Monday.
Based on their information, they expected to catch him in his exit.
Chuck made one trip to the Lavin house on Saturday and saw that
David Ackerman's BMW sat in the driveway. Lavin had borrowed
the car from David to drive after his car had been seized at his
arrest. Reed assumed that if the car was still there, so was Lavin,
and he returned home. He had no way of knowing the car had
purposely been abandoned in the driveway because it would be too
easy to trace.

On Monday around midday Perry and Reed met at the shopping
center in King of Prussia, got into Chuck's car, and drove to
Devon, where they introduced themselves as FBI agents to a
neighbor who lived directly across the street from Larry and asked
if they could park in her driveway to observe his house. She
amiably agreed, and they settled in for what they expected to be a
rather dramatic confrontation. The afternoon was slow and un-
eventful. By focusing their sight on the rearview mirror, they could
easily tell that nobody came and nobody left. When darkness fell,
they were able to get out of the car and move to a place where
they could see better without being seen. Taking turns crouching at
various spots on the neighbor's lawn, they tried in vain to get a

glimpse of activity inside the house. Nothing. By now the chill of the raw October day had eaten through their jackets and they were both shivering.

Finally, around nine P.M., a large white truck pulled into Lavins' driveway, quickly followed by Weidler in his Saab. Paydirt. This is it. The tip was right. Weidler and the driver of the truck entered the house and began hauling out furniture and stacking it in the truck. It was a black night with heavy clouds blocking the moon and stars. To improve his view, Perry crawled under a bush by a neighbor's mailbox, which practically put him in the street and nearly gave him a heart attack when an evening jogger running by almost tripped over him. It would have helped the agents if Weidler had turned on the lights in Lavin's house, but he did not. He stealthily moved in and out in total darkness. Larry had promised him several pieces of furniture, so he wasn't stealing. He just didn't want to arouse the suspicion of the neighbors by illuminating his activity to their curiosity.

The darkness was Reed and Perry's first clue that something might be wrong. Had Lavin already gone? If so, would Weidler lead them to him? Was Weidler taking the furniture to him? Was Lavin there in the dark with Weidler, helping with the packing? What the hell was going on?

Toward midnight, the truck and the car left. Perry stayed to watch Lavin's house, huddling on a neighbor's porch and trying to keep warm by imagining he was sweltering in the city on a ninety-degree day. The lady of the house kindly brought him a thermos of hot coffee and a plate of freshly baked chocolate-chip cookies, the chips still so soft they melted on his hands. He planned to share the plate with Chuck, but cookies were his weakness and he was starving. Sorry, partner.

The truck stopped first at Mrs. Osborn's Spanish-style condominium complex nearby and dropped off a few things. Then it proceeded to Weidler's house and unloaded. Kenny made a second trip to the Lavins' that night for a few smaller items that he couldn't fit in on his first round. Once more, Chuck followed him, still hoping he'd lead the way to Larry, but the trail dead-ended at his house. Weidler locked the car, walked inside, turned off the lights, and went to bed.

By now it was after three A.M. and it made sense for Sid and Chuck to do the same thing, so they rented a room at a nearby motel. The tightness in Sid's belly didn't come from hunger. Hour by hour it was becoming more apparent that Lavin had already gone.

"I told you so," Chuck said, more in resignation than anger as they flopped into bed. "From day one, I told you he'd flee." There was no gratification in being right.

They both fell into a dead sleep, fixating on the remote possibility that some activity at the house on Tuesday would retrieve the situation. Whatever hope they'd been holding on to evaporated when Mrs. Osborn arrived the next day to pick up the mail and told a neighbor that her daughter and son-in-law had left for a vacation. She didn't say how long they'd be away.

Lavin, his pregnant wife, and his two-year-old son had vanished. The house was empty, the furniture and the occupants gone. All that remained was a table sitting on the front lawn that Weidler had forgotten to load. The FBI agents stared at it all day, a wooden symbol of Lavin's victory in what, until now, had been an FBI storybook case. Sid grew increasingly depressed. Chuck got mad. Not at himself. He'd done his job. As far as he was concerned, the justice system was at fault, unnecessarily making him work harder. If the judge had paid more attention to the FBI's request and not let Lavin out on bail, if the U.S. attorneys had been more aggressive, none of this would have happened. They had given Lavin a license to run, and now the FBI would have to catch him.

It was nearly dinnertime when the agents returned to the shopping center where Sid had left his car the day before. They'd been on the stakeout for thirty-eight hours. Normally they had a great deal to say to each other. Now they drove in silence, unwilling to voice the frustration and embarrassment they shared. How could they have been outwitted? Actually there was no need to talk, since each of them knew exactly what the other was thinking: what a long, hard haul lies ahead of us. Of course they'd find Lavin. That was a given. But they knew they'd work their tails off to do it, and nobody would pay them overtime for all the extra hours they'd have to put in.

Sid got out of the car and Chuck called after him, "Don't worry. We'll get the guy if it's the last thing we do. And don't forget, this round's mine. You gotta buy me lunch." Despite his exhaustion, Reed could already feel a small surge of excitement as he relished the challenge to come.

The two agents took Halloween as a day off and went trick-or-treating with their kids. On Thursday the car Lavin had used surfaced back at the agency in Devon where he'd rented it. The speedometer showed four-hundred miles. Mistakenly assuming Lavin had used the car to escape, they took a map of the mid-Atlantic states and drew a circle with a two-hundred-mile radius. The mileage was their first clue, and even though it would prove useless, the chase was on.

19

PHILADELPHIA
1985

Nothing would have pleased Sid Perry and Chuck Reed more than to focus all their time and energy on the capture of Dr. Larry Lavin. Unfortunately there was far too much happening with the rest of the case to make that possible. For much of the year after Lavin fled, he was left simmering of the FBI's back burner, to be stirred when the agents had a free moment, which wasn't often.

Dozens of new indictments lay ahead, in addition to the activity generated by the ring members already arrested. Twelve of them pleaded guilty, and there was a great deal of presentencing work on each of their cases—arranging plea agreements, preparing reports for the court, outlining the extent of each defendant's involvement, meetings with probation officers, and so on.

Those defendants who chose to cooperate had to be debriefed, and the information they provided generated new investigations that either led to additional indictments or strengthened some already in progress. It was a bit like Alice's dilemma in Wonderland: each door opened into a room with more doors.

Of the more than eighty people ultimately charged in the drug ring federal prosecutors dubbed "The Yuppie Conspiracy," only a handful would opt to have their guilt or innocence determined by a jury. The first to make that decision was Kim Noramatzu, Suzanne's blond younger sister. Kim was unquestionably a minor figure in the conspiracy. As Bruce Taylor's girlfriend, she'd assisted him in his business before Suzanne came into the picture, which, in the government's eyes, made her guilty of a crime. However, their reason for indicting her went beyond punishment. They were warning her she was in serious trouble with the anticipation she'd react by cooperating. Having hung around the fringes of the group, she'd observed a lot of the activity and was perceived as a potentially valuable witness. The tactic didn't work. Kim recognized the insignificance of her role and believed that since she hadn't been active for the last year, she could beat the rap. Instead of flipping, she pleaded not guilty and her trial was set for Monday, December 10, 1984.

Three days before the trial, a shake-up occurred at the Philadelphia U.S. attorney's office, resulting in the removal of the two lawyers who had been handling the Lavin case since its inception. The official explanation was their reluctance to prosecute what they viewed as a weak case against a pregnant nineteen-year-old girl. But in the office corridors, it was whispered they'd lost their taste for battle. Reed and Perry received the news with mixed emotions. All along, they'd felt this pair of prosecutors lacked aggression, but there was no way of telling whether their replacements would be an improvement.

Assigned to handle the Lavin conspiracy at the end of that brisk, windy Friday were Tina Gabbrielli and Ron Noble, relative newcomers to the U.S. attorney's office, who described their previous trial experience as "green" and "pale green." Noble was the novice. An open, spontaneous twenty-seven-year-old with a wavy pompadour, a clipped mustache, and a terrific smile, he'd entered the Justice Department three months earlier, directly from a clerkship with a federal judge. He'd never seen a complete trial, had no idea how to pick a jury or play a tape in court, and didn't even know what FBI agents did, although he'd always admired them. What he lacked in expertise, he compensated for with brains and personality. Raised as an army brat who attended seven different schools before enrolling at the University of New Hampshire, he was the 1983 Pennsylvania state karate champion and had been elected president of his class and president of the student body at Stanford Law School. "I planned to graduate and have a very successful practice and do a little something for humanity on the side so I wouldn't feel guilty." During his clerkship his priorities shifted, and Ron Noble moved directly into the public sector.

The other half of the prosecutorial team was twenty-nine-year-old Tina Gabbrielli, who'd been at the Justice Department only three months longer than Noble, but was considered the senior member because she already had two trials under her belt and had spent four years with a large private law firm. Slender, with dark brown curly hair trimmed just above her shoulders and no-nonsense brown eyes, the Georgetown University Law School graduate was the daughter of immigrant parents who had scraped enough money from their Italian restaurant to give their child the education they never had. Married, with no children, Gabbrielli had grown up in a small town in northern New York, where she developed a love for music and the outdoors. Unlike Noble, who'd been told since boyhood that he should be a lawyer because he liked to argue, the bookish Gabbrielli had been advised by a junior-high-guidance counselor that if she continued to work hard and didn't get married right out of high school like all the other girls, she might become a nurse or a secretary. She had much bigger plans in mind, like becoming a concert flutist. When she became attracted to the law, her father told her, "You can always give flute recitals as a lawyer, but you can't practice law as a musician."

As the Friday sun was setting, Tina Gabbrielli and Ron Noble faced Perry and Reed for the first time across a table in a conference room at the U.S. attorney's office. None of them had the slightest inkling this case would occupy the next two years of their lives. All they realized at that moment was that they had two days to prepare for a trial. Sid picked up the indictment and began to explain Kim Noramatzu's role as a player in the Larry Lavin conspiracy.

"Whoa," Ron Noble said, throwing up his hand. "Who's Larry Lavin?"

Sid shot Chuck a "we've-got-a-long-night-ahead-of-us" look and took a deep breath. "Larry Lavin was a dental student at the University of Pennsylvania . . ."

By the time they parted company that evening, it was too late to watch the eleven-o'clock news, and Ron Noble had a splitting headache. They met again from eight A.M. to midnight on Saturday and on Sunday. Every name, every piece of evidence that seemed so clear to the FBI agents had to be explained in detail to the attorneys. When they turned out the office lights Sunday night, Ron and Tina knew a great deal about Larry Lavin and his friends.

Monday morning they arrived in court nervous but prepared, only to learn the case had been postponed because Kim had changed lawyers. It was finally tried several weeks later. Gabbrielli presented the opening argument, much less tense than she would have been without the extra time to fortify her grasp of the case and the witnesses. "I like to be as prepared as I possibly can because that way I'm most comfortable," she says. Noble was so afraid of making a mistake during the trial that the most he could swallow for breakfast was a glass of orange juice. When his parents asked if they could watch his closing argument, he told them absolutely not.

"I was so frightened of failing. I didn't know if I could cut it as a prosecutor," he remembers. "I kept thinking: Why did I ever come here? I could have been hiding away in some big law firm getting rich."

The verdict restored everybody's confidence. Kim was convicted on all counts: conspiracy to possess and distribute cocaine, using the telephone for a criminal enterprise, violations of interstate commerce. The judge, apparently influenced by her youth, vulnerability, and swollen belly, sentenced her to a work release program. The light sentence was a minor glitch in what was otherwise considered a major strategic victory. It didn't matter that Kim was nothing more than a minnow in a school of sharks. By prosecuting even the smallest defendant, the government delivered a loud and clear message to those yet to be indicted or tried that it intended to play hardball: if you plead not guilty, you can be absolutely certain we'll take you to trial and turn on all our guns. Had they lost, their signal would have been greatly weakened, and many who later pleaded guilty and cooperated might, instead, have opted for their day in court.

The government was keenly aware of how closely Kim Noramatzu's trial was being observed by defense attorneys for people like David Ackerman, Kenny Weidler, and the rest of Lavin's ring who knew it was just a question of time before they'd be indicted too. This was the time to decide whether to plead guilty in exchange for a lighter sentence. Several had already told Noble and Gabbrielli, "We'll see what happens after Kim's trial." Now the word was out that plea agreements made sense.

The public often views plea agreements as another form of criminal coddling. The government sees them as one of the law enforcement's most useful tools. They save the taxpayers the expense of going to trial and produce key information leading to more convictions, while still giving the court plenty of leeway for appropriate punishment. Because the Lavin case had such a huge number of indictments, plea agreements developed into the chief mechanism for dealing with defendants.

At its simplest, a plea agreement is nothing more than an admission of guilt. It may or may not involve cooperation. If it does not, a defendant has simply agreed to save the public a costly trial by pleading guilty, in return for which the government reciprocates by reducing the number of criminal counts against him. Criminal indictments generally involve multiple charges, each carrying a specific punishment, so cutting down on the counts directly affects the ultimate sentence.

Suzanne Noramatzu Taylor fell into the uncooperative category. She maintained a fierce sense of loyalty to her colleagues and refused to sell them out to buy herself less jail time. "I knew I was guilty," she said. "I was told I could get a lighter sentence if I cooperated, but I didn't. I told my lawyer that I didn't think it was fair to use those people I considered friends to help myself when I was probably guiltier than a lot of them."

Suzanne's was not the typical response. For most of the defendants the government's offer was hard to refuse, and frequently their attorneys advised them to try to shorten their stay in jail by cooperating. The overture to cooperate triggers a complicated barter system in which the government always has the upper hand. The bottom line in plea bargaining is based on the quality of the seller's information. Those who can supply the most succeed to the greatest degree, and the more a defendant tells, the sweeter the deal. Depending on the value of the revelations, the prosecutors have a number of options.

They may just reduce the number of counts they bring and promise nothing else.

Or they may agree to a specific number of counts, and while promising no sentencing recommendation, will detail to the court the extent to which the defendant cooperated. Lawyers often prefer this kind of agreement on the theory that judges tend to give more lenient sentences when the prosecutors have relinquished their right to make suggestions to the court.

The third type of plea agreement—the one used most frequently in the Lavin case—combines a reduction of counts with the promise to fully set forth at sentencing the breadth of cooperation and recommend to the court what the sentence be. That doesn't mean the judge will follow the recommendation. A specific sentencing deal cannot be guaranteed. At the hearing, the FBI and U.S. attorney can only suggest whatever terms they deem appropriate, but the decision on whether somebody is freed on probation or is put away, and for how long, rests entirely with the presiding judge.

There is one exception to this rule, commonly know as a C plea, in which a fixed sentence, or cap, is negotiated in advance. It's rarely used because it requires approval of the court prior to actual sentencing and eliminates the opportunity for judicial discretion.

Sometimes the wisdom of cooperation doesn't hit people until after sentencing. Bruce Taylor, despite his nervous ramblings to the FBI after the raid on his house refused to assist the government until he was given ten years without parole. The fear of testifying against Billy Motto and Franny Burns, which he claimed was his reason for keeping his mouth zippered, was suddenly mitigated by the prospect of a decade behind bars. He agreed to tell the FBI all in the hope that his help would have an effect on his request for a sentence reduction. All prisoners are entitled to file a Rule 35 from jail which asks the court to consider shortening their sentences. The government must inform a judge if someone has cooperated *subsequent* to sentencing, and the expectation is that this will have a benign influence on the Rule 35 application. In Bruce's case, it lopped off five years.

There's a good precedent for coming clean. The United States Supreme Court expressed its positive attitude toward criminals who give prosecutors a helping hand in the case of *U.S. versus Roberts;* it established that cooperation is "a deeply rooted social obligation" and an important indication that a defendant is prepared to sever ties with his former criminal associates, reform his bad habits, and abandon "his war with society."

Sometimes potential defendants see the light even before they're indicted, and appear at the U.S. attorney's office with their lawyers to make an "off-the-record proffer." In this situation the prosecutors say, "You show us what you have and then we'll tell you what we can offer in the way of reduced counts when the indictment comes out." This was the path Kenny Weidler chose.

Ever since Larry's departure at the end of October, Kenny Weidler had been nursing a sense of impending doom. He had a constant tightness in his chest and jumped whenever his doorbell rang at an odd hour. The three phone calls he'd received from Larry only exacerbated his tension. They'd talked once in November, once in December, and once in January, according to their prearranged plans. Before he left, Larry had copied the numbers from the pay phones at a shopping center, a gas station, and a train station within twenty minutes of where Kenny lived in Villanova and labeled them, A, B, and C. The day before Lavin made a call, he'd telephone Marcia's brother-in-law at his office in New Jersey, telling him to relay a message to Kenny, such as to be at location C tomorrow at 6:30. They'd agreed that if the feds somehow found out about their system and were tapping the phones, Kenny was to tip off Larry by referring to him as "Lawrence" at the start of the conversation. That would signal him to hang up before the call could be traced.

Larry had a way of making their occasional conversations seem as normal as if they'd spoken the day before. He never gave any indication of his whereabouts, and Kenny, content to hear his voice and know he was okay, never asked. Mostly Larry wanted to catch up on the news. He asked what was happening in the dental practice but was more interested in the federal investigation. Had anybody new been indicted? Had anybody been sentenced? Had

Reed or Perry been to visit him? He said he'd heard the FBI was hot on getting his brother, Rusty, and David Ackerman, but didn't reveal where he'd gotten that bit of gossip. And he even told Kenny a little about himself. He was building a house and planning on settling down, maybe even practicing dentistry sometime in the future.

During his last call, on the first Sunday in January to pay phone C, Larry reiterated the concern he'd expressed before leaving Philadelphia that Kenny wouldn't be able to withstand the pressure if Reed and Perry really leaned on him. Weidler replaced the phone in the cradle and stared out at the deserted train tracks. How he'd love to board a train and leave this mess behind him. Was Larry right? he wondered.

He buried the question in a cold place in his mind until a month later when a call from his lawyer forced him to examine it. The lawyer told Ken that Ron Noble had telephoned asking whether Weidler would be willing to assist the government on the Mark Stewart tax-evasion case. Weidler had invested hundreds of thousands with Stewart and could be helpful tracing money-laundering patterns. Noble made a point of stressing that Kenny was in very serious trouble. Kenny barely had time to adjust to the news he dreaded hearing when the phone rang again. It was David Ackerman. He'd just gotten a similar call from his lawyer, who without mincing words told the government to "take a hike."

Kenny and David met that same afternoon at a bar. Ackerman, now drug-free, was winding up his last requirements at the University of Pennsylvania Dental School and looking forward to going into practice with his father in New York in the spring. Neither Kenny nor Larry had seen much of David since he'd left the business. They'd really had little in common outside their mutual interest in cocaine. David felt they'd never have had much to do with him if he hadn't made money for them. "Kenny and Larry were my business associates. Our friendship was based on circumstance. I couldn't make any friends outside our circle while I was dealing. You can't very well meet new people and say, 'Hi. I'm a coke dealer.' To me a friend is somebody who'd do anything for you, and vice versa. My real friends were back in New York. Kenny was a golfing and disco buddy. An acquaintance. And Larry and I never would have hung out if it weren't for the coke."

As they chatted over drinks, David appeared almost nonchalant to Kenny, and certainly far less concerned than Kenny himself was about the future. From what David told him, Kenny got the impression that his lawyer, a former Philadelphia district attorney, was opposed to cooperating with the government. David's responses seemed to have been programmed by his legal adviser. "Who are they going to believe?" he said. "A couple of felons or a dentist? Sure, they'll promise you immunity, and then they'll indict you on information they got from somebody else."

Kenny was convinced David had been brainwashed and was acting on legal counsel. He was absolutely right. Fortunately for Weidler, his own attorney had a more realistic approach.

Kenny tugged on the end of his mustache in little nervous gestures while he spoke. "I'm telling you, David, you're taking this too lightly. These feds aren't fooling around. My lawyer says we're going to jail."

David insisted he was overreacting. Although his heart told him Kenny was right and he ought to talk to the government, his head told him to follow his lawyer's instructions and do nothing.

Another week passed and Kenny's lawyer called again, making it absolutely clear from his subsequent conversations with Ron Noble that Kenny would be serving a long prison sentence. They discussed the possibility of going to trial and rejected it, since there wasn't the slightest chance he'd be found not guilty. The lawyer urged Kenny to think about cooperating. He said everybody in the conspiracy was already tumbling like dominoes, and Ken didn't have any secrets that others weren't rushing to divulge. That conversation left Weidler with three possible options. One: he'd go to jail for twenty years. Two: he'd cooperate. Three: he'd kill himself.

For the rest of February he seriously contemplated option three. It seemed the best way to avoid the disgrace to his family. His wife could collect his life-insurance and start anew. He even planned how he'd take his life, sitting in the car in the garage with carbon monoxide from the exhaust pipe easing him into the sleep of death. At the end of the month his father came into Philadelphia so Kenny could drive him to the airport for his annual ski trip out West. On the way back, Kenny's tears made it hard to drive. Never again would he see the stubborn old man who had never shown him the affection he wanted, but who wasn't such a bad father after all. He knew his death would be hard on him. His mom, drifting in the fog of Alzheimer's disease, would at least be spared. And his wife's future would be made comfortable with his life-insurance policy.

What prevented Weidler from ending his life was his little daughter. Rocking her in his arms one night before he lowered her into the crib, he couldn't bear the thought of her growing up without a father. Her tiny hands rubbed the wet spot on his cheeks and she laughed. Suddenly it seemed cowardly to desert this innocent child.

The next morning he called his lawyer to discuss the procedure for cooperating with the government.

Larry had been right, after all.

On March 8, 1985, Kenneth Weidler arrived with his lawyer at Ron Noble's office and opened the floodgates of his memory. If he was going to cooperate, he was going to do it one hundred percent. When he left three hours later, having given the government over eighty pages of testimony, he remembers "It was the first time in months that I could breathe without a weight in my chest."

The next ordeal was telling his father and in-laws he was about to be indicted in a criminal conspiracy for selling cocaine, before they read about him in the newspapers. Ken's dad knew vaguely that his son was in some kind of trouble. He wasn't sure exactly what it was. In May, Kenny went home to see his mother, and during the visit, his father asked how things were going. That's when Kenny told him the whole story. It was a less emotional encounter than he had anticipated, but then again, they'd never had a very emotional relationship.

Telling his in-laws would be much more painful. He'd grown quite close to his father-in-law, who treated him more like a son than his own father and was the man he increasingly relied on for guidance after Larry had fled. Finally, in the car on a Sunday afternoon after they'd played tennis, he turned to him.

"Dad," he stammered, "I have something to tell you and it's going to hurt a lot, but I can't lie anymore." He paused and stroked his mustache with his forefinger, trying to summon the courage to say the awful words. "I might be going to jail for selling drugs. It's something I did a long time ago that I'm very sorry for now." He couldn't go on.

His father-in-law looked at him as if he'd announced he'd had a sex-change operation. His daughter's husband, a drug dealer! He couldn't believe it. They talked for a long time and decided not to tell Kenny's mother-in-law just yet. It was Mother's Day, and they didn't want to spoil her celebration.

The public humiliation was even worse for Weidler than the private disclosures. He felt the whole world now knew he was a criminal and he had no idea how to behave. Should he talk to his patients or ignore it? When one of them asked if that man in the drug ring in the paper was his brother, he was tempted to say yes. But he didn't. And he felt wonderful when the patient replied, "Far as I'm concerned, you've been a good dentist. I'll keep using you."

The June indictments were delivered the Monday after Father's Day. Among the thirty arrested along with Weidler were Billy

Motto, Paul Mikuta, Willie Harcourt, Jeff Giancola, Lavins's room-mate from Phillips Exeter, and David Ackerman. Agents took Ackerman into custody at his apartment in New York City, where he'd moved that spring to work in his father's dental office in Queens. He'd buried his high-living days along with his coke habit and now lived modestly in a studio apartment. Instead of riding in limousines, he took the subway to work. His lawyer was still telling him he had little to be concerned about and thus he was shocked to learn at his bail hearing the following day that the government wanted him detained without bail—one fugitive was enough. Tina Gabbrielli and Chuck Reed traveled to the hearing in New York and presented an effective case before a magistrate there for jailing Ackerman. They detailed his participation as a manager and owner in the cocaine business, brought up the gun used to frighten fellow dental student Paula into returning money she had stolen, and indicated there were witnesses who felt their lives were endangered by Dr. Ackerman. The last assertion by the government was un-founded and referred to the cocaine ramblings of Bruce Taylor, who ranted one night on a wiretapped phone call that Ackerman was going to kill him because he'd stolen Suzanne. Actually they'd broken up before she started seeing Taylor.

More damaging to David's hope for temporary freedom were some careless remarks he'd made himself. He'd mentioned to Kenny that he might consider the possibility of fleeing to Israel because he'd invested $100,000 there and he believed they had no extradition. He'd also bragged in anger to the agent who'd arrested him that his family would go to any length, legal or illegal, to keep him out of prison, and that his mother, in particular, had the connections to get him released from custody regardless of the cost. There was an audible gasp from the Ackerman family, seated in the courtroom, when Reed released this information into the record.

David's attorney, the one who had advised him he had nothing to worry about, was unable to persuade the court that his client was not the type to jump bail. Despite the offer from his parents to hire private guards to watch him, the magistrate did not feel reassured. After listening to two hours of arguments pro and con, she said, "You haven't satisfied me that if released, the defendant wouldn't hop on a plane and go somewhere. . . . I am going to order detention."

David fell apart at the decision. Now his attorney was telling him he'd finagle the best sentence possible. At worst, he said, David would go away for fifteen or twenty years and do his time like a man. David reacted like a boy and called his parents, sobbing:

"Get me another lawyer." But by then it was too late. Had he gotten the same sound advice as Kenny, he might have turned himself in before the indictment and cut a decent deal with the government. Instead he wound up held without bail in pretrial detention, angry that he'd been advised against doing what he'd been willing to do from the start. He'd never have squirreled away some of the organization's drug records if he hadn't considered using them as a bargaining tool. After languishing the long hot summer in jail, arrangements were completed for him to become a government witness. Despite his total cooperation, the real opportunity had passed. Rather than risk facing a hanging judge and a possible maximum sentence of life imprisonment without parole under the drug-kingpin statute, Ackerman's new lawyer opted for a "C" plea—the preset sentencing agreement. The term was to be 15 years without parole.

As late as mid-May 1985, Sid Perry and Chuck Reed had no intention of including Billy Motto in the June 17 round of indictments. Franny Burns continued to shield Motto in his dealings with the FBI, and while Weidler had been helpful to them, most of his information about Billy South Philly was secondhand. Motto's case needed more work.

All that changed when Nicholas Bongiorno unexpectedly sauntered into the FBI office on May 13.

Nicky B. and Billy M. were closer than brothers; they were bosom buddies. Nicky, tall, dark, and dangerous, and Billy, slight, fair, and flamboyant, met when Nicky began buying pot and Quaaludes from Billy. Before long he was Billy's chief worker and main man. He collected his debts, threatened his deadbeats, delivered his drugs, sometimes even carried Billy's $2,000-a-week protection money to the mob so they'd let him operate his drug business in their territory. Billy would tell people, "I raised this guy. I taught him everything. Me and him, we're real tight." What times they'd had together: ringside seats in Vegas for championship fights, weekend jaunts to the Islands and Acapulco, dates with two hot Canadian chicks vacationing in Miami—and two weeks later they were on a flight to Montreal just to take the girls to dinner. The pair of them were making a fortune and spending it like it was confetti.

Nicky not only worked for Billy but also became a substantial drug buyer with a cadre of his own customers. And that's where the trouble had started. Nicky felt that Billy resented his rising success as a coke dealer and was particularly jealous of his increasing sales in Los Angeles to a group that included a well-known soap-opera star. "Billy watches too many gangster movies," Nicky told friends. "He's afraid I'll get bigger than him and throw him over." Billy told the same friends, "Nicky's tryin' to cut my throat. You can't trust nobody no more." They bickered a lot throughout the summer of 1984, and their differences were exacerbated as much by the drugs they used as by the drugs they sold. Nicky was an indiscriminate addict. He smoked pot, snorted coke, swallowed Quaaludes. Billy, except for a little coke now and then to keep going all night at a party, and Quaaludes on a regular basis to mellow out, had stayed relatively clean from hard drugs since he'd graduated from the drug-rehabilitation center that served as his high school. What got him back in trouble was a potent prescription cough syrup.

One afternoon a guy who sold him Quaaludes and bought coke in return took a swig from a small bottle of something that looked like Karo syrup.

"Whaddya drinking?" Billy asked.

"It's called Tussionex. It's a cough medicine you get from the drugstore. Some kinda mix of codeine and morphine. Tastes like shit, but it's a great high."

"Lemme taste some." Billy took a healthy belt and so did Nicky. Soon they were off in the spacey twilight zone induced by powerful painkillers, where the FBI couldn't touch them.

Within a week they had a doctor who was a coke customer write them a refillable prescription for Tussionex. Billy was afraid his family would discover he was using drugs again, so in the beginning he got high only when they were alone together at Nicky's town house. But eventually, as the seams of his world began to fray with Burn's arrest and Larry's flight, he was hiding a bottle of the cough medicine in the glove compartment of his car and drinking two to three ounces of the stuff a day. Nicky's case was much worse. He downed twelve-ounce bottles daily as if they were soda pop.

Their relationship slid from bad to worse around the time of the first indictment, not too long after the murder of one Gregory Cavalieri—an impressionable kid who began hanging around Billy in his early teens. By the time Cavalieri turned twenty he had taken over Nicky's role of making drug deliveries. He mysteriously disappeared in August 1984 and parts of his body were later discovered in a wooded area of South Jersey. The police identified him from a portion of his skull with the teeth broken off at the gumline as if they'd been knocked out by the butt of a gun. The rest of his remains had been either devoured by animals or scattered elsewhere. It was an especially vicious murder, one that neither Billy nor Nicky had a motive to commit. Still, they were prime suspects and the local police suddenly became interested in their daily activities.

Nicky decided to beat the heat by taking a little vacation. He met with Billy in a downtown Philadelphia hotel to tell him was taking off for a while.

"I'll hit you on the beeper and let you know where I'm going," he told him, and went home to pack.

On the way he stopped to put gas in his Corvette and a police car pulled up beside him. The cops wanted to have a little chat about Gregory and, in particular, they wanted to search Nicky's house. He thought to himself: This is stupid. There's no dead body in my house. Maybe if I let them do it they'll stop harassing me. As far as he knew, the house was clean. No drugs. No money. Nothing more incriminating than a safe the size of a refrigerator, a closet full of nine-hundred-dollar suits, and a drawer loaded with gold jewelry bought and paid for. There was a false floorboard underneath which he hid cash, but at present the niche was empty. So without bothering to check with his lawyer, he led the police to his town house. Sitting there in full view on the kitchen table was a nine-ounce bag of coke.

Son of a bitch! He takes the police to his house to look for a body and gets busted for coke. Someone obviously left it there and had forgotten to come back for it.

After the drug bust, Billy wanted as little contact with Nicky as possible. Billy suspected that whatever the police knew about his business, they got from his former best friend, who'd suddenly become a hot potato capable of burning him very badly. But Nicky Bongiorno wasn't about to let go of his supplier. After posting his own bail and paying his lawyer, he needed to do some deals to raise capital. When he approached Billy to sell him coke, he was told, "Pay me the fifty-five thousand dollars you owe me and I'll bring you some stuff. I can't front you no more. You're too hot." After Nicky scraped up the cash, Billy lied and said he had no coke on hand to sell. In effect, he put Nicky out of business, and that sent him into a frenzy of revenge. "That little bastard. I risked my life for him all these years and he won't get me no product. He's through."

It was a long cold winter for Nicky and a nervous one for Billy. In April, Nicky's lawyer told him he was going to be indicted soon, and if he was smart, he'd turn himself in. The only thing he had of value to trade with the feds was Billy Motto, but before he did that, he'd give him one last chance to redeem himself. He pumped himself up with drugs, put on a bulletproof vest, and waited for

Billy one night outside a Nautilus club in South Philadelphia where he liked to train.

"Yo, Nicky. How ya doin'?" Billy greeted him with his five-hundred-watt smile.

"Not good, Billy. It's really fucked up, the way you're treating me. You been a scumbag. Didn't even pay my bail. You wouldn't bust a grape for Welch's. Then I paid you that fifty-five thousand dollars bein' a stand up and straight guy like I've always been. I didn't have to do do that. Anytime you had a problem, I took care of it. I beat people up for you. I never beat you outta a dollar. Christ, I put millions away in the Holding Company safe-deposit place. Did I ever rob you?"

"You're crazy, Nick. Whaddya talkin' crazy for?"

"You're jerkin' me, Billy. Tellin' me you won't give me no product. I ain't afraid of you or nobody else." Nicky knew that no one in their crowd, least of all Billy, was as mean as he was and would have the stomach to shoot him. "You know what, I'm gonna be the star witness against you when we get indicted."

"Nicky. Nicky. We're buddies. Why you talkin' this crazy nonsense?"

"You remember what I'm telling you, Billy. Unless you got a gun on you and you're gonna shoot me, it's over. Unless somebody's across the street working for you that's got me in the scope of their rifle, you better give them the signal now because I'm testifying. You listen to what I'm tellin' you because I mean it."

Two weeks later, Nicky surrendered himself to the FBI.

Pacing nervously, his penetrating coal-black eyes darting around the room, Bongiorno spit out information about Motto's drug dealings like a machine gun. Bam. Bam. Bam. Precise and matter-of-fact. Despite the clarity of his delivery, he was obviously strung out on drugs. Reed and Perry immediately saw they had a diamond in the rough whom they'd have to clean up before they could use him as a witness. It was actually Nicky's idea that he be sent to a drug-treatment center, and he was shortly packed off to a twenty-eight-day inpatient detoxification program. The government paid the six-thousand-dollar fee.

Loaded with the overwhelming evidence against Billy Motto supplied by the man he once considered closer than a brother, the FBI accelerated Motto's case so they could include him in the June indictment. One of their first moves was to confiscate his car. Not only did they want it for evidence—assuming it would vanish after Billy was arrested—they also figured that seizing the car might put Billy off guard. Perhaps, he'd reason that if the FBI took his car, it might still be a while before they came after him. They sent word to the surveillance squad: if you see Motto's black Volvo on the street, grab it. It was easily spotted parked in front of his house in South Philly, a sleek customized model with a long, low hood and narrow darkened windows in this working-class neighborhood of Chevrolets and Dodges.

The agents decided it never hurts to do things the easy way, so they knocked on the door of Motto's house and asked his father, who opened it, if they could have the car keys. He slammed the door in their faces. Then they called a towing company, which brought the car to the parking area in the basement of the Federal Building. By that time, Peter Motto had called his son, who'd called his lawyer, and just as the car arrived, the phone rang in Ron Noble's office.

"You have no authority to seize that car without a warrant," Motto's lawyer insisted.

Noble turned to Sid Perry, who just happened to be standing nearby. "Do we have the authority to take this car?" he asked.

"Sure do," Perry answered. "And if they wait a minute, I'll read them the specific statute." When he called back in a few minutes later prepared to recite, "Under the law, government agents have the right to seize a vehicle if they have a probable cause to believe it has been used to transport, purchase, or facilitate a narcotics transaction," he was cut short.

"Fine," Motto's attorney said. "You're right." The FBI later gave Motto the opportunity to challenge "probable cause," as the law instructed them to do, but he filed no objection.

Perry walked down to the basement to inventory the car. It was locked. A mechanic managed to pick the lock on one of the doors, but he couldn't repeat the trick with the locks on the trunk and the remaining doors. Apparently the security system was connected to the ignition, and without turning the engine on, which was impossible since they had no keys, they couldn't unlock anything else even from the inside. Finally Sid taped the one door open so no one would close it accidentally, and the car sat for months in the parking compound bandaged as if it had been wounded in action. They were eventually able to break the trunk lock and found inside a switchblade, a billy club, a small-caliber bullet, and an address book that included Lavin's and Burns's names.

Any respite Billy may have thought he gained when he lost his car was short-lived. A few weeks late federal agents yanked him out of bed and brought him to the Bureau in handcuffs. The government was determined to ensure that Motto didn't embarrass them as Lavin had. A pretrial-detention law passed in the interim gave them the basis for demanding at Motto's hearing, as they were also doing at David Ackerman's, that he be held without bail until trial. Because of the request, the hearing lasted two days, and in the course of it, a startling piece of information was made public for the first time.

Sid Perry had been on the witness stand for over an hour as Ron Noble questioned him. Without indicating he was about to drop a piece of dynamite, Noble asked Perry to explain the purpose of the $500,000 that Motto had paid to Larry Lavin in the bedroom of a casino in Atlantic City in the fall of 1984. Perry responded that part of it was to pay a debt Motto owed to Francis Burns, part was for hush money to keep Burns quiet, and part was to hire an assassin to kill FBI agent Chuck Reed.

Motto's lawyer practically jumped out of his seat. This was news to him. A hit on Chuck Reed. Was the government planning to charge Motto with attempted murder as well? Billy leaned over and whispered, "It was nothin' but talk. Nobody'd be dumb enough to try to kill an agent. And if you did, it wouldn't cost a half-million bucks." His lawyer nodded and asked permission to address the witness. He needed to find out if the government had any hard evidence about this murder plot that they could use against his client.

"Mr. Perry, did you get this information from recorded conversations?"

"Yes."

"Was there anyone else present at this exchange?"

"Yes."

"Who was it?"

"Objection," Noble yelled. At a bail hearing the government is not required to identify confidential sources.

The government went on to present an airtight argument for Motto's immediate incarceration. In further questioning, to support their contention that the twenty-nine-year-old produce wholesaler posed a serious threat to the community, Perry repeated the remark that Larry Lavin had circulated before fleeing: "I'd rather commit suicide than testify against Motto." Larry's purpose had been to protect Billy by scaring people into silence, but taken out of its intended context, the comment made it seem that everybody was afraid of Motto and his imagined connections to organized crime. Damn the feds, Billy thought. They don't play fair.

Although two lawyers and a priest testified that Billy was a calm and peaceable person, the court was not convinced. When Motto's attorney pleaded that there was no real reason his client should not be freed on bail, the magistrate asked incredulously, "How can you argue such a ludicrous and ridiculous point? Can you explain a ten-thousand-dollar-a-week income solely from his produce business? Bail denied." Billy Motto was led from the court in handcuffs and taken to prison to await trial.

The headline in the morning paper on the second day of Motto's bail hearing screamed "Coke Suspect Paid to Have FBI Agent Hit." Chuck Reed's wife read it and turned pale. She called him at the office in a state of near-hysteria. He did his best to convince her there was nothing to worry about and partly believed that was true. Once the threat became public, the chances were it wouldn't be carried out. Nonetheless he quickly crossed the gleaming marble corridor that connects the FBI office to the Justice Department wing, took the elevator to the third floor, and entered Ron Noble's office without knocking, visibly upset. It was the first glimpse Noble had had of the human side of Chuck Reed. Before him was a man very worried about protecting his wife and children.

"Please, Ron," he said in his flat low voice. "Do everything you can to see that Motto gets held without bail."

Sometime after the first series of indictments, it had become popular among the members of the Lavin ring to hate Chuck Reed. The aggressive investigator was not an easy man to like. Although he was a nice-enough guy in a social setting, when he switched into his work mode, his personality was ruled by his contempt for criminals and his rigid sense of right and wrong. Out in the field, his speech was blunt, and his interrogative style ranged from brusque to nasty. Reed made no attempt to hide the fact that he didn't get mad, he got even—and enjoyed every minute of it. Other than his family and his tinkering with sports cars, his work was his life and he savored his reputation as a relentless pit bull who, once he got his teeth into something, wouldn't let go. While he and Sid Perry complemented each other as partners in their mean-guy/nice-guy roles, Reed suffered from the constant comparisons made between them by the defendants.

They all saw Reed as a man with a lust for vengeance and preferred dealing with Perry, whom they perceived as a compassionate person capable of judging them apart from the crimes they committed. As David Ackerman put it: "Sid sees me as I am— someone who made a large mistake but is sorry and has changed. He would trust me to work on his children's teeth. Reed sees me as dirt." It was universally acknowledged that both agents strongly believed in what they were doing. But because they had such different fighting styles, it was less apparent that they were equally focused of the jugular. When Perry said over and over, "I hate to lose," he wasn't kidding. He simply disguised his drive with Southern manners, gentlemanly finesse, and talent for dealing with people in particular, his awareness of the importance of giving suspects a chance to save face. Perry got mad once in a while too, but unlike Reed, he rarely felt compelled to get even.

Thus it had been shocking but not surprising several weeks earlier when Ken Weidler turned to Chuck Reed as he was negotiating his plea agreement and said, "There's a contract out on you."

"Oh, really," Reed replied casually, not a trace of emotion betraying his inner fury. "What do you know about it?"

Weidler didn't know very much. He'd heard from Lavin that Motto, Mikuta, and Burns were all in on it, and Burns was the point man. Sid Perry drove out to question Burns about the rumored hit on Reed, and Franny claimed it was just a joke, something kicked around in anger.

"That's fine and dandy," Sid told him, "but if Chuck gets hit by lightning, you're gonna be blamed."

He left sensing he'd defused the threat and Chuck was safe. Reed was somewhat relieved, but found himself much more wary around Burns than he'd been in the past, and he no longer went to interview him alone. He'd never trusted the big thug anyway, and now he was convinced he was a no-good double-crosser. He'd make sure that Burns would get a very healthy prison sentence. His resolve was fueled by a conversation that took place between an FBI informant and Paul Mikuta, Lavin's college roommate who'd become a substantial coke dealer and one of the ring's preferred customers. The FBI had targeted Mikuta for the June 1985 indictment, and to solidify their case, they sent an informant wearing a wire out to visit him at his business, a wholesale ice-cream distributorship. The agents were parked in a car about a quarter-of-a-mile away listening to the conversation over a special radio. At one point Chuck Reed's name was mentioned.

"I thought Burns was supposed to take care of that guy," Mikuta said.

"Did you hear that?" Reed asked Perry. At that moment, for him, any possibility the hit had been mere rumor vanished.

The government was never able to prove there'd been a plot to murder the agent. Reed believed there had, when Burns failed a polygraph in which he was asked, "Were you paid by anyone to have Chuck Reed killed? . . . Did you pay anyone to kill Chuck Reed? . . . Regarding your answer just now about Chuck Reed, are you deliberately lying or withholding information?"

"No," he answered to all three questions.

"Now, listen," the polygrapher said, "you're lying to me." As he prodded Burns to come clean, he discovered that, as Reed and Perry had surmised all along, Burns had been deceiving the government since he'd been arrested and agreed to cooperate.

The overheard conversation with Mikuta only confirmed Reed and Perry's early suspicions. The more they now sniffed around, the stronger the stench of lies became. Little by little they learned that Burns had lied to the grand jury about his contact with Billy Motto, his collection of drug debts, his possession of cocaine, and in general the promise made in his plea agreement to provide the FBI with "truthful, complete, and accurate testimony and information." Two days before the July Fourth holiday, they'd amassed enough evidence to have Burns rearrested and his bail revoked. That's when he agreed to take the polygraph and revealed that, along with everything else, he'd also lied about surrendering the entire assets of his drug business. Apparently he'd given his uncle more than a half-million dollars in hundred-dollar bills to bury in his backyard.

It was a beastly hot and humid day in mid-July when a three-car caravan set out to recover the money. Reed was on vacation, so Perry was in the first car with another agent; behind him was Franny Burns in the custody of two federal marshals, with more agents and marshals in the last car. They drove to a working-class neighborhood out in Chester County and pulled into the driveway of a small house with a wooden porch, a patch of front lawn turning brown from lack of watering, and a narrow backyard.

Uncle Tony, an elderly retired man with a bad limp, was expecting them. Unable to get to the basement because of his disability, he directed Perry down the stairs and said he'd find some of the money buried in the crawl space. Perry took a screwdriver from a table and poked about until he hit something hard, and then with his hands dug up two pieces of plastic sewer pipe about fifteen inches long and four inches in diameter, capped at both ends. He tossed them to the agent standing behind him, who smashed them with a hammer. Out tumbled pack after pack of hundred-dollar bills—more than a quarter-million dollars.

Uncle Tony couldn't remember exactly where he'd hidden the rest, other than that it was somewhere near the toolshed in the backyard. Perry asked for shovel, removed his suit jacket, carefully folded it, and rolled up his sleeves. He was not pleased about getting sweaty and dirty. It took him about twenty minutes to find and dig up the remaining two pipes—a few shovels of earth in one spot and then another until he hit paydirt. Together the contents of the pipes totaled $528,200. He put the pipes in one bag, the money in another, and walked out front to where Burns was waiting, handcuffed, in the car.

"Is there any more?"

"No," Burns replied sullenly. "That's all there is."

"Is there any money buried anywhere else?"

"No."

The marshals returned Burns to jail to await sentencing, and Perry and his associate took off down the Schulkill Expressway with a half-million dollars in the back seat. Suddenly the car sputtered and died. Fortunately, they were close to an exit and able to push the vehicle off the highway and into a gas station, where they managed to get it started. Then they nursed it back to the city.

In the middle of July 1985, seven more men in western Pennsylvania were indicted as part of the Lavin conspiracy. They included a landscape architect, a former elementary-school principal, a stockbroker, and a real-estate executive who had all been connected to Lavin through a former classmate at the University of Pennsylvania, who, leaving Philadelphia after he graduated from college, continued to buy cocaine from Larry and sell it through his own coterie of dealers. This brought the total number charged to fifty-seven, and the FBI hadn't even begun the indictments in New England.

Only four of the people in the second batch of thirty indictments pleaded not guilty. They included Billy Motto and two of his workers, Vito Mirro and Pasquale "Pat" Giordano.

Motto chose to put his fate before a jury because he believed that if he got a chance to tell his story, he could show the world how different he was from Lavin and the others. *They* sold to him. He didn't sell to them. Surely the court would see that he was a major customer, not a major player in the conspiracy, and compared with the college boys, he was nothing but a small-time operator. He was willing to take his medicine for being a drug dealer and face prison if he had to, but he was going to battle the conspiracy charge to the hilt. And he looked long and hard until he found a lawyer who agreed he had a fighting chance.

As for pleading guilty and cooperating, that was to Motto a more heinous act than any of the things of which he'd been accused. Within the framework of his world, Billy South Philly was a man of very high principles. "It's tempting to save your neck and say the hell with everybody else. But I wasn't raised that way. What kinda world would it be if everybody sold their friends down the river? How you gonna look yourself in the mirror? It ain't my job to put people in jail. It would be more shame to my family if I flipped than to go to prison as a stand-up guy. If I was going away, I was going like a man, not a rat."

Motto's trial began in early October 1985 and lasted seven weeks. Although it had been less than a year since the Kim Noramatzu trial, Tina Gabbrielli and Ron Noble entered the courtroom this time with much greater confidence. They'd taken these indictments from their inception to their finish and probably knew more about the Lavin conspiracy than they knew about the lives of their closest friends. Tina, being the more methodical member of the team, presented the opening argument. Standing in the paneled federal courtroom in a tailored dress-for-success suit with a flared skirt and a bow at the neck of her blouse, she brilliantly laid out the complicated conspiracy in simple terms and promised that the government would show that "Billy Motto was an organizer, supervisor, and manager of a criminal drug enterprise." Ron, immaculately groomed as always in a starched white shirt and navy suit, elected to do the closing because he was more emotional, and the end of a trial is the appropriate place for histrionics.

Because neither of them was a seasoned prosecutor, they made what could have been two costly errors. The first occurred during the jury-selection process. One of the potential jurors had once been indicted for a crime and the charges later dropped. When Noble asked him how this experience had affected his view of the justice system, he replied, "It showed me the system works." They accepted him for the jury. A more experienced trial lawyer would not have taken the chance.

The second mistake was acknowledging in their opening statement that the prosecution witnesses were convicted criminals. The entire case against Motto depended on the testimony of other members of the conspiracy. His voice never appeared on any of the recorded conversations; he'd never been directly identified on tape other than as BSP or Billy South Philly, nor had he been observed by the government buying or selling coke. Everything the jury would hear about Motto would come from others involved in the same crimes. The government's difficult job was making those people appear credible. It would have been preferable to refer to them as "eyewitnesses who participated along with Motto and who will take you where he was." The defense picked up on the label "criminals" and repeatedly pointed out to the jury that they should not trust the word of lawbreaking witnesses attempting to save themselves.

Criminals or not, the government's star witnesses performed beautifully. David Ackerman's razor-sharp mind easily parried the

defense's attempt to disarm and discredit him, and Franny Burns
partially recouped his damaged reputation with the FBI by spilling
every detail of his relationship with Motto. Only Nicky Bongiorno
worried Noble. He was so unpredictable and could be utterly
charming one moment and downright frightening the next. He was
nervous when he first took the stand, and not very convincing. His
agitation was understandable. To make him uncomfortable, Motto's family had packed the courtroom with about fifty people from
the neighborhood. Noble reversed the intimidation by asking Nicky
to identify everybody seated in the room who had anything to do
with the conspiracy. He pointed at Motto's father. "He delivered
money." He singled out Billy's wife. "She counted money."

"You're a liar," Billy screamed.

The judge called a recess, and when they reconvened, only a
handful of the neighborhood crowd remained. Nicky relaxed and
gave Noble everything he wanted.

Except for that outburst, Billy Motto contained his frustration,
although he never got to tell his side of the story as he'd envisioned, because his lawyer advised him not to take the stand. He
did manage to give Ron Noble a laugh. Every day the federal
marshals would walk Billy into the court through the parking
basement, past his beloved Volvo with the door taped open. Billy
kept that car so clean there wasn't even dust on the tires when it
was seized by the FBI. One day as the court recessed, he paused
by Ron's table as he was being led back to jail.

"Thanks for washing my car, Mr. Noble." He always called the
prosecutor "Mr. Noble." "It looks real nice."

When the jury filed out late on a Tuesday afternoon, the government felt satisfied it had presented the strongest possible case. Its
optimism was shattered the next day at three when the foreman
reported to the judge that one of the members refused to accept
the testimony of known criminals and asked how they should
proceed. Noble knew instinctively which juror it was. The judge
called the jury in and instructed them that criminals are considered
competent witnesses. Their testimony must be considered and either accepted or rejected on its merits. The next two hours seemed
like two years to the two young prosecutors. They feared either a
hung jury or a not-guilty verdict. But at five P.M. the jurors marched
in and announced they'd found Motto, Mirro, and Giordano guilty
an all counts.

At Billy's sentencing hearing it was apparent the leash on his
freedom had very little slack. Still, his lawyer made a valiant effort
to persuade the judge that just because Motto, who was only a

preferred customer, chose not to cooperate, he did not deserve a stiffer sentence than the leaders of the conspiracy. A parade of witnesses—two priests, a lawyer, the mother of a boy whose life Billy had saved, a niece he'd raised—all spoke emotionally about the other Billy Motto, the good boy they knew and loved. Billy delivered a long, eloquent plea on his own behalf. His natural flair for theatrics, combined with his passion for the cause, created a bravura performance. He began by talking about his frustration.

"At the trial you can't say what you want. After the trial you can't tell the truth neither when you don't plead guilty." He addressed the issue of violence by contending that he carried a big stick but there was no proof he ever used it. He explained at great length why he could not in good conscience cooperate with the government and how he feared retribution against his family if he rolled over. "I beg the court don't punish me for what I didn't do but what I did." The further into the speech he got, the more animated he became, and he talked about wanting to make an example of his life by writing books on drugs, reaching out to kids and speaking in schools.

Finally he raised his face to the judge and said, "I realize now that I justified my doing wrong by trying to help people and do good deeds. There was a side in me busting out to be good. It was true I was greedy. I was wrong. I was influenced by the professional people. I wanted my family to live more comfortable. I wanted to get out of the ghetto, so I sold drugs. I did wrong. But I'll not put my family on the line for my own selfishness. How can they say because I didn't cooperate, I was foolish? My life is shaking now. My daughter is eleven months old and I never seen her. I'm a human being. I bleed. I am emotional, I know. Please believe that I have grown from prayer. God uses and life abuses. God forgave me. I forgive myself. I only hope you can forgive me. Thank you."

Pandemonium broke out in the courtroom. The crowd burst into loud applause. Women cried. Men shouted, "Go for it, Billy. We're with you, kid." It was a reaction unprecedented in the staid federal court. But it did not effect the judge the way it moved the audience. He sentenced Motto to twenty years, the longest jail term imposed on any of the defendants.

Sid Perry and Chuck Reed walked out of the courtroom barely able to conceal their elation. The score stood: fifty-seven indictments, fifty-six convictions, one fugitive.

It was time to go after Larry Lavin.

20

VIRGINIA BEACH
1985

The phone rang at 7:30. Despite the early hour, the sky showed signs of developing into a perfect May day. Brian O'Neil, who in a previous life had been Larry Lavin, picked up the receiver. Marcia was busy feeding the children their breakfast.

"Hi, Brian. It's Roy. Got any plans for today?" Roy, one of the dozens of friends Brian had made since moving to Virginia Beach, lived in a high-rise facing the ocean. Often, after surveying the water in the morning, he called Brian to go fishing.

"Nothing special. Why?"

"I'm looking out my window and the sea looks very calm. How about it?"

Brian would have preferred to spend the day scuba-diving. But Roy had just been fired from the hospital where he worked as a result of a nasty political confrontation and needed emotional support, so he said yes. There weren't that many guys available during the week to go fishing on a moment's notice.

"Okay. I'll pick up the sandwiches on my way to the dock," Brian said.

"Great. See you in about an hour."

Brian, juggling the day's planned schedule, mentally postponed his morning gardening for the afternoon and put off the stock-market newsletters he'd intended to read until that evening. He entertained the fleeting thought that he'd never been happier. He had everything he wanted: a beautiful family, good health, devoted friends, plenty of money, and all the time in the world to enjoy life. It had been over a year since he'd fled from Philadelphia, and he hardly ever thought anymore about getting caught. He'd figured that time was on his side. The FBI would look hard for six months and then abandon the chase. As far as he knew, his expectations were accurate. Despite his totally fabricated identity, he could not have felt safer.

It had been different when he, Marcia, and Chris arrived in Virginia Beach just before Halloween, 1984. Fortunately Christopher was only two and a half, still too young to miss trick-or-treating in the old neighborhood or realize that overnight he'd become Chris O'Neil. Sometimes he'd refer to himself as Chris Lavin, but he didn't speak clearly yet, and his parents were able to attribute his slips to baby talk. When the toddler told the dentist cleaning his teeth that this daddy used to be a dentist too, Larry laughed and made a joke about children's imaginations.

In the beginning it was hard for Lavin to adjust to waking up in the morning with nothing to do and nowhere in particular to go. For the first month or so as a fugitive, he moved about cautiously and weighed whether it was wise to remain so close to Philadelphia. But after spending so many of those early days driving around to acquaint themselves with their new environment, he and Marcia decided they really liked the area and, by the start of the new year, bought a house.

Before long the O'Neils were so totally integrated into the neighborhood that it felt like they'd lived there for years. Virginia Beach, a resort community of tourist hotels and suburban enclaves, is an easy place for a stranger to be assimilated, especially one as gregarious as Larry Lavin. Situated on a peninsula bordered by the Atlantic Ocean and the Chesapeake Bay, the city has a temperate climate with very little snow and is the northernmost region on the eastern seaboard where vegetation indigenous to the South can be cultivated. Yet it's not so Southern that a New Englander like Lavin would be conspicuous. The residential population has a higher percentage of newcomers than natives, marked by a concentration of transients and retired government personnel. One of them, a former naval officer who had lived across the street from the Lavins in Philadelphia, owned a summer house within a mile of where Larry and Marcia settled. Call it Lavin's luck that he never happened to bump into his old neighbor, or Lavin's arrogance that he knew about the summer home and moved there anyway.

Once the Lavins made the decision to stay, Larry thought he'd like to build his dream house, perhaps on the waterfront. However, there wasn't enough time because Marcia wanted to have the baby's room furnished and ready before her due date in the spring. Their daughter was born on April 5, 1985 and christened Tara, a name Larry thought was "just neat" when he found it in a book he'd bought. He'd known and liked a girl named Tara in high school back in Massachusetts, and the positive association definitely influenced him. That and the solid Irish sound of Tara Erin O'Neil. Actually, he was beginning to regret the choice of "O'Neil." It was bad enough that people always misspelled "Lavin." Was it "Lavin" or "Laven?" Now he was constantly being asked if "O'Neil" had one L or two. He told Marcia he should have called himself Kevin Reilly.

In preparation for Tara's arrival, the Lavins purchased a home under construction in Middle Plantation, a newly developed area of custom colonial houses on heavily wooded lots a mile or so from the bay. Larry was disappointed that his block, Royal Oak Close—which bore a striking resemblance to Timber Lane—turned out to have more traffic than he'd anticipated. He liked playing football in the street with the neighborhood kids, and the cars interfered with their games.

Lavin paid $200,000 (in a cashier's check) for his red brick hideout and then poured in another $50,000 in extras: a kidney-shaped pool in the backyard, equipped with a special ozone purifying filter and a self-sweeper to clean the leaves that fell from the towering elm trees; a sprinkler system to maintain the meticulously landscaped grounds; a custom outdoor slide and play gym for the kids; and a screened-in porch at the rear of the house, extending to a deck adjacent to the greenhouse, where Marcia could raise her African violets and orchids. He and Marcia swept through the local furniture stores, buying top-of-the line pieces off the floor in order to reconstruct as rapidly as possible the life they'd left behind. A homey note was struck by the knickknacks they'd carried with them in the U-Haul, along with a smattering of photographs with friends like Weidler and Mikuta that gave no hint of where they'd been taken.

Creating a history for the inhabitants of the house was a much more imaginative feat than furnishing it. This time there were no gold records to explain his wealth and unemployment. Larry generally told people that he'd sold a computer company and a seat on the stock exchange because he had a heart condition and his doctor had advised him "to sell the stuff and get out of the rat race." Now he was using his financial expertise to manage his investment portfolio. Most of their new friends envied him. For them, he epitomized the American dream: the young guy who'd hit it big.

To the next-door neighbors whom the O'Neils asked to serve as Tara's godparents, Larry felt he owed a more detailed explanation. He said the reason there were never any friends or family visiting from Philadelphia was that he was in the government's witness-protection program. The couple was touched to have this confidence shared with them and happily accepted the honorary responsibility for the infant.

The paper underpinnings to support the myth required a bit more ingenuity, but Larry was fully prepared for that too. He'd left Philadelphia with all the necessary forms for producing the family's phony documents but didn't actually do the work on them until he was settled in Virginia Beach. One rainy afternoon, he took out the blank birth and baptismal certificates he'd had printed in Philadelphia and typed in the information that transformed Christopher Lavin into Christopher O'Neil and Susan Marcia Osborn Lavin into Susan Marcia O'Neil. Marcia had always been known by her middle name and would continue to use it.

For the first few months, Larry kept Marcia grounded without a driver's license because he worried that the state would keep a duplicate of her picture on file. The excuse they gave to people for Marcia's not driving was Brian had so many license violations that the last time he'd been caught speeding, she switched places in the car with him, and her license had been suspended. Since he had plenty of time to chauffeur her around, it wasn't a problem. Larry continued to drive with his Massachusetts license in a friend's name and another one from Connecticut both doctored with his picture. Eventually Marcia applied for a license as Susan M. O'Neil after a series of phone calls to state agencies assured Larry that a picture license was not risky. How could the FBI search through all the licenses granted in Virginia without a name to initiate the trace?

About two months after getting Marcia her Virginia license, a speeding ticket spurred Larry to apply for one in his new name too. He'd always been the kind of driver who ran stop signs just to see if he could get away with it, but he'd been careful to change his habits since fleeing. He no longer disobeyed the speed limits or accelerated on yellow lights—until the one morning he got careless. It was just after dawn and he was rushing to pick up some people for a diving expedition in the Voyager mini-van when a cop stopped him for going thirty-five miles in a twenty-five-mile-an-hour zone. His heart was thundering. What if the information went into a computer and showed up in Massachusetts? Could it give the FBI a clue? The next day he telephoned the local sheriff, who happened to be one of his fishing buddies, and casually inquired about a friend who'd gotten a ticket using a license borrowed from someone in Boston and was worried the ticket would affect the insurance rates of the person who'd loaned it to him. The sheriff checked into it and reported back that information on out-of-state speeding tickets isn't transferred to the home state if the fine is paid. Still, that was too close a call for Larry, and he decided he'd better get a license for Brian O'Neil.

Little by little, Larry built an impressive dossier in his new name. In addition to the fake birth and baptismal certificates, he obtained mail-order blank employee-identification cards to which he affixed his photo and typed in information presenting himself as a programmer for Epsom Computers. He chose that job as his cover because he owned an Epsom and knew enough about computers to bluff his way into sounding like an expert. He also sent away for a metal social-security card engraved with the name Brian O'Neil and a bogus number. While these plates cannot be legally substituted for the government-issued paper cards, they look official, and most people will accept them as a secondary source of identification. Slowly he added other things to his wallet: a Red Cross volunteer-blood-donor card—type O negative; preferred-customer cards issued by local places like the nursery and the marina where he did business; his "open-water" diver certification from the Lynnhaven Dive Center; a Cashflow bank card. The only thing he didn't carry were credit cards. He paid for small purchases in cash and large ones with cashier's checks.

In his scramble to amass as much cash as he could before running away, Larry had assembled $1.6 million, which he packed in two suitcases along with his personal belongings. After arriving in Virginia Beach, he transferred the money to safe-deposit boxes. But not for long. He couldn't bear having his money sit idle and soon was overcome with the same compulsion that had driven him to give his early drug profits to Mark Stewart to invest. After that disastrous experience, he was not about to trust anyone but himself to handle his clandestine fortune. And one thing he couldn't do was plunk it in an interest-bearing bank account in one lump sum without attracting undue attention. So he devised a clever plan to augment his wealth. He'd create a group of fictitious people and furnish each of them with genuine social-security cards applied for in their invented names.Then he'd spread his money among high-yield mutual funds, using their names as investors. He'd even file legitimate tax returns for them!

The keystone of the plan was obtaining social-security numbers for these nonexistent people. Larry tackled the problem with typical verve. He found a book on the social-security system and thoroughly familiarized himself with the way it worked. He learned, for instance, that when a social-security number is punched into a computer to verify an identity, the age of the person is not part of the information that appears on the screen. Thus, when he eventually took Marcia to get her driver's license, she presented to authorities a birth certificate Larry had made with her true age on it and a social-security card he'd gotten using another birth certificate that showed she was twelve years old. There was a special reason for making Marcia so young. Individuals under eighteen did not have to register for their cards in person. The application could be made for them by any adult, like Larry, armed with the proper identification.

There were two necessary kinds of ID that Larry dubbed the hard set and the soft set. The hard set included a birth or baptismal certificate. The soft set could be a student card, a report card, a driver's license, a Boy Scout or Girl Scout membership, or a voter's registration card. The hard ID's Larry made from his printed certificates. For the soft ID's he created high-school records on his home computer.

Researching and implementing his plan occupied much of Larry's time those early months in Virginia Beach. He telephoned all kinds of state and national agencies, meticulously checking whether there was any possible way the phony identities could be traced to his doorstep. Every strategy was logically designed to draw the least attention and minimize the risks. He plotted the location of social-security offices within several hours of Virginia Beach and then searched for private mailbox providers in the same vicinity. He didn't want a sharp clerk asking what he was doing in her neighborhood if he lived somewhere else. In fact he didn't want to run into any bright clerks who might scrutinize his documents too carefully, so whenever possible, he filed his applications in run-down neighborhoods where he reasoned that the pleasure of dealing with someone as intelligent and charming as himself would allay the civil servant's suspicions. Finally, after weeks of preparation, he was ready for action.

He chose Richmond for his initial foray and set out from home dressed in a tie and jacket with his documents in a briefcase. He would be presenting himself as a lawyer obtaining social-security cards for his nephews who'd be working for him this summer at, respectively, a swim club, an ice-cream store, a flower shop, and so on. He'd decided it was most efficient to apply for two cards at once. He carried a birth certificate for Eric Thomas Wright, son of Andrew and Barbara, born January 11, 1974, in Haverhill, Massachusetts, and a baptismal certificate from St. James Church for his brother, Todd Robert Wright, born in the same town, December 26, 1972. He also had school records for them typed out on his computer.

Even before Lavin visited the social-security office to apply for a number, he needed a safe place where the cards and the money they'd later generate could be sent. That meant obtaining private mailboxes, since he could not have anything traceable to his home. Getting a mailbox often required some proof of identity too, and sometimes companies that offered them wanted two different documents. For one, the birth certificate would do. For the other, until he had real social-security cards, he relied on the metal kind, which he ordered in advance with a name to match the birth certificate and a made-up number.

Larry's first stop was the Mail Depot, one of hundreds of places that have sprung up all over the country in recent years to handle the demand for mailboxes that the post office can't accommodate. A primary advantage of these private companies is that the address appears to be that of an office rather than a box number. Most people use them for purely legitimate reasons: a small business operating from a home doesn't want to mix personal and corporate mail; a salesman who lives far from headquarters finds it more convenient to have his mail delivered closer to his home. Getting the initial box proved to be no problem at all. The clerk easily accepted Larry's bogus identification, and when he left The Mail Depot the imaginary Wright brothers had a real home—900 N. Lombardy Street, Apt 166, Richmond, Virginia. Still, that didn't take away the butterflies in his stomach as he walked into the closest social-security office, holding in his hand the hard and soft ID's and the application forms he'd already filled out at home.

Larry consciously planned on taking advantage of his gift for making people comfortable to facilitate the transaction. "Getting by clerks is my forte," he told himself as he pushed open the glass entrance door of the building. Once he stated his business, he began disarming the clerk with chatter about what a cold winter it had been, how difficult it was to get kids to work these days, and wasn't he lucky his nephews had the old-fashioned work ethic of their parents. Everything progressed smoothly until the woman commented that the boys' signatures looked kind of sloppy for youngsters' handwriting. Larry panicked. He hadn't considered that children have much neater writing than adults and tried to paper over his mistake with a remark about what a disgrace it was that schools didn't teach penmanship anymore. Hereafter he'd fake a signature that was closer to the precise way children write their names. The clerk agreed that he was right, gave him a receipt for the two applications, and told him to expect the cards in six to eight weeks.

"Have a nice day," she said.

"You too," Larry answered. There was no doubt he would. This was going to be a piece of cake.

Over the next several weeks he geared up into mass production, traveling by plane or car to Washington, Arlington, Baltimore— every town in a several-hundred-mile radius that had a social-security office. Slowly he accumulated fifty-eight social-security numbers. Only once did he have a problem—when a recalcitrant clerk refused to process the applications because his nephews weren't with him. He'd done this enough times by now to know the ropes and demanded to see her supervisor.

"Look," he said angrily, "I'm a busy lawyer. I've taken the time from my practice to come down here. I could have sent my secretary, but I didn't. These are my nephews. I've got all the right documents and there is no legal reason for you not to put this through."

Her boss looked at his papers and told her to go ahead with it.

As time passed, he'd detour on his application trips to collect the cards as they began to arrive. With these in his possession, he could now shift into phase two: investing his money.

From the original $1.6 million, he'd already spent $600,000. Half went into the house and its landscaping and improvements. They'd paid $25,000 in one shopping spree for furniture, $30,000 for two cars, and $80,000 on boats. Then there were business investments—a luxury home he built with a partner on speculation, $25,000 into a scuba-diving shop, and $43,000 to buy a special cement pump to start a company that would build swimming pools. The least of his expenses was their life-style. The Lavins were not ostentatious people. Their world revolved around family activities and Larry's hobbies. His gardening, computer, and saltwater fish tanks didn't involve much expense, and he didn't have a wife who pressured him for clothes or jewelry. They drove good dependable cars that wouldn't stand out in a parking lot—a Nissan Maxima and a Plymouth Voyager mini-van—and Marcia continued to clip supermarket coupons as she'd always done. Larry's big expenses were, as always, his toys and gadgets. He bought a $35,000 speedboat and within months traded it for a $75,000, thirty-two-foot Wellcraft St. Tropez with $7,000 worth of gear such as a microwave oven, a ship-to-shore phone, and a sophisticated navigation system. With those big purchases out of the way, he estimated they could live quite comfortably on $20,000 a year, which he set aside, leaving himself with approximately $930,000 to invest. Marcia wanted him to keep a cash reserve in the safe-deposit box in case anything went wrong, but he insisted on investing the whole amount. He wouldn't let go of his money-had-to-earn-money fixation.

What he wanted to avoid at all costs was any possibility the IRS would audit his fictitious investors. To evade scrutiny, he kept the amounts in each of his various holdings below $50,000, which he believed was a figure that wouldn't elicit interest from an Internal Revenue agent. There was another advantage to having multiple small accounts. If any one of them happened to be scheduled for an audit, he could abandon it, and lose only a small fraction of his whole portfolio. He set up thirty-six separate accounts under thirty-six of his false identities and distributed the monies among twenty different high-performing money-market funds—Vanguard, Evergreen Trust, Fidelity Overseas Investment Fund, Fidelity Growth, and the like. Each "nephew" had holdings in anywhere from one to four funds, and each fund had several "nephews" in it. Larry kept track of everybody in his computer. After a while, he forgot they were cardboard creatures and started to see them as flesh-and-blood people with distinct personalities. For example, he considered the Wright brothers conservative investors and he put their money in risk-free investments. Kevin Hecht, another of his "nephews," was more of a plunger, so Larry steered his money into the volatile Fidelity Overseas Fund.

Larry's investments augmented more than his pocketbook. He used them to broaden his "nephew" identity packages and establish banking connections for when he needed cashier's checks. Whenever he opened a money-market fund, he'd check the box next to "Send me a checkbook." The checks would arrive from say, Chase Manhattan Bank in New York. Now he had an account at Chase although no one there had ever set eyes on him. Suppose he next wanted an account at Mellon Bank in Philadelphia in order to get an automatic-teller-machine card (which he could also use as another soft proof of identity). He simply filled in the three-by-five application with his "nephew's" name, put the checking-account number at Chase Manhattan in the space for "bank reference," and wrote out the initial deposit on a Chase check. As long as his account at Chase was in good standing, Mellon hadn't the slightest compunction about sending him an ATM card and welcoming him as a new customer.

Like many legitimate savvy retirees, Larry carefully chose to trade in mutual funds because they did not require a registered stockbroker for doing business. He relied on his own background in securities to make decisions and move money around, and did extremely well. Within a year he built his $930,000 nestegg to $1.5 million, a tidy sixty-percent return. He attributed his success to timing. "It didn't take any particular genius. When I entered the market, the Dow Jones was thirteen-hundred and it rose over time to eighteen-hundred. Had I not been as conservative, I would have tripled my money." But it was more than luck. He employed an investment-tracking system recommended by one of his newsletters that followed the moving average performance of his mutual funds over a thirty-nine-week period. If the fund rose a certain number of points, he stayed in it. If it decreased a certain number of points, he withdrew his money and put it somewhere more productive. Larry liked having systems to direct him because they took the emotional component out of buying and selling.

Once Larry had his financial empire established, managing it occupied only a few hours every day. As soon as the system was humming, he closed a number of his mailboxes in distant places like Baltimore and consolidated them at companies closer to Virginia Beach so he wouldn't have to spend so much time driving around to collect his statements and his checks. He mapped the locations in such a way that he could make a sweep of all his boxes in a one-day trip that he embarked on monthly, with Marcia and the kids in the car to keep him company.

His typical day began with a three-mile jog. When the mail was delivered, he'd take it upstairs to the small room above the two-car garage that he'd made into a spartan office for himself and leaf through the latest of the ten-to-fifteen mutual-fund newsletters he subscribed to. After that, he'd sit down at his computer terminal and flip through his accounts to check on their performance. If one thing didn't meet his criteria, he'd phone the fund's 800 number and either shift his money into one of the company's other types of funds or withdraw it completely and reinvest his cash in something more profitable. By midmorning he was finished and ready to move on to the serious work of filling his considerable leisure time.

Larry Lavin told his brother Rusty that he was so well-liked in Virginia Beach, he could have run for mayor and won. The remark wasn't pure hyperbole. As Brian O'Neil he garnered a reputation for being an exemplary father, a trusted neighbor, and a valued friend.

He devoted endless hours to his son, Christopher, vowing to be the kind of father he wished he'd had. They went to the circus and to Easter-egg hunts. They played golf in the backyard with a set of miniature clubs Larry bought to fit a three-year-old's reach. Just as he'd helped his father maintain the grounds at their home in Haverhill, he let Chris dig in the earth with him and Marcia. They put in one thousand bulbs, sprayed and fed the roses, trimmed the azaleas. He spent hours almost daily in the yard, pruning, planting, and puttering as his own father had. But he tried to make the work fun for Chris instead of the chore it had been for him. His youthful memories were very vivid, especially those of his family's financial struggle, which had been such a motivating force in his passionate pursuit of money. He never could forget how tough it had been for him, always scrounging to make a buck. That was one of the reasons he overpaid the youngsters who baby-sat or cut the lawn. He felt they were all spoiled and complained to Marcia that it was hard to find kids today anywhere near as ambitious as he had been.

For the neighborhood kids who took to hanging around the O'Neil house, Larry became a role model. The same easy manner that enabled him to connect with young patients in his dental practice now made him the adult that kids sought out to discuss their problems when they weren't speaking to their parents. Lots of the fathers in the neighborhood traveled frequently on business, while Larry was not only always available, he actively offered himself as a surrogate dad. He helped the teenagers next door with their math homework and persuaded the sixteen-year-old boy to stop chewing snuff because it was dangerous to his health. He introduced the kids on the block to water sports, took them out diving with him, even lectured on computers at the local high school.

Parents never resented Larry because he was equally generous with them. He dispensed free stock market advice the way he had in the corridors at dental school, designed computer systems for people going into business at no charge, supported a diving buddy through a traumatic emotional breakup with his girlfriend, and was the man other people turned to for assistance when they had boating difficulties at sea. "Brian had a terrific rapport with people," said Walter Heller, a staffer at the dive shop. "It didn't matter whether you were five or one-hundred-and-five. He treated everyone on the same level and was always there for anybody who needed him. His attitude was, if you need help, let's look at the problem and get it squared away."

Heller had a special reason to idolize Brian. He had been adopted as a baby and was engaged in a search to find his natural mother when he became Larry's scuba diving instructor. Heller's quest ended successfully in California, but he was unable to scrape up the money for the trip to visit her. "One day I got a call from Brian that there were problems at the dive shop—some of the equipment had been busted. He told me to stop at his place and we'd take his pool vacuum over to help out. When I got there, a bunch of guys were standing around drinking beer and they handed me a check for my trip. Brian had organized the collection."

For the most part, Larry put his wild days behind him. Occasionally he'd sneak off to a bar to meet a friend and eye the women, but he no longer indulged in paid sex or drugs. If a joint were passed at a party, he usually refused. Marcia saw him as a reformed man, especially since she got a bigger chunk of his attention than she ever had before. Of course Larry would still do the kind of thing that annoyed her: go down to the boat for an hour to wax the molding and disappear for the whole day. Or drag her to huge outdoor barbecues with the boat crowd, who now filled the void left by his drug companions. But he placated her by also doing the things she enjoyed, like piling the kids in the car for a browsing excursion at the local mall. For Marcia this was the most wonderful period of their married life. No longer did their intimate friends have to be selected from the pool of Larry's drug associates. Without the cocaine business overshadowing everything, they could live a normal life as a normal couple for the first time since she'd met him. Larry even went to church with her regularly, mainly because it gave him the opportunity to put on a suit and hobnob with friends. Who cared if he perceived it as more of a social event than a religious experience. That was fine with her as long as he was by her side.

Their new friends, like the former crowd, found Marcia to be much more reserved than Brian. She was supermom, totally wrapped up in her children and her home. He seemed to have time for everybody, and his own interests, too. He dabbled in construction by forming a partnership with an established builder to erect a custom home they sold for $360,000. He also started a business importing and selling scuba wet suits that he purchased abroad for about one-third what they cost in the United States. As busy as he kept himself, he sorely missed dentistry and was surprised how little the passage of time diminished his craving to practice his profession. Once he got so involved discussing some new materials used for fillings with a dentist working on his teeth that the man remarked he seemed unusually knowledgeable for a layman. Marcia happened to be standing nearby and said that Larry's brother was a dentist and Larry, who had a photographic memory, liked studying his journals and remembered whatever he read.

Fortunately Larry found a new outlet for the energy he'd poured into the dentistry and drugs and that was diving. He enrolled for scuba lessons the spring after they'd arrived in Virginia Beach and by June was certified for his first dive. It was the perfect sport for Larry's thrill-seeking personality. It fed his appetite for adventure and slaked his thirst for risk. He even dove in winter, relishing the danger added by the icy cold waters. Twice he nearly died diving when his tanks ran out of oxygen. Once of those times was almost funny in retrospect. He'd gone down one-hundred-ten feet and when he broke the surface, barely conscious, he couldn't get the attention of the men on the boat to pull him out of the water. They were too busy aiding a seasick passenger heaving his breakfast into the ocean. Larry particularly enjoyed taking his own boat forty-five miles out into the Atlantic and scouting around for sunken

World War II wrecks to explore. He wasn't interested in buried treasure. What he loved was the excitement of swimming through a ship frozen in time and hunting for souvenirs, like brass bells crusty with barnacles that he'd retrieve from the ocean's bottom, polish at home and display on a knickknack shelf. Marcia thought they were ugly and would gradually move them behind her ceramic figurines and hope Larry didn't notice.

In good weather when Larry wasn't diving he was usually fishing. Although trawling in deep-sea waters was tame compared to diving in them, he savored the camaraderie of drinking beer, hanging out with a nice bunch of guys and supplying the neighborhood with free, fresh fish. It was the closest thing he had to replace the friendships left behind in Philadelphia, but it wasn't enough for him to cut those ties completely.

Larry always had an insatiable need to know what was happening to the people at the intimate core of his life, which exile only exacerbated. He could follow the general news of his case by reading *USA Today* and was shocked by the breadth of the indictments and length of the sentences. He never thought the case would get so big or that so many people would be arrested. "When I read Paul Mikuta's name in the paper, it practically killed me. I felt so helpless. I'd expected Bruce and Billy to go, but never Paul." Sometimes when he was in Washington applying for a social security card or emptying a mailbox, he'd pick up the *Philadelphia Inquirer*. He didn't do that very often. It made him too nervous, especially during the seven weeks that Billy Motto was on trial when he feared his picture might appear in the paper and somebody would recognize him. He was spared because there was a major newspaper strike in Philadelphia during the trial, so it got almost no local coverage.

The problem with the papers was that they didn't give him *details*. And the press was certainly no source of information about his parents, his brothers and sisters, and his former patients. Larry believed that he could remove himself physically from his past and survive, but his soul would wither and die if he didn't have some kind of emotional contact. He'd never been much good at the written word. The telephone line had always been his umbilical cord to the world. It remained that way in exile.

Before fleeing, Larry made an arrangement with his brother, Rusty, similar to the one he had with Ken Weidler. Rusty copied the numbers from seven pay phones in different towns an hour from where he lived in Massachusetts and coded them from A to G. When Larry left he took these phone numbers, along with a handful of others, including the home phones of his dental-office girls. He felt it was safe to occasionally go to a pay phone and call one of them at home for a bit of gossip. He couldn't imagine their lines would be tapped and trusted their loyalty because of all the favors he'd done for them—he'd set up the husband of one girl in the roofing business. By contrast, he was always a little leery calling his former dental partner. Lurking in the back of his mind was a statement Weidler once made that his own family came before everything else. After their third conversation about four months after he'd left, Larry's instincts made him cancel the next scheduled call. He telephoned one of the office girls and told her to tell Kenny he would not be calling him again.

That left Rusty, his brother and former drug worker, as his sole link to his old life. They talked every other week, setting the time, date, and code letter for the location of the next call at the completion of each conversation. After the calls, Larry would return home and pencil the next phone date in their big Sierra Club wilderness calendar alongside Marcia's neatly printed notations of medical appointments for the children and the dog, an oyster roast or Tupperware party, and reminders to feed the violets and the orchids. When the time came for the call, Larry usually awakened feeling vaguely apprehensive, with his jitters increasing as the day went on. Over and over he'd tell himself there was no way the calls could be traced. He traveled a minimum of an hour from home to make them and never used the same phone twice. Gradually he developed a little ritual to reduce his tension by making the phone trips into family outings. He'd put Marcia and the kids into the car and they'd drive somewhere for dinner. At seven he'd be at a phone booth with a handful of quarters while Marcia stayed with the children, aching as much as Larry was for news from home.

It was difficult for Larry to finish a call and difficult to stay on the line too long. He'd end with the intructions, "The eighteenth at seven at E," hang up, and rush back to Marcia. Oblivious of the parking lot, they'd hold tightly to each other in the front seat of the car, momentarily wrapped as one in nostalgic longing for the past and chilling fear for the future.

The calls became a focal point in Rusty's life too. He looked forward to each call with a mix of anticipation and fear, always leaving for the phone booth far earlier than necessary so he could take a circuitous route just in case he was being followed. After each call, he'd hang up feeling terribly lonely, and worried always that he might never hear from his brother again.

Rusty was a good reporter. Sometimes he'd have talked to Mrs. Osborn and could relay news about Marcia's family. Other times he'd update Larry about the lives of mutual friends, the health of Mom and Dad, or the progress of the case. A recurrent theme of Rusty's conversations was that Larry ought to consider turning himself in and coming home. The uncertainty about his own future and his role as Larry's sole connection was wearing Rusty down. "I was in this mess up here alone," he felt, "and Larry was out there not worrying about anybody but himself. He didn't have to see how miserable Mom and Dad were." After one of their calls, Larry got so exasperated with his brother's harping on the subject that he suggested maybe they shouldn't talk anymore. Rusty tried another approach. He drove to Philadelphia and arranged for Larry to call his attorney at an appointed time at a phone booth downstairs in the lawyer's office building. By then Reed and Perry had visited the attorney with a tempting offer that he conveyed to the fugitive: surrender and we'll lay off Rusty and Jill. Lavin toyed with the idea of exchanging himself for his brother's and sister's freedom until he realized that to save them he'd have to sacrifice his life with Marcia and the children. He told the attorney, "Not yet. I'll wait and see what happens to them."

Aside from these phone calls to Rusty, Larry lived very much in the present and rarely thought about Sid Perry or Chuck Reed. He told Ken Weidler in one of their last conversations that he slept well at night. What guilt he had surfaced in a recurrent dream: one of those ray guns from the *Star Trek* series came into his possession. With it he could miraculously zap out all the evidence from his past. A spray from his magic gun made the whole conspiracy disappear and enabled him to save his friends from going to jail. Sometimes during the day he'd get a little tense over a banking transaction or a license application and worry that he might somehow be establishing a lead the FBI could follow. The concern was fleeting. Lavin was optimistic by nature and not the sort to look over his shoulder. He viewed himself as similar to the heroes in the Hemingway novels he'd devoured in college—as a man always in total control. His current situation was simply another phase in the adventurous style he'd chosen to experience life. The way he saw it, "When you'd taken as many big risks as I had, one more little risk was no big deal."

There were two times, however, that the potential danger was great enough to make him think about pulling up stakes and fleeing again.

The first was when he discovered that one of his closest new friends, Pat O'Donald, was a retired FBI agent. There were quite a few agents—active and retired—living in the Virginia Beach area. Many of them came into the dive shop for scuba lessons. If Larry happened to be around, he always made himself scarce. When he met Pat, he had no idea of his background other than that he currently worked for the state police in some kind of white-collar-crime unit. A mutual friend had referred O'Donald to Larry because he was interested in purchasing a Loran system, a costly electronic navigational device that Larry had installed on his boat. They hit it off immediately. Both were take-charge captains who adored boating and could go out in the stormiest waters without ever getting seasick. They soon began fishing together, along with some other men, on a regular basis. On one of those outings when everybody had had too much to drink, Pat, obviously distressed, took Larry aside. Clearly he needed to talk to somebody, and he could tell this was a man he could confide in.

Out gushed the awful story of his wife's death. She'd seemed depressed when they'd moved to Virginia Beach, and he assumed she was just having adjustment problems. One day after he'd taken her out on the boat—God, they'd even made love in the cabin—she shot herself twice in the head. Her sister, who'd been horrified that his wife could have done such a thing, later tried to kill herself too. And to cap it off, their son, a rebellious teenager, attempted suicide after his mother's death. Pat was distraught. Did Brian think this kind of thing was genetic? What should he do? Lavin reassured him that it was circumstances, not genes, that caused this kind of behavior. They talked for quite a while, Larry comforting the anguished man as best he could. After that, it rare for three days to pass without them speaking.

It was on one of these fishing outings that Larry discovered Pat had been with the FBI. The men on the boat were reminiscing about their pasts and what they'd done with their lives. Larry told his finely crafted lie about making a fortune selling his computer business, and Pat regaled the crowd with stories of his exploits as an FBI agent. Luckily for Larry they were all just tipsy enough not to notice how white he turned under his tan or how his hands trembled when he tried to reel in a fish.

Marcia sensed something amiss as soon as her husband walked in the door carrying the day's catch. They talked late into the night about whether they were in serious jeopardy and what they ought to do. The relationship was too advanced at that point and he and Pat had too many friends in common for Larry to distance himself without raising questions. Maybe they should move away? Tara was too young to be affected by a change, but it didn't seem fair to wrench Chris away again. He was so happy in the neighborhood and had such a good friend next door. Could they destroy his life by running every time there was a threat? Finally they decided the answer was no. They pinned the decision on Chris's welfare, but in truth, Larry and Marcia were much too content to leave Virginia Beach.

So things continued on as before. Larry and the former agent actually became closer. There was a fishing-club Christmas cocktail party at his home, and Larry choked on the hors d'oeuvres looking at the FBI commendation plaques all over the den. He calmed himself by reasoning that perhaps if he ever were discovered by the FBI, Pat could protect him. He would realize how much more important it was for Larry to remain free and be a loving father to his children than to go to jail. Pat knew what a decent guy he was. Whom did the retired agent turn to when he came home early one day and found his son smoking pot in the living room with his girlfriend? About to call the police and turn in his son for breaking the law, Pat sought assistance from his good friend Brian O'Neil instead. The reformed drug dealer rushed over and restored calm by explaining to the boy that he had to consider his father's rigid response in the context of his law-enforcement background.

Typically, Larry concluded that his relationship with Pat wasn't that great a threat. He found the irony of it almost amusing and chuckled when he told Rusty during one of their calls, "Hey, you won't believe this. I just found out that one of my closest friends down here is a retired FBI agent."

"What?" Rusty shrieked. "That's awful."

"There's nothing to worry about," Larry answered. "He's a really good guy. Wouldn't do anything to hurt me."

The second time Larry and Marcia wrestled with leaving Virginia Beach was in April 1986. They'd just discovered that Marcia was pregnant for the third time when *Philadelphia Magazine* published a lengthy feature about the Lavin conspiracy, filled with pictures of Larry and Marcia. Rusty read him the entire article over the phone. There was a chilling silence at the other end from the normally garrulous dentist, broken only by an occasional expletive. Surely it was reasonable to expect that someone they knew in Virginia Beach might visit a friend in Philadelphia, see the article, and recognize them. By the time they got around to seriously considering starting over somewhere else, Chuck Reed and Sid Perry were already closing in.

21

FBI HEADQUARTERS, PHILADELPHIA
1985–86

The fog was so thick that Sid Perry could make out only the dim outlines of the man he was chasing. A glimpse of a leg. A long, thin arm. A head of coarse black hair. Still, as he ran for what seemed like hours, he knew with absolute certainty that it was Larry Lavin he was pursuing. He'd get close enough to almost touch the fugitive, when Lavin would disappear around a corner and momentarily elude him. Perry's legs were beginning to give out. He reached inside his jacket and, as much as he hated to use it, pulled out his gun and aimed into the mist. This time Lavin would not get away from him. Perry fired one shot, and the instant the bullet hit its target, the shadowy figure vaporized, leaving nothing but a small pile of white powder and the cruel sound of taunting laughter.

Perry awoke with a start. The clock by his bed said 3:43 A.M. He'd been having another one of the frustrating dreams that had been periodically disturbing his sleep ever since Larry Lavin fled. Perry's thoughts were hardly ever free of the missing dentist. He'd be jogging on one of the tree-lined country roads near his house and his mind would wander to Larry. Out to dinner with his wife and kids, he'd find himself drifting from the conversation, thinking about clues he might have missed. Many nights he'd even climb into bed with Larry Lavin on his mind and his wife would gently remind him that he'd been neglecting his conjugal duties.

As quietly as he could, without disturbing her, Perry got out of bed and padded barefoot down the stairs, past the powder room with the garish wallpaper left by the former owners that he kept promising to replace, and into the colonial-style den where he kept his large saltwater fish tank. This was the hobby that had replaced his Cambridge glass collection. Usually just watching the brilliantly colored fish swimming back and forth could stop the pages of evidence from turning in his head. Tonight, it didn't seem to be working. Finally, at 4:30 he went back upstairs, showered, and dressed. By six, Perry was at his desk in the large communal office space that FBI agents share, busying himself with one of the new cases assigned to him until Chuck Reed arrived and he could get his opinion on a new strategy he had for finding Larry Lavin.

Ever since Lavin had skipped town under their very noses, Perry and Reed had been obsessed with tracking him down. Reed saw Lavin's flight as a personal affront: "As hard as it was to acknowledge every day he was free, he thought he'd beaten the system, it was worse to know he was laughing because he'd beaten us." For Perry, nabbing Lavin was less of a vendetta issue than a game he'd played well and still intended to win.

This kind of determination developed into a more dogged commitment on the part of the FBI than Larry Lavin had bargained for. From all the books he'd read on living as a fugitive, he expected the FBI to look hard for six months; then their investigation would peter out. According to his calculations, time was on his side. Reed and Perry knew better. Time was on *their* side. It had been proven over and over that as months grow into years, fugitives relax and get careless. Lavin would be no exception.

A week after Larry Lavin disappeared in October 1984, Chuck Reed and Sid Perry began their manhunt. First they followed the routine procedure in a case like this and put a stop notification on all the things that might indirectly lead to Larry: credit cards, passport, social-security number, dental records, university records. Then they sat down and tried to analyze his character, putting themselves in his shoes in order to predict his moves. "We may not live like he did," Reed explained, "but we can certainly think like he'd think." This process helped them evaluate the tips on Lavin that trickled into the Bureau after the newspapers reported his flight. Every one of them was examined and ultimately discarded—from the anonymous phone tip reporting that Larry had been spotted in San Juan without his family to the fellow who contacted Sid Perry identifying himself as a former CIA operative with worldwide connections. He offered to help them find Lavin if there was a reward involved. Sid told him to come back when he knew where Larry was and they'd talk about compensation then. He never heard from him again and wondered if Larry had sent the man to sniff out how much the FBI knew.

A natural step was to ask Marcia's mother, Agnes Osborn, to allow them to enter the house on Timber Lane to rummage for

clues among the contents left behind. She refused. But when
Larry's lawyer told her the FBI would get a search warrant and do
it anyway, she handed over the key. Reed and Perry were surprised when they entered the house at how many things had not
been taken, although it was obvious from what was missing that
the Lavins had no plans to return and were not on vacation as Mrs.
Osborn had told the neighbors. The search provided several useful
leads, in particular Chris's christening book. The page displaying
the family tree had been carefully filled in with the names of all the
close relatives on both Larry's and Marcia's side, and there was
also a list of the good friends and family members who'd given
baby gifts. This created a host of potential sources who might
make contact with the Lavins or know something about where they
were. The agents immediately subpoenaed phone records for almost everybody in the book and studied them for patterns of calls
to a particular area, especially calls placed to pay telephones,
which would have been a dead giveaway. While this path yielded
no direct links to Larry, it unexpectedly led the FBI to a couple of
previously unknown drug customers who were eventually indicted.

More directly helpful was the cache of photos they found of
Marcia, Larry, Chris, and even the dog, Rusty, which could be
circulated for identification purposes. The paid doctors' bills in
Larry's desk drawer led them to the family's physicians, on the
outside chance their medical histories turned up anything traceable. The closest they came to a potential avenue was in a interview with Marcia's obstetrician, where they learned that she had
an Rh-negative blood factor and required the administration of a
special medication called RhoGAM at delivery. Reed, whose wife
was a nurse, had heard that the pharmaceutical company manufacturing the drug sometimes did follow-up studies on patients receiving it. Unfortunately, it turned out that no such studies were ever
made. The agents even considered calling Rusty's veterinarian in
case the dog had special problems, but that seemed a bit too
farfetched. So did the idea of showing Larry's picture to the
prostitutes who worked the casinos at the Jersey shore on the
remote possibility that his affinity for call girls and gambling might
draw him back to Atlantic City.

Other things found in the house served to broaden general
information about Larry, such as the briefcase with a hidden recording device that revealed his interest in electronic spying, and
some abandoned seals and embossers left in a drawer which verified the agents' hunch that Larry was fabricating his own phony
documents. These latter items tied in neatly with the invoices from
a stationery company in downtown Philadelphia which had been

found earlier in the briefcase seized at Larry's arrest. What didn't
jibe was the name on the sales slips: McDermitt and Sullivan.
That was the phony law firm Larry had created to purchase the
seals because he mistakenly believed that official stamps had to
bought through an attorney.

Reed and Perry visited the store where the seals had been
ordered. Yes, the clerk remembered a tall, slender guy with dark
hair named McDermitt. Did he have an address? Certainly: Suite
305, Lancaster Pike, Malvern. The agents drove out to suburban
Philadelphia to look for the law office and instead found at that
address a private post-office-box company. Unfortunately Mr.
McDermitt was no longer receiving any mail there. Still, this was
an important piece for the puzzle. It gave the FBI a pseudonym
that Lavin might still be using and verified something Franny
Burns had told them about Lavin using mail drops—although they
didn't yet know what he used them for.

Within weeks after Lavin fled, that question was partially answered when Bruce Taylor got a letter postmarked White River
Junction, Vermont, in which Larry apologized for dragging Taylor
into his problems and gave him permission to tell everything he
knew to the authorities if he felt it would help his case. Later Larry
sent a Christmas card to another drug customer with an Arizona
postmark. And he also wrote to Franny Burns: "Just a quick note.
Hope you enjoyed Florida. I saw a girlfriend of yours before I
went on vacation. [He was referring to having made arrangements
for Priscilla New England to pay Franny a substantial amount of
money she owed him.] Don't worry, you know my track record,
and I'll take care of you, probably through David, after the trial or
as soon as things die down. I'll send you a postcard soon. You
better go find a match now." In other words, burn this letter.

Burns did not follow Lavin's instructions. Instead he turned the
note over to the FBI and reported that before leaving, Larry had
said he planned to fly or drive to a location far from where he was
living to mail his letters or make phone calls. Eventually Reed and
Perry traced some of the letters back to mail-forwarding services in
Phoenix and Buffalo. By furnishing the services with a list of
aliases Lavin might have used, they were able to confirm that he
circulated letters through two or three mail drops before getting
them delivered to their final destination. But the agents were never
able to track the correspondence back to where it had originated.

It didn't take long for the stop on Lavin's credit cards to show
activity in the form of a series of purchases in the New England
area—shoes, clothes, a television, a three-wheel trail bike. The

agents knew Lavin wouldn't be stupid enough to be buying these things himself, but perhaps the transactions would lead to him. Had the television been shipped to Lavin? No. It had been taken home by the purchaser. The agents took the serial number anyway just in case the set came back for service. Ditto for the trail bike. What they conjectured was that Lavin had instructed friends to use his credit cards for the purpose of setting up a false trail to confuse the authorities.

This diversionary tactic was confirmed when Chuck Reed accidentally located a copy of *New ID in America*, and there in a chapter titled "Losing a Past Identity" was the advice on how to create a misleading paper chase. Reed knew from interviewing defendants in the case that Larry had once owned the book, and had since been looking for it unsuccessfully in libraries. One afternoon another agent in his office, a gun collector, found the paperback advertised in a rifle catalog and Reed ordered it. The lively little how-to for fugitives laid out in detail what Lavin would be expecting from the FBI and ironically became a helpful reference book in guiding the direction of their search for him.

One of the things it said was that investigators always pump the fugitive's family for clues to his whereabouts. The question of which family members to approach was one Reed and Perry hotly debated as they weighed the value of potential information against the risk of alerting Larry to their covert pursuit. The agents wanted Larry to think they were too busy to hunt for him. That way he'd be more likely to make the kind of slip that would lead to his capture. At the same time, they needed to interview the people close to him for leads. They chose not to talk to his parents. It was doubtful they'd give up anything valuable, and by avoiding them the FBI might lull Larry into thinking the investigation had been scrubbed because it wasn't following the pattern outlined in his book.

They did, however, decide to play a long shot and contact Larry's eldest brother, Paul, a prominent Ohio obstetrician who had no connection with the drug ring. They asked him not to mention the call to anybody and reminded him that a leak could damage an investigation that it was his duty as a law-abiding citizen to assist. But they assumed he'd talk anyway—which he did—and they used that likelihood to their advantage. When Paul Lavin asked Chuck Reed at the end of their brief conversation, "How's it going?", Reed deliberately lied. "Well, we're pretty sure Larry's left the country," he said, hoping the physician would relay that message to his brother, who would then relax his guard.

The agents believed it would have been more productive to

question Larry's other brother, Rusty, but they felt he was even less likely to be trusted. Always in the back of their minds was a remark Franny Burns had made right after Lavin fled. "I don't know where he is," Burns had said, "but if you watch Rusty, you'll find Larry." That was early in the investigation, and the geographical distance between Philadelphia and Boston made the suggestion too difficult to pursue actively.

Burns, in a move to curry favor for his own cause, offered to help the FBI find Lavin by threatening to kill his parents unless he gave himself up. The agents laughed at him. When and if all avenues to Larry had been exhausted, the FBI would apply its own kind of pressure on family members. Somewhere down the line they might squeeze something from Marcia's brother-in-law—the one who received the occasional Friday-afternoon phone messages—or the dental-office girls Larry sometimes called, by prosecuting them for aiding and abetting a fugitive. There was even the chance they could smoke Larry out by developing a case that threatened to send his parents to jail for obstruction of justice unless he turned himself in. But that was the last option on their list.

Having temporarily ruled out putting pressure on Larry's family, Reed and Perry turned to the one relative in Philadelphia who, they were convinced, maintained contact with the missing couple. That was Marcia's mother, Agnes Osborn. What did she do with her time? Who were her friends? With whom did she share her confidences? Off and on, the FBI tailed the plump retired nurse, clandestinely acquainting themselves with her life. She had few close friends, and one of them was a woman named Maureen Collins who owned a ceramics shop, where Mrs. Osborn could often be found. Painting and glazing porcelain figurines had been a favorite hobby of Marcia and her mother, and Mrs. Osborn continued with this interest even after her daughter was no longer around to accompany her. A routine FBI check showed that Osborn and Collins had more in common than ceramics. The shopowner had a relative who'd been in prison. Reed reasoned that if Mrs. Osborn were going to share her family secret with anybody, this would be the most likely person, and he filed that assumption in his mental computer.

Six months after Lavin jumped bail, the FBI gained an unexpected ally in the search when Kenny Weidler decided to cooperate with the government. Until that time, Reed and Perry had been only intermittently involved in tracking Lavin, occupied as they were with the other indictments. While they'd amassed a lot of information, they still had no strong leads as to where he was, although they'd learned a lot about where he might be by interviewing other defendants. They knew, for instance, that he liked water and warm weather. A very close friend had said, "They loved the Williamsburg area. I bet that's where they'll move." And one of the defendants believed it would be typical of Larry to hide right under the government's nose and pat himself on the back that the FBI wasn't smart enough to spot him. It wasn't a whole lot to go on, but it was a start. Perhaps Weidler could help them move forward.

At first they didn't ask Kenny to do anything but provide information.

"Do you know where Larry is?"

He didn't.

"Are you in contact with each other?"

"Yes, but I haven't heard from him since January. He's not calling me anymore. He does sometimes call one of the girls from our office."

This was great news for Reed and Perry. It confirmed their suspicion that Lavin was in the United States and that he was already making mistakes by contacting people.

Several interviews with Weidler finally assured the agents they could count on him not to double-cross them, and they began to lobby for a more active kind of assistance. Over and over they told him that the most important thing he could do to influence the outcome of his sentence was to help them find Larry. Perry was especially skillful in transferring Weidler's loyalty from Lavin to himself.

"Larry was very successful in winning trust from people," Perry felt. "We had to take his allies and make them our allies by convincing people he didn't deserve their allegiance." It wasn't terribly difficult because the FBI now held all the bargaining chips, while Lavin was left with none. When he judged the time was ripe to approach Weidler, Perry sat down across from him, comfortably flipped open a can of his ubiquitous diet cola, and locked the nervous dentist into the friendly gaze of his sky-blue eyes. "Think about this, Kenny," he said in a confidential tone. "Larry really isn't your friend. Which one of you is going to jail and which one is going to come out of this okay? Should you *suffer* while he's getting off scot-free? Who got you into all this trouble in the first place? If Larry was such a good friend of yours, would he have run off and left you holding the bag?"

Those were the same arguments advanced to Kenny by his family when they'd urged him to become a government witness.

Slowly he let go of his loyalty, and that made it easier to say yes when Perry finally asked him to join their search team.

They wanted him to get closer to Mrs. Osborn and squeeze every bit of information from her that he could, including having her unwittingly arrange another call between him and Larry that the government could record. Reluctantly Weidler agreed. He felt awful taking advantage of a sweet old woman who was grieving for her daughter, but he had promised his full and complete cooperation to the government and would not back down. Perry had successfully persuaded him that Larry didn't deserve to be protected at the cost of sacrificing himself.

As instructed, Kenny called Marcia's mother to say hello and see how she was doing. She responded by inviting him and his wife to dinner on April 26. The evening of the meal, he drove first to the parking lot of a motel near Mrs. Osborn's condominium complex, and while his wife and their child waited in the car, he went off with Reed and Perry to be fitted with a hidden tape recorder. Weidler was nervous. They reassured him that his questions would seem perfectly natural and cautioned him not to interrupt Mrs. Osborn once she started talking. He was specifically to find out if the baby had been born yet, was it a boy or girl, had the Lavins bought a new home, was Larry working, did she know whom they were communicating with? Thus prepared, the Weidlers drove off to dinner while Reed and Perry followed and parked a few blocks from the apartment, where they could comfortably eavesdrop on the taped conversation.

Mrs. Osborn was a short, heavyset, square-built woman with beauty-parlor-styled gray curls. She greeted the Weidlers warmly and cooed over their toddler. From her attentiveness to the little girl, it was easy to tell she was a devoted granny who despite having several grandchildren from Marcia's brother and sister, still missed Christopher terribly. She proudly gave them a tour of her apartment, from the walk-in closets to the laundry room, and paused by a wall of family pictures—her "rogues' gallery," she called it—to talk about Marcia, "my sunshine," and Larry. Kenny didn't even have to ask about the new baby. The news just bubbled out.

Later, at the table, as she passed the chicken and rice, Agnes Osborn told Kenny that she believed Marcia and Larry didn't trust her because she gave the FBI a key to enter their house on Timber Lane.

"What could I do? Their lawyer told me either I let them in or they'd get a court order. I hate those FBI agents. I wouldn't give them the right time of day."

Reed and Perry, listening to the conversation in their car, looked at each other and grinned.

Agnes Osborn's complaint was the perfect opening for Kenny to mention that he also felt Larry didn't trust him, because he was no longer calling as he'd done in the beginning. Kenny sympathized with her. He was hurt too. Could she pass a message to her son-in-law, Richard, whom Larry sometimes called on Friday afternoons, that Kenny would really love to hear from him again?

The Weidlers were the perfect guests. They helped with the dishes and then apologized for taking off so early. They had to get their little girl to bed. Before leaving, they insisted that Marcia's mother allow them to reciprocate, and come to their home for dinner in two weeks.

It was a miserable rainy night in May when Agnes Osborn arrived at the Weidlers'. The FBI had been there first and wired the dining room and living room with hidden recorders. Reed and Perry parked in a car nearby, munched on a meager dinner of peanut-butter crackers, and sipped warm Cokes while they listened to Kenny rave about the excellent leg of lamb his wife had prepared and praise the wine. Mrs. Osborn, delighted to be in the company of Marcia and Larry's good friends, was in a garrulous mood. She reminisced about her missing family and explained the mail-drop system they used to send her occasional letters and pictures. She was content they were doing just fine, although she had no idea where they were living. In one letter they'd promised her she'd see them in the future. "Larry says they'll pop up and surprise me one day when I least expect it. Isn't that just like him?"

Sid Perry's watch showed midnight when Mrs. Osborn finally put on her raincoat and said good night. He was tired and hungry but satisfied. Mrs. Osborn had told Kenny she'd delivered his message to her son-in-law, who'd already passed it on to Larry.

The wheels for the call having been set in motion, there was nothing to do now but wait. The response didn't take long. One evening in early June, Larry telephoned his former dental assistant and asked her to tell Kenny he'd call him at 11:30 on June 8 at location D.

In the hours prior to the call, Kenny kept repeating to himself that he was doing the right thing, that he really had no other choice. Miles away, Larry was wrestling with a different kind of apprehension. Something instinctively told him he shouldn't make this call. Marcia reminded him of that troubling remark of Kenny's: "My family comes first."

"I know. I know," Larry answered, and promised to talk no more than three minutes so the call couldn't be traced.

Lavin didn't realize that tracing the call was the least of his problems. The recent breakup of AT&T had placed long-distance phone service in the hands of a host of different regional and local operators, which made it extremely difficult to do a reverse trace. All the FBI could get was a promise that the phone company would do the best it could.

When Weidler and the agents arrived at the appointed phone booth on the appointed day, it was just before lunch and they could hear the bell of an ice-cream truck summoning the children in the next block to buy their dessert treat. The booth was in use and Weidler worried that he'd lose the call and with it his ticket to a shorter sentence. But the caller finished quickly, nodded in a friendly fashion, and walked away. Within minutes Ken's heart jumped to the sound he both welcomed and dreaded.

He picked up the receiver and chortled, "Yooo, WaWee." The two of them had developed an affectionate baby-talk patois that Kenny fell right into without thinking. "I couldn't believe this fucking guy wouldn't get off the phone."

"I was just about to give up," Larry said. "I figured it was some signal you weren't there or something."

"Ken-nee here. Ken-nee was going to the shore but Ken-nee didn't go because he had to be here for Wa-Wee."

They both started to laugh. That quickly, it was just like old times, and Larry forgot about his three-minute limit. They talked for over half an hour.

"First of all," Larry began, "I want to tell you that I'm sorry. I heard you told Marcia's mom that I probably didn't trust you. Well, I didn't trust her—though I do now. She's just not that smart. She took the FBI to my house."

"Well, your lawyer told her to let them in or they'd come back with a court order."

"Oh, really? I didn't know that. Well, I don't want to waste too much time with the past. The real reason I didn't call was I heard you're under all this pressure and I didn't want to add any temptation, especially after I took this little course and found out that these suicide hot lines can tap a phone in two minutes. So anyway, what's going on? Beth [the dental hygienist Larry sometimes called] tells me you're going to sell the practice."

Kenny answered that he was working on a deal and then said, "Beth told me your daughter had a spinal tap or something."

"No, they were considering doing it. These fucking doctors scare the hell out of you. They catheterized her and did blood work for three days in a row and all she had was a virus. It just went away."

"Did she have a temperature?"

"No. She just wouldn't stop screaming. She's just the best baby. Sleeps all the time, wakes up and cries to be fed. But she wouldn't stop screaming for three days. Nonstop. Just yelling so that she was hoarse. You could barely hear her anymore. I don't think a virus gives you a temperature. Bacteria does that. But since I'm no longer medical-orientated, I can't be sure."

"Beth also said you took Chris to a pedodontist and you were dying to get back."

"It killed me. He's telling me he's got some kind of overjaw and overbite. I felt like saying: You mean a class II? 'The kid's only three years old. Isn't his jaw still supposed to do some growing?' And he said, 'No, they grow at the same rate from here on out.' "

"Oh, Jesus," Kenny groaned.

"In general he's an excellent guy, though. I wouldn't want to take my kid to anybody but a pedodontist. They're so much more together than we are when it comes to treating kids."

"Did he have any cavities?"

"Nope."

Kenny changed to their other favorite subject, sports. "So you lost your Super Bowl again, Wa-Wee. You never could pick a Super Bowl."

"Yeah. I can't believe the Celtics, too. It just breaks my heart. It's not just because they're ours. It's because they're white. I hate to see that Magic Charger weave in between them. It pisses me off. They look like the Sixers looked when they played the Celtics. So how much are you going to be able to sell the practice for?"

"It looks like eighty-five."

"Not too bad. I'm sure that's forty grand less than what you wanted."

"It's a little depressing, but what the fuck?"

"So what happened with your case?"

"I don't know what's going on. Two or three months ago my lawyer got a call from the U.S. attorney saying they wanted help against the laundry case on Stewart. He got four years last week." They both laughed. "I thought you'd like that," Kenny continued. "Believe me, I hate the guy. Anyway, they told my lawyer I had a big problem. A drug problem."

"Exact same thing they said to me. You should have given whatever you could just for the hell of going against Mark. Tell them, if it helps, that Mark called me up before the arson and told me about it."

"But that can't be corroborated. What if the boy decided to say that, if he got in trouble? ["The boy" was what they often called David Ackerman behind his back.] It looks like the boy has a problem too, but the boy doesn't think it's serious."

"It probably looks like we all conspired on the arson, and actually we didn't have much control. We were just listening to what Stewart was going to do."

"Didn't he promise to give you an insurance settlement or something?"

Reed and Perry, listening to the tape in their car, liked this line of questioning. Weidler was going just fine.

"Right. When the insurance paid the mortgage that would free up the four-hundred-thousand-dollars in CD's and I was supposed to get two or three of them. But each week Mark used up more money, and I'd advance him more. I can't believe how stupid I was. Every month I get older, I think about how I've handled things in life and I can't believe it. I think back to my pot-selling days in the fraternity and I would have handled that so differently now. So you're in the same limbo you were when I left?"

"That's one of the reasons I'm liquidating," Kenny explained. "I was there to pick up your pieces and I wouldn't want to dump the girls if I go. Hey, my daughter started to walk last week. Guess what she calls me? 'Ya-Ya.' "

"Like Chris did. I try to remind him of that once in a while. He won't shut up, by the way. We used to worry about him talking, and now sometimes I have to put my hands over my ears 'cause I can't handle his jabbering. This new baby is totally different. Like right from birth she can hold her head up. He couldn't do that for months. You know, I told some people it was a boy to get a false rumor started, but it's a girl."

"I know. Beth told me. You know Reed came to see her."

"Yeah. She told me not to call anymore, that they've been to see everyone."

"That's the weekend I was supposed to talk to you but you didn't call. Ken-nee out on a limb here. No friends. No boy. No WaWee."

"Is boy in New York now?"

"Boy in New York. Boy setting up with Dad. Doesn't think he has a problem and thinks you're in the witness-protection program."

Larry chuckled. "No, I'm in a better situation than that. I like it. If everything could clear up and change, I don't think I'd go back anyway. I'm just having too much fun. I'm not into playing dentist anymore. I like talking to people, but I didn't like drilling. You really see how people think about doctors when they don't know you're a doctor."

"Yeah, that's true. Hey, did you know your picture's in the post office? You're wanted, La-Wee."

"Is it really?" Larry sounded shocked. "I looked in the post office here and didn't see it."

"Well, maybe it's just local. It's not posted on the wall. It's in this book you flip through of wanted people."

Larry's tone changed to bitterness. "It just kills me to know that. Those pictures are for really severe people—murderers and kidnappers." He was quiet for a moment and then resumed his lighthearted tone. "How about that girl you were playing tennis with when I left?"

"No. No. No extracurricular activities. Ken-nee good boy."

Larry wanted to know if his house had been sold—it hadn't—and what had happened to various people in the conspiracy like Paul Mikuta, Suzanne, and Bruce. Weidler gave him an update and then asked, "How's Rusty. Are they hot on him?"

"Not at all. He's had some wild times in Atlantic City that really bring back memories when he tells me. He got a notice from his bank they'd subpoenaed his records, but nothing else. I find it weird that the FBI does some of the shit like the post office, yet they haven't been to see my parents."

Perry turned to Reed. "A point for our side," he said. "And he's talking to Rusty, just like we thought."

They chatted some more about other friends and Kenny said, "I gotta tell you this story. You got a tax bill from the city for seventy-two-thousand-dollars, some business and occupancy tax on our office that you missed. I go in to talk to the tax guy and he pulls out a portfolio with three huge newspaper articles about you. He just shakes his head. I told him I had nothing to do with it and I don't know where you are."

Larry found the anecdote quite amusing. "I guess they figured any money I made in drugs I made within the city limits and they're entitled to the taxes. Well, I'm glad to hear you're not going to jail."

"Not yet, at least. But if Ken-nee go to jail, will Wa-Wee help my wife and family?"

"Yes. Yes. I'll make sure your wife gets a constant amount of sex." He laughed. "Don't worry. It's not gonna happen."

Kenny then bought himself a little extra FBI insurance. "All I can say is, if it does, I'd like you to maintain an open communication with me."

"Well, I didn't mind calling you today because I'm several states from where I live, so they can fuckin' do all they want. Hey, Ken. I'm in the real world now. I've got a job."

Kenny was surprised. "You do?"

"Once in a while I do some financial consulting. Mostly I work out and take it easy. Read books."

"Playing any golf?"

"No. One of my neighbors is an excellent golfer and that bums me out so much I don't want to play with him. I'm swimming a lot."

"Losing any weight?"

"No, I'm about the same. I run Marcia around and that takes up time. It's the same old life. Going to malls. Going to stores. Buying this and that. Fixing up the house. I'm heavily into my lawn and gardening. I've got a sprinkler system and I put paper under my flowerbeds so no weeds grow. Things you'd never dream about. I've got the nicest place here and that's kinda neat. I won a little award for the best lawn." He went on to explain a special chlorine system he'd put in his pool and then returned to the gossiping. "I heard that Doc had gotten arrested for something else and was in jail." Doc was another name for Bruce Taylor, who was sometimes known as Dr. Misery.

"Yeah, I heard that too. Some kind of sex crime. Really stupid."

"Oh, what a web we weave," Larry sighed.

"Oh, what a tangled web we weave, Wa-Wee."

"You know what kills me, Ken? When someone talks about gambling. Like I could never go to Atlantic City or Las Vegas. I know I have a file in some of those casinos."

"I'm going down there right now, as a matter of fact," Ken said, prompting Larry to give him a short lecture on how to take the $85,000 he expected from the sale of the practice and launder it in the casinos so he wouldn't have to pay taxes. Then Kenny asked him, "What am I gonna do if I get indicted? You don't have any suggestions on how to leave, do you?"

Larry liked that. "You can't leave," he chortled. "You don't have the personality for it. Listen, is anybody hanging around there?"

Kenny shot a glance at Reed and Perry. "No. Why?"

"A security guard just walked through here. So do you want to set up another call at another number?" They worked out an arrangement and Larry suggested, "If something happened and you wanted to get in touch with me, you can always get to Marcia's mother and have her tell Richard. By the way, you can tell her we just wrote her another letter that will take a while to get there because of the way it goes. I worry about sending her little things like pictures because they could research the fabric in our clothes, so we're real selective. I know that sounds farfetched, but I like to think I don't have to worry when I go to sleep. That there hasn't been one thing I've done so far that's traceable. So I'll talk to you in a few months."

"You want to set up a time?" They fixed another call for the first Wednesday in August at nine A.M. "Any message you want me to deliver?" Kenny asked before hanging up.

"Tell Paul I won't be able to make it this year. We'd promised we'd set up a day, same day every year, same spot, that he'd be looking for me, but obviously I'm not headed there this year."

"I'm really glad to hear you're doing okay," Kenny said.

"It sounds like you're doing okay too," Larry repeated. "This was better than we could have expected."

"I still see myself in your shoes. I just hope it doesn't come out the same way."

"In the end, Ken, we know you didn't do what I did, so that's going to help you. Look for you in August. 'Bye."

Kenny replaced the receiver. It felt like Larry had left yesterday. No conversation in his life had ever been so good and so bad simultaneously. How he resented Larry for taking off and robbing him of his friendship. And how he hated himself for what he'd just done. When he'd agreed to cooperate with the government to the fullest, Kenny hadn't counted on betrayal being part of the package. And he hadn't realized how far he'd go to save his own neck. He wrapped his arms around his belly and vomited his guilt into the gutter.

The telephone company was unable to pinpoint the precise location from which Larry Lavin had placed the call to Kenny Weidler but they could confirm it had come from the North Maryland area. That jibed nicely with Larry's comment that he had a sprinkler system and a prizewinning lawn. He wasn't living in Maine. The call generated several other suggestive avenues for the FBI to explore, but the real prize had been the mention of a letter en route to Mrs. Osborn. That was one piece of mail the agents intended to read before it reached its destination.

Here their knowledge that Lavin used mail drops came in handy; obviously the letter wouldn't be delivered to Mrs. Osborn's home along with her utility bill. Either it would go to a mail drop or through somebody. Reed and Perry assumed that, given his mother-in-law's age, Larry would use a mail drop in a convenient nearby location. They canvassed the private mail companies in her general vicinity for boxes under the name Osborn or one of Larry's aliases

and came up dry. That left family and friends. They took a shotgun
approach that covered all bases by obtaining a court order allowing
the post office to monitor the mail of Mrs. Osborn's relatives and
the friends she'd most likely to turn to for assistance. "Everybody
confides in somebody," Reed said to Perry. In Mrs. Osborn's case
he guessed it would be the woman from the ceramic shop with the
jailed relative. He was right.

After alerting post-office officials to be on the lookout for anything with the name "Osborn" sent to the people they were checking, they sat back and waited for their phone call. It came in early
July. There was a letter addressed to Mrs. William Osborn c/o
Mrs. Maureen Collins. They hastily gained court approval to inter-
cept the ceramic teacher's mail and by noon they had the letter in
their possession.

It wasn't even necessary to steam open the envelope because it
had been sealed by Scotch tape, which they carefully slit with a
razor. A handful of colored photographs tumbled out of the folded
pages—pictures of the Lavins' home, their new baby, Christopher.
Reed stared at the photos of the yard, and something clicked. "I
know where he is," he yelled. "That's Virginia." His parents had
once lived in Virginia, and although Chuck Reed couldn't tell a
pine tree from a maple, something about the reddish color of the
soil together with the look of the shrubbery in the yard triggered a
buried visual memory. "I'm telling you, Sid, Larry is in Virginia."

The letter was written in a clear feminine hand on paper with a
rose in the corner:

Dear Mom,
"Hi! I finally got my pictures back. Isn't the baby *cute*! He's
doing okay now [Marcia was still disguising the sex of the child])
but at 2 wks. he had a cold, then got a virus that lasted over a
week. I had him for all sorts of tests & then they finally decided
it was a virus. The poor baby screamed for a week—everything's fine now. Chris had a great birthday. We took him & his
best friend to one of those pizza places like I used to go to at
home, with video games and rides, & the bear brought out his
birthday cake & sang him a song. He was thrilled! He loves this
one little boy from across the street who's 4-1/2. They have so
much fun together. They are out in the sandbox right now. I
enrolled Chris in a nursery school for 2 mornings a wk. starting
in Sept. The place is so neat with tons of toys, puzzles, play
dough, jungle gyms. I want to go too! Chris is very anxious to
go. The only catch is that he *must* be toilet-trained so I've been
trying for three weeks now with limited success. He just doesn't

care if he pees his pants or on the floor or in the pot—and you can forget BM's. We've been bribing him with his latest favorite toys—little trucks that turn into robots, "Transformers." I even bought Transformer underpants. Oh well, I have time yet. I am well. I still have 10 pounds to lose but it's coming off slowly and I'm still nursing the baby. Larry is doing great. We are very happy. We went on a barbecue at the neighbors' on Memorial Day. They have 4 kids and the people next door came with their 3 so we all had fun. Chris is so happy here & he's talking up a storm. He really loves the baby and plays on the floor next to him. It's so nice to see. He hasn't shown any jealousy at all & I don't think he's going to. Well, that's all for now. I'll send more pictures when I can. I hope you are happy and taking care of yourself. We love you and are always thinking of you.

Love,

Marcia

Then, on a fresh sheet of paper, there was an added note obviously written after the call to Ken Weidler:

Hi again. I'm glad I didn't mail this letter. I'm so sorry I made you feel as though I didn't trust you. The only information I get about you is secondhand & the way it sounded was that the FBI was really pushing you & that you were having a hard time dealing with it. So I felt I must keep saying to be careful with what you say to the jerks and with what you have (letters and pictures) since you think they broke in once. I may have made my point too often and too strongly in my letters to you, but please remember that our lives & the happiness of our kids are at stake and I cannot take chances. So please overlook any harsh words I may have used. Larry also felt that we can finally say we have a daughter. I'm glad for you to know the truth so I can send you pictures of her as a girl. As usual, if you are ever asked the sex, *refuse to answer*. I'm also sorry Ken was offended by Larry not trusting him. Again, I wish that everybody would realize we have to protect ourselves first and worry about others' feelings last. Our lawyer told us not to contact him so we didn't. I'm glad you're seeing the Weidlers. I think of them often and hope that everything works out for them. Well, I hope I made you feel a little better—please still be careful. I know Ken was able to get a phone # to us so Larry could call him. Please try to do the same through the same channel. I would

really love to talk to you. It's been so long. Chris wants me to write a note to you: "Dear Grammy Mommy, Me got robots, toys, new house. Me love you."
He misses you & I do too.

Love,

Marcia

Just as Reed had instantly reacted to the photographs, Perry had a gut response to the line in the letter about Christopher's birthday party at a pizza parlor where someone dressed as a bear brought out the cake. His son Jason had been to a similar celebration at one of those places when they lived in Tempe, Arizona. It was part of a chain called Chuck E. Cheese Pizza Time Theater. Now all he had to do was find which of the franchises Larry and Marcia had used.

This was the first time since Lavin fled ten months ago that the agents actually felt optimistic. They photocopied everything and retaped the envelope, which was so battered from its trip through the mail drops that they had no trouble disguising the fact they'd tampered with it. When Maureen Collins handed the letter over to Agnes Osborn the next day, she hadn't the slightest indication that the FBI had already read it.

Sid Perry wasted no time in contacting a Chuck E. Cheese franchise in the Philadelphia area. "Is this the place that uses a bear to bring out birthday cakes?" he asked.

"No," the manager answered. "We use a rat. Showbiz [another fast-food chain] uses the bear."

Perry thanked the man and called the first Showbiz he could find in the phone book. He introduced himself as an FBI agent and indicated he needed some help finding a missing child. It was nobody's business that he was really seeking the father attached to the boy. Yes, all the Showbiz franchises had a bear named Billy-Bob, he was told.

"How does the party work?" Perry wanted to know.

"Well, we have a form that gets filled in with the name of the person making the reservation, their phone number and address, the child's first name and age, any special instructions for the cake, and the number of people in the party."

"Great," Perry said. "Thanks a million. You've been more help than you could know."

Perry contacted the Showbiz national headquarters in Texas and learned they had just purchased the Chuck E. Cheese chain, which gave him access to all the franchises through one source. The company could not have been more cooperative. If the FBI would send them a letter requesting the information about a birthday party for a boy named Chris, they would gladly distribute it to their three hundred outlets. Perry created a flier, mailed it to the main office and pinned his hopes on the results.

Over the next three months the responses dribbled in from around the country. One of the first came from North Carolina, but a utility check on the last name showed it was the wrong Chris. The family who'd given the party lived in a low-income neighborhood and had been there for many years. Of the 275 franchises that answered the FBI request, there were less than a dozen birthdays for boys named Chris and none of them fit the Lavin profile. Ironically, the one Showbiz that never wrote back was the place the Lavins had attended. This particular franchise routinely discarded its reservation forms every few weeks and had no records to submit. Slowly Reed and Perry's hopes that Billy-Bob the Bear would lead them to Larry Lavin began to fade. But not entirely. At least they had a list of all the places featuring a Billy-Bob, which gave them a geographical fix on where Larry might or might not be. Any future lead that didn't have a Showbiz in the vicinity was automatically rejected.

By the first anniversary of Lavin's escape Reed and Perry were only slightly closer to locating him than they'd been when he left, and the general attitude at the FBI and the Justice Department was that Larry would never be found. There was little official encouragement for sustaining an active search. The Bureau is willing to put in only so much money and so many man-hours on a project. When it begins to look futile, it's time to move on. There are other assignments waiting and performance statistics to be met by building new cases. Had Reed and Perry not been so personally committed to pursuing Lavin they might at this point have slackened the net and he'd have successfully slipped through. But frustration only increased their determination. It was now November 1985. The Motto trial had ended and they finally had the time to concentrate on the various leads they'd been accumulating. And what they couldn't pursue during the workday, they'd do on unpaid overtime.

Both of them believed that Lavin was living somewhere in the four-state Virginia/Maryland/Carolinas region. Everything pointed in that direction. There were eight Showbiz franchises there. The Weidler call had been traced to North Maryland. So convinced was Chuck Reed that Lavin was in Virginia that he half-expected to bump into him when he rented a house in Virginia Beach for the family's summer vacation. Even his sons were aware he was on the lookout for the fugitive, because he never went anywhere without his gun.

"What will you do if you run into him, Dad?" the youngest asked one morning on the way to the beach.

"I'll grab him and throw him in the trunk of the car," Reed answered, giving the boy a playful punch. Then for a moment he turned deadly serious. "Sooner or later, we're going to catch him and send him to jail for dealing drugs. It would be a slap in the face of justice for him to get away with this."

All along, the basic strategy of the investigation had been to branch out in as many directions as possible so that whenever they reached a dead end there was another path to follow. With that in mind, Reed and Perry activated several fronts, regardless of how remote they seemed. For instance, Larry had mentioned in his phone call to Kenny that he'd taken Chris to a pedodontist—a dentist who specializes in treating children—for a particular bite problem. Chuck zeroed in on those specialists concentrated in the four-state area they'd mapped out and telephoned several asking if they had a three-year-old patient named Chris. None responded positively.

Reed also explored the possibility of tracing Larry through the birth records of the new baby. The intercepted letter had told them the child was a girl, and friends of Marcia's remembered that she had once mentioned the names Tara and Kelly. Reed explored the feasibility of conducting a search through the birth records of all white females born in Virginia in April 1985. A phone call to an official in the state department of vital statistics affirmed that such a task, although quite tedious, could probably be done. He temporarily tabled the project, but didn't abandon it.

Perry, meanwhile, was toying with the idea of circulating Larry's picture to state troopers, FBI agents, even marinas throughout Virginia, Maryland, and the Carolinas. He was also considering publishing the photo in *Time* magazine, *USA Today*, and the national newsletter distributed to retired FBI agents. He worried that the quality of the reproduction in the newsletter was so poor the fugitive might not be recognized. Even more, he feared the photo would fall into the wrong hands and end up warning Lavin, rather than snaring him. "Our biggest fear was that we'd ID Larry and he'd be spooked and run off again." How much to reveal was their ongoing dilemma. The more public they became with their investigation, the greater the danger they'd reveal their progress and Larry would get away. This was the main reason they hadn't recruited more informants, although they knew that route was the tried-and-true one for producing the best results.

As Reed and Perry slowly exhausted their creative investigative techniques, it became apparent they had no other choice then to risk what they'd been avoiding. They'd taken Kenny and Mrs. Osborn as far as they could. Only the Lavin family remained. They'd learned that Pauli Lavin's health had been failing, and she was recovering from a stroke suffered in the midst of an operation to improve a blockage in her carotid artery. Surely, they thought, Larry's situation had contributed to his mother's stress. There was no telling whether the indictment of another son and daughter might just kill the poor woman. Reed and Perry concluded the time was ripe to tighten the screws and pay a call on Jill and Rusty. They drove to New England and arrived at Jill's house around dinnertime. Perry could smell the food cooking when her husband answered his ring. He introduced himself, showed his badge, and asked to speak to Jill. The door was slammed in his face. The call on Rusty was equally unproductive. He wasn't home, and his wife gave them the same cold shoulder as Jill's husband when they reached her by phone. The agents said they were searching for Larry and needed some assistance. Her answer was, "Look somewhere else."

A few weeks later, while vacationing with his parents, who still lived in New England, Reed made another attempt to contact Rusty. They had a brief telephone conversation. The agent told Lavin's brother the FBI was broadening its cocaine case into Massachusetts and his name had been prominently mentioned. Rusty was as icy as his wife and sister had been, showing no trace of his inner turmoil. He didn't have to. Perry was all too familiar with preindictment panic. "Every person I've faced in twelve years who's waiting to be arrested goes nuts wondering what's going to happen tomorrow or the next day. What direction is this case going? Where do I fit it?"

Rusty's trouble with the government was compounded by crushing problems on other fronts. His marriage was crumbling and his business on the brink of bankruptcy. He felt like he was driving a bumper car that had spun out of control. Things were crashing into him on every side. "I was in a constant state of worry. Unable to function. Unable to carry on daily activities. I had problems in my marriage. Problems with my business. Problems with the case. Everybody knew about Larry. It was all people around me talked about, and some of them kept asking, 'When will it be your turn?' " Rusty had to find some area where he could apply the brakes and climb out to safety. When a lawyer he'd hired in Philadelphia called a few weeks later saying the FBI wanted to talk to him, Rusty was more more than ready to fly down and listen.

The man who rose in the lawyer's office to curtly shake hands with Reed and Perry did not fit their expectations. Larry's older brother bore little resemblance to the fugitive they'd come to discuss. Slightly shorter and of a huskier build, Rusty Lavin was impeccably dressed in a finely tailored conservative suit, a striped shirt with monogrammed cuffs held together by small gold-and-diamond cufflinks that matched the pin of his patterned tie. The bright red hair that gave Charles Ford Lavin his nickname had thinned on top and faded like a fabric left too long in the sun. His round, ruddy face was sprinkled with boyish freckles, and under different circumstances they'd have seen more of his easy grin and perfect straight teeth. What little he said during that meeting was spoken in a deep, heavy voice with an eastern Massachusetts accent similar to Larry's but less broad. Although Rusty's hazel eyes displayed little emotion, the agents could tell he was frightened by the way his hand shook when he drank a cup of coffee. They took that as a good sign. Actually they were a little edgy themselves. If they failed to lure Rusty into their camp, he would surely relay the essence of their meeting to Larry, who'd probably pull up stakes and send their investigation back to the starting line.

The agents did most of the talking and pulled no punches. They told Rusty in no uncertain terms that he and his sister, Jill, were scheduled to be indicted for distributing cocaine and faced substantial jail sentences. Aware of the enormity of their request, they asked for his help in general terms without stating that he had to lead them to Larry. While they scrupulously avoided promising what they would trade for his cooperation, they indicated that one of the possible considerations was dropping the indictments. On the other hand, they were quite specific about what would happen if he did nothing.

"We haven't contacted your parents yet, Rusty, but we will as time goes on. Even if it has to be every month for the rest of their lives, somebody will be knocking at their door asking if they've heard from Larry. Do you know where Larry is?"

Rusty ignored the question. He was thinking of his parents, who in his eyes had been through too much already. The FBI could make their lives even more miserable; they didn't deserve that. He remembered the time he'd taken them with him to one of the phone booths so they could talk with Larry, and how his mother had sobbed afterward. "I don't like what he did," she'd said, "but at least if he was in prison I'd know where he is and that he's safe."

There was a lot Rusty needed to think about. "I'll let you know," he said, signaling the meeting had come to a close. His lawyer walked the agents out to the reception area and left them with his opinion: "There's no way in the world he'll help."

Rusty flew back to Boston so agitated that the stewardess had to remind him twice to fasten his seat belt. He held in his hands the awesome responsibility for a decision that would determine his family's future, that would destroy the freedom of one person he loved to gain peace of mind for four others. Give up Larry and spare himself, Jill, and two frail aging parents who might never recover from the shock of having three of their children convicted as drug dealers. Despite the agents' threats, jail was not his primary concern. "I knew my involvement in cocaine wasn't all that great, and whatever they'd get me for wouldn't be a long sentence. What tortured me was how this ongoing mess was wearing down my parents, my sister, her husband, my family. It had to stop somewhere. I realized the FBI would not let go until they had Larry. So many people had given in. It made no sense for me to hold out. None at all. For Larry to get away with this just seemed unfair. The family was suffering more than he was."

For a week Rusty agonized over his choices. He slept very little the first few nights following the FBI meeting. Talking to his wife brought little comfort because of the acrimony of their marital situation. By the third day, ravaged by sleeplessness and crying jags, he went to his parents and confessed he was cracking under the strain of what Larry had gotten them into. He was somewhat relieved when they said he'd taken care of his brother's problems long enough. It was time for him to take care of himself. On day four Rusty did something he'd thought he'd never do: he saw a psychiatrist. He admitted to the doctor that he'd done something wrong. "But should I have to pay for my brother too?" he asked. "Larry was always the kind of person who could put you right where he wanted you and make you feel good about it. But now I feel like he's using me." He left the office assured that he should cooperate. That advice was reiterated on the fifth day by a lawyer he consulted in Boston. At the week's end he called the FBI and said he wanted to meet with them again.

Reed and Perry were pleased but not surprised. "We felt he had no choice but to come back with some form of cooperation. The worse case scenario was that he'd just surrender himself. He had a good attorney who we figured had probably told him to plead guilty or wind up getting convicted at trial. For us it was now a question of whether we'd get everything at once or stretch it over the next five years."

Sitting in his lawyer's well-appointed office, Rusty knew enough to recognize—even after the agents repeated they could make no deals and give no guarantees—that he had no option except to help the government.

The significance of asking this man whom they hardly knew to help capture his brother was not lost on Sid Perry, who understood: "We were telling Rusty to make what was probably one of the biggest decisions of his life entirely on faith." Still, under the law Perry could do no more than tell him in his convincing Southern drawl, "You're gonna have to believe that when we say we'll do what's right, we'll do it."

Instinct told Rusty to trust them. From that first meeting, they hadn't been the awful characters he'd been warned about. He especially liked Perry, who'd been a real gentleman. Later, when he'd had the chance to think about his response, Rusty would say, "I had something they wanted. They had something I needed. I like to gamble. For me, this was the ultimate game of twenty-one." Rusty agreed to cooperate fully, understanding exactly what those words implied.

The next time he talked to his brother Larry, the FBI was listening on the line.

Rusty was given no special instructions on what to discuss with Larry or where to steer the conversation. He was told only to let Larry hang up first and stay on the line a few seconds afterward. Sid Perry never even bothered to play the tapes when the Boston agent who accompanied Rusty to the phone booths sent them to Philadelphia. His only interest was tracing where the calls came from. Ten months had gone by since Weidler's taped call with Lavin, and AT&T now had the capability to back-trace long-distance calls in twenty-four hours. Just as the agents had predicted, Larry had gotten lazy and was no longer traveling great distances to use the phone. The three calls they ultimately taped came from phone booths within a half-hour of Virginia Beach, where there also happened to be a Showbiz franchise with Billy-Bob the Bear. The target area was getting smaller and smaller.

Rusty Lavin had assumed that once he'd agreed to assist the FBI, he'd gain some emotional relief. Instead his anguish turned into a worse case of guilt. "The first time they wired me, God, it was awful. I went home afterward, put my gun in my pocket, and went out and got drunk. I just wanted to die. That was all. The feeling wouldn't go away. For weeks and weeks I kept thinking I'd shoot myself. I wished I'd wake up one morning and find out I had cancer and it would be all over." To make things worse, he had to suffer in silence. "Who do you tell you're helping the FBI catch your brother? My wife knew a little, but because of our own problems, I couldn't trust her. I never told Jill what I had done and I certainly wasn't going to tell my parents. The only one I could confide in was the psychiatrist, and he'd tell me to do this or that, but nothing really helped." Ironically, his sole ally and support system became, of all people, Sid Perry.

After each of the three taped calls, and often in between, Perry would telephone Rusty from Philadelphia to see if he was okay. The tone of Rusty's voice told Perry he was anything but all right. "Rusty was in a deep, deep depression. Sometimes he didn't even want to talk. Just said he'd call back when he felt better." Even after the FBI had the information it needed to find Larry and there was no self-serving reason to continue calling, Perry kept checking in with Rusty. "I realized what kind of predicament he was in, how anguishing . . . how hard this decision had been. The fact that I believed what was done was right and should have been done didn't make it any easier. I was worried about him. I wasn't acting as an agent anymore. I was acting out of being moral, being human."

Perry's concerned attention wasn't enough to keep Rusty from going over the edge. "Every day I felt more depressed, like I was in a foggy dream world. What have I done? How did I do this? I wished I could die. So many days I sat and cried, feeling sorry for myself, trying to figure how to overcome everything in my life that had gone wrong. I constantly thought of killing myself. I'd hold the gun to my head and get angry because I didn't have the guts to pull the trigger." One night, hell-bent on suicide, he left notes for his family and went to a local tavern planning to drink until he could summon the courage to put a bullet through his head. Before he reached that point, he was arrested for threatening people with his pistol and asked to be committed to a psychiatric hospital. Aside from his family, the only person who called every week of his ninety-day stay was FBI agent Sid Perry.

The phone calls that Rusty Lavin permitted the FBI to tape provided geographical leads to Larry's whereabouts, but the content of the few taped conversations between the brothers added nothing of value to the search. However, Rusty did supply other information in debriefing sessions that proved to be critically important. He remembered that in past calls whenever an operator had come on the line asking for money, she had a Southern accent and the amount she requested for each time increment was usually seventy-five or eighty-five cents. That was added reinforcement that they were targeting the right area. And there was one other thing: Larry had mentioned once that he had a fishing buddy who was a retired FBI agent!

Immediately Reed and Perry realized that agent could be the key person in helping them nab Lavin. The question was how to connect with him. A mass mailing of Larry's photo risked what they'd been worried about all along: tipping their hand to the wrong party. Maybe they ought to drive to the area and deliver an in-person pitch at local meetings of retired agents. That didn't seem like a very sensible idea. They didn't know what percentage attended—and what if the guy they were looking for didn't come? Finally, however risky, they settled on the mail.

Sid Perry telephoned the national association for retired FBI agents, found they had a directory of all members, and mailed them ten-dollars for a copy. Then he ordered several hundred three-by-five four-color glossies of Larry Lavin and composed a letter to accompany them:

Dear Fellow Agent:

Enclosed is a photograph of Bureau subject: fugitive Lawrence Lavin, also know as Larry. This photo and the following information are being provided to retired FBI agents residing in Maryland, Virginia, North and South Carolina, in an attempt to identify and locate Lavin. This investigative procedure is being utilized in that information has been developed to indicate that Lavin has made an acquaintance-friendship with a retired agent residing in the above area who is unaware of Lavin's criminal or fugitive status. The current name used in unknown.

Perry included some brief biographical data and was about to end the letter when it occurred to him that he really didn't know the extent of the friendship between Larry and the agent. What if Larry were very close to the man they were relying on to turn him in? He'd better add something that would influence the agent if necessary. He tacked on another two paragraphs:

During the course of the investigation, information was also developed, through interviews of witnesses and intercepted recorded conversations, regarding Lavin paying money to a co-conspirator which in part was to fund a contract on an FBI agent.

Your attention to this matter and any assistance you can provide in the apprehension of a major narcotics dealer is greatly appreciated.

There, he thought. That ought to do it.

It took Sid Perry two weeks after the directory arrived to sift through alphabetical list of thousands of former agents and pull out the seventeen hundred names of retirees living in the designated four-state area. Each time he wrote a name, he said to himself, "I wonder if it's him."

The first batch of photos was targeted to agents in the vicinity of Norfolk and Virginia Beach. Perry had decided to begin there and branch out if necessary. On Monday, May 12, 1986—almost nineteen months after Lavin had fled—one hundred envelopes left Philadelphia. Another hundred were mailed on Tuesday, Wednesday, and Thursday. All week Sid Perry stayed very close to the phone.

On a sunny Thursday morning, May 15, retired special agent Pat O'Donald walked outside to the mailbox in front of his Virginia Beach home and wondered what was in the envelope with the Philadelphia postmark. The contents stunned him. He stared at the picture of a man identified as Larry Lavin, a fugitive cocaine dealer. There was not the shadow of a doubt this was his friend Brian O'Neil. O'Donald had been with the Bureau too long to question the truth of what the letter said. Still, he read it twice, hoping to discover some mistake. When he was absolutely certain there was none, the loyalty to the Bureau that Reed and Perry were banking on took over. He picked up the telephone and dialed the Norfolk bureau of the FBI.

At the moment his fate was sealed, Larry Lavin was twenty miles off the Atlantic coast tossing back into the ocean a toadfish he'd just caught. These little things made lousy eating and weren't worth hauling back to shore. For a split-second he allowed himself to reminisce that if none of this had happened to him, he'd be back in Philadelphia right now preparing to attend the fifth reunion of his University of Pennsylvania Dental School graduating class. But that life was dead. He walked to the cooler and took out a can of beer.

Larry hadn't planned on fishing that morning. He'd recently emptied the safe-deposit box where he kept the fifty-eight phony identities created for his investments, and he'd intended to transfer them today to a box closer to home. Instead, when a friend invited him out, he postponed the chore because the weather was just too beautiful to waste riding around in his car. He stuffed the papers into a briefcase on his desk, kissed the kids good-bye, and left Marcia in the kitchen preparing a ham for that night's dinner. Whatever he'd catch, he'd put in the freezer or give away.

*   *   *

Sid Perry was at his desk assembling a list of the next group of agents to receive his letter when a call came from the Norfolk office.

"Sid, it's Phil. We located your man." Perry jumped out of his chair and waved his free hand in a victory sign at his secretary. She came running over, and he scribbled "Lavin" on his scratchpad. He was grinning from ear to ear. "He goes by the name of Brian O'Neil and right now he's out fishing with a friend. He's due back around five or six and we'll be waiting."

"Be very, very cautious," Sid warned. "If you miss him, you'll never get a second chance." He hung up the phone, let out a schoolboy's whoop, and called the radio room. "Get Chuck for me."

Reed had left the Philadelphia office shortly before the call from Norfolk and Perry knew he was somewhere on the road. It only took five minutes to locate him.

"We got Larry," Perry announced.

"I knew it as soon as I heard them call me on the radio," Reed said. "What name was he using?"

"Brian O'Neil."

"When are they gonna get him?"

"Around dinnertime, as soon as he steps off the fishing boat."

Both of them were thinking the same thing, reliving the painful memory of that cold October night when they realized they'd been outsmarted. This time they had to make certain there was no chance Larry could get away. It was decided that Chuck would work with Norfolk on the arrangements. He spent the remainder of the afternoon on the telephone giving the Virginia agents background on Larry. "You can't screw this up," Reed said over and over. "The guy is very clever. If he sees a gang of people waiting on the pier, he'll be suspicious and take off in the boat."

Sid Perry left the office early because the Little League team he coached had a game that night. He changed from his suit into jeans and a T-Shirt, packed his son and his wife, who was the team scorekeeper, into the car, and drove to the field. The ballgame was a total blur. Every five minutes he'd look at his watch and wonder if they'd arrested Larry yet. Oddly enough, he wasn't sorry that he wouldn't get to witness Larry's face. "I think I actually enjoyed not being there," he'd say later. "For eighteen months Larry was sitting in Virginia so smug, laughing at us and thinking he'd gotten away with it. Now here I was out at the ballpark thinking of Larry on the bay fishing and having a beer, and knowing that in a few minutes the tables would be turned."

By four that afternoon the Virginia Beach marina where Lavin would soon dock was swimming with FBI agents, including Larry's pal Pat O'Donald. Twenty agents, practically the whole local office, had been commandeered into duty. They'd dressed down into casual clothes to blend in with the boat crowd, and spread themselves around the dock where people were cleaning fish or sipping cocktails on their decks. A speedboat was stationed in the water in case Larry tried to escape by sea.

The twenty-five foot sport fishing boat carrying Larry Lavin returned from the day's outing with no great fish tales to tell. As expeditions went, this one wasn't very successful, and all they'd caught was a six-pound tautog. Still, the men were in high spirits. The beer, sandwiches, and conversation always overshadowed the fish. As the boat nosed into the slip, Larry waved to Pat standing on the dock with a man and woman he assumed were his friends.

"Come on board and have a beer," he called. Two of them hopped onto the deck. O'Donald went straight to the wheel and removed the boat's key from the ignition, while the other agent confronted the dark-haired man in the jeans and rugby shirt.

"Are you Larry Lavin?" he asked, flipping an FBI badge in front of his face.

"Yes," he answered very softly, his green eyes saying what his heart knew. It was over. His body felt numb, like it used to after staying up all night snorting cocaine. He was filled with fear for his wife and children. What would happen to them? Were there agents at his house now too? And he was furious with himself. Why had he kept on making those phone calls when he knew better?

The FBI man grabbed his arm, in case Lavin had any thoughts of running, and he leaned forward to deliver a message: "Chuck Reed says hi."

Epilogue

By September 1987, the last batch of indictments was issued for the Lavin conspiracy. Included among the fifteen charged was Philadelphia Eagles football star Dennis Franks. Although the government estimated that Burns and Lavin together had peddled over fifteen hundred kilos of cocaine with a street value of eighty-five million dollars, it wasn't the dollars that made this the largest cocaine case ever handled in the Eastern District of Pennsylvania. It was the eighty-three successful prosecutions. Everybody indicted either pleaded guilty or went to jail. In addition, the FBI found eighty-three kilos of cocaine and impounded thirteen vehicles. It seized over two-million dollars in cash, including $528,200 from Franny Burns, $400,000 from David Ackerman, and $90,000 taken from the safe in the raid on Bruce Taylor's house. But the king's ransom came from Larry Lavin.

The briefcase with the phony investment identities that was sitting in Lavin's home office the day he was arrested, along with a key to a safe-deposit box found in a search of his home, enabled the FBI to put its hands on $1.4 of Larry Lavin's drug money. They also confiscated his Virginia Beach home and its contents, his two cars, and his boat. Lavin's other properties, in Philadelphia and at the Jersey shore, were taken by the IRS, leaving the dentist and his family virtually penniless.

For Sid Perry and Chuck Reed, the close of the Lavin case marked the end of what would probably be the most demanding four years in their FBI careers. Reed went on to develop other drug indictments and Perry returned to investigating white-collar crime. There were no special commendations from the Bureau—only the immense satisfaction of nailing Larry Lavin.

On a balmy Tuesday following the Labor Day weekend in September 1986, the thirty-one-year-old Larry Lavin, looking pale and thin in a dark blue suit that accented the circles under his eyes, stood in a small wood-paneled federal courtroom and publicly apologized for the crimes he had committed. The courtroom was packed with people from Virginia Beach who'd traveled to Philadelphia to speak passionately as character witnesses on behalf of Brian O'Neil, a man they admired and respected even after discovering the earlier life he'd led. Marcia Lavin sat among their Virginia friends wearing a flowered maternity smock, her round, girlish face now grim.

The sentencing took place in two separate sessions. The morning portion dealt with the criminal charges stemming from the drug conspiracy. Tina Gabbrielli pointed out that Lavin's organization had distributed the street-level equivalent of two million grams of cocaine—or 16 million individual doses. In response Lavin's lawyer told the court that in Virginia Beach his client "had turned the corner and put the dark side of his life behind him." He dutifully pointed out that since his arrest, Larry had cooperated fully with the government, turned over his complete assets, and assisted in retrieving money from the investments made under the false identities he'd created.

The leading defense witness to appear for Lavin in his plea for leniency was Dr. Albert Levitt, chief psychologist of the Court of Common Pleas of Philadelphia, who'd been hired to examine Lavin and had already submitted a seventeen-page evaluation to the judge in which he detailed among other things the results of various standard psychological tests he'd administered to Lavin. He described the dentist as a man with 126 IQ who was compulsively driven to acquire money, wealth, and status and suffered from a character disorder labeled "histrionic personality with some compulsive features." As a result Larry tended to bend reality to fit into his own thinking, which enabled him to twist wrong into right. In addition, the psychologist found, "Dr. Lavin . . . does not adequately enjoy or benefit from sexual and social relationships. This means he has a need to seek other areas of stimulation, and risk-taking is one of these alternatives."

In his courtroom testimony, Dr. Levitt likened Lavin to the protagionist in Theodore Dreiser's novel *An American Tragedy*. "Larry was from a family where the father had boom-and-bust business involvements but aspired to be very rich. Lavin had to pay a lot of bills for his father, who was, at times, an embarrassment to him. He goes to schools where very rich people go, and sees their toys are drugs. That influences him in a very negative way. He sees that selling drugs is an avenue for what he aspires to be, and the rich are happy to pay him to do their dirty work for them. While he's selling, he's still interested in becoming a professional. So he starts to lead a double life and this life of contradictions goes on and on. His activities are illegal, but they are condoned by a large segment of society who participate with him by creating the demand for what he sells."

Judge Louis Pollack viewed the *American Tragedy* analogy differently. He looked around the jammed courtroom of what he described as "mostly white, upper-middle-class, upwardly mobile" people and said, "The fascination of Dr. Lavin is that he is one of us. We identify with him and are frightened by what he did. . . . And because we connect with this person, we are fascinated and terrified by his downfall. . . . We do have here an American tragedy, the fall from extraordinary grace of someone who, on the record, is clearly capable of doing very good things, who in fact had done good things for friends and family. But Dr. Lavin has also done terrible things to our society by distributing a terrifying poison. His dreadful crimes deserve no sentimental glossing over. They deserve punishment." He found Larry Lavin guilty of all five counts with which he'd been charged and sentenced him to twenty-two years in jail and a fine of $100,000. Many in the courtroom thought the fine was surprisingly low, but it actually was commensurate with the federal-court practice of using fines to offset government costs rather than mete out punishment.

In the afternoon, Larry Lavin arrived in handcuffs for the second portion of the sentencing, in front of a different judge, the honorable Louis Bechtle, assigned to handle the charges related to tax evasion. He'd already acknowledged earning as much as six million dollars between 1979 and 1984, on which he'd paid under $100,000 in income tax. With his long delicate fingers pressed to his lips, he heard the silver-haired jurist harshly declare that "with the possible exception of the *U.S. vs. Alphonse Capone*, I can't think of a more appropriate case for the application of full sanctions under the tax laws." He sentenced Lavin to twenty years in prison and fined him $140,000 for concealing his earnings from the Internal Revenue Service. Then came the worst blow of all: rather than exercising his option of assigning the prison time for tax evasion to run concurrently with the drug punishment, the judge declared the tax sentence was to be served consecutively.

That meant a total of forty-two years, at least seventeen of which would pass before Larry Lavin could even be eligible for parole. Never would he experience the joy of watching his children grow up. There would be no relationship at all with Kelly Marie, the daughter who would be born four months after he was behind bars. She would move from toddler to teen knowing her daddy only as a man she visited occasionally in jail. With good time earned, he might be out by his fiftieth birthday.

Immediately after leaving the courtroom, Lavin—because he was a security risk who'd been convicted under the drug-kingpin statute—was shipped to Leavenworth Federal Correctional Institution in Kansas, a Level V prison reserved for the most vicious criminals in the federal prison system. Within weeks of his arrival, word spread through the inmate grapevine that he'd cooperated with the feds. Prisoners walked by spitting the word "rat" in his face. One afternoon in the television area, five men surrounded Lavin, raised a metal chair over his head, and would have smashed it into his skull had not a guard intervened. Lavin asked to be placed in isolation for his own safety while his lawyer petitioned the court to have him moved to a prison where he'd be incarcerated with less-violent, white-collar criminals. As a result, he was transferred to a sixty-six-acre Level IV correctional facility in Oxford, Wisconsin, where he will probably remain until his release sometime in the next century.

Lavin's attorney was more successful gaining him a change of residence than he was in getting him a sentence reduction. The court denied his Rule 35 application—a routine procedure filed in almost all criminal cases asking the court to reconsider and hopefully shorten the sentence imposed at trial. The prison refused Lavin's request to practice dentistry on the other inmates, citing the risk of potential malpractice suits against the prison system. Instead, he works as a quality-control clerk in the prison cable factory, where he sometimes gets to use the computer. He spends his leisure time reading and exercising. Friends send him old issues of *Omni* and *Discovery* so he can keep up his interest in science and technology. He jogs several miles a day and plays softball, volleyball, and any other league sport the prison offers. On lucky days he falls into bed too tired to think about his past and berate himself for "the greed and stupidity that got me here." He'd like to take courses at the prison's college program but can't afford the tuition, since half of his sixty-six-cent-an-hour wages are taken by the government to pay his court-imposed fines. What little remains he sends to help his wife and children.

Marcia Lavin, along with her mother and three toddlers, has moved to a town near the prison so she can be close to Larry. The government decided not to indict her because it saw no benefit sending a mother of three to jail for harboring a criminal who happened to be her husband. At present Marcia is collecting welfare and hopes to return to work as a physical therapist.

*   *   *

Lavin's classmate and cocaine partner David Ackerman forfeited $400,000 in assets to the government. His original fifteen-year prison sentence with no parole was reduced after the rule 35 appeal to ten years. With good time earned, he expects to be free in 1991. Determined to make the most of his years behind bars, Ackerman reports, "I can't remember anytime I felt more productive. I feel I'm moving ahead every day. I've learned to overcome the limitations people put on themselves in prison. It's not where you are but what you do with yourself." He's pursuing an MBA degree from an accredited university program designed for shut-ins and has immersed himself in computer technology. After completing a prison course in computers, he uses his expertise to teach other inmates and help the prison administration computerize its records.

Of the three dentists in the conspiracy, Kenny Weidler received the lightest sentence. Because he cooperated with the government in apprehending Larry Lavin and because of his early withdrawal from the daily activity of the cocaine enterprise, he was sentenced to thirty months and a $10,000 fine. He actually served 13 1/2 months at the Allenwood Federal Prison Camp and was released in June 1987. He plans to reapply for his dental license and return to practice if his request is granted. At the present time he's working for an advertising agency.

Billy Motto received the most severe sentence of the drug conspirators—twenty years without parole plus five years' probation and a $125,000 fine. With time earned for good behavior, he could be released in 1999 from the Petersburg Federal Correctional Institution in Virginia. Motto has decided to use his prison time to get the education he missed on the outside, a decision made after a standard test administered to all inmates revealed that Billy South Philly had the reading and math comprehension of a fourth-grader. He subsequently attended prison school every morning and within six months raised himself to the eighth-grade level and managed to pass the Adult Basic Education exam, although he had to take the test four times.

Despite his difficulty, Billy was determined to continue until he finished high school. In the spring of 1987, dressed in a cap and gown, the thirty-one-year-old former coke dealer received his high-school diploma and was singled out as as the honor student of the prison class. Billy was disappointed that his family could not be present to share his triumph. Currently he is tutoring illiterate inmates and taking junior-college courses. His goal is to get an associate degree in social services, which he'd like to someday combine with his personal experience with drugs to help young addicts.

At his sentencing, the tough-talking Franny Burns dissolved into tears and sobbed in front of the judge like a child. Over and over he begged for mercy and kept repeating, "I'm sorry. I'm sorry." The court was not moved and his greed cost him a half-dozen more years in jail than he would have gotten had he played it straight and cooperated with the government the way he promised. Burns received eleven years on the charges stemming from his drug activities, but because of his attempts to double-cross the FBI, the government indicted him a second time and he received five additional years for obstructing justice, lying to the grand jury, and possessing cocaine. He surrendered $528,200 in assets and is serving a sixteen-year sentence. With good behavior, he will be eligible for parole in 10 1/2 years.

Bruce Taylor, the former machinist, received ten years for his part in the Lavin conspiracy. The sentence was later reduced to five years based on his postindictment cooperation with the government. His wife, Suzanne Noramatzu Taylor, was given two years and split her jail term between a prison in West Virginia and one in California. After completing her time in May 1986, she returned to her job as office manager for a small construction company in Philadelphia and is living with her parents until her husband's expected release in late 1988.

The remaining members of the Lavin conspiracy received the following sentences:
Glenn Fuller, who, as a boy, organized the snowmobile heist and handled drugs for his high-school pal Larry Lavin, faces two state charges for assaulting an officer and possessing cocaine and one federal charge for participating in the conspiracy. When his sentencing is completed on all three, he will spend at least seven years in prison.
Paul Mikuta, Lavin's college roommate, best man, and major customer, ran a substantial drug business of his own, selling the coke he bought from Larry. The married father of two was given twelve years, with five years' probation, and fined $15,000. He is serving his sentence at the prison camp of the U.S. Penitentiary at Lewisburg.
Jeffrey Giancola, the Washington lawyer who was Lavin's prep-

school roommate, was convicted of cocaine possession, fined $3,000, and given three years' probation along with four hundred hours of community service.

Willie Harcourt, the college dropout who bought coke for the conspiracy in Florida and managed it after David Ackerman's departure, is at the Federal Correctional Institution at Loretto, Pennsylvania, serving a sentence of eight years, with five years' probation, and a $10,000 fine.

Brian Riley, who succeeded Harcourt as manager and introduced Bruce Taylor to the conspiracy by bringing him to Philadelphia to work as his bodyguard, received twelve years without parole.

Nicky Bongiorno, once Billy Motto's right-hand man and enforcer, was released from prison in August 1987 after serving seventeen months. He has been drug-free for more than two years.

Vito Mirro and Pat Giordano, the two Motto workers who pleaded not guilty along with their boss and were convicted at the same trial, are serving sentences of respectively, eight years, with a $10,000 fine; and four years, with five years' probation.

Sandy Freas, Franny Burns' girlfriend and sometime drug-runner, received probation for her minor role in his cocaine business.

Christine, the cocktail waitress hired by Suzanne Noramatzu to assist her in counting money and filling cocaine orders, spent three months in a work-release program, was fined $1,000, and is now free on five years' probation.

Mark Stewart, whose bankrupt record company provided the thread that unraveled all these lives, was indicted separately from the drug conspiracy. Convicted on charges of tax evasion, he received four years in prison, five years' probation, and was ordered to pay $316,000 in restitution to his creditors. In addition, he pleaded guilty to a second crime of arranging the arson of the Martin Luther King Arena in order to collect insurance money and was given ten years in prison to be served concurrently with the tax-evasion sentence.

Diego Arbelez, the Colombian drug dealer arrested in the raid set up by Franny Burns, was sentenced to sixteen years in prison without parole.

Michael and Karen, the two young workers in Bruce Taylor's drug business, were granted immunity and not charged because of their extensive cooperation in providing information and assistance to the government.

Rusty Lavin and Jill Lavin were never indicted. At present the two brothers are not speaking. Rusty has recovered from the depression that prompted his suicide attempt and is struggling to rebuild his life. He is divorced and works for a construction company. "I'm at the bottom crawling out," is how he sees his life. But he's trying to be optimistic. "I'll most definitely get out. It will get better."

To Chuck Reed and Sid Perry, Larry Lavin is history. "We won. He lost." For them, it was that simple. The mega-million drug case closed exactly the way the FBI agents wanted it: eighty-three indictments, eighty-three convictions, no fugitives.

Neat and clean.